Tutankhamun's Trumpet

Professor Toby Wilkinson is an internationally acclaimed Egypto-logist and the prize-winning author of twelve books, which have been translated into twelve languages. They include *The Rise and Fall of Ancient Egypt*, which was awarded the Hessell-Tiltman Prize, *The Nile* and *A World Beneath the Sands*. He is a Fellow of the Society of Antiquaries and the Royal Historical Society, and a member of the international editorial board of the *Journal of Egyptian History*.

Also by Toby Wilkinson

A World Beneath the Sands

Aristocrats and Archaeologists (with Julian Platt)

Writings from Ancient Egypt

The Nile

The Rise and Fall of Ancient Egypt

Lives of the Ancient Egyptians

The Egyptian World (editor)

The Thames & Hudson Dictionary of Ancient Egypt

Genesis of the Pharaohs

Royal Annals of Ancient Egypt

Early Dynastic Egypt

TUTANKHAMUN'S TRUMPET

*The Story of Ancient Egypt
in 100 Objects*

Toby Wilkinson

PICADOR

First published 2022 by Picador

This paperback edition published 2023 by Picador
an imprint of Pan Macmillan
The Smithson, 6 Briset Street, London ECIM 5NR
EU representative: Macmillan Publishers Ireland Ltd, 1st Floor,
The Liffey Trust Centre, 117–126 Sheriff Street Upper,
Dublin 1, DOI YC43
Associated companies throughout the world
www.panmacmillan.com

ISBN 978-1-5290-4598-7

1 3 5 7 9 8 6 4 2

A CIP catalogue record for this book is available from the British Library.

Typeset by Palimpsest Book Production Ltd, Falkirk, Stirlingshire
Printed and bound by CPI Group (UK) Ltd, Croydon, CRO 4YY

Visit **www.picador.com** to read more about all our books
and to buy them. You will also find features, author interviews and
news of any author events, and you can sign up for e-newsletters
so that you're always first to hear about our new releases.

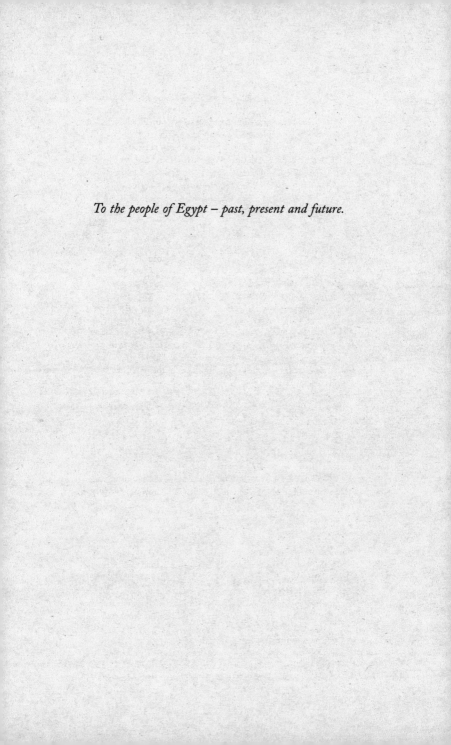

To the people of Egypt – past, present and future.

CONTENTS

List of Illustrations

Figures in the text

(Found in Amarna. New Kingdom Period, eighteenth dynasty, *c.* 1335 BC. Neues Museum, Berlin. Adam Eastland/ Alamy)

Fig. 32. Sistrum (Photograph by Harry Burton. © Griffith Institute, University of Oxford)

Fig. 33. Model solar barque (Photograph by Harry Burton. © Griffith Institute, University of Oxford)

Fig. 34. *Wedjat* eye bracelet (Photograph by Harry Burton. © Griffith Institute, University of Oxford)

Fig. 35. Ritual torch with *ankh* (Photograph by Harry Burton. © Griffith Institute, University of Oxford)

Fig. 36. Floral collar placed on Tutankhamun's coffin (Photograph by Harry Burton. © Griffith Institute, University of Oxford)

Fig. 37. The king's mummified body (Photograph by Harry Burton. © Griffith Institute, University of Oxford)

Fig. 38. Bier figure (Photograph by Harry Burton. © Griffith Institute, University of Oxford)

Fig. 39. The royal sarcophagus (Photograph by Harry Burton. © Griffith Institute, University of Oxford)

Fig. 40. Black resin scarab (Photograph by Harry Burton. © Griffith Institute, University of Oxford)

Fig. 41. Hussein Abdel Rassul (Photograph by Harry Burton. © Griffith Institute, University of Oxford)

Fig. 42. Tutankhamun's 'wishing cup' (Photograph by Harry Burton. © Griffith Institute, University of Oxford)

Fig. 43. Linen glove (Photograph by Harry Burton. © Griffith Institute, University of Oxford)

Fig. 44. Black guardian statues (Photograph by Harry Burton. © Griffith Institute, University of Oxford)

Fig. 45. Statuette of a deity carrying the king (Photograph by Harry Burton. © Griffith Institute, University of Oxford)

Fig. 46. Bandsman Tappern playing Tutankhamun's trumpet (BBC, 16 April 1939. Keystone-France/Gamma-Rapho/Getty Images)

Timeline

Note: all dates before 664 BC are approximate

Dates	Period	Significant Developments
700,000–5000 BC	Palaeolithic Period	Earliest humans in the Nile Valley
5000–2950 BC	Predynastic (Neolithic) Period	
2950–2575 BC	Early Dynastic Period (first to third dynasties)	Unification of Egypt
2575–2125 BC	Old Kingdom or Pyramid Age (fourth to eighth dynasties)	Giza pyramids and Sphinx
2125–2010 BC	First Intermediate Period (ninth to eleventh dynasties)	Civil war
2010–1630 BC	Middle Kingdom (eleventh to thirteenth dynasties)	Annexation of Nubia
1630–1539 BC	Second Intermediate Period (fourteenth to seventeenth dynasties)	Foreign occupation ('Hyksos')
1539–1069 BC	New Kingdom	Egyptian Empire
	Eighteenth dynasty, 1539–1292 BC	
	Thutmose III, 1479–1425 BC and Hatshepsut, 1473–1458 BC	Battle of Megiddo, April 1458 BC
	Amenhotep III, 1390–1353 BC	
	Amenhotep IV, 1353–1336 BC	Foundation of Amarna, 1349 BC
	Neferneferuaten, 1336–1332 BC	
	Tutankhamun, 1332–1322 BC	
	Ay, 1322–1319 BC	
	Horemheb, 1319–1292 BC	

Dates	Period	Significant Developments
	Nineteenth dynasty, 1292–1190 BC	Battle of Kadesh, May 1274 BC
	Twentieth dynasty, 1190–1069 BC	Tomb robberies begin
1069–657 BC	Third Intermediate Period (twenty-first to twenty-fifth dynasties)	
664–332 BC	Late Period (twenty-sixth to thirty-first dynasties)	
332–309 BC	Macedonian dynasty	Alexander the Great conquers Egypt
309–30 BC	Ptolemaic Period	Reign of Cleopatra (VII)
30 BC–AD 395	Roman Period	Last hieroglyphic inscription, AD 394
395–639	Byzantine rule	
639–1517	Islamic rule	
1517–1914	Ottoman rule	Decipherment of hieroglyphics, 1822
1914–1922	British Protectorate	
1922–1953	Kingdom of Egypt	**Tutankhamun's tomb discovered, November 1922**
1953–	Republic	Arab Spring, 2011

Maps

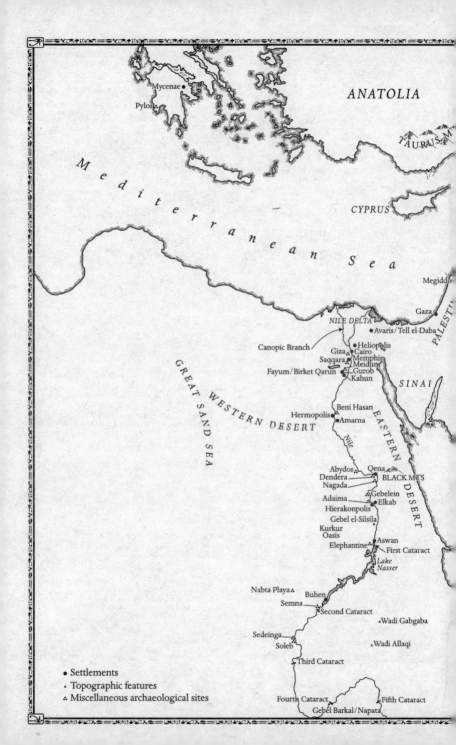

ANATOLIA

TAURUS MTS

Mycenae

Pylos

M e d i t e r r a n e a n   S e a

CYPRUS

Megiddo

Gaza

PALESTINE

NILE DELTA

Avaris / Tell el-Daba

Canopic Branch

Heliopolis
Giza • Cairo
Saqqara • Memphis
Meidum
Fayum / Birket Qarun • Gurob
Kahun

SINAI

GREAT WESTERN DESERT

Beni Hasan
Hermopolis •
Amarna

EASTERN DESERT

Nile

Abydos • Qena
Dendera • BLACK MTS
Nagada
Gebelein
Adaima • Elkab
Hierakonpolis
Gebel el-Silsila
Kurkur
Oasis
Elephantine • Aswan
First Cataract
Lake Nasser

Nabta Playa • Buhen
Semna •
Second Cataract
Wadi Gabgaba

Sedeinga
Soleb
Wadi Allaqi

Third Cataract

Fourth Cataract
Gebel Barkal / Napata
Fifth Cataract

• Settlements
▴ Topographic features
⁘ Miscellaneous archaeological sites

EGYPT AND THE LEVANT

Caspian Sea

HITTITES

MITTANI

ASSYRIA

Euphrates

Tigris

ZAGROS MTS

Kadesh

Byblos

SYRIA

Babylon

The Gulf

Red Sea

N

| 0 | 50 | 100 | 150 | 200 miles |
| 0 | 100 | 200 | 300 km |

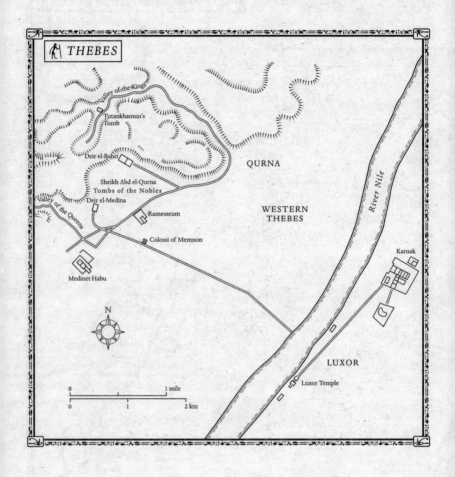

THEBES

Valley of the Kings

Tutankhamun's
Tomb

Deir el-Bahri

QURNA

Sheikh Abd el-Qurna
Tombs of the Nobles
Deir el-Medina

Valley of the Queens

Ramesseum

WESTERN
THEBES

Colossi of Memnon

Medinet Habu

River Nile

Karnak

N

LUXOR

Luxor Temple

0		1 mile
0	1	2 km

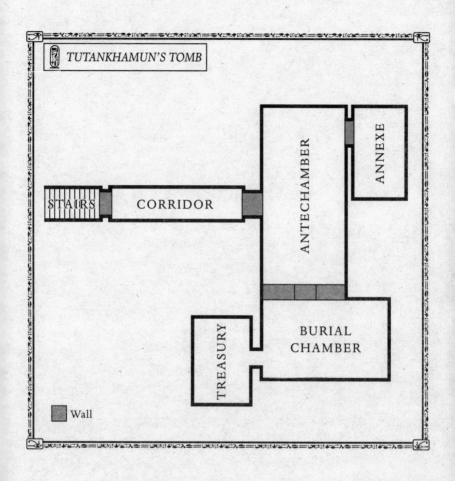

TUTANKHAMUN'S TOMB

STAIRS

CORRIDOR

ANTECHAMBER

ANNEXE

TREASURY

BURIAL CHAMBER

Wall

Introduction

On 5 November 1922, in the Valley of the Kings, Egyptian labourers under the direction of the English archaeologist Howard Carter uncovered a series of steps cut into the valley floor. A few hours later, clearance revealed a descending staircase, terminating at a rubble wall that blocked further access. This was the moment for which Carter and his patron, Lord Carnarvon, had been toiling for fifteen long years in the heat and dust. Carter immediately sent a telegram to Carnarvon, who was 2,500 miles away at Highclere Castle, his stately home in southern England: 'At last have made wonderful discovery in Valley. A magnificent tomb with seals intact. Re-covered same for your arrival. Congratulations.' When Carnarvon arrived in Luxor seventeen days later, he and Carter proceeded to clear the rubble wall and the corridor beyond. Eventually, on 26 November, they gained access to the royal tomb itself. Peering into the darkness with a lighted candle, Carter could not believe his eyes. Carnarvon, unable to bear the suspense any longer, asked, 'Can you see anything?' Carter's now-famous reply came back. 'Yes, yes, wonderful things.'

What Carter and Carnarvon had discovered was, in every sense, a treasure trove, a hoard of precious objects fit for a king. In total, the grave goods interred with the boy pharaoh numbered over 5,000 objects, an unprecedented collection for a single discovery. Together, they comprised, in the words of Carnarvon himself, 'enough stuff to fill the whole Egyptian section upstairs of the B[ritish] M[useum]'. They ranged from the mundane (the boy king's loincloth, shaving equipment and first aid kit) to the highly symbolic (his leopard-skin cloak, wooden paddles with which to row to the afterlife, and a ritual torch shaped like the hieroglyph for 'life'). There were poignant objects with personal family resonance (the king's mummified, stillborn children and a lock of his grandmother's hair); food and drink for the next world (chickpeas and lentils, joints of meat, a basket of dates and wine from the royal vineyards). Practical tools (a scribal palette, a cubit rod and chisels) were buried alongside weapons (bows and arrows, fighting sticks, scimitars, leather scale armour and the king's prized chariots). Precious objects (a linen glove, a blue glass headrest, gold and silver staffs) demonstrate the sophistication of ancient Egyptian taste and craftsmanship, while exotic imports from distant lands (ebony and ivory from Nubia, and a jewel of Libyan desert glass, formed by an ancient meteorite strike) show the range of Egypt's trading and diplomatic networks. Objects of daily domestic use (board games and oil lamps, make-up and furniture, baskets and sandals) provide a vivid picture of life in the Nile Valley over 3,000 years ago.

In the hundred years since the most famous archaeological discovery of all time, Tutankhamun has become the most famous ruler of ancient Egypt. A few objects from his tomb have achieved worldwide renown: his spectacular funerary mask, fashioned from beaten gold, is recognized as an icon – perhaps *the* icon – of pharaonic civilization. His gold coffins and royal throne are frequently illustrated in books on archaeology and ancient Egypt. However, most of the other myriad objects interred with him in the Valley of the Kings remain largely unknown, their stories untold.

To mark the centenary of Carter and Carnarvon's great discovery, this book focuses on the objects buried with the boy pharaoh as the source material for a portrait of ancient

Egypt – its geography, history, culture and legacy. One hundred artefacts from the king's tomb, arranged in ten thematic groups, are allowed to speak again, as witnesses of the civilization that created them. The treasures of Tutankhamun bring us face to face with the culture of the pharaohs, its extraordinary development and its lasting impact.

⋖◌⋗

Tutankhamun was barely known before 1922. None of the classical authors, on whose accounts of Egyptian history most European scholars relied, made mention of him, and nor did he feature in the king list compiled by the third-century BC Egyptian priest Manetho. Only after Jean-François Champollion's decipherment of hieroglyphics in 1822 was it possible to read ancient Egyptian inscriptions directly, and antiquarian visitors to Egypt began to notice the occasional mention of a little-known pharaoh bearing the throne name 'Nebkheperura' and the birth name 'Tutankhamun'. In the late 1820s, the English antiquarian John Gardner Wilkinson, on a trip into the remote Eastern Desert, noticed a stone block bearing these names. In 1828, he discovered a tomb cut into the hillside of western Thebes that, the inscriptions revealed, had been created for a high official during the reign of Tutankhamun.

Another English adventurer, Lord Prudhoe, was exploring in Upper Nubia when, at the ancient religious capital of Gebel Barkal, he found two magnificent statues of recumbent lions, each carved from a single block of red granite. Reused and reinscribed, they had originally been carved by the eighteenth-dynasty pharaoh Amenhotep III, and one of them bore a rededication inscription of Tutankhamun. In 1835, Prudhoe presented both lions to the British Museum, where they became the first two objects to be registered in its nascent collection of Egyptian antiquities.

Further evidence of Tutankhamun came to light during the French archaeologist Auguste Mariette's excavations at Saqqara in the 1850s. In the catacombs of the sacred bulls, known as the Serapeum, one of the burials was revealed to have been prepared during the reign of the little-known king. Towards the end of the nineteenth century, Mariette's compatriot Emile Amélineau found a gilded wooden box bearing Tutankhamun's name at Abydos in Upper Egypt. But it was the excavation by Flinders Petrie, the 'father of Egyptian archaeology', at the site of Amarna in the winter of 1891–2 that caused the real breakthrough, when it revealed the ruined city built by the 'heretic' pharaoh, Akhenaten. Numerous inscribed objects, including a cache of diplomatic correspondence on clay tablets, mentioned Tutankhamun and made it clear that he was Akhenaten's son and successor.

With the dawn of the twentieth century, Tutankhamun's name began to crop up more frequently. In 1905, investigations in the temple of Karnak uncovered a stone slab bearing a restoration inscription dated to the early part of his reign, while an expedition in the Valley of the Kings, sponsored by the American financier Theodore Davis, found a small faience cup bearing the name Nebkheperura. Two years later, Davis found a pit containing a cache of embalming materials left over from a royal burial; once again, hieroglyphic inscriptions mentioned Tutankhamun, which seemed to indicate that the king's tomb lay somewhere in the Valley. When Davis subsequently found a small undecorated chamber containing further objects with the king's name – a stone statuette, fittings from a horse's harness and several fragments of gold foil – he thought he had his prize. He published his discovery as the 'Tomb of Touatânkhamanou' (his rather tortuous rendering of the king's name) and relinquished his excavation permit two years later, declaring that 'the Valley of the Tombs is now exhausted'.

Waiting in the wings to prove Davis spectacularly wrong was a man who had worked for him a decade earlier. By 1914, Howard Carter was one of the most experienced archaeologists excavating in Egypt. He had begun his career as an artist, recording tombs and objects for various missions, including Petrie's dig at Amarna. He went on to work in western Thebes as an official expedition draughtsman. Wandering the hills, valleys and embayments over the course of six seasons, he developed an unerring eye for potential archaeological sites and came to know every inch of the Theban necropolis, including the Valley of the Kings. His appointment as chief inspector of antiquities for Upper Egypt followed in 1900, allowing him to carry out excavations in the Valley on behalf of various wealthy patrons. However, his promotion to chief inspector of antiquities for Lower Egypt in 1904 did not end well, an altercation with a group of tourists leading to his resignation. He returned to Luxor and fell back on his artistic skills, selling watercolours to well-heeled visitors in order to eke out a living. It was thus, in 1907, that he met a new patron, the fifth Earl of Carnarvon. The two men decided to join forces – Carnarvon's wealth matched Carter's expertise – and in doing so forged a partnership that was to result, fifteen years later, in the greatest archaeological discovery of all time.

As soon as Davis gave up his concession for the Valley of the Kings, Carnarvon snapped it up: it was the plum site in the whole of Egypt. In February 1915, Carter began work, his meticulous approach rescuing a number of overlooked finds from the debris of earlier digs. In light of the clues previously found by Davis, Carter was convinced that Tutankhamun's final resting place might yet reveal itself, and he resolved to leave no stone unturned in his search. Over the next five years, he oversaw the systematic clearance of the remaining unexcavated section of the Valley, but all this strenuous and expensive work yielded little: a few finds, and no tombs. Carnarvon started to lose faith and interest. By the summer of 1922, he had decided to call it a day, but Carter remained convinced he was on the right track and begged his patron to fund one final season. Reluctantly, Carnarvon agreed.

Carter arrived in Luxor on 28 October 1922 and excavations resumed a few days later. Just three days into the dig, the first step was uncovered. Twenty-four hours later, a flight of twelve descending steps had been exposed, leading to a blocked doorway covered in plaster and impressed with the seals of the ancient royal necropolis. Carter cabled his patron with the news and awaited Carnarvon's arrival. On 24 November, the two men watched together as the staircase was cleared to its full depth, revealing the whole of the plastered doorway. Now there could be no doubt what they had found:

> On the lower part the seal impressions were much clearer, and we were able without difficulty to make out on several of them the name of Tut.ankh.Amen.[1]

In due course, the blocked doorway was dismantled, revealing a sloping tunnel filled from floor to ceiling with limestone chippings. As workmen struggled in the dusty, confined space to clear the tunnel, they encountered a second doorway, likewise covered with sealings naming Tutankhamun. To Carter's horror, this inner doorway, like the first, showed signs of earlier forced entry. Robbers had clearly entered the tomb in antiquity. The question was, had they left anything behind?

By four o'clock in the afternoon on 26 November, the corridor had been fully cleared. Watched by his patron, Lady Evelyn Herbert, Carnarvon's daughter, and an English engineer called Arthur Callender, Carter prised some of the stones from the top of the second doorway. He recorded in his journal what happened next:

> Candles were procured – the all-important tell-tale for foul gases when opening an ancient subterranean chamber – I widened the breach and by means of the candle looked in, while Ld. C., Lady E, and Callender with the Reises waited in anxious expectation. It was sometime before one could see, the hot air escaping caused the candle to flicker, but as soon as one's eyes became accustomed to the glimmer of light the interior of the chamber gradually loomed before one, with its strange and wonderful medley of extraordinary and beautiful objects heaped upon one another.[2]

What they had found was a treasure in every sense. But all too quickly, the magnitude of the discovery began to dawn. Carter later reflected:

> I suppose we had never formulated exactly in our minds just what we had expected or hoped to see, but certainly we had never dreamed of anything like this, a roomful – a whole museumful, it seemed – of objects.[3]

Indeed, this 'seemingly endless profusion' of objects numbered 5,398 in total, distributed among the four rooms of the tomb: the Antechamber, Annexe, Burial Chamber and Treasury. It would take Carter and a team of specialists a decade to catalogue and conserve the contents.

◁◖▷

Among the myriad precious artefacts piled high in Tutankhamun's tomb were 'some familiar, but some the like of which we had never seen'.⁴ Indeed, many remain unique examples of their kind, unparalleled from any other ancient Egyptian site. It was fortunate that, by 1922, Egyptology had developed to a point where Carter and his assistants were able to recognize the importance of what they had found.

The orgy of treasure-seeking that characterized antiquarian interest in the Nile Valley throughout the first half of the nineteenth century had resulted in many thousands of objects entering European collections, to be admired as curios and *objets d'art*, but the proper interpretation of Egyptian antiquities only really began with Champollion's decipherment of hieroglyphics, which allowed ancient Egyptian culture to be studied in its own right and on its own terms. At the same time, Wilkinson's careful on-the-ground observations brought new breakthroughs in understanding. He recognized the pyramids of Giza as the tombs of fourth-dynasty kings, while his accurate drawings of the scenes in the Tombs of the Nobles at Thebes enhanced the picture of pharaonic culture by illuminating daily life in ancient Egypt.

Building on these foundations, nineteenth-century scholars brought a sharper focus to the study of ancient Egypt, elucidating the different periods of its long history and charting the development of its art and architecture. Thanks to the efforts of the Prussian scholar Richard Lepsius, pharaonic civilization gained texture and nuance: instead of being seen as a single amorphous entity, it came to be understood as a succession of distinct epochs, which were named the Old, Middle and New Kingdoms. Lepsius resolved many of the outstanding historical questions and also enabled sentences of ancient Egyptian – as opposed to just names and titles – to be translated for the first time.

With the establishment of the Antiquities Service in the late 1850s, new discoveries came thick and fast. The Pyramid

Age was revealed in all its glory, from life-sized royal statues to the world's oldest body of religious writings. From the 1880s, Petrie's insistence on meticulous, systematic excavation led to some of the most elusive and fragile remains being discovered, recorded and studied. His attention to detail revealed the long prehistory of ancient Egyptian civilization, the sophistication of Graeco-Egyptian culture at the end of its immense time span and much in between.

As knowledge grew, so further discoveries in the late nineteenth and early twentieth centuries added yet more colour and detail: the superlative craftsmanship of Middle Kingdom jewellery, the material remains of Egypt's earliest dynasties, and scenes of daily life from every epoch. Hence, by the time Carter and Carnarvon began to dig in the Valley of the Kings, ancient Egypt was no longer just an amalgam of garbled classical accounts or a mythical realm of esoteric knowledge, but a complex and vibrant civilization, inhabited by real people.

Even so, the sheer scale and scope of Tutankhamun's treasures demanded a multi-disciplinary team unprecedented in the annals of Egyptology, and the vast hoard of antiquities interred with the king was studied with unusual care and attention. The insights – which are still being refined and analysed, a century after their discovery – are perhaps even more remarkable than Carter could have imagined. As the following pages will show, objects from the tomb shed fascinating light on every aspect of ancient Egypt. They are not just a collection of precious artefacts, but a kaleidoscopic reflection of the culture that produced them. Perhaps most poignant is an object that conjures up a lost world of human experience: Tutankhamun's silver trumpet. The instrument itself survives, but the music it produced, and the occasions on which it was played, are lost forever. The world that surrounded the king has vanished; all that remains are echoes of the past, the stuff of interpretation and reinterpretation. But through the treasures buried with him, his world and the civilization of which he remains the ultimate symbol can be brought back to life.

ONE

Geography

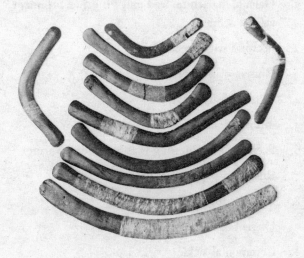

Fig. 1. Throw sticks.

1. Galena, malachite, lead and tin oxide, orpiment, yellow ochre

2. Pectoral with green glass

3. Chisels of meteoric iron

4. Ostrich-feather fan

5. Throw sticks

6. Scene of bird-hunting (Little Golden Shrine)

7. Rush and papyrus sandals

8. Model papyrus skiff

9. Osiris bed

10. Ceremonial sickle

Every culture is a product of its environment, and ancient Egyptian civilization was shaped by the distinctive geography of the Nile Valley and the surrounding deserts. To understand the richness and complexity of pharaonic Egypt, it is necessary to start with an appreciation of the Egyptians' physical world. The deserts that bordered the Nile Valley to the west and east afforded a sense of protection and emphasized the fertility of the river's floodplain. Inhospitable they might have been, but they were not impenetrable: evidence shows that they were widely explored, and they also provided a wide range of materials. Mineral ores and pigments, precious and semi-precious stones, and game: for those who knew where to look, the deserts were as valuable as the banks of the Nile. Yet it was the river that made life in Egypt possible, and ancient Egyptians considered themselves blessed by the narrow strip of fertile alluvium that threaded its way through the surrounding expanses of sand and rock. The banks of the Nile provided bountiful food and materials, while the river's remarkable regime – the annual inundation – brought fertility to the fields and underpinned Egypt's agricultural economy. Objects from Tutankhamun's tomb reflect and illustrate the varied geography of ancient Egypt, helping us enter the world of a people whose lives were shaped by such a special natural environment.

⊲◦⊳

'Egypt', as the ancient Greek historian Herodotus observed, 'is an acquired country – the gift of the river.'[1] His remark alludes to the fact – as true today as it was two, three, four or even five thousand years ago – that without the Nile, there would be no Egypt. Certainly, without the river, people would not have been able to settle, nor a civilization to develop, in the north-east corner of Africa. It is only the presence of the Nile that enables life to flourish amidst the arid vastness of the Sahara; either side of the narrow strip of green that consti-tutes the Valley, the lone and level sands stretch far away.

The area of irrigated land along the Nile constitutes only one-twentieth of Egypt's current land mass, yet it supports more than 96 per cent of its population. Indeed, in ancient Egyptian, the word for 'black [alluvial] land' was also the word for 'Egypt'. On the face of it, it would be easy to agree with the Roman geographer Strabo, who asserted that 'Egypt consists of only the river-land',[2] or with a later traveller, Samuel Cox, who wrote that 'Egypt is the Nile . . . The Nile has created its limits.'[3] But to do so would be to ignore the crucial role that desert – the other 95 per cent of Egypt's area – has played in the country's geography and in the formation of its ancient civilization.

Pharaonic Egypt may have been rooted in the Nile Valley and sustained by the river, but it was deeply shaped by the surrounding deserts. When, in the late nineteenth century, archaeologists came across the burials of prehistoric Egyptians, they were intrigued by the abundant signs of cultural influence from Egypt's arid hinterland: pottery that shared stylistic char-acteristics with wares from the Nubian wastes, ostrich eggs from the dry savannahs and mineral pigments from remote deserts. So alien did these grave goods appear at first, that they were believed to be the remains of a 'new race' of invaders who had entered the Nile Valley from the east. Subsequent excavations and studies proved, however, that the prehistoric (today we call them 'predynastic' – standing before the sequence of historic dynasties) Egyptians had been there all along.

If we go back 7,000 years to the first stirrings of Egyptian civilization, the country would have looked very different. Instead of desert, the lands either side of the Nile Valley were dry grasslands, watered every year by summer rains. In addition to the wildlife that is characteristic of such habitats today – ostrich, elephant, giraffe, antelope – the grasslands also supported groups of nomadic cattle herders who followed their herds from pasture to pasture according to the season. It was among these pastoralists that the seeds of pharaonic culture first took root. When the climate across North Africa started to dry out in the fourth millennium BC, the wandering herders were forced to retreat to the nearest source of permanent water – the Nile – and to settle in communities, thus paving the way for the emergence of a great civilization.

Just as much of the symbolic vocabulary of ancient Egypt can be traced back to the predynastic world, so, too, can some of its most deep-rooted cultural traditions. The love of bodily adornment, and especially of cosmetics, is a case in point. Bodily decoration is a hallmark of nomadic societies, among whom, in the absence of permanent structures, people display their wealth and status largely through their own bodies. Some of the earliest and most characteristic objects recovered from predynastic graves are cosmetic palettes – flat pieces of stone, often carved into geometric or animal shapes, that were used to grind up mineral pigments for make-up. Occasionally, traces of the pigments themselves have survived: deep green malachite, red and yellow ochre, white tin oxide and black galena. The custom of facial decoration continued long after the early Egyptians had settled in the Nile Valley. Throughout pharaonic history, whenever ancient Egyptians are depicted – for example, on the walls of tombs – they are shown wearing eye paint. Dark lines of make-up ring the eyes, ending in a 'fishtail' cosmetic line.

The raw materials for face paints – ingredients that found added use in the preparation of paints for art and writing – not only harked back to an ancestral way of life in the arid lands that became the Sahara; they were derived from desert mines and quarries, thus reinforcing the importance of the 'red land' as a vital component of Egypt's geography and identity. Long after the Egyptians had settled by the banks of the Nile, they continued to mine the desert for its resources, and they were probably more familiar with the lands to the east and west of the Valley than their modern descendants. Expeditions would have regularly brought back supplies of mineral pigments: lead and tin oxide from the Red Sea hills, malachite from the Nubian Desert and the Sinai Peninsula, ochre from the low deserts of the First Cataract region.

As befitted any self-respecting Egyptian, Tutankhamun was buried with a wide variety of mineral cosmetics, to enable him to maintain his appearance in the afterlife and to assist in his scribal and artistic endeavours. Pieces of galena were found tied up in a linen bag and deposited in the Annexe of his tomb. Also among his grave goods were lumps of malachite, a small piece of lead, fragments of tin oxide, orpiment and ochre. They are a reminder that ancient Egypt owed its origins and its flourishing as much to the desert as to the Nile.

⊲◦⊳

The deserts not only supplied ancient Egyptians with pigments for face and wall paints; the sand dunes and desolate wadis either side of the Nile Valley also yielded an abundance of rocks, minerals, precious and semi-precious stones that could be used for architecture, for sculpture and, not least, for jewellery. The abundant jewels buried with Tutankhamun are not the finest produced under the pharaohs – that accolade surely belongs to those from the Middle Kingdom royal workshops, seven centuries earlier – but they are among the most opulent. The sheer variety of materials from which the boy king's rings, bracelets, necklaces, pendants and pectorals were created demonstrates the wealth, reach and sophistication of ancient Egyptian civilization. In terms of rarity and exoticism, one piece in particular stands out; its true significance was fully revealed only twenty years ago.

Many of Tutankhamun's most valuable pieces of jewellery had been placed in sealed boxes in the chamber of his tomb dubbed 'the Treasury' by archaeologists. One of the caskets, found on the north side of the room, contained a veritable king's ransom of spectacular pieces: a pectoral in the shape of a scarab beetle, the insect's body made from lapis lazuli, with other elements inlaid in carnelian, turquoise and coloured glass; a second pectoral in the shape of a falcon, its feathers carefully depicted with cloisonné decoration; and a third pectoral, chunkier and heavier than the other two, which combined a variety of carved and inlaid religious symbols – lunar disc, sacred eye, solar barque, winged scarab, lotus and papyrus plants, rearing cobras, fruits and flowers – in one complex, extravagant composition. The central element, the beetle's body, was fashioned from a single piece of a pale green stone. It was initially identified as semi-precious chalcedony, but the truth is altogether more surprising.

In Egypt's Western Desert, straddling the border with Libya, there is a vast expanse of dunes, known as the Great Sand Sea, that stretches from the Siwa Oasis in the north to the Gilf Kebir in the south. The feature covers an area of some 72,000 square kilometres, and includes individual dunes that are one hundred kilometres long and one hundred metres high. It is as remote, inaccessible, inhospitable and forbidding as any place on earth. In modern times, it has been visited by just a handful of intrepid explorers. The first to do so, a German adventurer named Gerhard Rohlfs, surveyed the area in 1874. He nearly died of dehydration, but was saved by a chance thunderstorm. Before hurrying home, he marked the spot with a cairn, and wrote in his journal, 'Will ever man's foot tread this place again?'[4]

Among the many mysteries of the Great Sand Sea is the occurrence of lumps of pale green glass – ranging in size from small granules to substantial boulders – that are to be found lying on the surface, in a relatively small area of desert. First encountered by Europeans in the 1930s, the naturally occurring glass has been the object of a dozen geological expeditions to identify its composition and source. Volcanic activity can produce glass, but there are no volcanoes in the Great Sand Sea. The temperature and pressure required to fuse silica sand into glass are so extreme that there is only one other plausible explanation: meteorite impact. A potential impact crater, named the Kebira Crater, has been identified from satellite images; with a diameter of nearly twenty miles at its widest point, it must have been created by a sizeable meteorite. However, the crater lies about fifty miles from the main area of desert glass. The clues, while tantalizing, are, as yet, inconclusive.

In 1998, an Italian geologist was granted permission to examine the 'chalcedony' pectoral from Tutankhamun's tomb and discovered that the scarab's body was made of natural silica glass. The ramifications of this discovery are astonishing. Thirty-three centuries ago, ancient Egyptians must have known about the deposits of natural glass in the Great Sand Sea. They were clearly able to obtain it, either through long-distance trade with desert nomads, or – more likely, given their expeditions to other remote locations – through direct exploitation of the deposits. The ancient Egyptians must have marvelled at the occurrence of natural glass in such a desolate location. And the jewellers of Tutankhamun's royal workshops chose this otherworldly material to represent the body of the scarab beetle, the god of the rising sun and rebirth, whose magic would aid the king's resurrection.

Above all, the green glass pectoral reminds us that Egypt's ancient inhabitants knew their country better than anyone, including their modern descendants. In search of costly and exotic materials to adorn their rulers and prosper them in the afterlife, ancient Egyptians were prepared to go, quite literally, to the ends of the earth.

⊲๐⊳

For most of pharaonic history, Egypt was a Bronze Age culture. By Tutankhamun's time, the process of forging iron had been perfected in other lands, notably the Hittite Empire of Central Anatolia, but the conservative Egyptians preferred to stick to tried-and-trusted bronze for their weapons and tools. They regarded iron as a novelty: mysterious and intriguing, but no substitute for the metal their craftsmen had been happily working for 1,500 years. For a start, unlike the copper and tin needed for making bronze, there were no sources of iron ore easily accessible; the nearest deposits were in the furthest reaches of Upper Nubia to the south or in Palestine to the north. The only naturally occurring iron in Egypt itself was meteoric iron, small pieces of which could be found in the vicinity of the impact craters dotting the Western Desert. Together with green silica glass, carnelian and a host of other precious and semi-precious minerals, lumps of meteoric iron were occasionally brought back by mining expeditions and fashioned into curios.

Tutankhamun's burial equipment contained a range of ritual and practical tools. There were sickles and hoes, adzes and knives, mallets and chisels, but we should not imagine the young king passing his time with handicrafts or farming: the tools were included among his grave goods to ensure an eternal supply of agricultural produce and manufactured goods in the afterlife. The most valuable tools were, like the costliest jewellery, kept in the tomb's Treasury. One toolbox contained sixteen chisels; all had been made from a nugget or nuggets of meteoric iron weighing no more than four grams in total. Even in a society that knew how to exploit the deserts' natural resources, meteoric iron remained a very rare commodity.

Indeed, the ancient Egyptian word for 'iron' was *biayt*; its alternative meaning is 'miracle' or 'wonder'. But there is evidence to suggest that the origins of meteoric iron had not escaped the ancient Egyptians' enquiring minds. A thousand years before Tutankhamun, Egyptian priests composed the earliest surviving corpus of religious writings. Inscribed on the walls of royal burial chambers, they are known today as the Pyramid Texts. In them, the king's afterlife is imagined among the stars. There are prayers to help him rise up and join the stars, spells to aid his transformation into a star and hymns to celebrate his becoming one. And there are tantalizing references to the stars' composition. According to the texts, they were made from

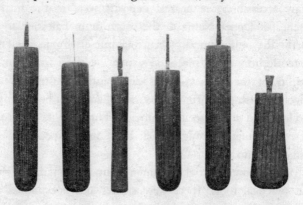

Fig. 2. Chisels of meteoric iron.

biayt. How could an Egyptian priest of the third millennium BC have known that the stars were made from iron, other than by knowing that iron fell from the heavens as shooting stars?

There is more: one of the most venerable funeral ceremonies in ancient Egypt, from the Pyramid Age onwards, was the 'opening of the mouth'. Its depiction takes pride of place on the wall of Tutankhamun's burial chamber, being performed by the king's successor, Ay. The symbolism of the ceremony was to bring the mummified body back to life by opening its mouth and allowing it to breathe. By tradition, the rite was performed with implements fashioned from meteoric iron. According to ancient Egyptian religious reasoning, there could be no better way of ensuring the king's resurrection to a celestial afterlife than by using an instrument of celestial origin to restore his breath.

A final link between meteorites and religion was especially vibrant in Tutankhamun's lifetime. One of the earliest priestly titles from pharaonic Egypt is 'Greatest of Seers', which came to be held by the High Priest of Ra, who officiated at the sun god's cult centre in Heliopolis (near present-day Cairo). The title probably pre-dates the cult of Ra and was likely accorded to a holy man who watched the heavens for omens and portents. It is probably no coincidence that the most sacred symbol of Ra, kept in the sanctuary of his temple at Heliopolis, was a stone named the *benben*. It has never been found, and there has been much speculation as to its nature. One possibility is that it was a meteorite: a rock of iron, a miraculous gift from the heavens. Tutankhamun's father Akhenaten, whose religious revolution sought to turn back the clock to the time of creation, showed special reverence for the stone, and he even had a version of it installed at the centre of his showpiece temple in his capital city, Akhetaten – the city where Tutankhamun was born and spent his childhood.

From shooting star and sacred stone to meteorite and source of iron, the web of associations conjured up by sixteen chisel blades illustrates pharaonic religion at its most inspired and insightful. All things in heaven and earth, it seems, were dreamt of in ancient Egyptian philosophy.

Alongside their abundant mineral resources, the deserts of Egypt were also famed for their wildlife. In the time of the pharaohs' earliest ancestors, the nomadic cattle herders, the vast expanses of grassland to the east and west of the Nile Valley teemed with a diverse fauna. Prehistoric rock art found across the Sahara depicts this wildlife in all its variety. Predynastic pottery, stone vessels and carved ivory knife handles likewise depict animals ranging from aardvarks to honey badgers, as well as the human hunters and their dogs who pursued such prey. But towards the middle of the fourth millennium BC, as the climate changed and the savannahs began to desiccate, many of the larger animals retreated southwards; by the Pyramid Age, elephants and giraffes had disappeared from Egypt, lions were rare and ostrich numbers had dwindled.

Nonetheless, desert hunting remained a popular pastime and a powerful display of status among Egypt's ruling elite. Tutankhamun had a hunting lodge built on the Giza Plateau, close to the Great Sphinx, where he could retire after a day's sport. Tales of hunting would be recounted to amuse and impress guests; Tutankhamun's grandfather, Amenhotep III, went a step further and issued commemorative scarabs to celebrate one of his more successful lion hunts and an epic hunt of wild bulls. Then, as now, trophies were brought back and displayed in a domestic or religious setting. Many were imbued with powerful symbolic associations. For example, the tail of a wild bull was worn suspended from the waistband of the king's kilt, a symbol of his power over nature. Leopard skins were highly prized and signified priestly authority: Tutankhamun's successor Ay is shown wearing one as he carries out the opening of the mouth ceremony.

When it came to hunting trophies that connoted pure ostentation, two products reigned supreme: the ostrich egg and the ostrich feather. The ostrich is an impressive creature, and it is not difficult to see why it was viewed with awe by those who encountered it. A tantalizing piece of evidence suggests that it may even have been venerated, or at least imbued with magical status: a prehistoric rock carving in the Eastern Desert shows an ostrich aboard a vessel, perhaps depicting an afterlife journey. Ostrich eggs also enjoyed a special status from predynastic times. For prehistoric people, they offered a valuable source of protein, and the shells may have doubled as water-carriers. Ancient campsites across the Western Desert are strewn with fragments of shell, attesting to the abundance of this natural resource. An intact egg decorated with wild antelope is a remarkable survival from a predynastic grave; other burials of the period were furnished with model ostrich eggs fashioned from clay. If you couldn't lay your hands on the genuine article, a substitute was the next best thing.

Ostrich feathers were also accorded great value and were widely worn as a mark of status. In tomb paintings from Tutankhamun's time, the archetypal Nubian chief is depicted wearing an ostrich feather in his hair. Six centuries later, the tables turned, a Nubian pharaoh contemptuously referred to his Egyptian rivals as 'the feather-wearing chiefs of Lower Egypt'. For Egyptians and Nubians alike, a feather in the cap was something worth striving for.

To possess a single ostrich feather was a mark of distinction; to possess enough to make a fan was the preserve of royalty. On one of the earliest monuments of pharaonic kingship, a carved stone macehead, the monarch is shown accompanied by fan-bearers. 'Fan-bearer on the king's right hand' was an honorific title bestowed on the most favoured courtiers. Tutankhamun's burial equipment included no fewer than eight fans. One was a hand-held rotating fan, fashioned from ivory and stored in its own box. The other seven were on longer handles, for a servant to wave before the king's face.

The most elaborate fan, which brings together multiple symbols of wealth and status, is one of the most beautiful objects from Tutankhamun's tomb. Measuring over a metre long, it was found in the king's burial chamber, nestled in the narrow gap between the third and fourth golden shrines that protected his sarcophagus. The handle and the semi-circular 'palm' into which the feathers were inserted are covered in gold foil, embossed and chased with scenes and inscriptions. On one side of the palm, Tutankhamun is shown in his hunting chariot, firing a hail of arrows at a pair of ostriches, which are also being pursued by a hunting dog. On the other side, the king is shown returning triumphant. An inscription on the handle records that all the feathers in the fan (there were originally forty-two of them, arranged in alternating colours, white and brown) were obtained by the king himself 'while out hunting in the desert east of Heliopolis'. Tutankhamun's ostrich-feather fan is a powerful symbol of his kingly status and an ostentatious reminder of the deserts' erstwhile abundance.

⊰⊙⊱

A final benefit of Egypt's desert margins was the protection they afforded: for most of its long history, Egypt enjoyed a secure position within impenetrable borders. The encircling deserts insulated it from the outside world and were a powerful deterrent against foreign incursions. However, they could not shield the Nile Valley from its jealous neighbours entirely. The fertility of the alluvial floodplain was a boon for the people of Egypt, but it was a perpetual source of envy for the inhabitants of the less fortunate lands to the west, east and south – the Libyans, Asiatics and Nubians. The river's bounty enabled communities and a sophisticated culture to develop and flourish along its banks, but the harsh conditions in Egypt's desert margins provided no such opportunities. On the fringes of the Sahara and in the Sinai Peninsula, semi-nomadic peoples had no choice but to follow their herds between water sources, their lives constrained by their unforgiving environment. The Nile Valley, with its permanent abundance, was a tantalizing prize that was worth fighting for; from prehistoric times onwards, border skirmishes between Egypt and its neighbours were common. Whenever Egypt was perceived to be weakened or vulnerable, the people of the desert margins took their chance.

In the Western Desert, tribespeople characterized by their curly hair, bellicose temperament and fighting prowess – the ancestors of present-day Libyans – proved a persistent thorn in Egypt's side. From the beginning of Egyptian history, they tested the young civilization's defences, launching raids on the western oases and along the west bank of the Nile. The earliest reference to one such encounter is on a ceremonial cosmetic palette dating from the decades immediately before Egyptian unification. Amid scenes of warfare, a vast haul of booty – mostly sheep and goats – is depicted, identified by the accompanying hieroglyphs as tribute from Libya. In ancient Egyptian, this land and its people were called *Tjehenu*. The term was written with the sign of a throw stick, perhaps indicating the primitive weaponry at the Libyans' disposal.

Throw sticks might have been primitive, but they could prove deadly at close range. A number were included in

Tutankhamun's grave goods; along with slings, clubs, boomerangs, bows and arrows, they constituted an arsenal of weapons designed to remind the king of his martial exploits during his lifetime and assist him in his battles in the next world. Throw sticks also served a non-military purpose, being used to bring down game birds during hunting trips in the marshes. A scene from an eighteenth-dynasty Theban tomb shows the tomb owner, Nebamun, hunting for fowl in a papyrus thicket, while brandishing in his upraised hand a throw stick carved to resemble a rearing snake. Two identical weapons were found on the floor of the Annexe of Tutankhamun's tomb.

The earliest recorded battle with the *Tjehenu* resulted in defeat for the would-be invaders, but they continued to try their luck. Eventually, in the dying days of the New Kingdom – two and a half centuries after Tutankhamun – they succeeded in penetrating Egypt's defences and establishing themselves in Egyptian society. Their military prowess now proved valuable to their hosts, and many Libyans rose to prominence in the Egyptian army. Eventually, following the collapse of the New Kingdom state, a dynasty of Libyan generals was able to seize power and gain the ultimate prize: the Egyptian throne. The men with throw sticks became pharaohs.

To the east of Egypt, a different group proved equally trouble-some neighbours, over an equally long period. On a small ivory label from the reign of Den in the middle of Egypt's first dynasty, the king is shown smiting an enemy in front of a sandy mountain. The victim, described as an 'easterner', belonged to one of the Asiatic tribes that inhabited a swathe of territory stretching from Palestine to the Sinai Peninsula. Campaigns against these people – whom the Egyptians referred to patron-izingly as the 'sand-dwellers' – continued sporadically throughout the succeeding centuries. The Egyptians never lost, but nor did they win a conclusive victory; their opponents melted back into their desert hills to lick their wounds. They, too, had their moment of glory: in the seventeenth century BC, some 300 years before Tutankhamun, they took advantage of Egypt's relative weakness to establish their own dynasty of kings. The so-called Hyksos (a Greek corruption of an ancient Egyptian term meaning 'rulers of foreign lands') ruled over the Nile Valley for a century.

In ancient Egyptian, the generic word for 'Asiatics' was *Aamu*. It, too, was written with the hieroglyphic of a throw stick. The connotation was the same as for the *Tjehenu*: both were uncivilized, primitive peoples, inherently inferior to the Egyptians, yet irritatingly aggressive. The throw stick-wielding foreigners who lurked beyond Egypt's borders reminded the inhabitants of the Nile Valley of their own geographical advantages and reinforced their sense of splendid isolation.

⊲○▷

While the 'red land' gave Egypt a measure of security, it was the narrow strip of 'black land' – the floodplain of the River Nile – that became synonymous with pharaonic civilization. As Herodotus recognized, a river was a prerequisite for the development of a great civilization, but it was not so much the waterway itself as its thickly vegetated banks that drew people from far and wide. Even in prehistoric times, when annual summer rains greened the desert and filled its shallow lake basins, the Nile, with its reliable flow and teeming banks, attracted semi-permanent settlement. In the fifth millennium BC – a thousand years before the unification of Egypt and the establishment of its first dynasty of kings – a group of semi-nomadic people known to archaeology as the Badarians migrated every winter from their savannah pastures to graze their herds and make their homes by the Nile's banks. While they kept watch over their animals and small plots of fast-growing crops, they built flimsy, temporary dwellings, clustered together in small villages.

The Badarians' seasonal settlements showed signs of repeated use over many years, but left only the merest of traces. Everything was portable, and when they packed up and left at the end of each winter, only the post holes and hearths betrayed their presence. The burials of those who died in the Valley were more permanent memorials, and probably served to connect particular family groups to specific stretches of riverbank. The grave goods tell of a people who loved decoration, traded widely and were beginning to organize themselves into a hierarchical society. There were objects from the deserts and also artefacts from their riverine way of life: pots made from alluvial clay and small copper fish hooks.

For hunter-gatherers, the river and its margins offered a rich ecosystem to exploit. There were plentiful fish, of course, ranging from the catfish lurking in the shallows to the great Nile perch that frequented the deeper channels. On the shore, wild cattle might be hunted when they came down to the water to drink at dusk. Above all, the papyrus beds that lined the banks teemed with waterfowl: ibis and egrets, cormorants and herons, ducks and geese. When a boat brushed the reeds, flocks of birds would rise up from their nests, providing a waiting hunter with an easy meal. From the days of the Badarians until the end of ancient Egyptian civilization some 4,000 years later, fowling in the marshes was an everyday feature of life in the Nile Valley, an activity enjoyed by rich and poor, whether as pastime or practical necessity. It is no accident that more than a dozen different water birds came to be used as signs in hieroglyphic writing, nor that a goose was the symbol of the earth god Geb and one of the animals sacred to the state god of New Kingdom Egypt, Amun-Ra.

Scenes of bird hunting can be found in tombs from every

period of Egyptian civilization, from the Pyramid Age to the time of Tutankhamun and beyond. The boy pharaoh himself clearly enjoyed spending time among the reeds as much as riding chariots in the desert. On the Little Golden Shrine from his tomb – an elegant gilded chest, which originally housed a statue of the king – the decoration on the gold foil includes a scene of one such excursion. Tutankhamun sits on the riverbank, bow and arrow in hand. There is no royal throne, just a portable folding stool, made more comfortable with a plump embroidered cushion. The king's pet lion cub stands alongside. Tutankhamun's young wife, seated on the ground, gestures towards the reeds, while passing her husband an arrow with her other hand. The king is shown poised to release the drawstring, while a covey of ducks rises from the reeds, abandoning nests that contain eggs and hatchlings.

On one level, this charming vignette depicts a royal day away from the rigours of duty, the young pharaonic couple relaxing in each other's company amidst the natural bounty of the Nile Valley. But there are layers of deeper meaning. In ancient Egyptian, the word for 'shoot' was the same as the word for 'inseminate'. Ducks were not just game birds, but symbols of fertility. So the image of a young man shooting ducks while his wife hands him an arrow would have been interpreted as a metaphor for sexual intercourse and procreation. Hence, the scene of fowling on Tutankhamun's Little Golden Shrine may be read as much as an idyll of conjugal union and an invocation for the continuation of the royal line as a depiction of a carefree hunting trip. Either way, it emphasizes the fecundity of the Nile's reedy banks, a sheltered environment where Egyptians came to enjoy nature's fertility.

The ancient Egyptians thought of their country as a papyrus plant: the long, narrow Nile Valley was the tall, sturdy stalk, while the delta was the flower head. This symbolic conceit was true in a very real sense: pharaonic civilization was dependent on central control of the economy, which was made possible by the written record, which relied on a convenient, abundant and portable medium of communication – papyrus. It is not known when the Egyptians discovered that the pithy interior of the papyrus stalk – cut into long strips, arranged in two layers at right angles, hammered with a mallet to release the fibres and knit the layers together, left in the sun to dry and finally burnished with a pebble – made an excellent writing material. The earliest roll of papyrus – tantalizingly blank – was found in the tomb of an official dating to the middle of the first dynasty, around 2850 BC. Before long, papyrus was being used to record land ownership, tax assessments, laws and regulations. The papyrus reed was hence both a metaphor for the land of Egypt and its underpinning technology.

Until very recent times, the Nile's banks were choked with dense reed beds. They can still be seen along stretches where human activity has been limited: in some areas of Middle Egypt, at the First Nile Cataract near Aswan and in remote parts of Nubia. The papyrus that once defined Egypt is now largely extinct in the wild, the victim of over-harvesting and wider ecological damage. Strictly speaking, papyrus is a plant that grows in swamps. It spreads quickly by means of horizontal rhizomes and grows at a rapid rate; as a result, when established, it soon smothers and out-competes other plants. Fast-growing and tough as it is, it nonetheless relies on saturated ground. As the swamps of Egypt were systematically drained, the natural habitat of the papyrus was reduced, eventually consigning it to the history books.

By contrast, other varieties of reed that live in the shallows along riverbanks continue to thrive. In ancient times, too, the humble reed and sedge are likely to have been more abundant than the noble papyrus. The common reed was so ubiquitous that it gave its form to one of the most frequently used hieroglyphic signs, with three flowering reeds together signifying 'field'. The sedge, for its part, was characteristic of the vegetation of Upper Egypt, and in prehistoric times came to be associated with the southern Nile Valley and its rulers. The most ancient term for 'king' – a term that endured for the entire 3,000 years of pharaonic civilization – literally meant 'he of the sedge'.

The ancient Egyptians were fond of symbols – Egypt's geographical environment was replete with natural features that lent themselves to reinterpretation and association – and this symbolic vocabulary was multi-layered. Hence, while Egypt as a whole was compared to a papyrus reed (and a stalk of papyrus was the hieroglyphic sign for the words 'green' and 'flourish'), the plant was also the emblem for the delta, while the waterlily stood for the Nile Valley. A favourite design in Egyptian art – seen, for example, on the fretwork of Tutankhamun's gilded throne – depicted intertwined papyrus and lily plants, symbolizing the inextricable union of Upper and Lower Egypt. The 'Two Lands' was a favourite moniker for the country as a whole, but Egypt was also known by other names: *Kemet* ('black land', from the colour of the alluvial soil), *Ta-meri* ('ploughed land', connoting its agricultural fertility) or 'Two Banks', indicating that the vast bulk of the population lived along the floodplain. The prominence of riverine motifs illustrates the central place of the Nile in the Egyptian consciousness.

The riverbanks not only defined the Egyptians' homeland, they furnished all life's essentials. The reedy margins provided food and a wide variety of supplies for everyday needs. Clay from the banks, tempered with a little reed straw, could be made into pottery. From earliest times, the Egyptians were among the greatest ceramicists of the ancient world; Badarian pottery, for example, with its eggshell-thin walls and rippled surfaces, ranks among the finest ever produced. The reeds themselves had multiple uses. Chopped straw, mixed with silt and dried in the sun, formed the quintessential building material for Egyptian houses, while longer stalks were woven to produce matting. Tutankhamun's tomb contained a variety of objects made from reed. One of his chairs had a back and seat of plaited papyrus strips, a supple yet hard-wearing material. Shredded papyrus was used as packaging material inside a compartmented wooden box that once held precious glass vessels. (To Carter's disappointment, the box was found empty, its contents probably stolen by tomb robbers soon after the king's burial.) Humblest of all, yet in many ways most characteristic of the ancient Egyptian way of life, were several pairs of sandals made from woven rush and papyrus. Everyday, throwaway objects, made from the most common of natural materials, they exemplify the bond between the Egyptians and their environment.

Ironically, the tomb of a ruler whose kingdom was built on the written word was entirely devoid of papyrus documents. In its most famous form – as the original paper – the reed that built a civilization had no part to play in the pharaoh's eternal afterlife.

◁◦▷

Sedges and reeds were plentiful in the ancient Nile Valley, but good timber was harder to come by. Palm logs were used as beams and roof supports, or as rollers for transporting blocks of stone, but were not suitable for carving. Small items of furniture could be fashioned from the native trees that grew along the banks of the Nile, but large pieces of hardwood – as required for statuary and boat-building – had to be imported from the cedar-covered mountains of Lebanon. Long-distance trade in exotic products was a royal monopoly, completely out of the reach of the average Egyptian, who had to make do with other materials to build the craft they needed to navigate the river.

Fortunately, papyrus was abundant and easy to work; moreover, its strong, pliable stalks have a natural buoyancy. Bundles of reeds, when lashed together, form an effective float. Spells from the Pyramid Texts refer to the 'double reed floats' on which the deceased king was believed to cross the sky in the company of the gods.

Better than a reed float was a skiff – a lightweight canoe made from papyrus bundles. They were usually big enough to carry one or two people, although larger craft for transporting cattle are known to have been built. Papyrus skiffs were probably the oldest form of river transport in Egypt; pottery models of such craft have been found in prehistoric graves. According to Pliny the Elder, the Roman historian of the first century AD, they were still a popular means of transport in his day, and they remained a feature of village life on the Upper Nile well into the twentieth century. Skiffs have been depicted in every period of ancient Egyptian history. Wall decoration in the tombs of Old Kingdom officials show papyrus being harvested, transported and woven into skiffs. Another famous scene, painted 500 years later in a Middle Kingdom tomb at Beni Hasan, shows the tomb owner and his friends standing in papyrus skiffs, wielding their punting poles to joust in mock battle.

Indeed, a long pole was the most common way to propel a skiff, but it could also be manoeuvred by means of a wooden paddle or even by hand. Skiffs were very occasionally fitted with a small sail, but this was the exception. Lightweight and drawing very little water, a skiff was the ideal craft to navigate the shallows along the banks of the Nile, avoiding the sandbanks and other obstacles that hampered navigation in heavier boats.

Gliding along almost silently, the papyrus skiff was the perfect vessel for birding and fishing in reed beds and marshes. Tutankhamun not only had himself depicted hunting waterfowl, but also made sure he had a model skiff among his grave goods, to enable him to pursue his pastime in the afterlife. The model is made from wood, its sides painted with stripes to resemble bundles of reeds. The prow is pointed and the stern is broad and flattened. Most full-sized skiffs would have had a small wooden platform in their middle to provide the rower with extra stability, but this detail is missing from Tutankhamun's model. Indeed, it is probably make-believe in other ways. For despite the skiff's practicality, it had largely fallen out of fashion

Fig. 3. Wooden model of a papyrus skiff.

among the ruling class by Tutankhamun's time. Larger boats made from imported timber had gained popularity among the elite. It is highly doubtful that the pharaoh would ever have travelled unaccompanied in a throwaway papyrus skiff. Nonetheless, because of its heritage and the fact that it was made from the Nile's iconic vegetation, the papyrus skiff had become the quintessential ancient Egyptian river craft and a ritually charged object.

In the Treasury of Tutankhamun's tomb, one of a series of shrines coated in thick black resin was found to contain a pair of gilded wooden statuettes, still wrapped in the linen shawls that had been placed around them to protect them from damage. Each one showed the king standing on a papyrus skiff, harpoon in hand. For Tutankhamun's contemporaries, this image would have called to mind the ritual harpooning of a hippopotamus, symbolizing the triumph of order over chaos. Whether it would have been possible to spear a hippopotamus while standing in a flimsy papyrus canoe was not the point: the skiff's symbolic associations were what mattered. The struggle between good and evil was one of the defining myths of ancient Egyptian religion; if the king was to participate effectively in a re-enactment of this epic encounter, it was appropriate that he should use a form of boat that dated back to before the beginning of recorded history.

Whether it was used for hunting large prey or for fishing trips and daily river journeys, the simple reed canoe exemplifies ancient Egyptian civilization, eminently practical and economical while also imbued with multiple layers of meaning.

<=10=>

Of all the different strands of myth and legend that were woven into the rich tapestry of ancient Egyptian religion, one story in particular had special resonance. It was a creation myth that summed up the defining phenomenon of Egypt's geography: the Nile and its annual inundation. According to the story, the world had begun as a watery abyss, dark, silent and infinite. Then, from the limitless waters, a small mound of earth appeared and a reed grew from it. On the reed, a god, in the form of a falcon, alighted, bringing divine blessings to the land and ushering in created order. All of civilization could trace its origins back to that moment, and the mound became a powerful symbol of rebirth. Early royal tombs were covered with mounds, to assist the king's regeneration into the afterlife; the pyramid began life as a series of mounds, piled one upon another, a 'resurrection machine' to ensure that the king would be born again; and every Egyptian temple was founded upon a mound of clean sand, recalling and channelling the power that had ushered the world into being.

The reality was no less miraculous than the myth. Each year in early July, heralded by the appearance of the 'Dog Star' Sirius, above the horizon just before dawn, the Nile rose, its waters swelled by the summer rains in the Ethiopian highlands. The flood was so vital that ancient Egyptians set their calendar by it, the first day of the inundation season marking the start of the new year. The impending arrival of the flood was first detectable at the First Nile Cataract, where the increased volume of water rushing over the granite boulders made a great crashing sound. Over the course of just a few days, the flow there rose fifteen-fold. On the island of Elephantine, a Nilometer measured the height of the floodwaters, for Egypt's prosperity in the coming year depended on it.

The measurements were pored over by priests and bureaucrats, as they gave an unerringly accurate prediction of the following year's harvest. Egypt's earliest historical records – a set of annals carved on a slab of basalt, noting the main events of each year, starting at the beginning of the first dynasty – give pride of place to the height of the annual Nile flood, measured in cubits, palms and fingers. As the Roman historian Pliny explained 2,000 years later:

> An average rise is one of sixteen cubits. A smaller volume of water does not irrigate all localities, and a larger one by retiring too slowly retards agriculture . . . In a rise of twelve cubits [Egypt] senses famine, and even at one of thirteen it begins to feel hungry, but fourteen cubits brings cheerfulness, fifteen complete confidence and sixteen delight.[5]

A flood measuring six feet below normal at Elephantine could reduce agricultural yields by three-quarters, bringing famine. By contrast, a flood six feet above normal would breach dikes, overwhelm settlements, destroy granaries, encourage plagues of insects and delay sowing, causing crops to wither under the hot summer sun. Fortunately, most years, the flood was neither too high nor too low. As the waters spread northwards, the entire floodplain was inundated to a depth of six feet, with only dikes and the towns and villages on higher ground remaining dry. Egypt stood poised to be reborn.

The floodwaters brought twin blessings: water to the fields and a fresh deposit of fertile silt, carried downstream from the Horn of Africa. After sixty days under water, the fields would emerge anew, the soil's fertility renewed for another year. The magical combination of water and nutrients, under the warmth of the Egyptian sun, gave the Nile Valley an agricultural productivity that was the envy of other lands. It was thanks to the annual inundation that Egypt was able to develop a sophisticated civilization.

As far back as the first dynasties of pharaonic rule, the generative and regenerative potential of the floodplain were worshipped in divine form. When such a god is first attested, in the Pyramid Texts, he is called Osiris, a mysterious name of unknown etymology that matched the mystery of Egypt's geography. In origin, he was probably a vegetation god. He is often depicted with skin of a greenish-blue hue, the colour of the Nile and the abundant plant life along its banks, or a lustrous black, the colour of the rich alluvial soil. As befitted a god of such ubiquitous yet intangible power, a web of myths grew up around him. In one of the most popular, he was murdered by his jealous brother Seth in a dispute over who should rule Egypt. Seth dismembered his brother's body and scattered the parts throughout Egypt. Osiris's grieving widow Isis painstakingly gathered up the pieces of her deceased husband – all save his penis, which Seth had thrown in the Nile. Using her magical powers, she revivified and stimulated her husband, conceiving a son, Horus, who subsequently grew up to avenge his father. Osiris, meanwhile, retreated to the underworld to reign as lord of the afterlife.

The story explicitly links the Nile with the power of regeneration, and describes a mystical bond between daily life in the Valley and the afterlife. Indeed, it was as god of the dead that Osiris achieved national prominence in ancient Egypt. A deceased person was customarily referred to as Osiris, and it was the dying wish of every Egyptian to be reborn into his presence and to live with him in his watery underworld, contributing to the fertility of the Nile Valley for all eternity.

The potency of the Osiris myth is expressed in one of the strangest of all the objects buried with Tutankhamun: a plain wooden frame nearly two metres long, shaped to resemble the mummified Osiris, with his distinctive twin-plumed headdress. Just before the king's interment, the frame was filled with moist Nile silt and scattered with grain. Miraculously, the seeds would germinate in the tomb, symbolizing the resurrection of god and king alike.

Fig. 4. Osiris bed.

Tutankhamun's 'Osiris bed' harnessed the essence of Egypt's prosperity to ensure that the king, his realm and its underpinning vitality might endure forever.

◁◌▷

The annual cycle of the Nile also determined the seasons in ancient Egypt. The year was deemed to begin with the onset of the flood in early July, with the first of the three seasons named *akhet*, or 'inundation'. During this period, fields were under water and the entire floodplain resembled a giant lake. For Egypt's largely rural population, there was relatively little to do on the land; it was at this time of the year that the state could most easily levy people to work on government projects, like pyramid building. Conveniently, the season of the inundation, when the waters of the Nile were deepest and spread furthest, was the time of year when it was easiest to move materials, especially large blocks of stone, from quarries to construction sites the length and breadth of Egypt.

Once the flood had passed and the waters started to recede, the season of *peret*, or 'emergence', began. The fields, newly watered and fertilized, would gradually emerge, as the Nile shrank back to its former limits. Artificial basins served to capture some of the water, which was used to irrigate land away from the main river channel. All over Egypt, farmers rushed to repair and dredge dikes and irrigation channels, to restore field boundaries and property markers, to till the soil and prepare it for sowing. Seeds germinated quickly in the warm, moist conditions, and before long new crops were emerging. Barley and emmer – a primitive variety of wheat – were the most common cereals in ancient Egypt. Both grew relatively quickly, and might, if conditions were favourable, supply two crops in the course of a year.

After *peret* came the heat of *shemu*, the summer season. In other parts of north Africa and the Levant, this was a harsh, unforgiving time of year. In Egypt, thanks to an intricate system of irrigation basins and channels, fields could be kept watered during the final few weeks of the growing season, enabling the grain to ripen in the sun. Then came perhaps the busiest period of the year: harvest time. Family members old and young would help gather the crops, before they were processed and stored. At Elkab, in southern Upper Egypt, the tomb of a local official named Paheri, who lived a few generations before Tutankhamun, is famous for its wall decoration showing the different stages of the harvest. At the start of the process, fields of corn are cut by men with scythes, while attendants gather the ears into stooks. These are transported on the backs of donkeys to the threshing floor, where livestock trample the crop. The grain is winnowed using large wooden scoops, before being taken to granaries for storage.

Every family depended upon its store of grain to see it through the year. If stocks ran short, famine loomed. That was one reason why the state maintained vast central granaries, as an insurance policy against lean times. Huge stores of grain also provided the pharaohs with currency for trade; Egypt's agricultural bounty could be exchanged for exotic products like timber and metal from less fertile neighbouring lands. The granaries of Egypt were both its food store and its central bank.

As well as storing the summer's harvest to provide food throughout the year, every farmer in the Nile Valley would set aside some of the grain as seed for the following growing season. Choosing the right amount and quality would determine the success or failure of the next year's harvest. The surviving correspondence of a farmer named Hekanakht, who lived around 2000 BC, describes what must have been a common concern among cultivators. He was temporarily away from his farm on business, and was eager to ensure that it was being properly managed. He wrote to his steward:

> As for all our land that is inundated, you are to cultivate
> it – take heed . . . Be extra dutiful in cultivating. Watch
> out that my seed-corn is guarded and that all my property
> is guarded. Look, I will hold you accountable for it.[6]

Once the harvest had been gathered, Egypt would prepare itself for the coming inundation. Flood defences would be strengthened, walls and banks reinforced, livestock moved to higher ground. Then it was just a matter of waiting for the river to rise and the agricultural year to begin again. This was the rhythm of life in the Nile Valley from prehistoric times up to the 1960s, when the construction of the High Dam at Aswan brought to an end a way of life that had endured for millennia.

Throughout the long sweep of pharaonic history, the familiar cycle of seasons remained a constant force, powering and shaping Egyptian civilization. Among the objects found scattered on the floor of Tutankhamun's tomb were a model hoe and a ceremonial sickle. The latter was made of wood and decorated with gold and electrum foil, with inlays of calcite and glass. It was inscribed with the king's names and the epithet 'beloved of Hu', the personification of food. It served as a reminder that, while the pharaoh's life was far removed from the fields in which his subjects toiled, his throne depended on the country's agricultural productivity.

TWO

History

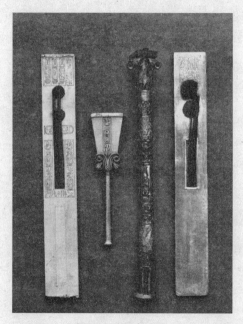

Fig. 5. Scribal palettes.

Ancient Egypt was the longest-lived civilization the world has ever seen. Between the unification of the Nile Valley as the first nation state and its conquest by the Romans, a period of some 3,000 years (one hundred generations) elapsed. While the ancient Egyptians never seem to have developed a sense of objective history, the sheer durability of their civilization gave them a profound sense of superiority. They exuded the confidence that they – and they alone – were the inheritors of a universe brought into being at the time of creation, a world unchanged and unchanging. Of course, the reality was very different. Throughout its long history, ancient Egypt experienced its fair share of upheavals: dynastic turmoil, political fragmentation, civil war, invasion and foreign occupation. Even at times of untrammelled state power, political, economic and climatic instability were ever present. The cycle of rise and fall would be repeated again and again over the course of pharaonic civilization. But throughout such vicissitudes, the Egyptians' fundamental belief in their own divinely ordained origins and destiny remained strong, shaping their civilization accordingly. While the objects from the tomb of Tutankhamun represent a particular moment in time – a single generation among one hundred – they also carry echoes of Egypt's past history, all the way back to its prehistoric origins, and glimpses of its future.

At heart and by instinct, the ancient Egyptians lived in the Stone Age. Even when metalworking – first in copper, then bronze, and only belatedly in iron – found its way to the Nile Valley from the Near East, Egyptian craftsmen seemed to prefer stone. Stone vessels remained highly prized, even though their bronze counterparts were quicker and easier to make. For centuries, a stone sarcophagus was a royal prerogative. Perhaps it was the ready availability of many kinds of hard stone that made it the quintessential Egyptian material. Or perhaps it was the Egyptians' concern with immortality: stone had a permanence, an immutability, that other materials could not match.

In the Nile Valley, as elsewhere, the earliest evidence for human activity comes in the form of chipped stone tools. The oldest such implements, which date back to the Palaeolithic Period, are roughly chipped hand axes fashioned from cores of flint. Examples have been found near Abydos in Upper Egypt and at various other spots along the Nile Valley, usually on raised gravel terraces high above the floodplain; and in the Western Desert, near ancient springs. Some sites are mere scatters of stone tools, suggesting a small, transient population. But a few, such as Arkin 8, close to the western shore of Lake Nasser, show evidence of more significant human activity. Blocks of sandstone laid in a trench and arranged in a semi-circle indicate a permanent structure of some kind, perhaps a ritual or residential building. The Egyptians seem always to have had a fondness for stone construction.

The sequence of Palaeolithic cultures within the borders of present-day Egypt reflects the importance of climate change in human development. A hundred thousand years ago, when Arkin 8 was occupied, a moister climate characterized by summer rains meant that the lands either side of the Nile Valley were grassland. Game was plentiful, and the early inhabitants were hunter-gatherers. Then, about 90,000 years ago, North Africa entered a hyper-arid phase; the savannahs turned into desert and the scattered population was forced to retreat to the oases and the Nile floodplain. When wetter conditions returned, people went back to the savannahs, which were now lusher than before. The combination of a more benign climate and abundant food sources led to population increase and a great flowering of culture. Sites of this period show dense concentrations of artefacts, dominated by more advanced stone-working technology. In place of the old hand axes made from flint cores, the new, smaller tools were made from individual flakes, carefully shaped for maximum efficiency. These, in turn, made hunting more efficient. Animal bones from Middle Palaeolithic sites show the variety of game that was consumed: aurochs and antelope, warthog and wild ass, gazelle and ostrich, fox and jackal.

Between about 37,000 and 30,000 BC, the climate entered another dry period. Faced with an unforgiving climate, people again migrated from the savannahs to the Nile Valley, where they encountered fishing communities. The different groups seem to have co-existed with little mixing, sowing the seeds for the cultural diversity that is characteristic of later phases of Egyptian prehistory. At a site near Qena in Upper Egypt, a camp provided temporary accommodation for a group of people who hunted and fished, making full use of the food resources at their disposal. A final wet phase, starting in about 17,000 BC, ushered in the Late Palaeolithic. Bands of people spread out across Egypt's diverse environments, from the grasslands to the oases and river valley. They ate a varied diet and fashioned objects purely for decoration – beads made from ostrich eggshells are among the earliest examples of jewellery discovered in Egypt. The key to the success of these peoples was, once again, their stone tools. The development of microliths, tiny flakes of flint used in compound weapons such as arrows and harpoons, brought unprecedented success when hunting and fishing.

The raw material for these advanced stone tools was quarried at a small number of sites in the Nile Valley. At one, Nazlet Khater in Middle Egypt, trenches were cut in the gravel, up to two metres deep, to gain access to the stratum of flint, with miners tunnelling along the flint-bearing layer. The best-quality flints must have been traded across a wide area, bringing different peoples into contact – and conflict. Bodies from this period often show evidence of violence – arrowheads embedded in bones, cut marks on the legs – suggesting warfare between competing groups. As so often in human history, an advance in technology could be used for good and ill, bringing benefits but also dangers.

As the Palaeolithic gave way to the Neolithic Period, Egypt's early inhabitants took the production of stone tools to new heights. Perhaps the most beautiful artefacts to have survived from the later phases of prehistory are ripple-flaked flint knives. They range in length from a few centimetres to half a metre or more, with each one representing a vast amount of skilled labour. First, the rough outline of the tool was fashioned from a flint core. Then the body of the knife was painstakingly thinned with a series of percussive strikes, giving an intricate ripple effect. Finally, razor-sharp edges were created by further flaking until the finished product emerged, practical and beautiful. The finest examples were probably objects of great ritual significance, carried in processions or wielded during sacrificial offerings. The antiquity of the technology, combined with the durability of the material, gave a flint knife a magical potency.

The Palaeolithic Period and the heyday of stone tool-making in Egypt drew to a close around 5000 BC, with the beginnings of agriculture and the advent of copper technology. Hand axes and flint knives may no longer have had any practical purpose, but they retained their symbolic associations. In an age of metal, the Egyptians continued to make stone tools for ceremonial purposes. Remarkably, the practice endured for millennia. Among the objects recovered from the floor of the Annexe in Tutankhamun's tomb were two finely polished flint knives, ten and eleven centimetres long. They are not the finest examples of their kind – that accolade belongs to the ripple-flaked knives produced some 2,000 years earlier – but they are artefacts of style and sophistication, made using the same technique as the stone tools of the Middle Palaeolithic, a 70,000-year tradition. Tutankhamun's flint knives are testament not only to the conservatism of ancient Egyptian culture but to the remarkable depth of Egyptian history.

⬳⬱

Many of the animals that Egypt's prehistoric inhabitants hunted with stone tools found their way into religious iconography and were revered as embodiments of natural phenomena. Giraffes may have been worshipped as solar symbols, perhaps because their long necks afforded them closer contact with the sun than any other creature. Elephants seem to have been imbued with protective powers, judging from scenes that show them trampling snakes. Likewise, the wild ass was temporarily worshipped as an incarnation of the desert god Seth. However, when the desiccation of the savannahs led to the extinction of large game animals, they seem to have been abandoned as religious metaphors and replaced by more familiar Nilotic species: hippopotamus and crocodile, catfish and heron. The one animal that retained its sacred status throughout Egyptian prehistory and the ensuing pharaonic period was not a wild species at all, but the most important domesticate: cattle.

The wild aurochs seems to have been tamed early on, and

herds of domesticated cattle were a key element of Palaeolithic subsistence. Certainly, cattle are the most frequently depicted creatures in prehistoric rock art. Paintings of cows from the fringes of the Sahara pay particular attention to their udders, suggesting that herds were kept for milk. Images of cattle etched onto the rocks of the Eastern Desert include beasts with artificially deformed horns, a sure sign of domestication. And on the rock walls surrounding a natural whirlpool in the cliffs above the Wadi Umm Salam, a frieze of tethered cattle illuminates the way of life of the prehistoric artist, who likely pecked the images while a herd grazed nearby. These ancient depictions are difficult to date precisely, but there is no doubt that cattle-herding was practised from at least Late Palaeolithic times. As in the pastoralist cultures of present-day East Africa, cattle were probably kept for their milk and blood; only at times of communal celebration would they have been killed for meat.

Cattle may be a reliable source of nutrition, but they require regular watering if they are to survive and thrive. As a result, prehistoric cattle herders were forced to adopt a semi-nomadic lifestyle, taking their animals from one water source to another. Even in wetter eras, the summer rains that fell over North Africa would have kept the grasslands green for only part of the year; during winter, communities would have been forced to migrate in search of water and fresh pasture. The rhythm of the seasons, so distinctive an influence on Egyptian civilization, was established early on as a key determinant of human culture.

The most remarkable evidence of Egypt's prehistoric cattle-herding peoples has come to light in one of the most unexpected locations. At a remote spot in the Western Desert, close to the modern border between Egypt and Sudan, lies a windswept plain surrounded by low sandy hills. At its centre is the bed of a long-dried-up lake. Nabta Playa, as the site is called today, would be easily overlooked, were it not for the great slabs of rock that dot the surrounding area, massive stones that were dragged from some distance away. A long line of monumental stones follows the crest of a nearby hill, while other monoliths stand as lone sentinels on the horizon. These towering rocks used to ring a collection of smaller stones close to the erstwhile lake shore. They were arranged in a circle, with two pairs of uprights facing each other. Two pairs were aligned north–south, while two more pointed towards the midsummer sunrise.[1]

The stone circle of Nabta Playa, dubbed the 'ancient Egyptian Stonehenge', can be dated to the early fifth millennium BC. It marks a site of great ritual significance to local prehistoric, cattle-herding peoples, the epicentre of seasonal fertility. Laying out the stones must have required a large degree of communal involvement, so Nabta Playa, like Stonehenge, would have been a gathering place, a focus of ritual and celebration. The purpose of the standing stones and calendar circle seems to have been to predict the arrival of the rains that fell shortly after the summer solstice. When the rains arrived, the community celebrated by slaughtering some of their cattle as a sacrifice of thanks. Large quantities of bones have been excavated at the site, as well as burials on a ridge overlooking the *playa*, the graves marked with large, flat stones.

Under one of these mounds, archaeologists found a huge sandstone monolith that had been carefully shaped and dressed to resemble a cow.[2] Also dating to the early fifth millennium BC, it is the earliest monumental sculpture from Egypt. Standing at the beginning of a long and distinctive tradition of stone sculpture, it celebrates the Egyptians' most revered animal companion. With its nurturing, nourishing qualities, it is not surprising that the cow came to be worshipped as the quintessential mother goddess. A pair of protective cows' heads watch over Egypt's first king, Narmer, on his carved ceremonial palette. The beneficent cow goddess was revered as the king's divine mother and worshipped as protector of ordinary Egyptians – at home and abroad, in this world and the next. She was still there at the end of pharaonic history, adopted by Cleopatra as her divine alter-ego, and was depicted watching over the last of the Ptolemies on reliefs at Dendera.

Sixteen centuries after Narmer and thirteen before Cleopatra came the boy king Tutankhamun. Carter and Carnarvon encountered a magnificent statue head of a cow goddess, Hathor, standing guard over his entombed body, facing west towards the land of the dead. Nearly a metre tall, it is made from wood covered in gesso. The upper part of the head is gilded, the lower part covered with black resin varnish. The eyes are made of inlaid glass with obsidian pupils, the horns of wood covered with copper sheeting. When it was discovered, the neck and base of the statue were wrapped in a linen shawl; only the gilded part of the head was visible, glinting in the light of the archaeologists' torches.

⊲◦⊳

Despite their long proficiency with flint, it is surprising that the Egyptians seem never to have learned how to make fire by striking sparks from a flint stone. Instead, the method they used, from prehistoric times until the end of pharaonic civilization, was a fire drill. A well-preserved example, discovered in Tutankhamun's tomb, displays all the main features. The body of the drill is shaped like a bodkin, with grooved sides to aid traction and a notch for easy removal of the detachable fire stick. The accompanying 'fire stock' is a rectangular piece of wood, nearly twenty centimetres in length; along each long side are six circular notches, lined with resin to promote friction. Carter himself described the method of use:

The rotation was effected by means of a bow alternately thrust forwards and backwards, the thong of which having been first wound round the stock of the drill in which the fire stick was fixed. In order to steady the drill, the upper end was held in a socket . . . The round holes in which the fire stick was rotated were made near the edges of the fire stock, so that a vertical slot was created . . . which allowed the spark created to have free access to the tinder.[3]

Fire played a key role in the early development of Egyptian civilization and the Egyptian state. Nowhere is this clearer than at the site of Kom el-Ahmar (better known by its classical name, Hierakonpolis), on the west bank of the Nile in southern Upper Egypt.

Beginning around 5000 BC, North Africa entered its most recent arid phase. The savannahs either side of the Nile Valley, which had supported many groups of prehistoric inhabitants, gradually turned into what we see today: dry, barren desert. People and herds who had depended on the summer rains migrated to the Nile Valley for good, with agriculture becoming the main form of subsistence. This transition marks the end of

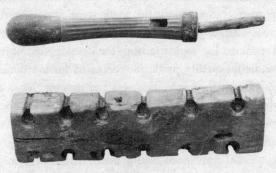

Fig. 6. Fire drill.

the Palaeolithic and the start of the Neolithic Period in Egypt. In Egyptological terminology, it marks the transition from 'prehistoric' to 'predynastic', with political and cultural developments in the Nile Valley leading directly to the formation of the Egyptian state under the kings of the first dynasty.

This process of societal transformation can be traced most clearly at the site of Hierakonpolis. It was a natural choice for permanent settlement: located at the junction of a host of trade routes and opposite one of the richest gold-mining regions in Egypt, its strategic position conferred significant economic advantages. The prosperity that flowed from the control of trade soon began to change the fabric of the community. Disparities in wealth between different sections of the population increased; society became more hierarchical, as an emergent elite emphasized its status through the acquisition of prestige goods, elaborate tombs in a special location and outward trappings of power.

One of the most important aspects of this social change was the centralization and professionalization of production. In prehistoric times, pottery and other manufactured goods were made by individuals or households. With the rise of permanent settlements in the Nile Valley, communities became sufficiently wealthy and settled that individuals could devote themselves full-time to craft production. This made sense from a practical perspective – large-scale production was more efficient – but also led to increasing sophistication. The development of more elaborate, better-quality products stimulated further demand, which reinforced the cycle. This was the process that led to the birth of a fully fledged state, and one with the experience and expertise to undertake massive government projects – culminating in the building of the pyramids.

The process of craft specialization began with the production of pottery, and ceramics are by far the most common type of artefact found at Egyptian sites. As containers for daily food-stuffs and precious commodities alike, pottery was an essential technology in the ancient Egyptian economy. Recent excavations have revealed how and where this most ubiquitous product was made, and the key ingredient was the management of fire.

Along the south side of the wadi linking Hierakonpolis to its desert hinterland, a large area of archaeological remains marks the site of a pottery factory. A man-made platform of burned mud was pockmarked by a series of horseshoe-shaped pits lined with broken pottery and burned earth. Unfired pots were placed at the back of each pit and a fire was prepared at the front, where the flames would be fanned by the prevailing northerly wind. The airflow was carefully controlled using temporary walls of earth and matting. Once the temperature had reached the necessary level, coals were heaped in the pits and the kiln was sealed to retain the heat. After firing, the finished pots were extracted from the pit and the process was repeated. Once the kilns had filled up with debris – no attempt seems to have been made to clean them out after each firing – replacements were built further up the slope.

This highly efficient factory produced everyday pottery as well as more specialist vessels, fuelling the expansion of Hierakonpolis from small village to large town. The scale of the installation shows that pottery production had become a full-time occupation, carried out by experts on an industrial scale. This specialization and the growing social complexity attested at Hierakonpolis and elsewhere propelled Egypt towards statehood – and all thanks to the humble fire drill.

⊲◻▻

Towards the end of the predynastic period, the rulers of Hierakonpolis and a handful of other rival centres began to extend their political and economic control over their surrounding regions. As they did so, loosely defined areas of influence were consolidated into proto-kingdoms, a process that ultimately led to the unification of the entire Nile Valley into a single nation in around 2950 BC.

Alongside control of production and trade, the early kings were adept at promoting and reinforcing their authority through the sophisticated deployment of religion, ritual and regalia. When used in a strategic and coordinated fashion, symbols constitute a particularly potent means for exercising control. Throughout human history, symbolic vocabulary has been used and abused to unite, inspire and intimidate, and the early rulers of the Nile Valley deployed it as effectively as any civilization since.

Take crowns, for example. Irrespective of era or culture, monarchs have invariably identified themselves by distinctive forms of headdress – accessories that have no practical use,[4] but which set their wearers apart and elevate them above their subjects. The earliest attested crowns were worn by the late predynastic kings of Upper Egypt. At the site of Nagada, the ruler wore a squat cap with a tall, tapering back piece and a curly protuberance at the front. His counterpart and rival at Hierakonpolis favoured a tall, bulbous hat. In due course, following the unification of the Nile Valley, these two head-pieces were recast as the crowns of Lower and Upper Egypt.

Other elements of royal regalia were adopted to symbolize the king's embodiment and mastery of natural forces. A bull's tail, for example, worn from the monarch's belt, associated him with the ferocity of the wild bulls that frequented the margins of the floodplain. The pear-shaped macehead was co-opted as a symbol of kingly authority, emphasizing his power of life and death over his subjects. The rulers of Hierakonpolis also adopted their local deity – a sky god in the form of a falcon – as their personal avatar. Not only did this tie royal and divine authority together in the minds of the people, it also sent a clear message about the scope of the king's power: just as the falcon looked down from on high over the Nile Valley, so the king kept watch over all his people with a hawk-like intensity.

While the image of the falcon would have resonated with the people of Hierakonpolis, so, elsewhere, would other local deities co-opted into the iconography of kingship: the vulture goddess of Elkab, the town on the other side of the river from Hierakonpolis, or a cobra goddess from the Nile Delta. But, in order to develop an iconography with national appeal, the early kings of Egypt also needed symbols that tapped into the psyche of all Egyptians, recalling shared ancestral myths and speaking to their sense of identity. And the first pharaohs found a rich vein of emblems and metaphors in the pastoral way of life of the Egyptians' prehistoric ancestors.

In the time of hunters and herders, people had used special implements to manage their livestock: goads to drive their animals forward and crooks to restrain them. At once familiar and ancient, these essential tools of animal husbandry provided the perfect metaphors for the king's powers of coercion and restraint. In some of the earliest examples of Egyptian royal art, powerful men are shown wielding a crook or a goad. Indeed, the crook was even adopted as the hieroglyphic sign for 'rule' or 'ruler'. In a neat elaboration of the underlying ideology, the goad – a series of knotted cords tied to a wooden handle – could be reinterpreted as a flail, a similarly shaped implement used for releasing the grains from ripened cereal. Together, crook and flail symbolized the king's control over livestock and crops.

Over the succeeding centuries and millennia, the crook and flail became the quintessential items of Egyptian royal regalia. Carried by the king on ceremonial occasions, they also accompanied him into the afterlife, being depicted on royal coffins crossed against the royal chest. The associations of these humble farming tools became so powerful that even the god Osiris was shown carrying them, signifying his position as king of the dead.

There are tens of thousands of representations of the crook and flail in ancient Egyptian art, but only two actual examples have survived – and both were in the tomb of Tutankhamun. They are made from cylindrical sections of dark blue glass, obsidian and gold, mounted on copper-alloy rods. The pendant beads of the flail are made of gilded wood, while the cap of the crook is inscribed with Tutankhamun's names. The blue-and-gold striped decoration of the boy king's crook and flail matches his famous funerary mask, blending the sacred blue of Osiris with the gold that was believed to form the bodies of the gods.

Ever since the time of the first pharaohs, monarchies around the world have developed their own distinctive accessories that identify the bearers as special and to be revered. But such symbols have never been more effectively deployed than in ancient Egypt. The early rulers of the Nile Valley – the first individuals in history to exercise authority over a geographically extensive nation state – were so successful that the basic elements of pharaonic iconography – and the form of government they symbolized – endured, unchanged and unchallenged, for the next 3,000 years.

⊲○▷

Of course, Egypt's first kings did not only exercise power through symbols: they also deployed more pragmatic means to assert and maintain their authority. Perhaps the most important tool of government, and one of the defining features of pharaonic civilization, was writing.

All the great civilizations of the ancient world developed

written communication as an instrument of economic and political control. Exercising effective government over a large territory requires control of the economy, which is dependent upon the systematic recording of property ownership and the routine accounting of income and expenditure. Although we tend to associate ancient Egyptian writing with religious texts and the celebration of kingship, the earliest written records are, in fact, economic. Small labels, inscribed on bone and excavated from the tomb of a late predynastic ruler at Abydos in Upper Egypt in the 1990s, recorded the provenance, contents or ownership of the commodities to which they were attached. The hieroglyphic signs are immediately recognizable from later periods, and the writing system itself – combining both phonetic and ideographic signs – is fully formed. It is as if ancient Egyptian writing sprang into existence without any preceding process of development.

One possible explanation for this sudden appearance is that writing was one of a number of concepts 'borrowed' by the Egyptians from the contemporary civilization of Mesopotamia. The Sumerians were the first to invent writing, and examples of their cylinder seals found their way along trade routes to the Nile Valley in the very period when pharaonic civilization was emerging. Functionaries at the Egyptian proto-royal courts of the time may have marvelled at these glyptic codifiers of complex information, before determining to develop such a system for themselves. If so, the system they came up with was quintessentially Egyptian, its structures ideally suited to the Egyptian language, its signs drawn from the Egyptian environment. A few symbols expressing complex notions of monarchy and theology were borrowed from Sumer, but these were swiftly abandoned in favour of indigenous Egyptian signs, like the crook and flail. Henceforth, hieroglyphic writing would become the most characteristic expression of ancient Egyptian cultural identity.

While the origins of hieroglyphic writing are obscure, its effectiveness as a method of exercising control was clear from the outset. During the process of political unification in the late fourth millennium BC, the written word was used to record taxation and to assert the royal court's ownership of Egypt's land and resources. Once a single nation state had been established at the beginning of the first dynasty, the uses of writing were expanded. Hieroglyphics now served to celebrate the achievements and authority of the ruler; to identify and empower officials of the royal treasury; and to denote the relationships between members of the king's inner circle, and the bond between the king and the gods. Egyptian writing was set on the course it would follow for the next thirty-three centuries.

Monumental hieroglyphics may be the most recognizable form of ancient Egyptian script today, but they were employed only in special, usually ritual, circumstances. Much more common was the cursive form of script – written in ink on sheets of papyrus or flakes of pottery or limestone – that was used for everyday communication. Indeed, so synonymous was the technique with the finished product that the sign used to denote 'writing', 'scribe' and all associated words depicted a typical scribal kit: a rectangular wooden palette with two circular inkwells, a water bag for mixing the pigments and a reed stylus.

The earliest surviving example of the hieroglyphic sign for 'scribe' occurs on the gravestone of a courtier who was buried alongside his king, Semerkhet of the first dynasty. It is a powerful demonstration of the power and prestige associated with writing at the beginning of Egyptian history. Over the succeeding centuries, boys of talent and ability – generally speaking, the sons of the elite – were selected for training in special scribal schools, where they learned to master the art of writing. In a civilization where no more than 5 to 10 per cent of the population could read and write, literacy held the key to influence, advancement and wealth.

The exalted status of writing is reflected in the numerous examples of scribal equipment buried in Tutankhamun's tomb. Carter recorded fourteen palettes, two writing horns, a pen case of gilded and inlaid wood and a papyrus burnisher of ivory and gold, as well as various pigments, four limestone paint slabs, a paint container, a small piece of shaped limestone used as an eraser and an ivory water dish. The two finest scribal palettes, one of ivory and another of gilded wood, were inscribed with the king's name.

In the sacred context of the tomb, this trove of writing equipment was included for the express purpose of assisting the pharaoh in the afterlife. For according to the ancient Pyramid Texts, the dead king would act as scribe to the sun god, recording the creator's words and promulgating his decisions. But on a more mundane level, the number of pens, palettes and inks in Tutankhamun's tomb remind us of the position of writing as one of the cornerstones of ancient Egyptian civilization.

<figure>⋘○⋙</figure>

The invention and deployment of writing by the early Egyptian state enabled it to exercise effective control over a vast geographic area. As the royal court began to harness the agricultural bounty of the Nile Valley and to benefit from a monopoly on trade, it grew increasingly wealthy. In turn, this wealth enabled the state to fund building projects that further reinforced its control over its inhabitants' lives.

One of the earliest projects was the construction of a fortress and customs post on the island of Elephantine, at the foot of the First Nile Cataract. To boats arriving from Nubia to the south, this imposing installation signalled the Egyptian state's control of its southern border, but it also enabled the royal treasury to monitor the movement of goods north and south, ensuring effective state control. State-sponsored construction for ideological and economic purposes would characterize ancient Egypt for most of its long history.

During the first two dynasties, the Egyptian government erected a host of administrative buildings, provincial shrines and palaces throughout the Nile Valley and Delta, facilitating the collection of taxes and projecting royal power throughout the realm. However, from early in the first dynasty, the major building project of each reign – the royal tomb – became even more closely associated with the monarch, a symbol of his earthly power and a guarantee of his rebirth into an eternal afterlife. The earliest surviving royal tomb, from a century or so before the unification of Egypt, took the form of a palace in miniature, complete with wine cellar, treasury and linked chambers.

As royal power began to develop during the formative years of the Egyptian state, the conception of the king's tomb started to change. By the end of the second dynasty, the burial was accompanied by a magnificent structure above ground – the funerary palace – which stood as a monument proclaiming and projecting the king's power. At Abydos, the last of these great mortuary enclosures still survives; known by its Arabic name, Shunet ez-Zebib, its walls still stand some eleven metres high and enclose an area of over 6,000 square metres. They are decorated with a series of recesses and buttresses, recalling the enclosure of the royal compound at Memphis. Its builder was the last monarch to be buried at Abydos and the last to associate himself in death with Egypt's prehistoric rulers. His successor, known today as Djoser, is regarded as the first king of a new dynasty and also a new era. Djoser's royal tomb and funerary palace were combined in a single monumental stone construction. Covering a vast area and dominating the skyline for miles around, it signalled the start of the Pyramid Age.

More than decorated tombs or columned temples, the great mountains of stone erected by the kings of the third to sixth dynasties are *the* iconic monuments of pharaonic civilization. They still stand proud, more than 4,000 years after they were built. Their scale and precision seem to defy their great age, yet it was clearly within the Egyptians' abilities to undertake projects of this size and complexity. Indeed, through the funerary constructions of Egypt's early kings, we can trace a growing confidence and ambition, a growing skill in stone architecture and a growing ability to harness the manpower and material required for such vast projects. It has been said that while the Egyptians built the pyramids, the pyramids also built Egypt. The direction of the state's resources towards a single grand scheme was a great engine of growth that was both enabled by and enabled the flowering of pharaonic culture.

In recent decades, painstaking archaeological work at Giza has uncovered the town built for the pyramid workers, with barrack blocks, granaries and food processing areas. But if feeding a workforce of several thousand was a feat in itself, the organization required to bring building materials to the Giza Plateau was an even more impressive undertaking. While much of the stone for the monuments was quarried locally, the casing blocks of fine white limestone had to be brought from Tura, across the Nile, while blocks of granite came from the First Cataract, hundreds of miles upstream. These heavy loads must have been transported by barge, docking at a harbour area at the foot of the plateau. Seven model barges were found in Tutankhamun's tomb, and they are typical of the cargo vessels used on the Nile for millennia. Mastless, with protruding prow and stern posts, they were steered with a pair of large paddles. All of them had a central roofed cabin and a smaller kiosk at either end. The models had a smooth finish, reproducing the carvel-built hulls of the full-sized versions.

Until just a few years ago, the use of barges to transport stone to the pyramid construction site at Giza could not be proven. In 2013, French archaeologists digging at the site of an ancient port on the Red Sea coast unearthed dozens of inscribed papyri, the oldest such documents found in Egypt. The port itself seems to have been used in the reign of Khufu, probably for expeditions to Sinai to obtain copper for the tools to dress the building blocks of the Great Pyramid. Many of the fragments of papyrus were from a daily log kept by a man named Merer, who was in charge of a barge delivering construction materials for Khufu's great monument on the Giza Plateau. Merer's journal records trips from the limestone quarries at Tura to the building site. Entries note the time of day when the crew undertook each operation, whether they were travelling up or downstream and where they spent each morning and night. A typical sequence of four daily entries runs thus:

[Day 26]: Inspector Merer sails with his team from Tura South, loaded with stones for the Horizon of Khufu [the Great Pyramid]; spends the night at the Lake of Khufu.

Day 27: sails from the Lake of Khufu, towards the Horizon of Khufu, loaded with stones; spends the night in the Horizon of Khufu.

Day 28: sails from the Horizon of Khufu in the morning; sails up the river [to] Tura South.

Day 29: Inspector Merer spends the day with his team, gathering stones in Tura South; spends the night at Tura South.[5]

Though brief and matter-of-fact, the Red Sea papyri provide a remarkable first-hand account of the building of the Great Pyramid and illustrate the role played by the humble river barge in the creation of Egypt's most enduring monuments.

Although the public works of the Pyramid Age helped build a sophisticated civilization, the seeds of its destruction were present from the start. The myopic policies of the royal court allowed Egypt's restive north-eastern and southern neighbours to build up their strength; the growing threat of incursion and disruption to Egyptian control of trade routes remained largely unchallenged, until it was too late. Within Egypt, the unremitting concentration of economic activity and wealth on royal projects established an uneasy relationship between the centre and the provinces; when a deteriorating climate and a series of low Niles put the economy under severe stress in the sixth dynasty, the pent-up tensions were unleashed. Powerful local families jockeyed for influence, as a diminished central government sought to buy them off with royal favours. Eventually, the court abandoned all attempts at large-scale building projects and retreated to its heartland around Memphis, the capital city. This admission of weakness was not lost on the ambitious dynasts in the southern Nile Valley, who used their local influence to launch bids for power – and for the throne. The result was civil war, within a generation or two of the last royal pyramid being completed.

A series of autobiographical inscriptions commemorate key actors in this period of internal strife, known to Egyptologists as the First Intermediate Period. Together, they allow us to recreate the different stages in the war that tore Egypt apart over four generations. As for the prosecution of the war itself, tomb scenes from before and after the fighting illustrate the types of combat in which the opposing forces were embroiled. There were river-borne assaults on enemy positions; siege warfare, as armies attempted to capture their foes' strongholds; and hand-to-hand combat, when rival forces met on the battle-field or in the streets.

The relatively small mercenary armies would have had access to a range of sophisticated weaponry – principally bows and arrows, but also daggers, clubs and maces – but the larger numbers of peasant soldiers would have had to make do with more rudimentary arms. Among the numerous weapons buried with Tutankhamun were six fighting sticks. Each had been fitted with a leather knuckle guard mounted with gold orna-ment. The sticks wielded in the civil war of the First Intermediate Period would have had no such fittings, but they were equally effective. A sharp blow from a fighting stick, wielded at close range, would have smashed the skull of an opponent.

One of the most poignant archaeological discoveries dating from this period is a war grave at Thebes, part of a larger cere-monial complex inaugurated by the Theban ruler Mentuhotep II, the eventual victor in the civil war. His great-grandfather had first laid a bold claim to the Egyptian throne, provoking war with the king in Memphis and resulting in a protracted internecine conflict. Seventy years later Mentuhotep finished the task, attacking the enemy stronghold of Herakleopolis, defeating the last of his adversaries and reuniting the Nile Valley under Theban control. But this final battle came at a heavy price. In a pit close to the king's own mortuary temple in the Theban hills, archaeologists found the linen-wrapped bodies of at least sixty men, stacked one on top of the other.

The men had been strong and tall, and some of them were battle-hardened veterans, but they had all been shot by arrows or crushed by missiles raining down on them from the battlements of an enemy town. Some had been killed outright, while others had been brutally dispatched on the battlefield, their skulls smashed by sticks and clubs. Their bodies had been left for the vultures – only when the battle was over could the victors gather up their dead, strip them of their blood-soaked clothes, scour the bodies clean with sand and bandage them with linen, ready for burial. In death, distinctions of age or rank were forgotten. Instead, each man had his name written in ink on his linen wrappings. Some had Theban names, but others bore names suggesting they came from far away, on the front line of the conflict.

The experience of civil war – of communities fighting their neighbours, of holy sites being desecrated, of political insecurity and economic hardship – changed Egyptian civilization forever. Gone was the self-confidence and easy superiority of the Pyramid Age. In its place, a certain world-weariness and a cynicism about the human condition came to characterize Egyptian art and literature. Gone, too, were the rigid social distinctions that had prevailed throughout the early dynasties: when thousands of ordinary inhabitants were expected to give their lives for their masters' regal ambitions, they expected to be rewarded with at least the promise of an afterlife. In civil war, conceptions of the next world were democratized, bringing the hope of resurrection within the grasp of Egypt's non-royal subjects for the first time. Presiding over this new, accessible afterlife was the figure of Osiris. Once a minor provincial deity, after the civil war he was worshipped as king of the dead, bringing to his followers the promise of a better life beyond the grave. On the back wall of Tutankhamun's tomb, the boy pharaoh is depicted being ushered into the presence of Osiris, ready to be born again into the next world. His fighting sticks remind us of the tragic circumstances in which the cult of Osiris came to prominence, a watershed in the history of ancient Egypt.

<◦>

One of the defining characteristics of pharaonic culture was an obsession with measurement. Perhaps the desire to quantify as a means of exercising control is symptomatic of all bureaucracies, or perhaps there was something in the ancient Egyptian mindset that elevated counting and recording to a noble art. Either way, metrics were used to shape Egyptian civilization. From prehistoric times, the height of the annual Nile inundation was regarded as an indication of the following year's harvest. As we have seen, too low a flood and the crops would fail; too high a flood and fields and villages would be washed away. Measuring the height of the inundation was hence a matter of life and death.

The annals of ancient Egypt's first six dynasties comprise a series of horizontal registers, divided by vertical lines into one compartment for each year of a king's reign. At the foot of each one is the height of that year's inundation. By means of such detailed measurement, the early Egyptian state was able to plan economic activity and maintain stability.

The annals record the height of the Nile in the ancient Egyptian units of length: cubits, palms and fingers. The cubit, roughly fifty-one centimetres, was traditionally the length of a man's forearm, from elbow to fingertip. It was divided into seven 'palms', each consisting of four 'fingers'. Although longer units were used in land measurement, the cubit reigned supreme in art, architecture, town planning and many other areas of state activity. Indeed, the importance of measurement in the life of the royal court is illustrated by the presence of cubit rods –

Fig. 7. Cubit measuring rod.

equivalent to modern rulers – among the grave goods interred in Tutankhamun's tomb. A set of six made from a dark red wood, probably cedar, were found in a box in the Antechamber; while a narrow wooden shrine in the Treasury, empty at the time of discovery, was believed by Carter to have been made for a metal cubit rod. A further wooden cubit rod made for Tutankhamun and inscribed with his name was excavated by Flinders Petrie in the late nineteenth century at Kom Medinet Ghurab, a royal fortress and palace complex north of Thebes.

This fixation with measurement bled into many areas of government activity, and again, the royal annals provide early examples. The upper part of each compartment contains a brief description of the salient events of the royal year. Sometimes these are religious in nature, such as the dedication of a new divine statue or the foundation of a temple. However, occasionally in the first dynasty and then every other year from the second dynasty onwards, the event that was singled out was the census of national wealth, known later as the 'cattle count', but originally encompassing fields and mineral resources. With their love of measurement, the kings of Egypt carried out a survey of their realm every two years. Later, in the Old Kingdom, the biennial 'cattle counts' replaced regnal years as the preferred way of dating government documents.

Accurate measurement and meticulous record-keeping were essential in the construction of the pyramids. However, even after the end of the Pyramid Age, when the royal court largely abandoned the building of massive funerary complexes, the bureaucratic mindset continued to flourish. Its zenith was reached in the twelfth dynasty, which – despite, or perhaps in response to, the civil war that preceded it – emerged as a period of overweening central control.

One of the clearest indications of a society's operating principles is the layout of its settlements. The building of a new town allows the directing authority to shape the environment – and people's lives – according to its own philosophy. The twelfth dynasty was a period of intense settlement construction; Thebes was entirely redesigned and brand-new towns were established the length and breadth of the Nile Valley, with whole communities resettled. This would have brought economic activity under closer state control, disrupting old patterns of local allegiance and replacing them with tighter state supervision – all the elements, in other words, of an authoritarian government.

Moreover, the new twelfth-dynasty settlements were characterized by regimented, grid-iron layouts, with carefully delineated zones for administrative and residential buildings and a clear distinction between ordinary and elite dwellings. The 'type site' was the town of Kahun in the south-eastern Fayum, which was built to serve the nearby pyramid of Senusret II but which functioned as a large regional centre in its own right. The town covered an area of around thirteen hectares. Within its stout mudbrick walls, the interior was laid out according to a strict orthogonal plan. Individual dwellings were built from a series of rectangular modules; a limestone tablet discovered there bears an inscription which reads 'A four-house block – thirty by twenty [cubits]'.[6]

The dwellings at Kahun fell into two distinct groups: very small houses for the general population and very large villas for the ruling class. Much of the town would have depended on rations held in large granaries adjacent to the villas. Surviving papyri from the town illustrate an obsessively bureaucratic mindset, in which scribes documented every activity with an almost religious zeal. As a noted Egyptologist has remarked:

> The whole reflects the prevailing mentality of the Middle Kingdom, which tended towards an extreme structured view of society, partly reflected in an inclination to devise arithmetic calculations for every facet of economic life, and to seek to control human behaviour and property by means of a strict bureaucratic framework.[7]

Yet even as the twelfth dynasty exercised an unprecedented level of control over its citizens, stirrings beyond Egypt's borders threatened to undermine the stability of the pharaonic state.

◁▭▷

In prehistoric times, Nubians from beyond the First Nile Cataract settled in Upper Egypt, shaping predynastic Egyptian culture in the process. However, from the first dynasty onwards, Egyptian expeditions took a more aggressive stance, sailing upstream into Nubia, intent on trade or conquest. From the beginning of the pharaonic state, the Egyptians – at least in the official record – had a condescending, colonial attitude towards their southern neighbours: while admiring the Nubians for their fighting prowess, they generally regarded them as undeveloped, unsophisticated barbarians, ripe for subjugation.

By the Pyramid Age, the first Egyptian colony in Nubia had been established, at the site of Buhen near the Second Nile Cataract. Together with the customs post on the island of Elephantine, it allowed for the control of riverine trade in the exotic products for which Nubia was famous: giraffe tails and ostrich eggs, gold and other minerals, ebony and ivory. The ivory trade gave its name to Elephantine, while the Egyptian word for ebony, *hebeny*, was borrowed from a local Nubian language. Throughout pharaonic history, these two contrasting materials were highly prized by the craftsmen of Egypt's royal workshops, and many of Tutankhamun's grave goods are fashioned from imported Nubian ebony and ivory. Among them are two fine pairs of casting sticks and an accompanying box for board games. Casting sticks were used in ancient Egypt, like dice in more recent times, to determine the number of places a player would advance. One pair of Tutankhamun's sticks has ends that are carved to resemble fingers; the other pair are shaped like animal heads, and all four sticks are decorated with bands of cross-hatching.

Towards the end of the Old Kingdom, a series of expeditions to Nubia led by a man named Harkhuf brought back vast baggage trains of ebony, ivory and other sought-after Nubian products – along with a pygmy that particularly delighted the infant king Pepi II. The expeditions also noted worrying political developments along the Upper Nile – a series of minor chiefdoms had formed a unified territory spanning much of Lower Nubia. Egypt was soon too preoccupied with its own internal affairs to worry about its southern neighbour. But as soon as Mentuhotep II had emerged as victor in the Egyptian civil war, he reasserted control over Lower Nubia. Following his reconquest, the twelfth dynasty took Egyptian dominance in Nubia to a new level, building a series of massive fortresses throughout the Second Cataract region. They formed an impregnable line of defence and constituted an impressive show of force. In one of the forts, at Semna, a statue of the king Senusret III was set up to inspire loyalty among the Egyptian garrison forces. Its inscription left no room for any doubt:

> Aggression is brave; retreat is cowardly! He who does not defend his borders is a pansy! . . . As for any son of mine who strengthens this border which My Majesty has made, he is indeed my son, born of My Majesty, for the model son champions his father and strengthens the border of his begetter. But he who loosens [his grip] on it and will not fight for it: he is not my son; he is not born of me. Now My Majesty has had an image made of My Majesty at this border which My Majesty has established, so that you will strengthen it and so that you will fight for it.[8]

Alongside the fortresses, new settlements were established as a means of exerting political and economic control over the surrounding hinterland. The motive was not just defence or conquest, but wholesale colonization and annexation.

For a long time, archaeologists confronted by the number and scale of the twelfth-dynasty Nubian fortresses were at a loss to explain the vast amount of state resources expended on their construction. They were rather unconvincingly labelled as examples of Egyptian government propaganda, despite the advanced military technology employed in their design and construction. In recent years, the reason for this massive display of defensive capability has come to light. It is now clear that when the

Egyptians' backs were turned during the civil war of the First Intermediate Period, an incipient statelet beyond the Second Nile Cataract seized the opportunity to become the hegemonic power along the Upper Nile. By the time the rulers of the Middle Kingdom had regained control of Egypt, the Kingdom of Kush had emerged as a major rival. The string of forts at the Second Cataract were not just an affirmation of Egypt's strength, but a defensive border against attack by a powerful adversary.

As excavations in present-day Sudan shed new light on the Kingdom of Kush, discoveries in Egypt are also elucidating its role in the decline and fall of the Middle Kingdom. After the strong central control and ambitious territorial expansion of the twelfth dynasty, perhaps it was inevitable that subsequent generations of rulers found it too burdensome to maintain such rigid oversight of their realm. The garrisons were gradually withdrawn from Nubia and the colonial outposts were left to their own devices; the Kingdom of Kush was quick to step into the vacuum. In a tomb at Elkab, in southern Upper Egypt, an inscription describes an attack by a Kushite-led coalition, comprising all the peoples of Upper and Lower Nubia, as well as forces from distant Punt (coastal Sudan) and the Medjay of the Eastern Desert. This fearsome army ransacked and pillaged its way through southern Upper Egypt, before retreating back beyond the First Nile Cataract. For the Egyptians it was a cataclysmic shock, and a dire warning. Beset with troubles at home and abroad, Egypt's existence as an independent nation hung in the balance.

⊲⊙⊳

In the darkest days of the Second Intermediate Period, the century of disorder that followed the collapse of the Middle Kingdom, a letter was sent to the ruler of Kush, inviting him to invade Egypt:

> Come northward, do not flinch . . . There is no one who
> will stand up to you in Egypt . . . Then we shall divide
> up the towns of this Egypt and Upper Nubia will be
> joyful.[9]

The author of the letter, a man of Asiatic descent named Apepi, was another claimant to the Egyptian throne. For over a hundred years, his dynasty, known today as the Hyksos, had exercised authority over the delta and suzerainty over much of the Nile Valley. Apepi and his immediate forebears regarded themselves as legitimate kings of Egypt, even assuming pharaonic titles. The ascent to power of a foreign dynasty in the north of the country was the culmination of a gradual process of infiltration and migration that had begun at the height of the Middle Kingdom.

At the same time as the Egyptian government was building a series of fortresses in Nubia to counter the threat from Kush, it was also busy constructing and reinforcing a line of defences across the north-eastern delta. The intention behind the 'Walls of the Ruler' was to halt the tide of economic migrants from the Levant who were making their way to Egypt in search of a better life. But the vast marshy expanses of the delta were harder to police than the narrow Nubian Nile Valley; by the late twelfth dynasty, a substantial community of Levantine people had settled in and around the town of Avaris. They maintained their own cultural practices, proudly bore their Asiatic names and stubbornly refused to assimilate to ancient Egyptian norms.

With the demise of the twelfth dynasty and the succession of a series of weak kings to the Egyptian throne, the state became increasingly incapable of defending its north-eastern frontier. Migration from the Levant accelerated and the substantial Asiatic population in the delta began to recognize its own native leaders, a direct challenge to pharaonic authority. One of these minor dynasts ultimately achieved recognition as *primus inter pares*, thus founding a dynasty that eventually claimed the kingship of the whole of Egypt. The country's native rulers retreated from Memphis back to their ancestral heartland of Thebes, in order to lick their wounds and plan for the reconquest of the Nile Valley.

Several generations would pass before a Theban leader emerged with the charisma and leadership ability to mobilize an effective army. Around 1541 BC, Kamose launched a series of campaigns to break out of Thebes and start the long process of reunification. He took the fight all the way to the Hyksos capital of Avaris, but also suffered setbacks. The letter from Apepi to the king of Kush, which was intercepted on its way to Nubia, suggested a policy of divide and rule, showing how precarious Kamose's position was – Egyptian victory was not a foregone conclusion. But eventually, through a combination of brilliant battlefield tactics and astute psychological warfare, the Theban side prevailed. Kamose's heir, Ahmose, was able to drive the remaining Hyksos back to their Levantine homeland and see off the Kushite threat; with Egypt's northern and southern borders secure, Ahmose proclaimed himself king of a reunified Egypt, ushering in the golden age of the New Kingdom.

Ahmose and his immediate successors not only set about the creation of a new Egyptian state with a religious capital at Thebes, centred on the temple of Amun-Ra at Karnak; they also demonized the Hyksos as illegitimate rulers and cast the peoples of the Levant as 'miserable Asiatics'. Nubia was referred to, in a similar vein, as 'vile Kush'. But this xenophobic propaganda, designed to shore up the credentials of Egypt's new ruling family, masked a more complicated reality. The dominance of Levantine culture across a large swathe of Lower Egypt for 160 years had profoundly influenced its host communities. The Hyksos, with their strong ties to the wider Near East, had introduced a range of cultural practices and innovations, from new materials and technologies to new artistic styles and motifs. The kings of the eighteenth dynasty found that some of these foreign imports were worth keeping, somewhat against their instincts. In truth, while maintaining an outward pretence of cultural superiority, the ancient Egyptians had always been receptive to new ideas from outside.

Without doubt, the most influential of the many things introduced to Egypt by the Hyksos was the horse. Until the Second Intermediate Period, the only quadruped in Egypt that could be ridden was the donkey, which, while tough and sure-footed, was hardly speedy. Egyptian armies had to rely on infantry and marine battalions, but that changed with the introduction of the horse from the Levant.[10] From the time of Ahmose onwards, the Egyptian army embraced the tactical potential of cavalry and used the Hyksos's military advantage against them.

The horse was adopted by the Egyptian elite as a status symbol: the pharaohs of the eighteenth dynasty maintained royal stables and enjoyed riding trips in the desert around Giza. Amenhotep II, while still a young prince, is said to have

> loved his horses and delighted in them. He was strong-willed in breaking them in and understanding their natures, skilled in controlling them and learning their ways.[11]

The title 'chief of the stables' is attested from the beginning of the New Kingdom, and Tutankhamun's right-hand man and successor, Ay, began his career as 'master of the horse' at the royal court.

A delicate ivory bracelet, found in the Annexe of Tutankhamun's tomb, illustrates the transformation of Egyptian elite culture in the New Kingdom following its exposure to Levantine influences. Exquisitely carved with scenes of running animals – there are well-known species of native Egyptian fauna, including a gazelle and a hare, but also a horse in a flying gallop – it serves as a reminder that, for all its self-confidence and bluster, ancient Egyptian civilization was always susceptible to external influences. Tutankhamun's bracelet also reminds us that the golden age of the eighteenth dynasty began in a period of intense cultural and political rivalry, with a clash of cultures leaving its mark on the victors as well as on the defeated Hyksos. Challenged and transformed by its interaction with its neighbours, ancient Egypt in the age of Tutankhamun was no longer able to hide behind its natural borders.

Fig. 8. Ivory bracelet with running horse.

THREE

Supremacy

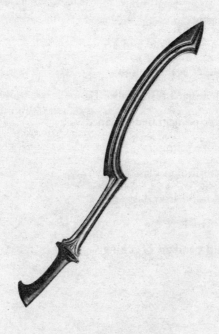

Fig. 9. Bronze scimitar.

The magnificence of Tutankhamun's treasures reflects a civilization at the height of its power and influence. When the founders of eighteenth-dynasty Egypt finally succeeded in driving out foreign invaders and reuniting the Nile Valley under Egyptian rule, they understood the importance of thinking creatively and acting decisively to maintain the country's security and prosperity. The solution they adopted was the deliberate widening of Egypt's borders, creating buffer zones of influence in Nubia and the Levant: an Egyptian empire. At its greatest extent, the pharaoh's writ extended from the banks of the Euphrates in Mesopotamia to the rapids of the Fourth Cataract in Upper Nubia, a distance of some 1,200 miles. Different administrative solutions were adopted in different regions, whether the direct annexation and colonization of Nubia or a looser system of vassal states in the Near East. But what all parts of the empire had in common was subjugation to pharaonic rule by force of arms. At the same time, new ideas, materials, technologies and fashions found their way back to the Nile Valley, making eighteenth-dynasty Egypt truly cosmopolitan. While the pharaoh was portrayed as a fearless leader and the unassailable conqueror of foreign lands, Egyptian taste was, more than ever before, shaped by foreign fashions. This paradox at the heart of eighteenth-dynasty court culture is strikingly attested in the objects from Tutankhamun's tomb.

◁◦▷

If a single piece of technology enabled and sustained Egyptian supremacy during the New Kingdom, it was the horse-drawn chariot. Developed by Indo-Aryan peoples in Central Asia, this new contraption revolutionized the art of warfare. The Egyptians encountered it during their battles against the Hyksos; their subsequent adoption of it allowed them to dominate swathes of the Near East for centuries. The chariot provided a fast-moving mobile platform for armed attack, bringing the element of surprise to the battlefield. A squadron of chariots gave an army the ability to launch a sudden attack from multiple directions and turn a defeat into a rout. The Egyptians mastered them with deadly efficiency, turning a foreign invention into an instrument of pharaonic power.

The earliest reference to chariots in an Egyptian text occurs in Kamose's account of the booty seized from the Hyksos, where they are described as 'that which belongs to a span [of horses]'. In the reign of Ahmose, chariots appear for the first time in Egyptian art, in battle scenes from a temple at Abydos. These early examples seem to have been rather simple vehicles, with primitive four- or eight-spoked wheels, limited manoeuvrability and little protection. Within a generation or two, however, significant advances had been made in chariot design and manufacture, assisted no doubt by the Egyptians' familiarity with more advanced examples from the Levant. In the battle reliefs of Thutmose III, the great warrior king of the eighteenth dynasty, chariots can be seen everywhere: carrying the king onto the field and paraded among the captured booty. The image of the pharaoh in his chariot became the quintessential icon of royal power and is ubiquitous in the art of the New

Kingdom. Yet until the discovery of Tutankhamun's tomb, only two complete chariots had been discovered, one of which was from the burial of his great-grandparents, Yuya and Tjuyu.

The boy king's treasure included no fewer than six chariots. Four were found in the Antechamber and two in the Treasury. All had been dismantled for ease of storage, and reassembling them was a long and complex task. Today, five of the six have been put back together for public display, and together they constitute one of the most impressive groups of artefacts from the tomb. The basic design consisted of a cab with a D-shaped floor plan, connected via a long pole with a yoke for two horses. The cab's floor was made from leather mesh to absorb shocks. Two wheels were rear-mounted for maximum manoeuvrability, with six-spoked wheels becoming the norm in the middle of the eighteenth dynasty; they could be fitted with outer tyres of leather or wood to protect the rim.

Just as the horse-drawn carriages of Victorian England came in various shapes and sizes, so the construction and appearance of Tutankhamun's chariots differed depending on the role they played. One of the six was a plain and ultra-lightweight example, with undecorated open sides. It would probably have been used for everyday riding or hunting. Among the few buildings with which Tutankhamun can be definitively linked, one of the most intriguing is the 'rest house' next to the Great Sphinx on the Giza Plateau. Here, it seems the young king and his eighteenth-dynasty forebears enjoyed practising their horse-riding and chariotry skills.

By contrast with Tutankhamun's lightweight 'runabout', his two finest chariots must surely have been intended for ceremonial purposes; with a nod to British imperial pageantry, Carter identified them as the king's 'state chariots'. The pharaohs of the eighteenth dynasty certainly used chariots in formal processions and on state occasions, and they would have been a central feature of Tutankhamun's ceremonial life. When Akhenaten made the official proclamation of his new capital city, Amarna, it was from the back of a glittering chariot, calling to mind the image of the sun god's appearance at dawn:

> His Majesty . . . appeared mounted upon the great chariot of electrum, like the Orb when he rises on the horizon and fills the Two Lands with his love.[1]

Once the city of Amarna had begun to function as the country's capital, Akhenaten instituted a daily chariot ride as the central element in the city's ceremonial life – perhaps to replace the regular festivals of the gods that he had abolished as part of his religious revolution. Every morning, he would travel by chariot with members of the royal family and various out-riders from the royal residence at the northern end of the city, along the Royal Road to the King's House in the Central City. Depictions of this spectacle are found in the tombs of Akhenaten's loyal courtiers. Tutankhamun's first 'state chariot' is a real-life example of the kind of vehicle his father must have used on such occasions. Its cab is over a metre wide and has a thin wooden floor. The frame has a waist-height rail to help the passenger maintain his balance, while the body is decorated with scenes of royal power, and reliefs showing the celestial falcon protecting the names of the king and his wife. The main surfaces are covered in gesso and gold leaf, and inlaid with semi-precious stones and coloured glass. The wheels have tyres made of raw hide, while the axle, the yoke and the pole are all decorated with gold. It must have been a dazzling spectacle: the king in his regalia, mounted on his finest chariot, and the horses wearing gilded crests topped with ostrich feathers.

Alongside the chariots themselves, Tutankhamun's tomb

yielded a large number of related fixtures and fittings: saddles, harnesses, blinkers, bridle bosses, fly whisks, 'check rowels' (to distract capricious stallions) and whip stocks; only the metal bits were missing, removed, perhaps, by early tomb robbers. Such a large array of chariot equipment illustrates how, within a couple of centuries, an entirely foreign invention had come to dominate the practice of Egyptian kingship.

⊲⊙⊳

The iconic image of the pharaoh in his war chariot shows him steering the vehicle with the reins wrapped around his waist, leaving him free to wield a bow and fire arrows at his enemies. While chariotry represented the most modern form of military technology in the New Kingdom, there was still an important place for its most ancient, archery.

The bow and arrow seem to have been developed very early in human evolution. Certainly, the earliest Egyptian figurative art – painted on pottery or etched into the rocks of the Eastern and Western Deserts – includes images of hunters and fighters armed with archery equipment. Like so many other accoutrements of military prowess, the bow and arrow became part of the iconography of kingship during the period of conflict that led up to the unification of Egypt. In the twelfth dynasty, a cycle of hymns to the king Senusret III lauded him as a ruler 'Who shoots the arrow like Sekhmet [a fierce lioness goddess] | When he overthrows thousands who ignore his power'.[2] The eighteenth-dynasty pharaoh Amenhotep II seems to have been something of an archery fanatic. One relief shows him firing arrows through a copper target while riding in a chariot; supremely confident of his own strength and ability, he challenged his followers to beat him, declaring, 'Anyone who pierces this target as deep as His Majesty's arrow shall have these things [as a prize].'[3]

The bow was thus a royal weapon and, because of its un-rivalled antiquity, symbolic of warfare as a whole. Perhaps not surprisingly, Tutankhamun was laid to rest with a plethora of archery equipment. It excited great interest at the time of the tomb's excavation, with a journalist for the *Daily Telegraph* commenting:

> In design they are not unlike the conventional bow and arrow of modern times, but they display a remarkable ingenuity and thoroughness in construction. It was apparent that they had been placed in the tomb with Tutankhamen to assist his ancient Majesty in combating any enemies who might attempt to retard his progress from this world to the next.[4]

Altogether, the tomb yielded at least forty-six bows and 428 arrows, as well as four bracers (to protect the inside of the arm from the bowstring), two quivers and two bow cases. The last were made of wood; one, 1.67 metres long, was painted white and contained seven bows and 254 arrows; the second was covered with linen, decorated in marquetry with bark, faience and gold leaf, and contained three bows. The fact that these were stored in such carefully crafted boxes points to their prized status; they were not ordinary bows, but the very latest composite models.

Introduced from the Near East during the battles against the Hyksos, the composite bow – like the chariot – represented a huge advance in military technology. Instead of being made from a single piece of wood, different types of wood were glued together, often with elements of sinew, horn and bark. It was much more time-consuming to produce, but it had far greater strength and penetrating power. Most of Tutankhamun's composite bows have a core of ash, wrapped with birch or cherry bark. The finest example, found laid on a bed in the Antechamber, is covered with gold leaf and granulated gold decoration. Carter labelled it the king's 'bow of honour', and described it as 'a work of almost inconceivable fineness'.[5]

Another of the king's composite bows has tips carved and painted to resemble enemy captives, their necks forming the indentations where the bowstring was tied – the king symbolically strangled his enemies every time he drew his bow. The symbolic association of bows and enemies in ancient Egypt went further. From an early period, the term 'bowmen' was used to refer to hostile forces. Nubia was known, in ancient Egyptian, as *Ta-Sety* or 'bow-land', for the inhabitants of the Upper Nile enjoyed a long-standing reputation as expert archers. Their skills were appreciated by the ancient Egyptians, who recruited Nubian auxiliaries to serve in Egyptian expeditions in the Old Kingdom and during the civil war of the First Intermediate Period. A wooden model depicting a troop of Nubian archers was among the grave goods interred with an Egyptian noble of this period, while a community of Nubian bowmen settled at Gebelein near Thebes: on their gravestones, they are shown with tightly curled hair, dark skin and a distinctive form of sash attached to their kilts. They are also shown carrying bows and arrows, emphasizing their particular skill and the reason they were welcomed by the Egyptians.

However, by the eighteenth dynasty, when the Upper Nile was firmly back under Egyptian control, the Nubians' greatest attribute was used against them as a term of condescension. An inscription from the beginning of the dynasty states:

Now after His Majesty had slain the Bedouin of Asia, he sailed upstream to Upper Nubia to destroy the Nubian bowmen.[6]

In Tutankhamun's Egypt, 'bowmen' were still occasionally welcomed into Egyptian society, but only if they pledged full allegiance to the sovereign. One example was a local Nubian prince from a region called Miam, which became the colonial seat of the Egyptian viceroys of Kush in the New Kingdom. The prince chose to adopt a loyalist Egyptian name, Hekanefer ('the good ruler', in reference to the pharaoh), and built his tomb according to the latest Egyptian design. He even befriended the viceroy himself, and was shown in *his* tomb at Thebes, along with a group of fellow Nubians. While retaining their dark skin, the 'bowmen' are shown wearing Egyptian-style robes, signifying their adoption of Egyptian cultural norms, and hence the triumph of pharaonic civilization. As one Egyptologist has remarked of Hekanefer, 'To Egyptians he remained a Nubian, but to his local community he presented himself as if he were an Egyptian.'[7]

The bows from the tomb of Hekanefer's royal master, Tutankhamun, were thus weapons perfected in the Near East and adopted by the Egyptians, but symbolic of the Nubians; instruments of royal prestige, but also of a subject people. They are illustrative of the multiple layers of meaning embodied in artefacts, and of the cultural complexity of eighteenth-dynasty Egypt.

◁○▷

The Asiatics and the Nubians were the traditional enemies of Egypt who, under Kamose, had threatened to divide and rule Egypt and who, under his successor Ahmose, had been expelled and defeated. Pharaohs had been contending with 'the miserable Asiatic' and 'vile Kush' from the end of the Pyramid Age. The peoples of Palestine and the Upper Nile were belittled in Egyptian texts precisely because they were known and feared. But once Ahmose's army had pursued the retreating Hyksos as far as their Levantine stronghold of Sharuhen, the Egyptian state found itself involved in the power politics of the Near East. Egypt's imperial expansion brought it into contact with foes whose languages, customs and practices were utterly foreign to the inhabitants of the Nile Valley.

Egypt's first contact with another 'great power' took place during the reign of Thutmose I, founder of the royal line that ended with Tutankhamun. Two generations after Ahmose, he decided to launch a pre-emptive strike against potential aggressors from Syria-Palestine, creating not just a buffer zone but a full-scale empire. In 1490 BC, he marched his army to Naharin, the 'river land' of the upper Euphrates, Tigris and Habur valleys. Some centuries earlier, a group of Hurrian-speaking people had established themselves in northern Mesopotamia and unified several small territories under their leadership. By the time of Thutmose I, the Mittani – as their Akkadian-speaking subjects called them – had forged a kingdom that stretched over much of present-day Iraq and Syria. They may not have left many written records of their own, but they left a great impression on everyone with whom they came into contact.

They fought and defeated the fearsome Hittites to establish control over southern Anatolia and northern Syria. They kept the Babylonians penned in the marshes of Mesopotamia and regarded the Assyrians as a vassal state. And they successfully fought the Egyptians, under Thutmose I, to a stalemate, limiting pharaonic ambitions.

Thutmose I celebrated his famous 'victory' over them with a triumphant elephant hunt and a haul of booty. To cement his authority, he encouraged the vassal states of northern Syria to rebel against Mittanian rule, but they defected as soon as his back was turned. This enabled the Mittani to gain control over a huge swathe of the eastern Mediterranean littoral, bringing it uncomfortably close to Egypt's backyard. Men with

Hurrian names were soon established as rulers of many Syrian and Palestinian city-states, and the Mittani strengthened their position by acquiring the client state of Kizzuwatna in south-eastern Anatolia. The stage was set for another major confrontation, two generations later.

The Mittani may have been a surprising and unwelcome new adversary, but the Egyptians were always adept at learning from an enemy. The Mittanian rulers excelled in chariotry and horsemanship, skills they had acquired from Indo-Aryan peoples in the early second millennium BC. They had their own term for an elite military equestrian: *maryannu*. Not only did the pharaohs of the eighteenth dynasty consciously emulate this warrior class, but Egyptian charioteers sometimes sported beards or wore their hair braided into three pigtails, in imitation of the *maryannu*'s distinctive appearance. It was from them that the Egyptians learned to perfect chariot warfare: not for nothing was one of the most mighty of all Mittanian rulers named Tushratta, Indo-Aryan for 'whose chariot surges forward violently'.[8] By the time Thutmose I had finished his Syrian campaign, his chariot corps was firmly established as the third key element in the Egyptian armed forces, alongside the infantry and the marines.

The other technology the Egyptians adopted from the Mittani was protective clothing. Apart from shields – Tutankhamun was buried with several, one of them gilded and covered with cheetah skin – Egyptian soldiers seem to have gone into battle singularly ill-protected. The combination of the climate and an emphasis on speed of movement apparently discouraged the development of armour. In some Old Kingdom reliefs, young recruits wear only a belt with three strips of cloth attached to it. It was Nubian auxiliaries who seem to have introduced the kilt (complete with a leather sporran) as a standard item of military uniform. As for the protection of the

Fig. 10. Leather scale armour.

upper body, Egyptian soldiers had to make do with crossed bands of linen, perhaps sufficient to parry a glancing blow from a spear. Egyptian infantry also went barefoot, and wore no face or neck protection.

The *maryannu* went into battle much better prepared. Scenes of Asiatic charioteers show them wearing scale armour on their upper bodies, and among the booty captured by the Egyptians following one encounter with Mittanian forces were twenty mail shirts made of leather and two made of bronze. The Egyptians quickly adopted this bright idea. A suit of scale body armour with a solid metal gorget was among the new year's gifts presented to Amenhotep II, as depicted in the tomb of one of his high officials. By the Amarna Period, Egyptian soldiers often wore protective gear, including leather overkilts, quilted torso coverings and jerkins made from overlapping leather or metal scales. One such leather mail shirt was found in the tomb of Tutankhamun, crumpled up and stuffed into a wooden box. Carter described it as 'made up of scales of thick tinted leather worked on to a linen basis, or lining, in the form of a close-fitting . . . bodice without sleeves'.⁹

When Egypt's second great warrior pharaoh, Thutmose III, set out to re-engage the Mittani, like his grandfather Thutmose I before him, 'in a chariot of electrum, equipped in the splendour of his weaponry like a strong-armed Horus',¹⁰ his equipment owed as much to his impending foe as to his own Egyptian civilization.

⊲✦⊳

At the end of winter 1458 BC, a formidable army of 10,000 men, led by the pharaoh Thutmose III, set out for Syria from the fortress of Tjaru on Egypt's north-eastern border. The king had taken the reins of power just ten weeks earlier, following the end of a fifteen-year co-regency with his stepmother Hatshepsut. Now undisputed ruler in his own right, he was determined to assert his authority and reassert Egyptian dominance in the Levant.

In the years since Thutmose I's military campaigns, Egypt's hold over its vassal states in Syria-Palestine had begun to slip. Under Thutmose I's son and daughter, Thutmose II and Hatshepsut, Egyptian foreign policy in the Near East seems to have swung from military action to diplomatic engagement. Hatshepsut, in particular, had been too preoccupied with a trading expedition to the fabled southern land of Punt to pay much heed to her northern protectorates. Unsurprisingly, the kingdom of Mittani had been quick to exploit the situation, winning over a series of Levantine city-states that had once been loyal to Egypt. By the time Thutmose III achieved sole power, most of Egypt's erstwhile vassal states in northern Syria-Palestine had defected. Worse still, the ruler of Kadesh had formed a coalition of princes that was intent upon throwing off the Egyptian yoke for good. The ringleaders had holed themselves up in the fortified town of Megiddo to plot their next move. It was a situation Thutmose III could not ignore.

The strategic value of Syria-Palestine to Egypt lay in its control of key trade routes with the eastern Mediterranean, Anatolia, Mesopotamia and the Zagros Mountains. The city-states fought over so keenly by Egypt and Mittani had grown wealthy from their commercial networks rather than their own resources. Megiddo, for example, controlled the Jezreel Valley, which was both the main north–south route through Canaan and the easiest east–west route between the Jordan Valley and the Mediterranean coast. As Thutmose III told his army in 1458 BC, 'the capture of Megiddo is the capture of a thousand towns'.[11]

Nine days' march from Tjaru, the Egyptian expeditionary force reached Gaza, capital of the Egyptian colonial province of Canaan. After a welcome night's rest, the army set off at dawn the next day, 'in valour, victory, power and vindication'.[12] A further eleven days' march through hostile territory brought them to Yehem, where the king held a council of war. The immediate challenge was tactical, for three different roads led to Megiddo: one to the north, one to the south and a narrow route through the Aruna Pass. According to the campaign records, Thutmose III argued for the last option, which was most direct, against the advice of his generals. It was a dangerous gamble, but it paid off. The enemy, not expecting the Egyptians to risk that route, had positioned their forces at the other two termini. In consequence, the Egyptian army encountered no resistance and pitched camp directly opposite Megiddo. Whether or not the story is true, it illustrates that in a world of great-power politics, it was no longer sufficient for the pharaoh to be presented as a strong superhero: he also had to demonstrate quick-witted, strategic thinking on the battlefield.

At daybreak on 27 April 1458 BC, Thutmose III appeared surrounded by his infantry, standing in his chariot and clad in shining armour. The rebellious prince of Kadesh and his fellow conspirators had not expected such a response, and

> fled in panic towards Megiddo with faces of fear, abandoning their horses and their chariots of gold and silver. By pulling on sheets, they were hoisted up into the town.[13]

After a long siege, the city surrendered, and the rebels prostrated themselves before the pharaoh, 'to kiss the ground before His Majesty's might, and to beg breath for their nostrils'.[14] They forfeited their lands, and Thutmose III appointed new rulers to the city-states that had rebelled.

In the wake of the battle, the administration of Egyptian-controlled lands was consolidated, to reduce the risk of further rebellion. The province of Amurru was governed from Sumur on the Mediterranean littoral. The province of Upe had its capital at Kumidi on the upper Litani River. The southernmost province, Canaan, was critical for national defence and remained most closely tied to Egypt. Authority over all three vassal provinces was exercised by a combination of civilian commissioners and military commanders. Egyptian garrisons were stationed at key sites and could be supplemented by mobile troops when necessary. This highly effective system of colonial administration was still in place in the reign of Tutankhamun, five generations later.

The Battle of Megiddo sealed Egyptian control of Syria-Palestine and effectively defined the limits of Egypt's Levantine empire for the remainder of the New Kingdom, but it was not just a one-off show of force. Thutmose III was determined to succeed where his forebears had failed. After Megiddo, he led a further sixteen military operations in the region over the following two decades, all of which had clear strategic objectives. Three consecutive campaigns were directed at the troublesome city-state of Tunip in northern Syria. To prevent it from mounting an effective opposition to Egyptian hegemony, Thutmose III's armies captured its coastal protectorates and transformed their harbours into fortified supply centres for the Egyptian army.

After the Battle of Megiddo – which Thutmose III immortalized in a great commemorative inscription on the walls of Karnak temple – the pharaoh's most significant campaign was his eighth, the purpose of which was to match, blow by blow, the achievements of his heroic grandfather. At Byblos, a safe port on the Syrian coast, the Egyptian army built a fleet of ships which they proceeded to haul over land to the Euphrates, in order to mount an impressive show of force to their Mittanian rivals. The Mittani declined to engage, allowing Thutmose III to claim a great victory and carve a stela on the riverbank, next to that left by Thutmose I. After a five-month-long campaign, the Egyptian army headed home, laden with tribute.

Over a century later, the royal treasury was tasked with gathering provisions for the burial of the newly deceased Tutankhamun. Among the numerous storage vessels brought to supply his tomb were two heirlooms dating back to the time of his illustrious great-great-great-grandfather. An unassuming ovoid jar and a large amphora, each made of calcite and incised with the name of Thutmose III, were reminders of the greatest pharaoh of the eighteenth dynasty, a king who extended the borders of Egypt 'as far as the Horn of the Earth, the marshes of Naharin'.[15]

The booty from Thutmose III's campaigns in the Levant, together with the regular tribute received from the conquered lands, gave eighteenth-dynasty Egypt the wealth to match its military might. The spoils from the Battle of Megiddo alone included 2,000 horses, nearly 1,000 chariots and a large quantity of silver. Following the king's eighth campaign, to the Euphrates, Mittani's enemies were quick to curry favour with the new regional superpower, sending envoys and diplomatic gifts to Egypt. Babylon sent lapis lazuli and the Hittites sent silver, gems and wood, while Tanaya (perhaps Mycenae) provided silver and iron. The first Asiatic campaign of Thutmose III's successor, Amenhotep II, yielded an even greater haul of treasure: three-quarters of a ton of gold and a staggering fifty-four tons of silver.

The arrival of these exotic objects and materials in the Nile Valley over a relatively short period of time caused a marked shift in fashion among the Egyptian ruling class. Artefacts of foreign manufacture – such as the 'large jar of Syrian workmanship'[16] mentioned among the spoils from Megiddo – were especially highly prized. Egyptian craftsmen adopted foreign styles and motifs, aware of their special cachet. One example is the so-called 'volute tree', a decorative symbol comprising sedges with pendant buds and heart-shaped volutes, forming a tree with three papyrus stalks sprouting from the top. The inspiration for the design seems to have come from the kingdom of Mittani; by the reign of Amenhotep II, this influence could be seen in Egyptian objects. A pink leather quiver given by the Egyptian king to a loyal servant named Maiherpri features three large volute trees and shows elements of Asiatic workmanship and decoration. Maiherpri also owned a fine glass vase that was likely to have been imported from Mittanian lands. In Thutmose III's reign, even the burials of middle-class Egyptians could boast objects of foreign origin, from pottery vessels to lyres, lutes and tambourines.

By the end of the eighteenth dynasty, craftsmen in the

Egyptian royal workshops were adept at making artefacts from imported materials and in foreign styles, to suit a discerning and cultivated clientele. One such object that was buried with Tutankhamun is a pomegranate-shaped vase. The finest of all the tomb's metal vessels, it is thirteen centimetres tall and fashioned from sheet silver, with a high proportion of gold – it may have been regarded as electrum, a naturally occurring alloy of gold and silver and the most prized of all metals. The vase is decorated with chased floral motifs and was originally closed with a rushwork stopper. The contents could not be identified but were most likely some sort of precious ointment. The pomegranate was one of several exotic flora Thutmose III brought back to Egypt from his campaigns in the Levant. A large dried pomegranate was among the objects found in the tomb of one of Thutmose III's generals, Djehuty, and its first mention in an Egyptian text is in another eighteenth-dynasty tomb. A relief in Thutmose III's Festival Hall at Karnak shows some of these strange plants, describing them as 'the plants which His Majesty found upon the hill country of Syria-Palestine'. Another encounter recorded in one of Thutmose III's campaign inscriptions was with 'the bird which gives birth every day' – in other words, the domestic fowl.

It was not only animal, vegetable and mineral products that flowed into the Nile Valley as a result of the eighteenth dynasty's imperial adventures. The booty from the Battle of Megiddo included '1,796 male and female slaves and their children' and numerous prisoners of war, including the wives of the ruler of Kadesh. Thutmose III himself brought back three Syrian women as concubines. He evidently doted on them, showering them with gifts that included jewellery and vessels of precious metal. Regular soldiers, too, returned from battle with foreign wives. Nearly 90,000 prisoners of war, including over 21,000 families, accompanied Amenhotep II's army back to Egypt from its first Syrian campaign.

This large influx of foreigners, most of whom quickly integrated with their host communities, turned New Kingdom Egypt into a thoroughly cosmopolitan country. One recent arrival, for example, a man named Pada-Baal, gained employment at Thebes in the workforce of the temple of Amun, and gave his children Egyptian names to speed up the family's assimilation. Nonetheless, most of his male descendants chose to marry women who were either immigrants or of foreign descent, thus quietly asserting their non-Egyptian identity. Another Asiatic immigrant at the court of Thutmose III, Ben-Ia, who adopted the loyalist Egyptian name Pahekamen, served as a royal page and architect. In his Theban tomb, decorated in the Egyptian style, he depicts his parents as Egyptians, but their Semitic names, Irtenna and Tirkak, betray their origins. They were not alone in eighteenth-dynasty Thebes. A gang hauling stone blocks for a temple on the west bank of the Nile is recorded as comprising twenty Egyptians and sixty Palestinians. In the Theban tomb of Thutmose III's vizier Rekhmira, a scene of construction workers is labelled as 'the captives which His Majesty brought back for the projects of the temple of [Amun]'.[17] Another inscription from the same tomb notes that 'the children of the princes of the northern lands, carried off as the pick of the booty' were brought to Thebes 'to fill the labour camps and to be the serfs of the temple estate of . . . Amun'.[18] Thutmose IV established similar settlements, while Amenhotep III surrounded his mortuary temple in western Thebes with settlements of Hurrians, immigrants from Egypt's erstwhile arch-rival, the kingdom of Mittani.

By Tutankhamun's time, even the royal bodyguard included men of Asiatic origin, alongside Libyans and Nubians. While

Egyptian art of the New Kingdom emphasized foreigners' distinctive facial features, skin colour and dress to make explicit their 'otherness', men and women from the furthest-flung regions of Egyptian influence and control were, in reality, shaping the civilization of the Nile Valley from the inside.

⊲◦▷

The eighteenth dynasty – the era of Thutmose I and III, Amenhotep II and III, Akhenaten and Tutankhamun – belongs to the Bronze Age. The three ages of human history – Stone, Bronze and Iron – were first delineated in the 1830s, based on the predominant material used for tools and weapons in Scandinavian burials. The three-age system was subsequently applied to the whole of Europe and western Asia, with a fourth age, Copper,[19] inserted between Stone and Bronze to reflect the course of technological development in the ancient Near East.

These designations may be a useful framework for classifying early human societies, but they take no account of local differences in tradition or technology. For example, in the Balkans, the addition of a small amount of tin to copper to make bronze may have been pioneered as early as the mid-fifth millennium BC. Copper-tin alloys were being made in some parts of the Near East by the late fourth millennium BC, while the earliest bronze objects from Egypt that have been found are from the early third millennium.

When tin is added to copper, there is an increase in the hardness of the resulting alloy, allowing a sharper edge to be created – an advantage for tools and weapons. The tin also increases the fluidity of the molten metal, making it easier to cast. Our most detailed information about New Kingdom metalworking comes from scenes in the Theban tomb of

Rekhmira. Workmen are shown producing copper-alloy objects, the process starting with the arrival of metal ingots and finishing with the casting of a temple door. Moulds were made from pottery or stone and an actual example, designed to produce the frame for a shield, has been excavated at the nineteenth-dynasty capital Per-Ramesses (modern Qantir) in the north-eastern Nile Delta.

Even once the Egyptians had become familiar with a new material, they did not always adopt it immediately – as we have already seen, they continued making stone artefacts many centuries after the Stone Age. Similarly, even when the rest of the Mediterranean world had entered the Bronze Age, the Egyptians stuck resolutely to copper for their tools and weapons. Copper-tin alloys were still rare in the Middle Kingdom and, even in the New Kingdom, pure copper and copper-arsenic alloys were used regularly in preference to bronze.

The reason was probably economic: while copper ores were found in abundance close to the Nile Valley and were easily mined, the tin required to make bronze was harder to come by. Tin-bearing ores do occur in the Eastern Desert, but they may not have been exploited in ancient times. Instead, pharaonic Egypt seems to have relied on tin imported from other parts of the Near East. The precise sources are uncertain, but analysis of a tin bead from a tomb at western Thebes, dated to the reign of Thutmose III, suggests that the metal may have originated in the Taurus Mountains of southern Turkey, where traces of mining activity date back to the early Bronze Age. Such sources would only have become readily accessible to Egypt following the creation of its empire in the early eighteenth dynasty. Indeed, the analysis of Egyptian pigments and glazes shows that tin was much more readily available in this period. Even so, Tutankhamun's tomb contained more copper than bronze.

Two of the objects from the boy king's burial that *are* made of bronze, the two scimitars found in the Annexe, show a Near Eastern influence, in form as well as material. The first is nearly sixty centimetres long – a heavy, full-sized weapon. Its sickle-shaped blade was cast in one piece with the handle. The grip is inlaid with panels of a dark wood, perhaps ebony. The second scimitar is much smaller, just forty centimetres long. It was also cast in one piece, and its grip was inlaid with dark wood. It was probably made for Tutankhamun to use as a child, whereas the larger weapon could only have been wielded by an adult.

The scimitar was originally a Levantine invention, but having been swiftly adopted by Egyptian armies at the beginning of the eighteenth dynasty, it became the primary long-bladed weapon used throughout the New Kingdom. It was designed to slash rather than stab, the curved blade having a sharp outside cutting edge. When wielded against an enemy, a leather loop attached to a ring at the end of the handle would be worn around the wrist, allowing the soldier to keep hold of his weapon in the cut and thrust of battle.

Just like the chariot, the scimitar soon found a central place in the militaristic iconography of the New Kingdom, where it came to stand for the king's power of life and death over his enemies. On temple walls, the chief deity is often shown handing a scimitar to the king as he prepares to slaughter his foes. Scimitars are particularly abundant in royal reliefs from the reigns of Tutankhamun and his father, Akhenaten. On one, from Amarna, the sun god Aten hands a scimitar to Akhenaten, while the king smites an enemy with a second weapon. Akhenaten's chief wife Nefertiti is also shown using a scimitar to slay a foe. In the colonnade of Luxor Temple, the reliefs carved during Tutankhamun's reign depict scimitars being carried by Egyptian infantry and brandished by the king and his young queen as they travel in a ceremonial barge. Two small gold amulets shaped like scimitars were found on the floor of Tutankhamun's tomb, alongside their full-scale bronze counterparts.

The popularity of the scimitar in eighteenth-dynasty Egypt illustrates the Egyptians' propensity for selective borrowing: when an object or technology proved useful, they had no hesitation in adopting it and making it their own. Bronze weapons were undoubtedly superior on the battlefield, and the scimitar, with its elegant and deadly form, made a perfect addition to royal iconography. While Tutankhamun's Egypt may have been a Copper Age civilization at heart, bronze undoubtedly gave it the edge.

⊲◦⊳

Sometime around the birth of Tutankhamun, a large merchant ship carrying a valuable cargo of commodities and precious objects taken on board at ports in Egypt, Syria-Palestine and Cyprus sank off the southern coast of Anatolia, with the loss of all hands. Coming to rest on the sea floor, it lay undisturbed for some three and a half thousand years, until archaeologists brought it to light.

The Uluburun shipwreck, named after the nearest spit of land, presents a time capsule of international trade and a vivid illustration of the interconnections between north Africa and the Levant in the late eighteenth dynasty. The ship itself was of a seagoing type known to the Egyptians as a *menesh*. It was fifty feet long, with a tall prow and stern, and fencing around the deck. The cargo suggests that the ship was travelling in an anti-clockwise direction around the eastern Mediterranean, following the prevailing winds and currents, when it foundered. Among the items recovered from the shipwreck were six tons of copper (a product of Cyprus); ingots of tin from Anatolia (or perhaps as far afield as present-day Afghanistan); nearly 150 amphorae of food and wine; ceramic vessels from all over the Mediterranean containing terebinth resin and other oils and perfumes; and a range of luxury items, including swords of Canaanite and Mycenaean designs, Baltic amber, elephant and hippopotamus ivory from Syria, Mesopotamian cylinder seals, ostrich eggshells from Libya and a gold ring inscribed with the name of Akhenaten's queen, Nefertiti. Perhaps most unexpected of all, however, were the disc-shaped ingots of dark blue glass, each fifteen centimetres in diameter and six centimetres thick.

Glass-making was a highly specialized industry in the late Bronze Age. It seems to have been first perfected in the Levant, where Syro-Palestinian craftsmen jealously guarded their knowledge while exporting their costly wares across the eastern Mediterranean. In Egypt, the use of glazes and glazed composition had been developed as far back as late predynastic times, but the art of true glass-making was unknown until Egyptian military expeditions encountered it in the early eighteenth dynasty. Two small fragments of glass were found in the tomb of Thutmose I, and glass beads have turned up in contemporary burials of high officials at Thebes. By the reign of Thutmose III, an embryonic glass-working industry seems to have been established in the Nile Valley; and by the time of Tutankhamun, sizeable workshops were in operation at Amarna, the city of his birth.

Contemporary diplomatic correspondence from Amarna makes reference to '*mekku*-stone', which seems to have been the term for raw glass. But until the discovery of ingots among the Uluburun cargo, the existence of international trade in it was pure supposition. Moreover, they confirm that dark blue glass, coloured with cobalt, was the most highly prized form. Achieving a reliable dark blue colour in any manufactured material was difficult and costly. Before the eighteenth dynasty, Egyptian craftsmen had access to small supplies of lapis lazuli, but they did not use this rare commodity as a colouring agent. The cobalt that provided a reliable dark blue pigment was most easily obtained by tapping into Aegean trade networks, which were outside the Egyptian sphere of influence until shortly before Tutankhamun's time.[20]

Among the inscriptions on statue bases from the mortuary temple of Tutankhamun's grandfather, Amenhotep III, are a series of strange-looking foreign place names, rather tortuously rendered in ancient Egyptian hieroglyphics. On closer inspection, they turn out to provide a comprehensive list of the most important sites in the Aegean world of the fourteenth century BC: Amnisos, Kydonia and Knossos; Mycenae, Phaistos and Lyktos; Nauplion, Boeotian Thebes and the island of Kythera; perhaps even Ilios, or Troy. Their order suggests the itinerary of a diplomatic mission to the leading city-states of the Mycenaean world. A major reason for such a mission may have been to obtain supplies of cobalt, for use in glass-making.

As a high-value commodity – and one that could be easily recycled – glass was especially prone to theft. Much of the glass that was buried in Tutankhamun's tomb is likely to have been robbed soon after his burial. Carnarvon noted having seen glass fragments in the passage leading to the tomb, for him 'proving that glass had certainly been there and was either broken going in or coming out'.[21] The only intact glass vessels discovered inside the tomb were three small cups: one of translucent white glass and two of deep blue glass. A handful of other glass objects – a headrest and an amulet of a squatting king (both also cobalt blue in colour), and a model scribal palette – miraculously survived the tomb robbers' attentions. But there were strong indications that the burial had originally been much richer in this most exotic of materials. Carter described 'a plain wooden box of oblong shape' whose contents had been 'completely cleared by the tomb-plunderers':

> Its gable-shaped lid had been replaced the wrong way on, and only the packing material in its eight rectangular compartments was left. This material comprised pieces of papyrus reeds, shredded papyrus pith and, at the bottom of each division, a small bundle of linen matting of long pile. There was not a trace of evidence as to what the original contents were, save that the careful arrangement of the packing suggested that the objects were of fragile nature – possibly glass.[22]

There is tantalizing evidence to suggest that Mycenaeans themselves reached the Nile Valley during Tutankhamun's lifetime. A fragmentary papyrus depicting members of Akhenaten's army seems to show Mycenaean auxiliaries, with their distinctive helmets and ox-hide tunics. Substantial quantities of Mycenaean pottery have been excavated at Amarna, reinforcing the impression of a significant Aegean population. Moreover, the reception of foreign tribute in Akhenaten's twelfth regnal year – perhaps the year of Tutankhamun's birth – included envoys from the islands of the Aegean: as the accompanying inscription put it, 'all foreign lands assembled on one occasion, even the islands in the midst of the sea, bringing presents to the king'.[23]

Within the last few years, further evidence has come to light of contact between the ancient Egyptian and Mycenaean worlds. In December 2019, archaeologists announced the discovery of a Mycenaean royal cemetery at Pylos in the Peloponnese. The tombs contained a wealth of ancient artefacts, including a gold pendant of the Egyptian goddess Hathor, the protectress of those who ventured beyond the Nile Valley. Although Pylos is a remote location, it is conveniently situated for maritime trade across the Mediterranean. If Mycenaeans were able to reach Amarna, it is equally possible that Egyptian merchants and envoys travelled in the other direction. The two small blue glass cups from Tutankhamun's tomb open up a whole new dimension to ancient Egypt's foreign relations.

⊲○▷

In 1887, villagers digging in the ruins of Amarna discovered a hoard of small clay tablets incised with strange wedge-shaped signs. Some of these curious objects, quite unlike anything else dug from the sands of Egypt, eventually reached the hands of collectors and scholars in Europe. At first, the tablets were dismissed as forgeries, but their authenticity soon became clear: the villagers had found a collection of letters inscribed in the cuneiform script of Mesopotamia, recording the diplomatic correspondence between Egypt, its Levantine vassals and other great powers of the Near East during the reigns of Amenhotep III, Akhenaten and Tutankhamun. The ruined building where the tablets had been found turned out to be 'the House of Correspondence of Pharaoh', the foreign ministry archive of the late eighteenth-dynasty Egyptian state. In the years since their discovery, the so-called 'Amarna Letters' have provided a wealth of new information about international relations at a crucial period of antiquity.

In the early eighteenth dynasty, Egypt's chief adversary in the Near East was the kingdom of Mittani. The two states vied with each other for control of vassals in Syria-Palestine, and for hegemony over the wider Levant. This uneasy state of affairs changed in the reign of Amenhotep II, as Mittani came under increasing pressure from the expansionary Hittite kingdom. From their power base in Central Anatolia, the Hittites began to extend their influence in the south and east. Mittani decided it could not defend its interests on two fronts so chose to sue for peace with

Egypt, the result being an entente that would last for sixty years. The alliance was sealed, in the reign of Thutmose IV, by the marriage of a daughter of the king of Mittani to the Egyptian pharaoh. This was followed, a generation later, by two further unions, as first King Shatturna of Mittani sent his daughter Gilukhepa and then his successor, King Tushratta, sent his daughter Tadukhepa to wed Amenhotep III.

The first of these events was marked in Egypt by the issue of a commemorative scarab. Its inscription begins with an extensive titulary of Amenhotep III, followed by the name and parentage of his chief wife, Tiye. Only at the end is the new Mittanian concubine mentioned:

> The marvel which was brought to His Majesty – life, prosperity and health: Gilukhepa, daughter of Shatturna, chief of Mittani; and the personnel of her harem, 317 women.[24]

From the pharaoh's perspective, the new addition to his court was nothing more than a gift from a foreign chief, but the kings of Mittani looked at things rather differently. When Tushratta succeeded to the throne, he sent his greetings to Amenhotep III. The preamble to his missive, preserved among the Amarna Letters, puts his sister in her rightful place:

> For me all goes well. For you may all go well. For Gilukhepa may all go well. For your household, for your wives, for your sons, for your magnates, for your warriors, for your horses, for your chariots and in your country, may all go very well.[25]

To avoid any hurt feelings, he sent a gift of Mittani's speciality: 'As the greeting-gift of my brother, I send you five chariots, five teams of horses.'[26]

Some years later, to cement the burgeoning alliance, Tushratta sent his own daughter to join Amenhotep III's extensive harem. This time, the dowry was not just confined to the princess's entourage. Among the glittering array of treasure that made its way from the Euphrates to the Nile were more horses, a chariot and various horse trappings, but also a large quantity of clothing – multicoloured 'Hurrian-style' shirts alongside coloured leather shoes, sashes and a 'pair of leggings, of shaggy wool'.[27] There were purely decorative objects, too, including a 'plaque with winged disks and Deluge monster(s), of ebony overlaid with gold',[28] and a veritable arsenal of military equipment, including bronze and leather cuirasses, a composite bow, bronze helmets, alabaster and malachite helmet containers, an axe and a spear. Perhaps most precious of all was an object that made use of the very latest technology: 'a dagger, the blade of which is of iron, its guard of gold'.[29]

Iron ore was found in the heart of the Hittite lands, and was hence of great rarity in Egypt. Moreover, ironworking would not become a widespread technology for another two and a half centuries – for a king of ancient Egypt or Mittani, an iron-bladed dagger was the ultimate status symbol. Remarkably, an object that bore a close resemblance to Tushratta's gift was among the most precious artefacts recovered from the tomb of Amenhotep III's grandson, Tutankhamun. While most of his grave goods were piled in the tomb's four main chambers, a few were evidently deemed so valuable that they were deposited within the mummy wrappings that protected his body. Foremost among these closely guarded treasures were two daggers, one with a blade of gold and one with a blade of iron. The ceremonial, gold-bladed version was tucked under one of the linen girdles wrapped around his waist. Its sheath is decorated with an inlaid feather pattern and a hunting scene in repoussé work. The hardened metal blade is chased with a palmette design, while the grip is decorated with granulated gold and inlaid with glass and semi-precious stones. The iron-bladed dagger, thirty-four centimetres long, was hidden among the mummy wrappings along Tutankhamun's right thigh. Its scabbard is made of sheet gold and finely decorated, terminating in the head of a desert fox. When the blade was discovered, according to Carter, it was 'still bright and resembling steel',[30] demonstrating the highest quality of metalwork. The pommel, being made of rock crystal, is equally unusual. (The dagger sent by Tushratta to Amenhotep III is described as having a pommel of '[. . .]-stone';[31] the crucial word is missing, but the material was evidently thought worthy of special mention.) Unlike Tutankhamun's gold-bladed dagger, his iron-bladed example bears no royal name, which suggests that it was made outside the Egyptian royal workshops.

It is tempting to think that Tutankhamun's dagger could be the same one that was given to his grandfather as part of the dowry of a Mittanian princess. If it was, the diplomatic support it bought turned out to be of limited value. For in the very year of Tutankhamun's birth, a new and vigorous Hittite ruler, Shuppiluliuma, invaded Mittani from the north, sacking its capital and conquering its vassals. Mittani had also lost territory to Assyria and threw in its lot with the Hittites, with Tushratta's son ruling as a puppet of his new masters. From now on, the Hittites would be Egypt's principal adversary in the Levant – until that rivalry, too, was brought to an end by a military stalemate and a diplomatic marriage.

⋖○⋗

If Tutankhamun's gold dagger represents a masterpiece of the jeweller's art and his iron dagger a triumph of advanced metalworking, the acme of the painter's craft must surely be the king's Painted Box. This remarkable object, found in the Antechamber, is sixty-one centimetres long and forty-four centimetres tall, with a vaulted lid. The entire outer surface is covered with detailed scenes painted in tempera on a thin layer of gesso. The box's original purpose seems to have been to store children's clothes – at least, that was what Carter found inside it when it was opened – but there is nothing everyday about the decoration. Executed with consummate skill and astonishing attention to detail, it is one of the finest examples of ancient miniature painting to have survived. The American Egyptologist James Henry Breasted called it, with just a touch of hyperbole, 'the work of a master artist of all time, compared with whom the greatest artists among the Greeks and of the Italian Renaissance and of the Louis XIV period are mere hacks'.[32]

Just as arresting as the technique of the decoration is its subject matter. On each end, the king is depicted as a sphinx, a mythical beast with strong connotations of divine supremacy.

Fig. 11. End panel of the Painted Box showing Tutankhamun as a sphinx trampling his enemies.

Tutankhamun is shown doing battle against the Syrians on one side of the box and against the Nubians on the other. In both tableaux, the king appears in his war chariot, brandishing a bow and shooting arrows into a confused melee of enemies. The foreigners are rendered in painstaking detail, in accordance with the ethnic stereotypes so beloved of ancient Egyptian artists. In each battle scene, the artist has drawn a deliberate contrast between order and chaos, a counterpoint that lends them energy and intensity.

There is growing evidence that the Egyptian army engaged in military action against Syrians and Nubians during Tutankhamun's reign. Fragments of wall relief from the king's mortuary temple in western Thebes show fighting against Asiatic foes, which might record a battle against the ruler of Kadesh. And a recently discovered stela from the Kurkur Oasis lends credence to the argument that Tutankhamun's armies fought a Nubian campaign. But whether or not the scenes on the Painted Box depict real events misses the point: their primary purpose is to present the king as the all-conquering hero, suppressing Egypt's neighbours in order to defend and assert Egyptian supremacy. According to ancient Egyptian thought, all military action was part of the struggle between order and chaos, because all foreign enemies lived outside pharaonic rule and were thus anathema to the divine order.

The ideological intent behind the decoration on the sides of Tutankhamun's Painted Box is reinforced by the scenes on the lid. On one side, the king is shown hunting wild gazelle in the desert, while on the other he pursues a lion. While we can be certain that Tutankhamun did take part in hunting expeditions in the desert close to Giza, the depictions on his Painted Box are not intended to record real events in his life. The parallels between the hunting and battle scenes rather emphasize the ritual significance of both and the deliberate contrast between order and chaos.

The symbolic connection between hunting wild animals and fighting enemies was a familiar trope in Egyptian thought, expressed in explicit terms by the twin architects of Egypt's empire. Thutmose I and then his grandson Thutmose III each took part in an elephant hunt after confronting Mittani forces on the banks of the Euphrates. In his war annals, Thutmose III recounts how he killed 120 elephants in the land of Niye, in direct emulation of his predecessor, and participated in a sporting conquest at Qatna on his return journey to Egypt. The hunting of big game expressed the same divinely inspired mission as the waging of war on foreign enemies: the preservation of created order through the destruction of the untamed forces of nature.

Tutankhamun's grandfather, Amenhotep III, may not have engaged in military campaigns, but he certainly recognized the propaganda value of hunting. At key moments in the first part of his reign, he issued special scarabs that were probably presented to influential members of his court. The choice of events that he celebrated in this way tells us about the priorities of Egyptian kingship in the late eighteenth dynasty: the excavation of a boating lake for the king's chief wife Tiye highlights the importance of the royal marriage; the arrival of Gilukhepa of Mittani in the royal harem emphasizes Egyptian superiority over other lands; and a hunt of wild bulls signifies the king's mastery of nature. The latter event was more a ritual slaughter than a sporting contest, as the inscription makes plain:

> Then His Majesty ordered a ditch to be dug to enclose these wild bulls, and His Majesty went forth against all these wild bulls. The number thereof: 170 wild bulls.

The number the king took in hunting on this day: fifty-six wild bulls.[33]

Even more important in royal ideology was the king's prowess against the king of beasts, the wild lion. To mark his tenth year on the throne, Amenhotep III issued a commemorative scarab recording the number of lions he had killed since his accession: 102. Over a hundred of this particular scarab have been found, not just in the Nile Valley but as far afield as Lachish (in present-day Lebanon) and Cyprus. It was evidently distributed to the king's foreign allies as well as his Egyptian lieutenants, an indication of the significance of the lion hunt in ancient Egyptian divine kingship.

In pharaonic Egypt, the lion was the ultimate adversary for an earthly ruler, and the symbolic power of the lion hunt dates back to predynastic times. A large palette from the period is carved with images of a lion hunt, strikingly similar to the scene on Tutankhamun's Painted Box, created eighteen centuries later – a remarkable example of the innate conservatism of ancient Egyptian art and culture. The hunters on the palette are on foot rather than in a chariot, but they bear familiar weapons: maces, clubs, throw sticks and bows and arrows. They are accompanied by hunting dogs – which also run alongside Tutankhamun's chariot on the Painted Box – and the lion itself is shown pierced by arrows at the end of the hunt.

As well as being the finest surviving example of painting from the ancient world, Tutankhamun's Painted Box also illustrates the antiquity and durability of pharaonic civilization. Once they had been established in the early days of the Egyptian state, the ideology of kingship and the iconography with which it was expressed continued for the next 3,000 years.

⊲∘⊳

> May my brother send me in very great quantities gold
> that has not been worked, and may my brother send me
> much more gold than he did to my father. In my brother's
> country, gold is as plentiful as dirt.[34]

These words, written by the king of Mittani to Tutankhamun's
grandfather, neatly sum up the main reason why Near Eastern
powers maintained diplomatic relations with the Nile Valley
in the late eighteenth dynasty. Egypt had access to almost
unlimited supplies of gold, the most prized of all raw materials
and the currency of international trade. This superabundance
of gold gave Egypt an economic advantage to match its military prowess. A foreign army might hold an Egyptian force to
an uneasy stalemate, but Egyptian gold always won the day.

Access to gold-bearing regions was a decisive factor in power
politics from the start of Egyptian civilization. One of the
earliest sizeable settlements to emerge in the Nile Valley was
the town of Nubt (modern Nagada), whose name meant
'golden'. Its early rulers were able to gain political and military
advantage over their rivals because they commanded access to
an area of the Eastern Desert that was dotted with gold mines.
Whoever controlled the so-called 'gold of Coptos' commanded
the wealth of the country, and the few surviving golden objects
from the Pyramid Age testify to the skills of ancient Egyptian
goldsmiths during the first flowering of pharaonic culture.

At the beginning of the Middle Kingdom, a major motive
for the annexation of Lower Nubia was the abundance of gold
in the surrounding deserts. The 'gold of Wawat' came from
mines in the Wadi Allaqi and the Wadi Gabgaba, and the
string of fortresses built along the Lower Nubian Valley

controlled access to these all-important sites. The surviving jewellery from twelfth-dynasty royal burials illustrates the levels of sophistication attained by Egyptian craftsmen, who used gold and other products of the desert such as carnelian and turquoise as their raw materials.

By the start of the New Kingdom, intensive mining seems to have largely exhausted the most accessible of the northerly gold deposits, so all eyes turned to Nubia. Not only did Lower Nubia have the gold of Wawat, but the Upper Nile Valley, between the Fourth and Fifth Cataracts, held the key to deposits further south, in Sudan and Ethiopia. Gaining access to these new sources, known as the 'gold of Kush', may have been the decisive spur to the Egyptian conquest of Nubia at the beginning of the eighteenth dynasty. In the Tombs of the Nobles at Thebes, scenes of tribute show Nubians bringing great quantities of gold as rings or baskets of gold dust. There was no more important product from Egypt's southern lands.

Modern archaeologists have uncovered some 130 ancient gold-mining sites in the Eastern Desert of Egypt and Sudan; the ancient Egyptians (and their Nubian subjects) were adept at finding reserves in some of the most remote places on earth. In the words of an early-twentieth-century scholar, 'no workable deposits have been discovered that they overlooked'.[35]

The Amarna Letters highlight the central role played by gold in international trade and diplomacy during the eighteenth dynasty. Scarcely a foreign ruler writing to the Egyptian court fails to mention his desire for gold, while Tushratta of Mittani, quoted above, opened his letter with a reference to earlier gifts:

> I also asked my brother for much gold, saying, 'May my brother grant me more than he did to my father and send it to me. You sent my father much gold. You sent

him large gold jars and gold jugs. You sent him gold bricks as if they were the equivalent of copper.'[36]

The ruler of Babylon wrote to the pharaoh with a similar request:

And as to the gold I wrote you about, send me whatever i[s on hand], (as) much (as possible).[37]

Not to be outdone, the King of Assyria also sent a demand:

If your purpose is graciously one of friendship, send me much gold.[38]

With gold playing such a decisive role in maintaining Egypt's status, the pharaonic state went to great lengths to preserve its access to supplies. Akhenaten's reign seems to have been characterized by diplomacy rather than aggression. It is conspicuously devoid of armed campaigns in the Near East, but he does seem to have launched a military operation against rebel nomads in an area called Akuyati in Nubia. A later inscription, from the reign of Ramesses II, mentions that a similarly named land, Akuta, contained 'much gold'. If Akuyati and Akuta are the same place – both representing an attempt to spell an unfamiliar Nubian toponym in Egyptian hieroglyphs – it is easy to understand Akhenaten's swift response to a rebellion: whatever his pacifist leanings, he could not afford to allow a major gold-bearing region to slip from Egyptian control. Indeed, the punishment meted out to the ringleaders of the insurgency was particularly grisly; they were impaled on stakes, a grim warning to anyone else who sought to disrupt Egypt's access to gold.

Just a few years after the Akuyati rebellion, Akhenaten's son came to the throne. One of the boy king's most treasured childhood possessions was a little statuette attached to a bead collar and a tasselled suspension cord. It shows him as a young boy, squatting, holding an *ankh* and wearing a crown. The miniature statue, just over five centimetres tall, was found wrapped tightly in a linen bundle inside two nested coffins: a prized keepsake and talisman, it was designed to protect the king and grant him a long life. It is made of pure gold, the material that had secured Egypt's status as a great power and given it supremacy in the Near East.

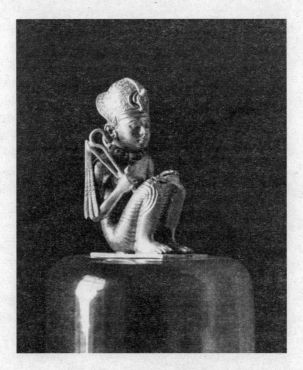

Fig. 12. Gold pendant of the boy king.

FOUR

Bounty

Fig. 13. Wine jars.

Diplomatic relations between the eighteenth-dynasty pharaohs and their imperial rivals may have been eased by abundant supplies of gold, but Egypt's fundamental wealth derived from the fertility of the Nile Valley. Pharaonic civilization was built on agricultural bounty. In Roman times, Egypt was famed as the breadbasket of the empire, and its economy had always been based on cereal production. Barley and wheat – and their products, bread and beer – were the staples of the ancient Egyptian diet, but the fields, orchards and gardens along the Nile also produced an abundance of pulses, fruit and vegetables. The river itself was full of fish, while cattle were reared in the lush pastures of the delta, and a host of other livestock on smallholdings the length and breadth of the country. All told, the Egyptians had a varied list of ingredients at their disposal; feasting was an important part of their culture. Cuisine is fundamental to any civilization, yet surprisingly little is known about how the ancient Egyptians prepared their food – all we have are the raw ingredients. The tomb of Tutankhamun yielded a veritable larder of foodstuffs, from everyday garlic and lentils to special-occasion jars of wine and joints of meat. While the king could enjoy exotic commodities that were the preserve of the elite, like dates and honey, he shared with his lowliest subjects a dependence on the bounty of the Nile.

'Give us this day our daily bread.' Bread was regarded as the staff of life throughout the Near East, and ancient Egypt was no exception. It was not only the staple foodstuff, it also had a symbolic potency. When an ancient Egyptian boasted that he had 'given bread to the hungry', it could be meant literally or metaphorically.

Due to the dry conditions along the desert edge of the Nile Valley, where ancient cemeteries tended to be located, the preservation of organic material in ancient Egyptian graves is unusually good. Among the foods that were interred with the deceased to nourish them in the afterlife, several hundred loaves have survived. Fragments of bread have been recovered from the graves of the Badarians, Egypt's first settled people, dating back some 6,000 years. When the tomb of Kha, a middle-ranking official of the eighteenth dynasty several millennia later, was excavated in 1906, it was found to contain tables piled high with loaves of bread and cakes. Among the ancient varieties that have been identified are bread flavoured with coriander seeds and fruit bread containing dates, sycomore figs and fruit from the Christ's thorn bush.

The evidence for the ubiquity and importance of bread in ancient Egypt is not confined to material remains: Egyptian texts mention many different kinds of bread, while scenes of bread-making are a common trope on the walls of tombs from the Old, Middle and New Kingdoms. A wooden model of a bakery found in the eleventh-dynasty tomb of Meketra provides further insights regarding the baker's art in pharaonic Egypt.

The principal ingredient of ancient Egyptian bread was emmer, a primitive form of hulled wheat that, when threshed, breaks into spikelets. These had to be moistened and pounded with pestles to release the individual grains, which were then winnowed and sieved to remove the chaff, before being ground into flour. Until the Middle Kingdom, quernstones were usually placed on the floor, which made grinding the corn, a task typically carried out by women, especially back-breaking. Around 2000 BC, the idea of placing the quern on a raised platform took hold, which considerably reduced the discomfort of milling. The result of this labour-intensive process was a coarse flour that contained a good deal of sand and other debris; not surprisingly, the teeth of ancient Egyptian mummies usually show heavy wear from chewing on coarse bread.

Once the grain had been milled into flour, it was mixed with water and baked. Bakeries, which have been excavated at a number of ancient settlement sites, are recognizable by the broken remains of discarded bread moulds that typically litter the area. At Giza, there was a large-scale bakery to feed the workers who built the pyramids, with heavy clay bread moulds laid in rows on a bed of hot embers. By the Middle Kingdom, the shape of the classic bread mould had evolved into a tall, narrow cone. Thousands of fragments have been found in settlements of the period, such as the pyramid town of Kahun.

The most impressive ancient bakeries to have been uncovered are in the city of Amarna. Situated close to the city's two major temples, they were designed to make bread on an industrial scale and comprised over a hundred individual chambers, built side by side. Each chamber was a single baking unit such as might have been found in a house, while the walls were lined with brick bins for grain or flour. Near the bakeries, a shed containing forty-eight mortars sunk into the ground was where the grain was pounded, while a concentration of quernstones identifies the grinding room. As the site archaeologist has noted, 'The rhythmic pounding of mortars and the sliding of quernstones rubbed together must have been some of the regular sounds that accompanied life at Amarna.'[1]

The surviving remains at Amarna are complemented by the artistic record: on a reused temple block at nearby Hermopolis, the decoration includes a representation of a bakery. Under a vaulted roof, a baker is tending an oven. Flat loaves are stacked on a table behind him, while cylindrical bread moulds are laid out behind another man, ready to be filled. The scene depicts the two main types of loaf that were popular at Amarna in the eighteenth dynasty. The flat loaves were either baked on trays or slapped directly onto the hot exterior of an oven, a technique that is still practised in Egypt today. Conical loaves were baked in moulds laid among embers.

In Tutankhamun's time, conical bread seems to have been preferred for celebratory and ceremonial occasions, and the bakeries adjacent to the temples at Amarna are littered with the fragments of tens of thousands of moulds. The loaves produced in them would probably have supplied the royal palace as well as the temples – the diplomatic gifts from the king of Mittani to Amenhotep III included bread shovels made of gold, silver, ebony and ivory.[2] By contrast, moulds are rarely found in residential areas, suggesting that domestic production focused on simpler loaves. It is odd, therefore, that the loaves found in Tutankhamun's tomb are of the domestic variety. In total, at least a dozen were found in the Antechamber and Annexe, having been discarded by ancient tomb robbers searching for more valuable items. Those from the Annexe were the best preserved, varying in size from nine centimetres to thirteen centimetres long, and including three small, semi-circular loaves (shaped similarly to the hieroglyphic sign for 'bread'), one of which was encased in a rushwork mesh – perhaps a rudimentary breadbasket.

Carter believed that some of the other specimens of bread from the tomb were intended for brewing beer, and it is possible that two wood and copper strainers buried with the king may have been used for this purpose. Certainly, in ancient Egypt, the two staples were inextricably linked. As an instructional text put it:

Pectoral with green glass (2)

Ostrich-feather fan (4)

Ceremonial sickle (10)

Gilded Hathor head (12)

Crook and flail (14)

Silver pomegranate-shaped vase (25)

Painted Box (29)

Gold dagger and sheath (28)

Detail of statuette of
the king harpooning (43)

Faience *nemset* vase (46)

Falcon pectoral (42)

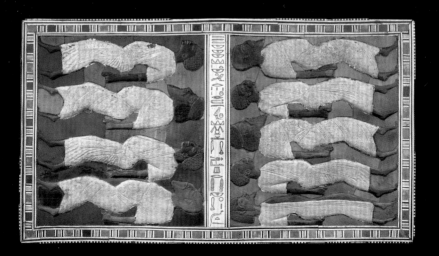

Footrest with enemies (44)

*Shabti*s with different crowns (45)

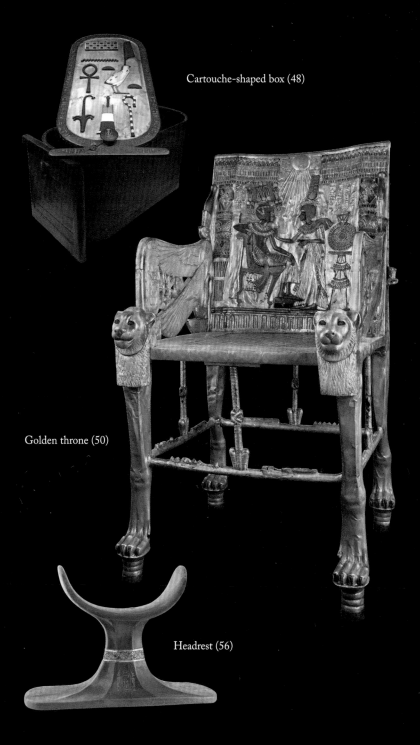

Cartouche-shaped box (48)

Golden throne (50)

Headrest (56)

Golden throne (detail) (50)

If you have stuffed yourself with three loaves,
washed down with two jugs of beer,
and your belly is [still] not full, fight against it![3]

Bread and beer may have been manufactured together, with coarse loaves forming the main ingredient for beer's fermentation. While emmer was the principal grain used in bread-making, beer was mostly made from barley, using a mixture of sprouted and unsprouted grains. The resulting drink was thick, cloudy and rich in carbohydrates and sugars, a source of nourishment in itself. Beer was also a key ingredient in offerings to the gods and the dead.

The word for beer is first attested in fifth-dynasty offering lists, and the standard offering formula, inscribed on countless coffins, offering tables and stelae, begins, 'May you say: a thousand bread and beer [for the deceased]'. With its alcohol content effective at killing bacteria, beer was safer to drink than water, and it was consequently an ingredient in many medicines. It was also an important economic commodity. Goods could be valued in terms of a number of beer jars and workers could have their rations paid in beer, to be exchanged for other commodities. Some people, however, may have consumed more than was good for them. One of the maxims from an eighteenth-dynasty instructional text warns against the ill effects of excess drinking:

Do not indulge in drinking beer, lest bad words come out of your mouth without you knowing what you are saying. If you fall and hurt yourself, no one will give you a helping hand. Your drinking companions will stand around saying, 'Out with the drunkard!' If someone comes to find you and talk to you, you will be discovered lying on the ground like a little child.[4]

Perhaps the omission of jars of beer from the teenaged Tutankhamun's tomb was a deliberate precaution.

⋖○⋗

The processing and storage of agricultural produce – including the raw ingredients for bread and beer – was a major activity throughout pharaonic civilization. Thanks to the fertility of the soil and the life-giving Nile, Egypt was one of the most successful agricultural economies of the ancient world, the roots of which extended back into prehistory. The first agricultural communities were established in the Nile Valley in the sixth millennium BC. Traces of emmer and barley have been found in early predynastic settlements, and these two cereal crops were the mainstay of the Egyptian economy for over 5,000 years. Cultural preference and innate conservatism must have been factors, but there were also pragmatic reasons: barley thrives in arid and saline conditions and was suited to the climate of Upper Egypt, whereas emmer grew well in the delta. Free-threshing wheats were introduced from other parts of the Near East in the Ptolemaic Period and Egypt was a major exporter of durum wheat while under Roman rule, but these were late additions to the country's agricultural scene.

The stages of cereal production are well known from archaeological, archaeobotanical, textual and artistic evidence. Decorated tombs of high officials from the Old, Middle and New Kingdoms often include tableaux that depict the agricultural year, but they reflect an idealized view of rural life from the perspective of the ruling class. In reality, a farmer's life was one of unrelenting hard work. It is no coincidence that the servant figurines (*shabti*s) interred with the dead from the New Kingdom onwards were routinely inscribed with the following:

you shall assign yourself to me every time the fields are
to be fertilized, the banks irrigated or sand ferried from
east to west.[5]

As we have seen, the year was divided into three seasons that
reflected the principal preoccupations of rural communities:
inundation, growth and harvest. The sequence of activities
associated with cereal production was carefully timed to take
advantage of the prevailing environmental conditions.

With little or no rainfall, ancient Egypt was dependent on
the annual Nile inundation, with the floodwaters being carefully managed to provide suitable conditions for agriculture.
Although artificial irrigation – the use of dikes to allow water
to flood a field – is attested from the predynastic period, only
in the Middle Kingdom, in the aftermath of a long series
of disastrous floods, does man-made irrigation seem to have
been widely adopted. The central government undertook land
reclamation and irrigation projects in marginal areas like Fayum
and the delta, but left the construction and maintenance of
irrigation systems to local communities.

Following the peak of the inundation each August and
September, water was retained in flood basins for between one
and two months, during which time it fertilized the soil and
washed away damaging salts. Once the waters had receded, the
earth was tilled with a hoe or plough and the seed was sown,
scattered by hand from baskets. Farmers kept their best grain
from each harvest to use as seed-corn for the following growing
season. After sowing, a field was either ploughed or had a flock
of sheep driven over it, to cover the seed and tread it in.
Thereafter, the crop was largely left to fend for itself. Clappers
were sometimes used to scare away birds, but weeding seems
to have been rare and fertilizer does not seem to have been
routinely applied – Nile silt was the perfect growing medium.

Six months after sowing, the grain ripened. Harvesting was a busy time and required the participation of the whole community. Lively harvest scenes are a feature in the tombs of many New Kingdom officials, such as the eighteenth-dynasty tomb of Menna at Thebes. As in many agricultural societies, sickles were used for harvesting, with stalks bound into sheaves and gleaners following behind to gather up any loose grain. Sheaves were then carried, either by hand or on donkeys, to the threshing floor, where they were trampled by animals to separate the ears, which were then sieved and winnowed. Rather than being discarded, the straw and chaff were valuable materials in their own right, being used as bedding, fuel, animal fodder and building materials.

The final stage in the process was storage. With some 95 per cent of its population working as subsistence farmers, ancient Egypt was extremely vulnerable to fluctuations in food supplies. The state's response was to maintain sizeable buffer stocks of grain to protect against shortages, a practice that was central to the stability of pharaonic civilization. Records from the New Kingdom workmen's village at Deir el-Medina show that the system was remarkably effective in keeping grain prices stable throughout the year. The scale of the operation can be judged by the facilities at the mortuary temple of Ramesses II at western Thebes, one of the largest land-owning institutions in the New Kingdom. Its granaries could hold over 16 million litres of grain, enough to support the population of a medium-sized ancient city for a year. Such wealth not only provided a national reserve but also gave the state huge purchasing power, paying the wages of government workers and funding major building schemes, foreign trade and other royal projects.

In addition to the large state-maintained grain stores, granaries were also built by private individuals to house their own produce, a personal store of wealth and a domestic insurance policy. The model granary from the tomb of Tutankhamun

Fig. 14. Model granary.

provides a good example. Measuring seventy-four by sixty-five centimetres and twenty-one centimetres tall, it is made of wood, painted white and divided into sixteen compartments, which were found filled with grain and seeds. Carter noted that similar storehouses, 'built of sun-dried mud bricks, are the mode for storing cereals in Egypt to-day. Their external architectural details are precisely the same as this very model of thirty-three centuries ago.'[6] Tutankhamun may have been pharaoh, but where his eternal sustenance was concerned, he was taking no chances. As a nineteenth-dynasty letter noted:

Don't let the granary be lacking in barley or emmer, for it is upon the granary that a house stands firm.[7]

◁◦▷

The ancient Egyptian diet revolved around bread and beer, but it was not without other foodstuffs and flavours. Even for the poorest in society, vegetables were relatively easy to come by, with members of the onion family among the most popular varieties. A block from the Aten temple at Karnak, built a few years before the birth of Tutankhamun, depicts a workman eating an onion. Garlic was appreciated both for its flavour and for the medicinal qualities of garlic oil, which were known from at least the New Kingdom. It was also used in the embalming process, and its consumption as a vegetable dates much further back: unbaked clay models of garlic bulbs, painted white, have been found in several predynastic tombs in Upper Egypt. The earliest surviving specimens of real garlic have been found at Amarna, suggesting that it was eaten at Akhenaten's court. This is confirmed by the small bunch of garlic bulbs found inside a chest in Tutankhamun's tomb.

Garlic, grown as a winter crop, was ideally suited to Egyptian conditions: it requires little water after the early stages of growth. In general, the cultivation of vegetables and fruit was an impor-tant part of the ancient Egyptian economy – horticulture and agriculture were complementary activities that made use of the Nile Valley's bounty. Vegetables and other summer crops were planted on the low-lying, late-draining land on the Nile banks, to take full advantage of the moist conditions. The higher land on the levees, meanwhile, provided the perfect environment for arboriculture, and together with natural islands of higher land in the floodplain, they were often developed as orchards.

The fifth-dynasty tomb of two high officials at Saqqara depicts a well-observed cross section of the Nile Valley. The scene shows vegetable plots, an orchard and a vineyard in the areas that were unsuited to arable cultivation. The wall decor-ation of a twelfth-dynasty tomb at Beni Hasan features a similar tableau; activities depicted include the watering and harvesting of vegetables, fruit being picked and grapes being harvested. Orchards also provided a suitable environment for keeping domesticated or caged waterfowl.

As well as growing fruit and vegetables on the Nile levees,

the ancient Egyptians were also keen gardeners at home. Throughout pharaonic history, the ruling elite idealized a large house set in a walled garden, with a pool and vegetable garden, with trees providing shade and produce. An eighteenth-dynasty instructional text encouraged its audience to

> Make a garden and enclose a plot, in addition to your fields. Set out trees in it to shelter your house.[8]

The most important feature was a permanent water source. This was a well or, more often, a deep pond – in fact, the word for 'pool' (*she*) could also mean 'garden'. A pond also had the advantage of providing a home for fish and waterfowl, which were prized both for decoration and as food. Trees were usually planted in rows around the central pool, sometimes with water rills running between them. A scene in the eighteenth-dynasty tomb of Amenemhab shows one such garden, its central pool surrounded by alternating rings of fruit trees and palm trees. The near-contemporary tomb of Sennefer depicts an even grander layout, with four separate ponds, each with waterfowl and surrounded by rows of fruit trees and palms; at the centre of the garden is a vineyard. Examples of walled gardens, attached to some of the large private estates in the North City, have been excavated at Amarna.

Amarna also provides the best archaeological evidence for vegetable plots, of the kind that would have been used to grow Tutankhamun's garlic. Because of the scarcity of water and the sandiness of the soil, the ancient Egyptians practised horticulture in raised beds. Potagers were generally laid out as a grid of low mud ridges, with each square one cubit wide and filled with alluvial soil. Animal dung and decayed mudbrick provided ready sources of additional fertilizer, if needed. Examples of such plots have been found across Amarna, from the humble workmen's village to the private estates of high officials and royal buildings. The material remains are supported by a detailed scene of gardens in the tomb of the high priest Meryra. It also shows, for the first time in Egyptian art, a *shaduf*, the water-lifting device that transformed horticulture in the Nile Valley from the eighteenth dynasty until the introduction of the ox-powered water wheel (*saqiya*) in the Ptolemaic Period.

Artistic evidence suggests that watering was carried out manually, with containers used to collect water from river, pool or well. As gardening was extremely labour-intensive, the scale of plantations was restricted to those that could be easily watered by hand. While the tombs of New Kingdom officials depict scenes of gardens overflowing with fruit and flowers, the reality is captured more accurately in the Middle Kingdom text known as *The Satire of the Trades*:

> The gardener carries a yoke; | his shoulders are bent as with age. | There is a lesion on his neck | and it festers. | He spends the morning watering vegetables | and the evening with the coriander, | while at noon he has done himself in in the orchard. | He works himself to death | more than all [other] jobs.[9]

◁◦▷

Visit any Egyptian market today and you will see fruit, vege-tables, herbs and spices piled high in woven baskets of all shapes and sizes. In ancient times, baskets were the containers of choice for a wide range of personal belongings and house-hold goods, and over a hundred were found in Tutankhamun's tomb. Most held foodstuffs, whether fruit, seeds, spices, nuts, wheat or bread. In ancient Egypt, baskets of food signified abundance. Carter noted that 'On certain festivals the modern

Egyptians still take similar baskets of fruits to the tomb of their deceased relatives,'[10] and the pharaonic baskets display a similar technique to modern Egyptian basketry. Baskets are easy to make – the only tools required are an awl or needle and a knife – and the process can be stopped and resumed at any time. Basketry was probably carried out largely by women as part of their household activities. Records from the New Kingdom settlement at Deir el-Medina show that the finished products – along with their contents – were bought and sold in the village market.

The baskets buried with Tutankhamun come in three main shapes: oval ones are the most numerous, followed by round and bottle-shaped baskets. Between ten and forty centimetres wide, they are woven from the stalks of palm leaves. The Nile Valley was blessed with an abundance of natural materials for basketry and matting, including reeds, sedges and rushes. Halfa grass was used in bundles and strands to make mats and ropes, but hard-wearing palm leaves were preferred for durable containers. These materials could be woven using a variety of techniques, from weaving, twining and plaiting to looping, sewing and binding. But by far the most common method, and the one used for every basket in Tutankhamun's tomb, was

Fig. 15. Basket of fruit.

coiling. The technique is simple: a twisted bundle of grass, papyrus or palm leaf is laid out in a coil, before being bound with a long strand of material. The result is a strong basket with rigid walls, perfect for fine-grained contents.

Coiled baskets are still sold in the market in Aswan, and similar examples have been found in the workmen's village at Amarna. But the technique goes back much further than Tutankhamun's time. The oldest examples found in Egypt were Neolithic and excavated on the northern shore of the Birket Qarun in the Fayum depression. They are remarkably similar to ones from Tutankhamun's tomb, yet they date from around 5500 BC, over 4,000 years before the boy pharaoh. Along with the manufacture of stone tools, the production of woven mats and baskets seems to have been one of the earliest crafts perfected by humans.

The Neolithic remains in the Fayum were unearthed in the winter of 1924, while Carter was cataloguing and clearing the objects from Tutankhamun's tomb. The archaeologist responsible was Gertrude Caton-Thompson, one of the most remarkable pioneers in the history of Egyptology. In what was still very much a man's world, she pursued her passion in the most testing of circumstances. While Cairo was in uproar following the assassination there of the British governor of Sudan, Caton-Thompson defied official advice and set out for the Fayum – not with a camel train, as recommended, but in a second-hand Ford motor car. A two-month dig produced the first Neolithic pottery ever discovered in Egypt, in addition to flint tools, grinding stones and cereal remains: in short, the earliest evidence of an agricultural lifestyle in Egypt. In a subsequent season, while studying the desert's underlying geology, Caton-Thompson uncovered the grain silos of Egypt's first farmers. A series of shallow pits had been carefully plastered with mud and lined with coiled mats made from grass fastened with palm leaves; most of the winding material had deteriorated, but the mats were in such good condition that Caton-Thompson was able to remove ten of them intact and send several back to England.

The silos were arranged in groups, suggesting a communal effort to bring in the harvest. Each pit could hold eight hundredweight of grain, the yield of two to three acres, so this earliest farming community seems to have tended a holding of between 200 and 300 acres. Although ploughing has long since destroyed the Neolithic settlement in the Fayum, a few silos survive, some of which still contain kernels of barley and emmer and some still lined with matting. The baskets in Tutankhamun's tomb thus take us back to the very origins of Egyptian agriculture. The productivity of the land and the pattern of food production and storage that built and sustained Egyptian civilization were its defining features from the beginning.

⊲⊙⊳

Tutankhamun grew up in a family whose religion had the celebration of food at its very heart. In *The Great Hymn to the Orb*, almost certainly composed by Tutankhamun's father Akhenaten as the credo of his new religion, the sun god Aten is praised as the creator of abundance:

> The earth is bright when you rise on the horizon.
> And shine as Orb of the daytime . . .
> All the herds are at peace in their pastures;
> Trees and plants grow green;
> Birds fly up from their nests,
> Their wings in praise of your spirit.
> All flocks leap on their feet . . .
> You put every man in his place;
> You supply their needs.[11]

In the temples of the Aten at Amarna, the power of creation – and of the creator – were celebrated through an abundance of food. Each of the two main Aten temples in the Central City acted as giant food displays. A large area within the southern part of the Great Aten Temple enclosure was taken up by 920 offering tables, and there may have been a corresponding field in the northern part of the enclosure. The main building, comprising a series of gateways and courts, was likewise filled with nearly 800 offering tables. Contemporary tomb scenes show the tables piled high with food, and this seems to have been the reality of cult practice at Amarna. Archaeologists have excavated an enormous food depot along the south side of the temple, which kept the offering tables supplied. It included an industrial-sized bakery, grain storage and processing facilities, cattle pens and butcheries.

But this obsession with offerings did not mean that the ordinary inhabitants of Amarna were well fed. Most of the people in the South Tombs Cemetery, where Tutankhamun's humbler compatriots were buried, suffered from a growth delay of at least two years and failed to achieve a normal height. Skeletons excavated there show signs of prolonged nutritional deficiency, including scurvy, rickets and the distortion of bone growth in the eye sockets, while banding of the teeth indicates acute childhood illness. Seventy per cent of the people buried there died before the age of thirty-five – so much for Amarna's cult of abundance.

Indeed, despite its famous fertility, the Nile Valley was prone to bouts of famine. A series of high or low inundations could easily lead to widespread food shortages, even with the state's buffer stocks of grain. And in times when the government lacked the resources, authority or the will to keep the granaries stocked, the threat of famine was ever present. Fifth-dynasty reliefs from the pyramid causeway of Unas at Saqqara show the effects of famine in stark detail: emaciated people sit help-less, their bodies reduced to bags of bones. The autobiographical inscription of Ankhtifi, from the First Intermediate Period, boasts of saving his people from 'dying on the sandbank of hell'. A slightly later inscription, dating from the eleventh dynasty, refers to famine, as do the letters of Hekanakht. Clearly, these were times of great vulnerability for much of Egypt's population. At the end of the New Kingdom, when law and order broke down once again, the wife of an apprehended tomb robber claims to have come by a quantity of silver 'in exchange for barley in the year of the hyenas, when there was a famine'.[12]

Part of the problem lay in the pharaonic system of land ownership. Much of the land was owned by the state and temples; individuals could own or rent land, but they had to pay a proportion of the yield as tax to the central authorities, which went towards funding the royal court and its lavish building projects. Even when the harvest was poor, the taxman still insisted on his share, leaving the farmer and his family with insufficient for their basic subsistence. In the New Kingdom, taxes were principally levied in emmer, the basic ingredient for bread. The letters of Hekanakht show that he cultivated more land than was needed to feed his household and had substantial reserves, but he was an exception. The average New Kingdom farm to support eight people was just three acres; a good harvest was essential if the family was not to go hungry. The ordinary inhabitants of Amarna, most of them migrants from the countryside and divorced from the traditional patterns of land tenure, were even more at the state's mercy.

Tomb scenes at Amarna and elsewhere reflect the perspective of the ruling class; in practice, the range of foods available to most people was much more limited. Current research on the ancient Egyptian diet suggests that alongside bread and beer, fruit and vegetables were the dominant feature. Meat was probably a rare commodity for most of the population; in its absence, pulses would have provided the main source of protein. Although rarely depicted in art or mentioned in texts, archaeo-botanical evidence suggests that lentils and chickpeas were staple ingredients, as they are in Egypt today. In the Nile Valley, lentils were grown as a winter crop. Unlike cereals, they can withstand up to twelve weeks of drought, making them particu-larly valuable in years of low Nile floods. They have been found in predynastic tombs, and faience models of chickpeas have been found in a Middle Kingdom burial.

Despite being the food of commoners, pulses were also consumed by ancient Egypt's elite. The tomb of Tutankhamun yielded a variety of legumes and pulses: chickpeas were mixed in with the grain in the model granary, and a wine jar found in the Annexe contained dried lentils. They remind us that in ancient Egypt, a secure supply of nutritious food could never be taken for granted.

⊏◯⊐

> The finding of canned beef 3,350 years old in Tutankhamen's tomb is admitted by cold storage experts to be a record. Mr. Raymond, hon. Secretary of the British Cold Storage Association, says the record, so far as cold storage is concerned in this country, stands at eighteen years.[13]

So ran a story in the *Daily Mail* on 20 January 1923, two months after the discovery of Tutankhamun's tomb, as the king's grave goods were being documented and catalogued. Among the most intriguing – and among the first to be glimpsed by Carter as he peered into the Antechamber – were a series of forty-

Fig. 16. Boxes of preserved meat.

eight two-piece boxes, covered with gesso and painted white. Most of them were roughly egg-shaped, giving little clue as to their contents. Upon opening, they were found to contain joints of meat – mostly from oxen, but also a goose. The sycamore boxes had been stacked underneath one of the ritual couches, and each of them had been waterproofed and sealed on the inside with hot resin. The joints of meat showed a remarkable degree of preservation, even though they were not, strictly speaking, 'canned' and nor had they been kept in 'cold storage'. Such 'victual mummies' have been recovered from other ancient Egyptian tombs, including that of Tutankhamun's paternal great-grandparents, Yuya and Tjuyu. Preserved joints constitute our most valuable source of evidence for meat processing in pharaonic times.

The date at which cattle were first introduced into the Nile Valley is disputed, but it is likely to have been very early, perhaps as early as the seventh millennium BC. Archaeological evidence from sites such as Nabta Playa shows that cattle had already been domesticated by the fifth millennium BC. Together with sheep and goats, they constituted the main types of livestock in the Nile Valley, depicted in countless tomb scenes throughout pharaonic history.

The ancient Egyptians showed a continuing interest in domestication and attempted to rear all sorts of exotic wild animals for the dinner tables of the royal court. A knife handle crafted for a high-status client in the years immediately before the first dynasty shows dogs guarding lines of oryx and Barbary sheep, suggesting that these animals may already have been domesticated. More explicit is a wall decoration in a fourth-dynasty tomb at Meidum that shows an oryx being slaughtered for food. An Old Kingdom tomb at Saqqara shows gazelle, ibex, addax, hartebeest and oryx collared, tethered and feeding from troughs, while another has a scene of hyenas being force-fed to fatten them for the table. Faunal remains from tombs and settlements confirm that the cuisine of the royal court during the Pyramid Age was unusual and eclectic.

However, among this plethora of potential food animals, only cattle had a status that merited inclusion in religious ritual. The connection between cattle and cult – seen already at Nabta Playa – remained strong throughout Egyptian history. The Nile Valley's earliest excavated temple at Hierakonpolis yielded an abundance of animal bones; examination showed that they had most likely been slaughtered on site. However, the cattle seem to have been kept long after they were fully mature, suggesting some reverence or symbolism besides their use as food. And on the carved stone macehead of Narmer, first king of the first dynasty, two cattle in an enclosure are shown in association with a religious ceremony.

Not only were cattle thought to possess a special sacred significance, but their slaughter was an important ritual. An ox would be wrestled to the ground with the aid of a lasso, then laid on its back and held by assistants. The butcher would cut the animal's throat while a priest might examine its blood and entrails for purity. Blood was drained from the carcass by pumping the foreleg, to force blood to flow from the severed vessels of the neck. This may explain why the foreleg assumed a special prominence in religious offerings – it played an essential role in bleeding the animal and preventing the meat from being spoiled.

Next to the Great Aten Temple at Amarna, pens with stone floors and brick mangers served as sheds for the cattle that were destined for the offering tables. The high priest of the Aten also bore the title 'Superintendent of the Cattle of the Aten in Akhetaten' and the dumps next to his house were full of cattle bones. In tomb reliefs from Amarna, cattle are garlanded with flowers as they are led to the slaughterhouse within the Great Aten Temple. Once they had been killed and butchered, choice cuts of meat – including the foreleg – were laid out on the offering tables. Other pieces were supplied fresh to the palace or cured and stored in large pottery jars. The ink labels on surviving jars identify the contents. One example states: 'Preserved meat: intestines, for the daily offerings, provided by the butcher Wepet.'[14] Experiments in modern times have shown that if they are hung in the shade, joints of meat can remain safe to eat for up to eight hours in the heat of an Egyptian summer. Tomb paintings show that the ancient Egyptians also air-dried meat, pounding pieces thin before hanging them up on lines.

Tombs and temples thus provide abundant evidence for the preparation and consumption of meat in ancient Egypt, from poultry and mutton to oryx and hyena, with beef at the top of the culinary pyramid. But there was another commonly eaten meat in pharaonic Egypt, the existence of which has been revealed by the excavation of the workmen's village at Amarna: pork. In ancient Egyptian religion, pigs were taboo. There are sound reasons for this: pork does not keep and is susceptible to infection in hot climates. Nonetheless, the inhabitants of the workmen's village kept pigs for food – and lots of them. There were specially built pig pens, and dedicated areas for butchering, salting and packing the meat. Pigs were fed on grain, with animals killed in their first or second year. Pork production was a significant and well-organized community activity. While cattle were reared by the thousand to satisfy Akhenaten's family and his god, his humbler citizens had to make do with lowlier flesh.

⊲◉⊳

Nothing marks an occasion – commemorative or celebratory, secular or sacred – like a feast. Preparing a special meal is one of the most ancient of human rituals. As we have seen, the ancient Egyptians had a wide variety of foods at their disposal – grains and pulses, breads and cakes, fruits and vegetables, seeds and nuts, fish and fowl, and, for some, meat. While we might not be able to write an ancient Egyptian recipe book, the raw ingredients are well known, and we may suppose that the Egyptians combined these ingredients in adventurous and flavoursome combinations to produce not just cooking, but cuisine.

To judge from the painted scenes in high-status tombs, banqueting was a favourite pastime of the eighteenth-dynasty elite. As a contemporary text urged its affluent readers, 'Give food to the despised, provisions to the uninvited guest.'[15] The banquet scene is one of the standard tableaux in the Tombs of the Nobles at Thebes. A classic example is found in the eighteenth-dynasty tomb of Nakht, where guests are shown smelling lotus blooms and being entertained by a blind harpist.

Another fine banqueting scene is in the nearby tomb of Ramose, which shows the tomb owner and his wife seated side by side alongside other couples in front of tables piled high with food.

Yet there is more to these scenes than meets the eye. The guests shown at such banquets often include dead relatives and friends. The scenes are not merely intended to serve as an evocation of happy times, a guarantee of abundance in the afterlife or the perpetual provisioning of the funerary cult, but as a permanent celebration of the funeral meal and its annual commemoration. The Beautiful Festival of the Valley was one of the principal holidays of New Kingdom Egypt, an occasion when families would gather for a celebratory meal at the tombs of their deceased relatives, who might participate vicariously. This annual commemoration may have also recalled the banquet that the tomb owner and his family took in the tomb's court-yard to mark its completion.

As befits the sacral nature of the Theban banqueting scenes, they are full of complex symbolism. Erotic imagery is particu-larly prominent – scantily clad waitresses proffer ducks (linked to procreation) and lotus flowers (associated with rebirth) – to ensure the resurrection of the tomb owner. Guests are shown dressed in their finest clothes, often with cones of scented wax or unguent on their heads – the smell of perfume was believed to imply and encourage the immanence of the gods. The frequent depiction of lotus flowers may have had connotations not just of rebirth, but of religious ecstasy: some waterlilies contain narcotic alkaloids, and these may have been used by guests to achieve an altered state of consciousness. Mandrake plants, which feature in some banquet scenes, may have played a similar role, as did copious amounts of alcohol: 'the shore of drunkenness' was a metaphor for the veil between earthly and divine realms.

Besides food and drink, the final essential ingredients in any good banquet were music and dancing. Rhythmic singing, accompanied by percussion instruments, may have helped guests enter a trance-like state, and the human voice was believed to revivify the souls of the dead while bringing good health to the gods. Music was closely associated with the mother goddess Hathor, protectress of the vulnerable and presiding deity of the hills of western Thebes, where the dead were interred. Female musicians are usually depicted shaking the sistrum (rattle), which was especially sacred to her. Other musical instruments included the flute, lute, pipes, cymbals and tambourine. The double flute, theorbo and seven-stringed harp appear for the first time in the eighteenth dynasty, and no Egyptian banquet was complete without a harp.

Banquets and banqueting scenes were not just popular at Thebes. The tomb of Paatenemheb at Saqqara, dating to the reign of Akhenaten, has a fine tableau of feasting, and the tomb of Huya at Amarna shows the royal family enjoying a celebratory meal, complete with courtiers, servants and musicians. The young Tutankhamun must surely have participated in similar occasions.

Among the array of food interred with Tutankhamun, one particular dish symbolized the luxury of feasting: a large pottery bowl containing dates. Across North Africa and the Middle East today, dates are presented to guests and as gifts of friendship. In ancient Egypt, too, they seem to have been highly prized. Their sweetness was savoured, either on its own or as a flavouring for cakes and even beer. Wine was made by the pressing and fermentation of dates as early as the second dynasty, while date stones have been found on archaeological sites dating from the eleventh dynasty onwards.

Although the date palm is among the oldest cultivated fruit trees and thrives in the hot, dry Egyptian climate, dates seem to have been widely cultivated only from the New Kingdom onwards. Its relatively late introduction may have been due to its need for a sustained water supply and artificial pollination to produce a reliable crop. But once it had been established as a mainstay of ancient Egyptian horticulture, it became a popular and productive tree; all parts were used, and the fruit was highly prized for its sweetness and longevity. Certainly, the bowlful and six small baskets of dates that were found in Tutankhamun's tomb were almost perfectly preserved. Together with his thirty-six baskets of Christ's thorn fruits, thirteen baskets of dom palm fruits, four of grewias and three of perseas, as well as assorted other fruits and seeds, the boy king had all the ingredients for a memorable banquet.

⋖○⋗

The oldest royal tomb in Egypt is dug into the sandy desert floor near the site of Abydos. Tomb U-j, as it is known, was marked out as royal not just by its architecture (it was designed to resemble a miniature palace) but by its contents. One of the chambers housed the king's ivory sceptre. Another contained a large number of ivory and bone labels, small dockets that constitute the earliest hieroglyphic writing found in the Nile Valley. But perhaps the most impressive demonstration of the status of the tomb owner was found in another chamber: forty-seven storage jars of Palestinian wine. The predynastic king of Abydos was interred with a cellar of the finest imported vintages. His fondness for wine set a trend that would characterize elite culture in the Nile Valley for the next 3,000 years. Seventeen centuries later, Tutankhamun was buried with twenty-six wine jars.

The contents of the storage jars found at Abydos were identified by the grape pips that remained inside. Eleven of them also contained strings of sliced figs that were perhaps added as a flavouring or sweetener, while others seem to have had resin added to the wine – retsina is clearly an ancient tradition in the eastern Mediterranean. Like other cultural practices that were imported from the Near East, wine-making was readily adopted by the Egyptians. The earliest evidence for viticulture is the grape pips recovered from predynastic settlements in the delta. The appearance of a hieroglyph depicting a wine press[16] and the first use of the word for wine, *irep*, both in royal contexts, indicate the presence of wine-making in the first two dynasties. Royal and elite tombs from this period were generally furnished with tall cylindrical storage jars, which archaeologists have identified as wine jars. If this is correct, it suggests that wine was important in a funerary context.

Because of its intoxicating properties, wine was considered to have divine qualities. The Pyramid Texts list five different kinds of wine that were offered in remembrance of the dead, and the drink was used extensively in temple rituals. According to twentieth-dynasty texts, Ramesses III presented 103,550 jars of wine to the temples at Heliopolis, and a further 25,978 jars to the Memphite temples. This gives an indication of the levels of domestic wine production in the New Kingdom.

Whereas the brewing of beer took place at a household level, there is little evidence for the private ownership of vineyards in ancient Egypt. Rather, they were located on royal estates in the delta and oases in the Western Desert, areas beyond the reach of the Nile flood where the soil was better drained and less fertile. Traces of an ancient vineyard have been uncovered at Tell el-Daba in the north-eastern Nile Delta.

The stages of wine production are depicted in the decoration of funerary chapels at Thebes. The drink seems to have become more popular in the New Kingdom, reaching a wider section of the population than before. The tomb workers of Deir el-Medina were sometimes given bonuses in the form of wine, while wine jar labels were recovered from the workmen's village at Amarna. The fashion for wine in the eighteenth dynasty is reflected in the decoration of nobles' tombs from the time: the ceilings in the tombs of Amenemhat and Sennefer are decorated with bunches of grapes and vine leaves, while the tomb of Kenamun depicts a pool surrounded by vines. A scene in an Amarna tomb shows Akhenaten and his mother, Queen Tiye, drinking wine together.

Grapes were harvested in the summer, after the grain harvest. The tomb of Nakht shows them being picked and trodden to release the juice. Treading was sometimes accompanied by music or singing to a rhythmic beat. An alternative way of extracting the juice was with a sack press, with a man braced between its two upright poles. Once the grapes had been pressed, the juice was poured into jars to ferment. When it was ready, the wine would be stoppered and sealed. Sometimes, as in four of the wine jars from Tutankhamun's tomb, a small hole was left in the stopper to allow gases to escape during secondary fermentation.

New Kingdom wine labels tend to record the date of the vintage, the name of the wine maker and the estate, the location of the vineyard and sometimes the quality of the wine ('good', 'double good' or 'triple good'). Labels recovered from Amarna name twenty-six different estates, mostly along the 'Western River' – probably the Canopic branch of the Nile. This was also the predominant source of the wine in Tutankhamun's tomb. Most of his labels are dated to the fourth, fifth and ninth years of his reign, although a jar from the thirty-first year of his grandfather's reign was also included. This was most likely for symbolic or sentimental reasons, since the porosity of jars meant that wine would not have kept for more than five years.

The artistic evidence suggests that red wine was the only colour produced in ancient Egypt, though there were a number of different varieties and styles. Labels from a palace of

Amenhotep III refer to 'blended wines', and a tomb scene at Thebes shows different wines being mixed together. Four of Tutankhamun's wine jars are labelled as 'sweet wine', which suggests that other wines were dry, while five jars were identified as containing *shedeh*, an unknown term that may designate a variety of wine that was regarded as more exclusive. Surrounded for all eternity by his cellar of the finest vintages, Tutankhamun was maintaining one of ancient Egypt's oldest royal traditions.

⊲◦⊳

In addition to furnishing the ancient Egyptians with a veritable larder of produce, the Nile Valley's bounty moulded their culture in other, more subtle ways. Perhaps the most characteristic feature of ancient Egypt, besides its monumental architecture, is hieroglyphic writing. Hieroglyphs define the lifespan of pharaonic civilization, appearing at its inception and disappearing with the arrival of Christianity in the late fourth century AD. Though the idea of writing may have been borrowed from Mesopotamia, the system developed by the Egyptians was all their own. It fitted their language perfectly and drew its inspiration from their world.

A student of hieroglyphics must master some 700 signs to achieve a reasonable proficiency in reading and writing. The twentieth-century British Egyptologist Alan Gardiner divided them into thematic sections, including parts of the human body (sixty-three signs) or loaves and cakes (eight signs). Some categories are small in number: there are just eleven signs to represent ships and parts of ships. Other groupings are more extensive, reflecting aspects of life that caught the Egyptians' attention: rope, baskets and bags; agriculture, crafts and professions.

The largest number of signs by far, 407 out of the list of 743, depict environmental features, plants and animals. Hieroglyphs thus reflect a society that saw itself as part of nature. It is curious that only six types of fish were adopted as hieroglyphic signs, but they are glimpsed through the distorting lens of water and are not so readily identifiable as other animals. Mammalian life was far more diverse, and this is reflected in the thirty-four signs that depict warm-blooded animals, from domesticates (cow, sheep, pig, dog and cat) to wild creatures (jackal, lion, panther, hippopotamus, elephant, giraffe, baboon, hare and several species of antelope). These animal hieroglyphs represent the fauna of the Nile Valley during the early phases of pharaonic civilization, when the writing system was developed and codified: by the New Kingdom, elephants and giraffes had long since disappeared from Egypt, and lions were increasingly rare.

As any traveller on the Nile will know, the river and its reedy shores support a dazzling variety of avian life. This aspect of the natural world is fully reflected in the Egyptians' writing system, with sixty-two signs representing birds or parts of birds. There are birds of prey – the Egyptian vulture is one of the most common signs, alongside the long-legged buzzard, falcon and vulture, the last being used to write the word for 'mother'. The owl and quail chick were both common phonetic signs, while a flying pintail duck wrote the word 'the'.

Other birds symbolized more complex concepts. The flamingo denoted 'red' and the sparrow 'small'. For unknown reasons, the lapwing represented the common people and the crested ibis the spirit of a deceased person. In a play on words, the heron (*benu*) was associated with the shining of the sun (*uben*) and became a solar symbol.

Alongside wild birds, domesticated fowl were also adopted as hieroglyphic signs. The white-fronted goose became a symbol of the earth god Geb and a walking pintail duck wrote the word 'son', a vital concept in a patrilineal society. Perhaps strangest of all, a trussed duck was used to denote the word 'fear'.

Geese and ducks were the main poultry birds in ancient Egypt, even after the introduction of the domestic fowl from western Asia in the early eighteenth dynasty. Poultry is particularly prone to bacterial infestation after death, so birds had either to be eaten immediately or preserved by drying, salting, smoking or curing. Geese and ducks could also be preserved in their own fat; scenes from a Theban tomb show birds being strangled, plucked, eviscerated and put into narrow-necked amphorae, possibly containing salt; one such amphora containing birds preserved in brine was found in another tomb. Another way of preparing poultry was to spatchcock and roast it: several examples have been found in a nineteenth-dynasty tomb at Deir el-Medina. Although dried poultry is usually tough and unpleasant, a scene in a New Kingdom tomb shows strips of duck being hung up to dry. Ducks, geese and pigeons were included among the grave goods in the tomb of Amenhotep II's wife, and were found 'thinly wrapped in linen that had been saturated with an oily or resinous substance, perhaps even honey'.[17]

Tutankhamun had a selection of poultry buried with him: there were duck breasts and a goose, the latter stored in a two-piece box alongside the king's other joints of meat. Whether a trussed goose was intended to bring the pharaoh good luck in the afterlife by confining the hieroglyph for 'fear' or was simply included as a handy packaged meal, it illustrates that the world of the ancient Egyptians was one of quacking, cackling and squawking.

◄○►

While the ancient Egyptians were adept at exploiting the resources of the Nile Valley, some aspects of their natural world remained unfathomable and were hence viewed with awe and reverence. The bee was a source of fascination and admiration for its extraordinary organization, hard work and its production of honey, a miracle substance. Among all hunter-gatherer societies, honey is highly prized, both for its natural sweetness and its health-giving properties. Across Africa, traditional societies have passed the skills required to locate wild honey from generation to generation, and there are indications that this was also true in ancient Egypt.

In the centuries preceding the foundation of the state, craftsmen created a remarkable series of prestige objects, designed to symbolize and celebrate the authority of the nascent elite. Among the most notable are a series of intricate artefacts carved from ivory. A knife handle from Abu Zaidan in Upper Egypt is perhaps the finest surviving example. Both sides are decorated with tiny animals: Barbary sheep, oryx, lions, elephants. There are also rows of honey badgers, also known as ratels, a member of the weasel family that is skilled at finding bees' nests.

On the Abu Zaidan knife handle and on other contemporary objects, ratels are depicted alongside a five-pointed rosette, a symbol known to have been associated with the king at the dawn of Egyptian history. One explanation for this juxtaposition of motifs is that, in prehistoric Egyptian tradition, the ruler derived his authority from an ability to harness the power of the natural world. The connection between honey, bees and royalty seems to date from the origins of Egyptian civilization.

In the first dynasty, this association was cemented by the adoption of one of the strangest elements in the royal titulary: the phrase *nesut-bity*, which literally means 'he of the sedge and bee'. In later periods, this title introduced the king's throne name, the principal name by which he was known. In the Ptolemaic Period, *nesut-bity* was translated as 'King of Upper and Lower Egypt', but in origin it probably signified a different duality: the role of the king as both god incarnate (*nesut*) and head of state (*bity*). The symbolism of the bee seems to have been attached to the secular authority of the monarch. Scholars have speculated endlessly about why the bee was chosen for the pre-eminent pharaonic title. In the Pyramid Texts, the sky goddess Nut is said to appear as a bee; but bees span two worlds, moving between land and air – just as the sedge has its roots in the water and its flowers in the air. Perhaps this suggested that both species bridged the physical and spiritual worlds.[18] Perhaps the dense thickets of sedge along the riverbank and the innumerable bees in a swarm epitomized the marvels of nature in all its limitlessness.

In one Egyptian myth, the tears of Ra are said to have become bees. Links have also been made with the goddess Neith, whose cult centre at Sais in the Nile Delta was known as 'the House of the Bee'. It is not difficult to see how the queen bee could have been worshipped as an early mother goddess, nor how a hive could have provided a compelling metaphor for the government of a country.

Whatever the mystic connotations of the bee, its principal product was equally revered. The antibiotic and soothing properties of honey were appreciated from an early period, and it is listed as an ingredient in some 500 prescriptions and remedies preserved on ancient Egyptian papyri. In a world before soap, a mixture of powdered calcite, red natron, salt and honey could be used as a body scrub. Honey was employed as a linctus to relieve coughing; as a balm on burns and ulcers; and as an anti-bacterial and anti-fungal agent to treat open wounds. It was also used in remedies for intestinal worms, skin diseases, stomach complaints, urinary disorders, gynaecological conditions and even for a prolapsed anus (salt, oil and honey applied externally for four days). In a sacred context, it was used as an offering to the gods; Ramesses III donated huge quantities to the cult of the inundation god, Hapy, while the cult of Amun maintained its own beekeepers.

The ancient Egyptian language distinguished between 'honey-hunters', who collected the substance from the wild, and 'beekeepers', who practised apiculture. In fact, the earliest evidence for professional beekeeping comes from Egypt. Domesticated bees were known, rather fetchingly, as 'honey flies'. While they thrive in a warm climate, they also need water; the Nile Delta would have been particularly favourable for apiculture. A relief in the sun temple of a fifth-dynasty king – a building designed to celebrate the wonders of the natural world – shows a series of beehives, and the harvesting, filtering and packing of honey. An 'overseer of beekeepers of the entire land' is identified in a Middle Kingdom text, while a scene in the tomb of Rekhmira shows a man carefully removing honeycomb from a series of horizontal hives while his assistant smokes the bees using a censer. Alongside honey, the Egyptians also prized beeswax, using it to make small models, in medical treatments and as a varnish for the paintings in New Kingdom tombs.

Tutankhamun's burial goods included two jars of honey, stored in the Annexe. One, a small amphora, has an inscription that reads 'honey of excellent quality'. A medicament, a foodstuff and a source of energy with connotations of ancient, mystic kingship: there could have been no better provision for a pharaoh's tomb.

FIVE

Monarchy

Fig. 17. *Shabti* of Tutankhamun wearing the blue crown.

'There's such divinity doth hedge a king':[1] nowhere and at no time in human history has this been as true as in pharaonic Egypt. The concept of divine kingship, forged at the dawn of Egyptian history, was the ideological glue that held Egypt together. The king stood at the apex of the societal pyramid, a link between his subjects and the gods. In theory, all land belonged to him; all art and architecture, explicitly or implicitly, served to glorify him and his position. It is impossible to understand pharaonic civilization without understanding the institution at its heart. As befitted a royal sepulchre, the tomb of Tutankhamun was filled with objects that illustrate the various facets of ancient Egyptian monarchy. While the king's own divinity was deliberately vague – sometimes he was god incarnate, at other times the gods' representative on earth – his role in preserving order and defending Egypt from its enemies was at the core of royal ideology.

The king's primary duty was to propitiate the gods, so that they might continue to favour Egypt and its people. To this end, he was the high priest of every cult, and he regularly travelled throughout his realm to visit important temples and participate in key festivals. Ritual and symbolism elevated him above the everyday and distinguished him from his mortal subjects, yet his was also a political office: the pharaoh was head of state and government, an absolute monarch who presided over a complex and bureaucratic administration. Merging these two distinct roles, sacred and secular, was the particular genius of Egyptian civilization.

⊲○⊳

The origins of ancient Egyptian kingship are lost in the mists of time. Among the Egyptians' prehistoric ancestors, there must have been individuals whose knowledge of the natural world gave them some degree of status or authority among their tribal group. Once people started to settle permanently in the Nile Valley, the types of knowledge and skill required for effective leadership may have changed, but they would still have involved an innate understanding of the environment. A few small statues of bearded, hooded figures have been recovered from graves of the early fourth millennium BC, suggesting that there were individuals in these early settled communities who were marked out as special – though a shamanistic or priestly role is as likely as anything overtly political.

As Egyptian society became more stratified, more explicit indications of kingly status began to appear. One of the clearest examples is the decoration of the so-called 'Painted Tomb' at Hierakonpolis. This otherwise undistinguished brick-lined chamber, dug into the desert close to one of the Nile Valley's first walled towns, remains the earliest known example of a decorated tomb, that quintessential pharaonic status symbol. The scenes that were crudely painted on the plaster lining of one of the internal walls present a ragbag of disjointed motifs, but their unifying feature is that all these elements would later be incorporated into the standard iconography of kingship. A flotilla of boats seems to denote a royal tour or religious procession. Elsewhere, the ruler is depicted smiting a bound captive, an image of power and authority that would endure until the very end of pharaonic civilization. And there is the scene which historians term 'the Master of the Beasts': the ruler stands between a pair of lions and holds them at bay. While this last motif was probably influenced by Mesopotamian art, its adoption into early Egyptian art shows that it resonated with the Egyptian psyche. The natural environment of the Nile Valley and its fringing deserts was precarious and hostile, and the awesome power of nature was embodied by the apex predator, the wild lion. The symbolic association of the ruler with big cats – whether subduing them or absorbing their strength and ferocity – would remain a feature of royal iconography for the whole of pharaonic history.

Alongside the Master of the Beasts, other elements were borrowed from Sumerian culture to help convey the complex and developing concept of Egyptian kingship. There was the rosette, which seems to have denoted the ruler, and made its final appearance on objects from the reign of King Narmer at the beginning of the first dynasty. There was the comb-winged griffin, a mythical beast that perhaps symbolized the unpredictability of the natural world, which features on a few elite objects from the centuries before unification. And there was another type of mythical creature, a long-necked quadruped (the 'serpopard'), which was depicted in pairs, their necks intertwined, and which may have symbolized the opposing forces of nature – day and night, life and death, valley and desert – that it was the ruler's duty to keep in balance. Serpopards are also depicted on the Narmer Palette, after which the royal iconographers seem consciously to have discarded Mesopotamian motifs in favour of indigenous elements. The result was a codified system of symbols that expressed Egyptian monarchy in all its mystery and majesty, but also had deep roots that extended back into prehistory.

While the institution of pharaonic kingship is uniquely Egyptian, a closer look reveals African roots. Perhaps the most striking illustration of this is the important role played not by the mythical serpopard but by the very real leopard. Leopards, like lions, were closely associated with the king. It was said of the eighteenth-dynasty warrior pharaoh Thutmose I:

> when he travelled upstream to Upper Nubia to crush rebellion throughout the hill countries and to drive away those who had infiltrated the desert region . . . His Majesty raged like a leopard.[2]

The context here is no accident, for leopards were found only in sub-Saharan Africa and not in the Egyptian Nile Valley.

In order to take on the power of the leopard, the pharaoh would garb himself in a cloak made from its skin. But obtaining such pelts required access to sub-Saharan trade networks. The ritual importance of leopard skins in ancient Egyptian religion may have been one reason why the pharaonic state took such pains to conquer and subdue Nubia, the gateway to tropical Africa. A thousand years before Thutmose I, the autobiographical inscription of the desert scout Harkhuf placed particular emphasis on the exotic products he brought back from journeys to Upper Nubia:

> I came back with 300 donkeys laden with incense, ebony, precious oil, grain, leopard skins, elephant tusks, throw sticks: all good produce.[3]

The wearing of animal attributes by priests, shamans and people of authority may be as ancient as humanity itself. In Egyptian art, there are early, predynastic examples of such figures in ritual settings: a man wearing an ostrich head, leading an ostrich hunt; a man with a dog mask and tail, playing a flute before a jumble of wild animals; hunters wearing dogs' tails in their waistbands as they set out to hunt game. At the time when the Nile Valley was in the process of being consolidated into a single nation state, the leopard-skin cloak appears in art as a signifier of high office. The earliest example is on a commemorative royal object, the Battlefield Palette; a figure clad in a long, spotted robe leads a bound prisoner to his fate, while a huge lion gores a defeated enemy.

In later periods, the leopard-skin cloak was associated with a specific religious office: that of the '*sem* priest'. Several examples of their feline pelts were found in Tutankhamun's tomb. While in theory the power of the *sem* priest resided with the pharaoh, in practice the office seems to have been held by his heir apparent. The *sem* priest officiated at important festivals and had a major role at funerals, where he would carry out the opening of the mouth ritual to enable the dead to be reborn to eternal life. Many of the eighteenth-dynasty Tombs of the Nobles at Thebes depict a *sem* priest acting in this capacity, while the tomb of Rekhmira shows Nubian tribute bearers bringing leopard skins to be turned into priestly robes. On the rear wall of Tutankhamun's burial chamber, the king's successor, Ay, had himself depicted wearing the leopard skin of a *sem* priest, carrying out the opening of the mouth for his deceased predecessor. In this way, he emphasized his legitimacy as the next pharaoh, even though he had been a mere courtier during Tutankhamun's reign. As Ay well knew, even the most ancient item of a priest-king's regalia could have powerful contemporary resonance.

⊰○⊱

As the early kings of Egypt cemented their political and economic authority over a newly unified country, new elements were added to the ideology of monarchy. One of the most confusing features of ancient Egyptian religion, to the modern way of thinking, is that old ideas were never discarded to make way for new ones: novel concepts were merely added, resulting in a gloriously complex, often contradictory accretion of myth and belief. This did not seem to matter to the ancient Egyptians, to whom the myriad layers of symbol and meaning simply reinforced the unfathomability of divine creation.

While the prehistoric attributes of the ruler such as the leopard-skin cloak endured, new, more theologically sophisticated elements started to be introduced. Foremost among these were the overt connections between the sovereign and the cosmos. The idea that the king was the embodiment of divine power on earth can be traced back to the predynastic period, but the association of that divine power with the celestial realm seems to have accompanied the process of state formation.

The site of Hierakonpolis was one of the early crucibles of royal authority. The most important local deity was a sky god, worshipped in the form of a falcon, called Horus (literally 'on high'). The bird of prey, which can still be seen soaring high above the Nile Valley, was the perfect metaphor for the king looking down on his people. Horus was adopted by the rulers of Hierakonpolis as their personal god, and this explicit association of the king with the transcendent powers of heaven marks the rise of the pharaonic state. The shrine of Horus at Hierakonpolis became an early focus for the royal cult, where successive kings dedicated votive objects and presented gifts to their divine protector. One of the most celebrated is a gold statue of the falcon god, gifted to the temple by Pepi I in the sixth dynasty.

As Egyptian theology was further elaborated, Horus graduated from being a local god of Hierakonpolis to playing a pivotal role in the story of creation. According to the most prominent creation myth, 'the time of the gods' ended with Horus, so the falcon god represented the link between his divine forebears and human successors. The king, embodying both human and divine strands, came to be regarded as Horus's incarnation on earth. This found frequent expression in Egyptian art, most notably in the seated statue of Khafra from his pyramid temple at Giza, which shows the falcon perched on the back of the royal throne, guarding the monarch with his outspread wings.

As part of the reinvention of kingship in the eighteenth dynasty, the mythical bond between king and god was taken to its logical extreme, and the person of the king was merged with that of Horus in official iconography. A statue, now in the Louvre, shows an unidentified pharaoh in falcon form, while a remarkable statue of a standing Amenhotep III from Karnak depicts the king mid-transformation, the feathers of the celestial falcon appearing on his back. Tutankhamun's official garments included a feathered dress, in which he could appear on ritual occasions to demonstrate his oneness with Horus. This unity was also expressed by one of the most magnificent pieces of jewellery from the king's tomb, a lavish pectoral in the form of the Horus falcon with outspread wings, holding the hieroglyphic symbols for 'life' and 'eternity' in its talons. The object, which the king would have worn around his neck, is a masterpiece of the jeweller's art. Made in gold cloisonné, it is inlaid with lapis lazuli, pale blue glass, obsidian (for the falcon's eye), turquoise and carnelian. Atop the falcon's head, which is shown in profile, is a solar disc formed from a single carnelian cabochon, mounted in gold.

Not originally part of Horus's iconography, the solar disc represents a merging of the sun god Ra and the sky god Horus to form a composite deity, Ra-Horakhty ('Ra-Horus of the two horizons'). The creative force and dazzling light of the sun were a powerful metaphor for royal authority that provided the king's role with the ultimate in divine justification. As a text of Tutankhamun put it:

> The son of Ra, Tutankhamun ruler of Thebes, given life
> like Ra forever and ever . . . appeared upon the throne
> of Horus of the living like his father Ra every day . . .
> His Majesty was in his palace . . . like Ra inside heaven.[4]

In some accounts, the falcon's eyes were the sun and moon,
but it was the fierce Egyptian sun that came to play the dominant role in religious myth. From the fourth dynasty onwards,
in addition to being regarded as the living incarnation of Horus,
the king was lauded as son of the sun. In this capacity, he had
a responsibility to defend created order. Conveniently, the king's
enemies could be presented not just as traitors but as nihilists
threatening the whole of creation. The association of the ruler
with the sun and the sky provided Egypt's absolute monarchy
with unchallengeable ideological underpinnings.

As the theology surrounding the king developed, aspects of
royal burial took on new meaning. From the beginning of
dynastic history, kings had been buried with boats to enable
them to travel to the afterlife. The boats buried next to the
Great Pyramid were explicitly identified with the barques of
Ra, and were intended to enable the king to travel across the
heavens and through the underworld in the company of the
sun god. But being part of the great rhythm of the universe
was not without its dangers.

⊲◦▷

The daily voyage of the sun god across the vault of heaven and
through the underworld was the eternal cycle that kept creation
alive. It was regarded as emblematic of the struggle between
good and evil. The king's role, as son of Ra and representative
of the gods, was to drive away the forces of chaos. When
the sun entered the underworld each evening and rose again
each morning, the barque of Ra was vulnerable to attack. The

evil-doer was imagined as a monstrous serpent, Apep, which lurked in the shadows and tried to ensnare the solar boat in his giant coils at sunset and sunrise. Ra always prevailed, but the blood of the wounded snake dyed the sky red at dusk and dawn. Royal tombs in the Valley of the Kings often include a depiction of the voyage of Ra and the defeat of Apep in their decorative scheme.

Being attacked by a giant snake twice a day was bad enough, but so terrible was the prospect of the ensuing chaos should Apep ever prevail, that the Egyptians imagined further dangers in the sun god's path. Ra's enemies were not only lurking in the shadows: one of their number was aboard his ship.

The ancient Egyptians, much like their modern descendants, lived in extended family units, with grandparents, parents, children and assorted relatives sharing the same household. The letters of Hekanakht reveal the fractious nature of Egyptian families. His children from his first marriage took a disliking to his second wife, sparking a protracted quarrel that seems to have drawn in other members of the household. The squabbles recorded in his correspondence are worthy of a novel – indeed, Agatha Christie used them as the basis of her murder mystery *Death Comes as the End*. Ancient Egyptian teachings are full of advice about how to deal with troublesome neighbours and family members.

In common with all societies, ancient Egyptians projected their experiences onto their concept of the divine. Their gods formed family units and had fallings-out, just like humans. Perhaps the most spectacular of such godly quarrels was a bitter rivalry that spanned two generations. The Pyramid Texts contain snippets of the myth, but the fullest account is found on a New Kingdom papyrus in a lengthy text entitled *The Contendings of Horus and Seth*. The story begins during the reign of Horus's father, Osiris. Osiris's brother, Seth, was envious of the throne and determined to reign in his place. He murdered Osiris, cut his body into pieces and hid them the length and breadth of Egypt. Osiris's grieving widow, Isis, devoted her life to finding and gathering up the pieces, after which she wrapped them in bandages, thus creating the first mummy. In time, she conceived a son, Horus, but wary of Seth's evil designs, she brought him up secretly, hidden among the reed banks of the Nile Delta. (The later story of Moses may have been influenced by the tale.) When Horus came of age, he resolved to cement his succession to the throne and avenge his father's murder. *The Contendings* relates the trials and tribulations as nephew and uncle battled it out for the kingship. Eventually, Horus prevailed and was declared king on earth. Osiris became king of the underworld, while Seth skulked off to lick his wounds.

But that was not the end of the story. For Seth, regarded by the Egyptians as a storm god and sower of confusion, tried to interfere in the running of the universe by helping the serpent Apep in his twice-daily assault on the barque of the sun god. From his position aboard the solar boat, Seth had the perfect opportunity to prosecute his treacherous designs. The king, as descendant and embodiment of Horus, had an especially important role to play in defending created order and patrilineal inheritance; Seth and his gang represented the threat to hereditary monarchy and the illegitimate assumption of rule. So the king would jab fiercely with a harpoon from the solar boat to drive away Apep and Seth. For Horus to triumph, Seth must be defeated.

This convoluted and colourful myth finds expression in both tomb scenes and three-dimensional representations. Tutankhamun's tomb may lack paintings of the sun god's journey, but among the gilded wooden statuettes from the tomb is one that shows the young king in the act of harpooning. Some seventy-five centimetres tall, the figure depicts Tutankhamun

Fig. 18. Statuette of the king harpooning.

wearing kilt, crown and sandals and standing on a papyrus skiff, holding a length of rope in his left hand and wielding a harpoon in his right. The intended prey is not shown, but nobody who saw the statuette would have been in any doubt: the quarry was the hippopotamus, which by Tutankhamun's time was closely associated with Seth.

<><

A pharaoh's potential enemies were not just in the cosmic battle to defend creation, but in the very real exercise of political power. Although it was hedged about with divinity, the institution of kingship was no doubt seen by some for what it was: a position of power, privilege and fabulous wealth that could be seized by force in the right circumstances. Threats to the king's position came both from within the royal family – there is tantalizing evidence of palace coups at almost every period of Egyptian history – and from without. Too harsh a regime or too punitive a tax might provoke the pharaoh's own citizens to desert their fields and become outlaws; even Thutmose I, the famous warrior pharaoh of the early eighteenth dynasty, faced such an internal revolt.

Too radical a break with orthodoxy might also place the king in a vulnerable position: when not riding through Amarna in a gilded chariot, Akhenaten seems to have holed himself up in a high-walled riverside palace at the far edge of his city, which was criss-crossed by tracks used by the police to monitor comings and goings. A contemporary text refers to 'those who would ascend the mountain': would-be rebels who planned to take to the hills to prepare an attack.

Threats also came from outside Egypt. Even during periods of strong central control, the Nile Valley remained a target for attack by 'less happier lands' to the west (Libya), north-east (Syria-Palestine) and south (Nubia). The autobiographical inscription of Weni, written at the height of the Pyramid Age, mentions repeated incursions by the 'sand-dwellers', the semi-nomads of Sinai and southern Palestine. At times of weak government, Egypt repeatedly found itself harried by foreign foes. Asiatics infiltrated the delta in the late Middle Kingdom, while Libyans raided Upper Egypt in the dying days of the New Kingdom. A pharaoh who wanted to keep his throne and his kingdom had to be on constant lookout for potential foes.

Foreigners were both feared and belittled in Egyptian discourse – it was easier to square up to a foe who had been dehumanized through the power of words. Pharaonic Egypt's oldest enemies, the Nubians, had long been referred to as 'bowmen', and 'bow' came to be applied to any foreign foe. Because the number three in ancient Egyptian signified the plural, and three times three signified a plurality, the term 'Nine Bows' came to be used to refer to all possible enemies. The great military strategist of the twelfth dynasty, Senusret III, was praised as a ruler 'whose terror kills the Nine Bows'.⁵ One of Tutankhamun's footstools, which accompanied a magnificent polychrome throne, has an inlaid top depicting nine bound captives, identified in the accompanying inscription as 'all foreign lands'. By resting his feet on an image of the Nine Bows, the king might symbolically trample his enemies every time he sat down.

Of course, by the time of Tutankhamun's accession, Egypt's fortunes had been thoroughly enmeshed with those of its Levantine neighbours – Mittani, the Hittites, Babylonia, Assyria and a host of vassal states. Foreign weaponry had given Egypt military supremacy, foreigners held office at the Egyptian court, foreign tastes had been embraced by the Egyptian elite and foreign concubines were ensconced in the royal palace. The court culture of the eighteenth dynasty was thoroughly multicultural.

But the complex reality did not prevent the pharaonic court, its scribes and artists from sticking to the official ideology: Egyptian civilization was superior to all other cultures, foreigners living outside the Nile Valley were anathema to created order and it was the king's sacred duty to dominate all foreign lands. At around the time of Tutankhamun's birth, his father Akhenaten staged an elaborate assembly at Amarna, the highlight of which was a parade of foreigners bringing 'tribute'. The Nubians who brought gold, ebony and ivory may have been genuine subjects of Egypt, but the other foreign delegations – Syrians and Mycenaeans – were diplomatic allies and trading equals. Yet it suited royal ideology to present them as paying homage to the pharaoh.

The origins of this xenophobia lay in the creation of the Egyptian state, when a nation was forged from a jumble of petty chiefdoms and proudly autonomous communities. The first kings of a newly unified Egypt realized that there are few more powerful ways to create a feeling of identity and bolster a government's legitimacy in the eyes of its people than to demonize outsiders.

⊲○▷

Egyptian kingship may have been shrouded in layers of ritual and myth, but it was, in origin and at heart, a form of government – the ideology was developed to cement the king's political authority, not the other way round. The pharaoh was god incarnate but also head of state. He appointed all officials, civil and religious, and was at the apex of the government machine, receiving reports from his advisers and taking all significant decisions on the running of the country. It is this aspect of Egyptian kingship that attracts relatively little attention, for the simple reason that it is less visible in the surviving record. Hieroglyphics were designed to record and perpetuate an idealized state of affairs; it is little wonder that official texts dwell on the sacred, transcendent aspects of kingship rather than the grubby world of day-to-day politics.

One of the rare exceptions is a remarkable work of literature written in the early Middle Kingdom called *The Teaching for King Merikara*. Set at the court of the eponymous First Intermediate Period ruler, it may reflect the experiences of the time: civil war, the breakdown of central authority, the erosion of royal privileges and the blurring of distinctions between the king and the rest of the population. The tone is striking for its pragmatic emphasis on the king's mortality and fallibility. It allows us a rare glimpse behind the veil of mythic kingship, revealing the vulnerability and loneliness of high office. So too does the broadly contemporary text, *The Teaching of King Amenemhat I for His Son*, in which the narrator recounts a fatal attack by agents within the palace, lamenting:

Be wary of subordinates who have not yet come into
      their own,
about whose plots one is not yet anxious.
Do not get (too) close to them; do not be alone (with
      them);
do not trust a brother; do not make friends;
do not promote intimates: there is no profit in it.

When you lie down, guard your heart yourself,
because a man has no helpers
on the Day of Suffering.
I gave to the poor, I promoted the orphan,
I gave the one who had nothing his due, just as I did
      for the one who had.

Yet he who ate my food made rebellion,
he to whom I gave arms plotted with them.[6]

Apart from these two extraordinary works, there is little
written evidence for the political aspects of kingship, but the
pharaoh's secular role finds reflection in artistic sources.
Monarchs throughout history have chosen different types of
clothing and accoutrements to signify different aspects of their
office. In our own age, a crown and robe denote the sanctity
and majesty of royalty, while a military uniform emphasizes
the ruler's role as commander-in-chief. Similarly in ancient
Egypt, the clothes – and, in particular, the headgear – sported
by a pharaoh conveyed a message about the particular aspect
of kingship being emphasized. For everyday wear, in the exercise of the king's governmental duties, the simple bag headdress
(*khat*) or folded linen head covering (*nemes*) was preferred. On
military occasions in the New Kingdom, the distinctive, helmet-
like blue crown was favoured. When the king wished to

emphasize his role as secular head of state, the red crown might be worn, while the white crown was often selected for more sacred occasions. If the king wished to underline his role as unifier of the Two Lands, the double crown (combining red and white crowns) was a natural choice. There were lots of other royal paraphernalia that conveyed further subliminal messages, but crowns were perhaps the most important category of regalia. From the New Kingdom onwards, combinations became popular, with ornaments and elements added and combined, to be read as 'iconographic sentences'.

The range of headdresses worn by Egyptian kings is illustrated by the collection of servant figurines interred with Tutankhamun. The purpose of a *shabti* (literally 'one who answers') was to serve as a substitute in the afterlife, should the tomb owner be summoned to carry out corvée labour or other unwelcome tasks. To deflect such unwanted demands, kings and commoners alike were customarily buried with servant figurines, which would magically come to life in the tomb. Over time, the practice assumed increasing importance; by the eighteenth dynasty, a high-status tomb might be furnished with a veritable army of *shabti*s. Tutankhamun had no fewer than 413, made from wood, faience and stone. What is notable, apart from the sheer number, is their appearance. More than three-quarters wear a simple wig, and these *shabti*s are best categorized as helpers. Among the remaining figurines, which are characterized by overtly royal accoutrements, fifty-six wear the *khat* and twenty-seven the *nemes*. Only nine of Tutankhamun's *shabti*s are shown wearing crowns, of whom four sport the red crown, two the blue crown and two the white crown. Only one wears the double crown.

If the king's collection of afterlife helpers reflects the balance of his duties, then his role as head of state and government – the political as opposed to the sacral aspect of monarchy –

was what occupied most of his time, even if it was largely unacknowledged in the official record.

⊲○▷

The scenes of Egyptian kingship that are most intact, and survive in the greatest numbers, are those carved on temple walls. Indeed, stone reliefs were designed to perpetuate an idealized image of the ruler for all time. Unsurprisingly, in such religious contexts it is the king's relationship with the gods that is the focus.

Part of the unwritten contract between an Egyptian ruler and his people was the notion that the king would intercede with the gods on his subjects' behalf. This, in turn, depended on a bargain the king struck with the gods: in exchange for him maintaining their temples and cults, they would legitimize his rule, confirm him in office, grant him a long reign and bestow their blessings on the populace. A responsibility to preserve, protect and beautify the shrines of Egypt's myriad deities was hence one of the most ancient duties of kingship. Labels from the tombs of first-dynasty kings commonly record the dedication of new cult statues; a large stone statue of a baboon deity, incised with the name of its donor – Narmer, first king of the first dynasty – illustrates what they would have looked like. The production of statues of the gods must have occupied the royal workshops from the inception of the Egyptian state and for the following 3,000 years. Examples in a range of materials, including stone, bronze and gold, have survived from every period of pharaonic history.

Before a cult statue could be dedicated, the king had a duty to establish the temple that would house it and provide a home for the god. A second-dynasty relief from Gebelein, south of Thebes, depicts the essential elements of the ceremony, which would remain fixed for the next three millennia. At the heart of the proceedings was a ritual known as 'stretching the cord', during which the king would mark out the ceremonial axis of the new temple on the ground. He would also dedicate 'foundation deposits' of ritual objects at key spots along the temple perimeter and mark the location of the sanctuary with clean sand, recalling the creation myth in which a sandbank emerged from the waters of chaos and formed the basis for Egypt's first temple. In this way, every temple foundation was equated with the moment of creation and identified the king with the creator god. Indeed, the king was probably involved in the establishment of every significant shrine, local or national.

Once the king had founded a temple, he had a duty to maintain it by ensuring a regular supply of offerings for use in divine ritual. Among the faience vessels in the tomb of Tutankhamun were several shaped like teapots, known in ancient Egyptian as *nemset*. They were originally contained in a box in the Antechamber, which had a label describing the contents as 'seventeen blue faience *nemset* ewers'. Another box contained further faience vases, many of them with tall, S-shaped sides, narrow necks and flared mouths. This type was modelled to resemble the hieroglyphic sign *hes*, which meant 'praise'. Indeed, both *nemset* and *hes* vases were types of ritual vessel used in temple ceremonies to make offerings to the gods. The inclusion of such vessels in a royal tomb demonstrates the central role of the temple cult in the life of the pharaoh. Although in practice, temple rituals would generally have been carried out by the resident priests, it was important to maintain the myth that only the monarch – as mediator between the gods and humanity – was qualified to perform this role. In temple reliefs, it is the ruler who is shown making offerings to the gods.

Another way in which the king could sustain temple cults was by donating land and commodities, to supplement their income. As an inscription from the reign of Tutankhamun averred:

> His Majesty made monuments for (all) the gods, [fashioning] their images from the best pure electrum from foreign lands; building their shrines anew as monuments for eternity, endowed with possessions for ever; laying down divine offerings for them – daily offerings – and endowing their food offerings on earth. He gave more than had existed before, surpassing what had been done since the time of the ancestors.[7]

The monarch might also grant temples other favours, such as exempting them from tax or providing perks to their workforce. As a result of such royal largesse, the major temples eventually became significant landowners, controlling vast swathes of the Nile Valley's most productive fields and owning a range of other productive resources, from mines to trading vessels. At the end of the Pyramid Age and again in the dying days of the New Kingdom, the balance of economic power swung so far in favour of the temples that it threatened to destabilize the entire apparatus of government. A register of landholdings from the twentieth dynasty, preserved on papyrus, shows that the great temple of Amun-Ra at Karnak – by then the primary focus of royal attention for four centuries – was by far the most important landowner throughout the Theban region. With such economic clout, it is little wonder that the high priests of Amun regarded themselves as important political actors on the national stage. Maintaining the cults of the gods while also ensuring the effective balance of power was not an easy task.

Just as the foundation of each new temple symbolized the moment of creation, the start of each new reign was represented as a resetting of the balance that had been disturbed by the passing of the old monarch. Given the symbolic and ideological importance of divine kingship, a king's death must have been seen as a threat to the very survival of ancient Egyptian civilization. Hence the first duty of each new ruler was to reassert order by reunifying the Two Lands.

The ceremonies associated with the royal accession and coronation can be reconstructed from a variety of written sources. According to the Palermo Stone, a sixth-dynasty compilation of earlier royal annals, each new reign began with a ritual called 'Uniting Upper and Lower Egypt', during which the king would symbolically take possession of both halves of his realm to restore order to a troubled world. But this was only one element of a series of rites that marked the beginning of a new era and sought to elevate a mortal prince into a divine monarch. A coronation did not simply confirm a king in office – it transformed him into a sacred being. After a coronation, there was no possibility of challenging the new monarch's right to rule.

Coronations must therefore have been especially charged for those whose path to power had been contested or controversial. A good example is Hatshepsut, the female ruler of the mid-eighteenth dynasty whose elevation to the kingship was anything but orthodox. To remind her subjects of her inalienable right to rule, she had an extensive description of her coronation carved onto the outside walls of her Red Chapel, a magnificent shrine of pink granite that she erected inside the temple of Amun-Ra at Karnak. Hatshepsut's coronation ceremonies began with her proclamation as king, which was performed twice – once when she assumed the throne and again the following New Year's Day. After waking and leaving the palace, the new ruler was purified before entering the temple for the coronation proper. The monarch received the crowns of office and was inducted into the presence of the gods. In Hatshepsut's case, she was symbolically nursed by the goddesses, before being formally installed on the 'throne of Horus'. Finally, her royal titles and names were announced, symbolizing the official start of the new reign.

The presentation and assumption of the royal regalia were at the heart of the crowning ceremony. According to mythology, they had been presented to Horus, the last of the divine kings, by the solar creator god Atum, thus setting a precedent for future reigns. King Thutmose III of the eighteenth dynasty claimed that

> I was elevated in dignity because of the crowns, which are on his [Ra's] head; his uraeus was fixed on my head . . . he has fixed my crowns and assembled my royal names for me.[8]

Egyptian crowns literally elevated their wearer above his subjects: in Hatshepsut's coronation text, one of her crowns is described as 'piercing the sky', bringing her into contact with the heavenly realm. In all, she was presented with twelve different crowns, reflecting the multiple aspects of kingship. The transformation of the monarch from mortal into semi-divine being was emphasized by other items of regalia: collars, bracelets, anklets and sceptres and staffs. Made from gold, silver and precious stones, everything would have been designed to make the king appear radiant, like the gods. In addition to the crook and flail from the tomb of Tutankhamun, two further items of coronation regalia were included among the king's grave goods: a pair of matching gold and silver staffs or sceptres, each some 130 centimetres tall and topped with a miniature image of the boy pharaoh.

Fig. 19. Gold coronation staff.

The symbolic power of the coronation rites notwithstanding, there remained a fundamental contradiction at the heart of ancient Egyptian kingship: while the sovereign was meant to be semi-divine, he was all too obviously human. As Tutankhamun himself demonstrated, kings fell ill and died. The eighteenth-dynasty answer to this conundrum was to add a further element to the mythology of kingship and to give it expression once a year, during a great annual festival. The Festival of the Sanctuary was instituted at the beginning of the dynasty. Its premise was simple: once a year, the god Amun-Ra of Karnak went to his Southern Sanctuary, Luxor Temple, to refresh himself before resuming his duties as chief god of Egypt. The cult statue of Amun-Ra would travel in a procession from Karnak to Luxor, before making the return journey some days later. It was an occasion for merry-making and feasting, a highlight of the calendar for the inhabitants of Thebes.

But there was more to the Festival of the Sanctuary than a

mere holiday; at its heart was the idea that the king derived his sacred status from the divine essence that dwelled within him. The real purpose of the Festival of the Sanctuary was to 'top up' this *ka* and reaffirm the monarch's right to rule. As soon as Amun-Ra had taken up residence in his Southern Sanctuary, he would be visited by the king. In the temple's inner sanctum, monarch and god would commune in private, with the god's *ka* rejuvenating the king's divinity. At the culmination of the ceremony, the monarch would emerge visibly restored, to be acclaimed by his courtiers and priests as 'foremost of all the living *ka*s'.

In a brilliant piece of political theatre, Tutankhamun's eventual successor, the general Horemheb – a man with no royal blood and no obvious claim to the throne – decided to use the Festival of the Sanctuary as the setting for his coronation. The combination of ancient accession rites and holy communion with Amun-Ra left no room for opposition.

⊲◉⊳

Appropriately enough, Horemheb's name means 'Horus is in festival'. In modern, Western societies, forenames are usually chosen for aesthetic or family reasons, rather than on the basis of etymological or symbolic associations. In other societies, however, names have retained their power. Chinese given names, in particular, reference a wide range of qualities, aspirations and auspicious omens.

Pharaonic civilization has much in common with non-Western traditions in this regard, for ancient Egyptian names were replete with meaning. In the ancient Nile Valley, where childhood mortality was high, the naming of a child was considered an important weapon in the fight against malign forces. Calling a baby boy Djedkhonsuiufankh, '[The god] Khonsu said he will live', was effectively daring death to contradict the promise of a divine oracle. Other common types of given name invoked gods or the king more directly: a child named Pepi-ankh ('[King] Pepi lives') would hope to be saved by association with the monarch, while a baby called Djehuty ('[the god] Thoth') would be placed under the protection of its divine namesake. Naming a boy Horemheb virtually predestined him to succeed to the throne. Thus, when Akhenaten and his wife called their newborn son Tutankhaten, 'The living image of Aten', they were making a theological point, emphasizing that a king's son – and future monarch – was the living incarnation of the supreme deity.

After Akhenaten's death and the abandonment of his religious reforms, references to Aten were swiftly replaced with the name of the traditional state god of the eighteenth dynasty, Amun. Tutankhaten thus changed his name to Tutankhamun, 'The living image of Amun', a clear expression of the new orthodoxy. Royal names are ubiquitous in the ancient Egyptian record, incised and painted on all sorts of objects, elaborated in jewellery, scribbled in ink on labels and dockets, carved in tablets of stone. Just about every inscribed object from Tutankhamun's tomb bears his name. One of the most splendid examples is a box found in the Treasury, which is made in the form of the oval ring ('cartouche') in which royal names were written as far back as the third dynasty. The cartouche was an elongation of the hieroglyphic sign for 'eternity'; it expressed the twin ideas of protection and everlastingness, an appropriate device with which to enclose the principal expression of royal identity.

The lid of Tutankhamun's cartouche-shaped box is decorated with large ebony and ivory hieroglyphs that spell out the king's personal name: 'Tutankhamun, ruler of Upper Egyptian Heliopolis'. The inclusion of this circumlocution for Thebes emphasized the city's status as the southern cult centre of the solar creator god

Amun-Ra, underlining the king's association with the god and his role as champion of the restored orthodox religion.

Just as the proliferation of different crowns reflected the multi-faceted ideology of pharaonic kingship, the multifarious names, titles and epithets borne by an Egyptian ruler expressed his diverse roles. As each new element of the royal titulary was added, the theology of kingship became increasingly elaborate. The birth name, written inside a cartouche, only became a standard part of the royal titulary in the fifth dynasty. Even then, it played second fiddle to the throne name, which was the principal name by which each king was known from the end of the third dynasty. Hence the king known to us as Tutankhamun would have been referred to as Nebkheperura ('Ra is lord of forms'). A throne name was typically a complex theological formulation which, while following a dynastic convention, served to express each new reign as a re-creation of divine order.

The earliest royal names, from the period before the unification of Egypt, were not enclosed in a cartouche but inside a special rectangular frame. Known as a *serekh*, its lower part was decorated with panelling, in order to resemble the façade of the royal compound in Memphis. Like the cartouche, the *serekh* denoted the concept of protection but also associated the king with the building that was the physical manifestation of his political power. This same idea would give rise in the eighteenth dynasty to the term 'pharaoh', a Greek corruption of the Egyptian *per-aa*, meaning 'great house'. The *serekh* was typically surmounted by a representation of Horus, expressing the ancient idea that the king was the earthly incarnation of the sky god. To reinforce this association, the name written within the *serekh* – the so-called 'Horus name' – was originally an attribute of Horus that the king wished to emphasize, but over the centuries it became increasingly elaborate; by the eighteenth dynasty, it often had a militaristic flavour.

The next element that was added to the royal titulary was the two-part title *nesut-bity*, 'he of the sedge and bee', which, as we have already learned, expressed the sacred and secular nature of Egyptian kingship. From the fourth dynasty, the *nesut-bity* title was paired with the king's throne name and typically compounded with the element Ra, signifying the importance of the sun god for kingship. Tutankhamun's throne name, Nebkheperura, maintained this centuries-old tradition.

A third element of the royal titulary was a name prefixed by the signs of a vulture and cobra, which symbolized 'the Two Ladies' Nekhbet and Wadjet, the tutelary goddesses of Upper and Lower Egypt, and thus emphasized the king's role as unifier of the Two Lands. Tutankhamun's 'Two Ladies' name made reference to the way in which he had unified Egypt by restoring orthodox religion.

A fourth royal title, 'Golden Horus', signified the divinity of the king. With the fifth and final element that was added, the title 'son of Ra', the king's descent from the creator god became an established part of royal theology. It also reinforced the ideal of patrilineal inheritance and the king's position at the apex of Egyptian society.

Incarnation of the sky god, divine and mortal ruler, unifier of the Two Lands, fashioned from gold like the gods, son and heir of the creator: the five-fold titulary of an Egyptian king expressed the ineffable, unchallengeable nature of his rule. The human being was transformed by his accession and assumption of royal titles into the supreme head of state, an intermediary between the people and the gods.

Besides the cartouche-shaped chest, Tutankhamun's burial equipment included a further fifty boxes. All the wooden containers seemed to have been ransacked by tomb robbers soon after the pharaoh's burial. Items of intrinsic value – glass, silver, fine linen – were carried off, leaving many boxes half-empty, their dockets testifying to their original contents.

Many of the boxes were made to accommodate specific items, their interiors divided into compartments or protected with secondary lids. The sheer variety of chests and containers, fashioned from stone, papier-mâché and various woods, including cedar from Lebanon and ebony from Nubia, illustrate the sophistication of ancient Egyptian craftsmen. There are carrying chests with retractable poles, rectangular boxes with gabled, curved and vaulted lids, boxes on feet, chests on fretwork stands, painted boxes, inlaid boxes – every kind of container.

As well as reflecting the superlative craftsmanship of the royal workshops, Tutankhamun's boxes emphasize the peripatetic nature of the royal court. Rulers have always made a habit of travelling throughout their realms. Queen Elizabeth I of England was renowned for moving between stately homes, not only to be seen and to gather intelligence, but to defray the cost of maintaining the royal household by imposing on the hospitality of her fawning courtiers. In modern times, Queen Elizabeth II moves between three official residences and two private retreats. Even a republican leader like the President of the United States travels between the White House, Camp David and his private home. If rulers are to be believed, they have to be seen, which requires them to visit different parts of their countries on a regular basis.

One of Tutankhamun's boxes exemplifies this lifestyle. Semicircular in shape and measuring thirty-seven by thirty-one centimetres, it is made from imported cedar with ebony veneers and ivory inlays. On the front, an inlaid panel is decorated with the sign for 'unification', surmounted by three gold-foil cartouches, with a pair of feathers and a solar disc above each of them. The cartouches contain the names of the royal couple,

Tutankhamun and Ankhesenamun, but originally named their ephemeral predecessors, Ankhetkheperura and Meritaten. The box, therefore, is one of several 'heirloom' pieces that were inherited by the boy king at his accession and repurposed for his own use. Its original function is not known, but it may have been used to store rolls of papyrus – essential documents that the king needed on his travels. Indeed, portability is a key feature of the box, which is fitted with four metal rings. A string or cord passed through them would have enabled it to be carried. The container may have been the ancient Egyptian equivalent of the British monarch's red dispatch box, in which state papers are kept and transported.

That the Egyptian monarchy was a mobile one is clear from the earliest royal records. They list visits to shrines, participation in major festivals and a biennial royal progress called the 'Following of Horus'. Details are sketchy, but we might imagine a flotilla of ships sailing up and down the Nile, led by the king's flagship and visiting important provincial shrines and major towns over the course of several months. The royal court would have relied on the largesse of regional governors to sustain itself during its travels. A twenty-sixth-dynasty inscription describes just such a journey, undertaken by a princess:

> Messengers had sailed upstream to the south to ensure provisions ahead of her . . . garnered from every provincial governor from his own stores – consisting of every good thing: bread and beer, oxen and fowl, vegetables, dates and herbs; every good thing (indeed) – one handing on to another until she reached Thebes.[9]

In return for this hospitality, the monarch would have confirmed his governors in their offices and beautified their local shrines, as well as dispensing justice and learning about developments in towns and villages far from the capital. The Following of Horus was an effective way of maintaining control over a geographically extensive territory, and the regular peregrination of the royal court remained a feature of pharaonic government.

A dazzling glimpse of this lifestyle is afforded by the spectacular treasure of Hetepheres, the mother of Khufu, builder of the Great Pyramid. Her burial at Giza, in the shadow of her son's massive monument, contained a fine set of gilded furniture: a bed, an armchair, a carrying chair and a canopy frame. All are lightweight and portable, notable for their simple, elegant design. The queen's grave goods also included a jewellery box for her set of fourteen silver bracelets, each decorated with inlaid butterflies of carnelian and turquoise. We can imagine Hetepheres being carried in her sedan chair from one royal rest house to another, her bracelets glittering in the Egyptian sun. On arrival, her furnishings would have been unpacked and reassembled, the wooden frame spread with a covering of fine linen to provide shade from the sun during the day and a tent for her bed and armchair at night.

Much of Tutankhamun's furniture speaks of a similarly peripatetic lifestyle. Inscriptions from his reign indicate that he spent time at Thebes and Memphis, as well as in his hunting lodge at Giza. There would have also been visits further afield, utilizing the campaign palaces built in Nubia by his forebears and the forts along the 'Ways of Horus' from the Nile Delta to the Levant. Despite his young age and physical frailty, Tutankhamun's life, like that of every Egyptian king, was spent on the move.

⊲⊙⊳

Despite all the pomp and pageantry, crowns and regalia, names and titles, a question continued to hover over the king: was or wasn't he a god? The Horus title asserted that he was god on earth, but 'son of Ra' suggested inherited power. Texts and images intimated that it was the gods who granted the office of kingship, but he claimed to be fashioned in their image.

During the eighteenth dynasty, the royal myth-makers sought to resolve the conundrum of the king's status once and for all. Hatshepsut promulgated the notion that she was the offspring of the god Amun, but after her demise, the myth of divine birth was temporarily shelved. Her successor, Thutmose III, exercised authority by force of arms, and his successor, Amenhotep II, championed the image of a superhero, whose political supremacy was underpinned by strength and skill. Then Thutmose IV, perhaps lacking his predecessors' martial vigour, began to identify himself more explicitly with the sun god. His son Amenhotep III developed the idea further, commissioning colossal statues of himself in red quartzite and pink granite – rocks with strong solar connotations – and adopting the epithet 'the dazzling Orb'. He built an enormous temple at Soleb in Upper Nubia, in which he had himself depicted making offerings to his divine self; and in the inner sanctum of Luxor Temple, he formally resuscitated the myth of the divine birth. By the end of his reign, no one could doubt – or would dare deny – the actuality of the king's divinity.

It is little wonder that Amenhotep III's son and successor should have picked up where his father left off. At Karnak, Amenhotep IV built a new set of courts and gateways to the east of the main complex, facing the sunrise and dedicated to the Orb of the visible sun, 'Aten', who soon became the sole focus of his worship. He changed his name to Akhenaten, abandoned Karnak and set out to found a capital city where he could dedicate his reign to the exultation of his new, all-encompassing deity.

Akhenaten's search led him to a dramatic desert embayment on the east bank of the Nile in Middle Egypt. He named it Akhetaten, 'horizon of the Orb' (known today as Amarna). Its limits were demarcated by a series of boundary stelae carved into the surrounding cliffs. Their dedicatory inscription, penned by the king himself, leaves no room for misinterpretation:

> Now as for what is within these four stelae, starting from the eastern escarpment and finishing at the western escarpment, it is Horizon of the Orb in its entirety. It belongs to my father, 'The living Ra-Horus-of-the-two-horizons who rejoices on the horizon in his name of Light which is the Orb, given life for ever and ever' and comprises the mountains, the hill country, the marsh-lands, the reclaimed land, the high ground, the fresh land, the fields, the water, the towns, the riverbanks, the people, the livestock, the copses and everything that the Orb, my father, brings into being, for ever and ever.[10]

To accompany his new name, capital city and purified theology, Akhenaten also introduced a radical new style of art. The traditional images of the gods were replaced by the symbol of the Orb, depicted on high, sending out its rays to all creation – but above all, to Akhenaten and his family. For in Akhenaten's theology, the king, queen and the royal children were the unique intermediaries between heaven and earth. As Akhenaten's credo, *The Great Hymn to the Orb*, put it:

> There is none other who knows you,
> Only your son, Neferkheperura [i.e. Akhenaten], Ra's
>   only one,
> You have informed him of your plans and your might.[11]

Akhenaten promulgated this uncompromising religion for the rest of his seventeen-year reign, and his son Tutankhaten maintained it for a short time. One of the objects made for him at his accession was a spectacular golden throne that provided a sumptuous illustration of the cult of the Orb. The outer arms are decorated with inlaid cartouches containing his original birth name, 'The living image of the Orb'. In pride of place is a richly decorated back panel, inlaid with sheet silver, carnelian and coloured glass. It depicts the young king, attended by his wife. Above them is the golden Orb, its rays extending the signs of life to the nostrils of the king and queen.

Yet Akhenaten's bold theological experiment did not endure. Scarcely a year after taking the throne, Tutankhaten presided over a wholesale restoration of the old orthodoxy, abandoning Amarna for Thebes, reinstating the traditional deities and changing his name to Tutankhamun. The cartouches on the back of his golden throne were altered; thus one of the boy king's most famous artefacts reveals that ancient Egyptian monarchy was a work in progress rather than a fixed concept.

SIX

Domesticity

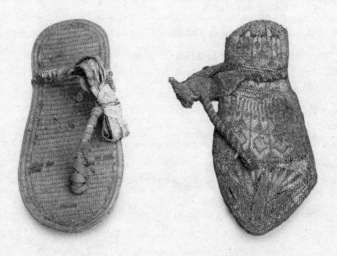

Fig. 20. Leather and beadwork sandals.

In ancient Egypt, kings and commoners alike lived in buildings made from the same mudbricks. Palaces, hovels and everything in between were created from the Nile sediment; only the scale was different. Ancient Egypt was a pre-industrial, pre-urban society; its cities were little more than agglomerations of villages. People lived close-knit lives, based on family units and small neighbourhoods. A warm hearth and a few items of furniture stood at the heart of every dwelling, whether opulent or ordinary.

Objects from Tutankhamun's tomb illustrate the common features of domestic life in the ancient Nile Valley. The emphasis on lightweight, portable furniture reflects a lifestyle in which people trod lightly on the land. Clothing was simple but not unadorned, for people took pride in their appearance and were conscious of their status. Life was not all hard work, with all levels of society enjoying leisure pursuits. With no locks on the doors, and houses built side by side, there was always the possibility of guests, both invited and uninvited. Possessions were closely guarded, love lives complex. Despite the outward simplicity of daily life, human emotions and relationships were rich, and it is in the material remains of domesticity that we come closest to understanding life as the ancient Egyptians experienced it.

Tutankhamun's gilded throne is the supreme surviving example of a chair from the ancient world. Its craftsmanship, decoration and iconography are striking and unique. It is also atypical in a less obvious way: it is significantly higher than other ancient Egyptian chairs; sitting on it would have felt, to the young Tutankhamun, like sitting on a high chair. The king, in common with his subjects, would have been accustomed to spending life closer to ground level.

Chairs were highly prized in pharaonic culture. They were items of significant value, which only the better-off could afford. Unless you happened to be a furniture maker, a chair would have represented a major purchase, a status symbol to demonstrate your material success to family and friends. The larger houses at Amarna were built around a central reception hall, with a low dais running along the wall facing the entrance. From contemporary tomb scenes, we can reconstruct how the room would have been used, with the owner and his wife sitting on their chairs on the dais to receive guests.

The average ancient Egyptian would be more likely to sit on a simple folding stool, which was cheaper, lighter, more portable and more stowable than a chair – important qualities in households where most activities took place in a single room and where space was at a premium. Even royalty, it seems, preferred stools to chairs for everyday use. Scenes in the tomb of Ay at Amarna show palace residents sitting on low stools, and Tutankhamun's tomb was equipped with no fewer than twelve stools. There were simple stools with straight legs and a double curved seat, strengthened with vertical and diagonal bracings. Then there were more elaborate models, with decorated panels and animal legs, or with turned legs and horizontal stretchers. There was a tripod with a semi-circular seat, and an even flimsier model made from papyrus and palm stalks. Finally, there were three folding stools, with feet carved and decorated to resemble duck's heads.

Sitting on a low stool may have been the custom at meal-times, but many other activities were carried out even closer to the ground. The aforementioned palace scenes show members of the royal family lounging on cushions, while a painting from the King's House at Amarna depicts Nefertiti squatting on a thick embroidered pillow, attended by her daughters. Other scenes show members of the royal court sitting on cushions while arranging their hair or playing musical instruments. 'Living the low life',[1] as the excavator of Amarna has described it, was no indication of lowly status. From the Pyramid Age onwards, one archetype was the figure of a scribe, squatting cross-legged on the floor with a length of papyrus over his lap. The judges of the underworld were similarly depicted.

The archaeological remains of houses confirm that the 'horizon of reach' was lower in ancient Egypt than in modern Western societies. A typical workman's house in Amarna or western Thebes had an open hearth at its centre. Consisting of a pottery bowl set in a brick surround, it was the focus of family life. A low platform built along two sides of the room would have allowed the occupants to sit around the fire on

Fig. 21 Folding stool.

mats or cushions; on chilly nights, householders would have squatted around the hearth to warm their hands.

For much of ancient Egyptian history, workers' houses were built to a standard layout. A front room housed a domestic altar that was dedicated to the ancestors. This room would have been used to receive visitors on special occasions and for other household activities. Off the front room was the central living space, where everything from cooking and eating to relaxing and sleeping would have taken place. At the back of the house, smaller rooms were used for storage and food preparation.

The house of a wealthier Egyptian family differed in scale but followed the same general layout. Cooking would have been done outside, to keep smoke and smells away from the living areas. A dedicated room with a special bed niche served as the master bedroom and might have washing facilities: a small cubicle lined with a thick layer of gypsum plaster and a limestone 'shower tray' with raised sides and a spout that drained into a pot or stone tank. For the wealthiest inhabitants, a latrine – a limestone seat with a keyhole-shaped slot, set on low brick walls with a chamber pot underneath – was the ultimate luxury.

In the city of Amarna, life seems to have been quite comfortable – at least for the upper classes. Limited amounts of rubbish found within settlement areas suggest the collection and disposal of waste. The air would have been scented with woodsmoke from abundant open fires, and with incense wafting on the breeze from the altars of the city's many temples and household shrines.

The sensations of daily life in ancient Egypt can only be guessed at from the surviving archaeological and artistic records, but we can be certain that settlements were more colourful than the stone and mudbrick ruins would suggest. The Egyptians had a fondness for bright colours, including in their houses. Even the modest village houses at Deir el-Medina had doorframes painted a rich red, while plaster fragments found in some of the larger villas at Amarna indicate a vivid decorative scheme. Red was the favoured colour for doors, columns and window grilles; for the upper parts of the walls, swags and friezes of flowers and foliage were particularly fashionable; the ceiling beams were plastered and painted in bright mineral pigments (red, blue, yellow and green), and the spaces between them filled with tartan patterns. The house of the vizier Nakht, probably the most sumptuous private residence in the whole city, had whitewashed walls and a long hall with a bright blue ceiling, to resemble the dazzling Egyptian sky. The floor was originally whitewashed, but it was subsequently painted in bright colours.

Amarna is the only well-documented city from pharaonic Egypt. Built, occupied and abandoned within a single generation, it presents the most complete picture of life in an ancient Egyptian city. Larger houses sometimes occur in groups, but more often they are each surrounded by a cluster of smaller dwellings, reflecting patterns of economic dependency. Although the ancient Egyptians were acutely status-conscious, people of different social standing lived side by side.

⊲◌▷

Ancient Egypt was rigidly hierarchical and economically polarized, yet distinctions of status seem to have been largely a matter of degree. Wealthy, powerful individuals lived in larger houses that were laid out to the same basic pattern as humbler dwellings. High officials sat on cushions while their attendants made do with simple rushwork mats, but rich and poor alike sat on the floor. The upper and lower classes ate the same food. And what was true of houses, furniture and food was also true of clothing. In ancient Egypt, everyone from the pharaoh to the lowliest peasant wore essentially the same items of apparel.

There was a limited range of garments to choose from, fundamental among which was a triangular loincloth. A well-preserved example was found in the Antechamber of Tutankhamun's tomb. Like most of his clothing – and like most clothing worn throughout the Nile Valley – the king's underwear was made from linen, the manufacture of which can be traced back to the Neolithic Period. Linen could be made in a range of grades, from coarse to fine, and many of Tutankhamun's clothes are of the finest type, almost akin to silk. Yet fragments of high-quality textiles have also been found in workers' settlements. The difference between rich and poor was, again, a matter of degree. Although the Egyptians used other fibres, ranging from sheep's wool and goat hair to palm fibre, everyone wore linen garments and aspired to have at least a few items of superior grade. As a popular song exhorted:

Put myrrh on your head,
Wear fine linen.
Anoint yourself with the real wonders that belong to a
    god!
Increase your joys,
Let not your heart be weary,
But follow your heart and your happiness.[2]

Tutankhamun's wardrobe illustrates the different types of garment worn by all classes of Egyptians throughout their history. Over the loincloth men wore kilts and women wore skirts; men might also wear an apron under their kilt, its front panel providing extra modesty. Sashes of all kinds were popular accessories and could be worn over the shoulder or wrapped around the waist. The quintessential garment for women was a long, close-fitting dress with a V-neck – although how frequently such restrictive clothing would have been worn in

Fig. 22. Linen loincloths.

the course of daily life is questionable. More common, one suspects, were simple tunics, shawls and cloaks. If circumstances required men to cover their upper body, a tunic was the garment of choice. The simplest type was made by sewing up the sides of a rectangular length of cloth that had been folded in half, cutting a slit for the head and neck, and leaving two gaps, hemmed with stitching, for the arms. Sleeves could be attached to cover the arms. Tutankhamun was buried with a number of short tunics, while the tomb of Kha at Deir el-Medina yielded a beautifully preserved long tunic with decorative stitching. Other items of clothing from the New Kingdom include scarves and kerchiefs, gloves and leggings. As a general rule, individuals of higher status wore more layers of clothing.

Rich and poor alike, however, seem to have favoured simple designs with little decoration. In everyday clothes, the most common form of adornment was a long fringe woven into one side and a knotted fringe along the bottom edge. Dresses and tunics might also be pleated in horizontal, vertical or herring-bone patterns. The corners of sashes were typically held together with knots rather than pins or brooches. Linen was usually left undyed, its off-white colour providing the perfect foil for the multicoloured jewellery so beloved of both sexes. However, as might be expected for a king's wardrobe, many of the garments buried with Tutankhamun were elaborately decorated. One of his tunics was covered with a dense net of beads, while another had panels of embroidery and appliqué featuring hunting scenes and mythical beasts. A tunic made for him as a child was decorated with small gold rosettes, and sequins were a popular form of decoration for royal clothing.

Perhaps the biggest change to Egyptian clothing came about in the eighteenth dynasty, following Egypt's imperial conquests in the Levant. Alongside the many exotic imports that reached the Nile Valley at this time were two non-native plant species, woad and madder. These yielded blue and red dye respectively, and would have been used to produce the coloured panels on one of Tutankhamun's tunics. However, as novel as these colourful garments may have been, they failed to change the Egyptians' long-held preference for simple, natural linen.

To transform harvested flax into linen cloth is an elaborate operation that was a household industry in ancient Egypt, carried out by womenfolk in their front rooms. A scene from an eighteenth-dynasty Theban tomb shows five servants preparing yarn while three more weave on vertical looms. The tell-tale signs of textile production – bone pin beaters, spindle whorls and spinning bowls – have been found in the residential quarters of Amarna. The site has also yielded a few fragments of looms, including the vertical looms that were introduced in the New Kingdom.

Households would have made textiles for their own use and under contract to state institutions. Temples needed a regular supply of fine linen for priestly robes. Inscriptions suggest that a household might surrender a portion of the cloth it produced, just as a farmer would hand over a portion of his harvest. In addition to this supply, the state maintained its own textile factories, which were often associated with the households of queens and concubines. Thutmose III established a harem palace at Gurob as a home for his foreign spouses and their retinues. Throughout the eighteenth dynasty, the palace employed its own weavers and was a major centre of high-quality textile production. While Tutankhamun's lowly loincloth is an everyday product, some of his highly decorated tunics may have been made by his father's foreign concubines.

⊲◦⊳

Linen was an everyday commodity in ancient Egypt, but it was still a valuable one. Garments were kept folded and rolled up when not in use, and were mended – often repeatedly – to prolong their life. Stocks of linen were kept in wooden chests as part of a household's disposable wealth. Tutankhamun was buried with a significant quantity, and one of his chests bore on its lid an inscription listing the original contents:

Royal linen . . . various *suh*-garments: 2
Royal linen . . . *idga*-garments: 10
Royal linen . . . long *sed*-garments: 20
Royal linen . . . long shirts: 7
Total of various choice linen: 39.[3]

Though the precise meaning of the terms is not clear, there is no mistaking the care with which the inventory of the royal wardrobe was carried out.

The king's linen chest exemplifies a phenomenon in pharaonic culture: the careful acquisition and storage of portable items of wealth, both as a means of exchange and as a security against financial distress. Although most people were farmers – growing what they needed for themselves, paying a portion in tax to the state and, in a good year, keeping a small part of the harvest back to barter for other necessities – natural disasters were not infrequent enough to be ignored. While the state might intervene, using its buffer stocks of grain to avert widespread famine, it made good sense to have something put by. Everyday crises, such as the death of the householder or a close relative, could also force a family into economic difficulty. The storage chest in the corner of the front room was thus both a bank account and an insurance policy. In the absence of locks and keys, boxes were held shut by means of a string or cord wound around two knobs, one on the lid and one on the side. The knot could be sealed with a lump of mud, into which a personal seal could be stamped, for extra security. The best defence against theft, however, was to have a chest of some size and weight.

One of the boxes in Tutankhamun's tomb was a wooden chest measuring eighty-three centimetres long, sixty centimetres wide and sixty-three centimetres tall. The only surviving example of its kind, it is made from cedar and ebony imported from the furthest reaches of the Egyptian Empire, with four retractable poles to allow it to be carried by two porters. This particular box was used to transport implements and materials utilized during the funeral service. When Carter opened it, he found an assortment of contents: stone vases, cups and bowls; seven stone knives; lumps of resin and balls of incense; fragments of ostrich feather; and dried fruit and garlic bulbs. While the contents may not be typical of an average household's stored wealth, the chest indicates how a wide variety of objects with intrinsic value might be placed together for safe keeping.

Scenes in the tombs of high officials at Amarna depict storage chests as key items in the daily lives and burial provision of the city's wealthier residents. One courtier named

Parennefer showed himself being rewarded by the king with an array of gifts, which his servants packed into a wooden crate. His colleague, the palace steward Huya, depicted the contents of his tomb; in pride of place, alongside a chariot and three folding stools, were three wooden chests.

The contents of a typical household store would have comprised a range of practical, durable and easily traded commodities: linen, small items of furniture, vessels, scraps of metal and grain. Many of these objects would have been made within the home, for the raw materials were readily accessible: clay for pottery, papyrus and sedge for basketry and cordage, flax for textiles, animal skins for leather, sand for faience and glass. More exotic materials – hard stones for jewellery, copper and tin for metalworking – were obtained through trade and exchange.

There is abundant evidence of craft production in pharaonic Egypt. Tomb scenes from every period include detailed depictions, supplemented by wooden tomb models, that allow the technologies employed by the ancient Egyptians to be reconstructed in detail. Manufacturing took place in individual households, larger workshops and specialist installations attached to temples and palaces.

Basketry and matting, woodwork, hand-formed pottery and textiles were made in a domestic setting with simple technology. Even simple items of faience jewellery could be made in standard bread ovens. At Amarna, metalworking was also carried out in the home. By contrast, more complex or labour-intensive technologies were carried out in larger workshops under the control of high officials. Rekhmira had responsibility for a range of craft production, while the royal steward Huya was rewarded for his service to the king with a set of workshops. In return, these facilities would have been required to supply the palace with manufactured goods in what was a neat reciprocal relationship.

The ancient Egyptians liked to poke fun at workmen who laboured over dirty, smelly, hot and uncomfortable jobs, yet to be master of one's craft was a mark of esteem. Even the great Imhotep, revered for centuries after his death as builder of the first Egyptian pyramid and a god of wisdom and healing, was proud to bear the title of overseer of sculptors and painters during his lifetime.

—◁○▷—

The redistributive aspect of the ancient Egyptian economy is well documented. Manufactured goods were subject to a levy, while farmers were required to hand over a portion of their harvest to the state. In turn, the royal treasury paid workers on royal projects and provided emergency stocks to guard against famine. Food was presented to the gods before being redistributed to priests and temple workers as part of their state rations. By such means, commodities circulated within society.

But this picture of a closed system is only partially representative. Close attention to the ancient sources reveals that private enterprise flourished in pharaonic Egypt; while the Egyptians had no word for 'profit', they still bought for the lowest price, sold for the highest and accumulated wealth. As one archaeologist has put it, the ancient Egyptians 'lived economics rather than thought it'.⁴ An early example is the farmer Hekanakht, who by means of shrewd stewardship of his estate was able to build up a surplus of grain, a herd of thirty-five cattle and a store of copper, oil and linen: all in all, a significant amount of wealth.

Although the business of buying and selling took place in a society without money, the operation of the ancient Egyptian economy was remarkably flexible and sophisticated. The underlying principle was barter, but everything had a notional value that was expressed in units that corresponded to precise measurements of grain, sesame oil, copper or silver. It was not necessary for any of these things to form part of the transaction: they simply provided a reference point for ascribing value. The most common unit of value was the *deben* of copper, a weight equivalent to ninety-three grams. Hence in one transaction, an ox was valued at fifty *deben* of copper. To purchase it, a policeman handed over a range of items totalling the same value: a jar of fat, two linen tunics, a quantity of vegetable oil and some scraps of actual copper. The purchaser no doubt went on to exchange some of these commodities for others, until everyone ended up with the items they wanted. In another transaction recorded at Deir el-Medina, a purchaser acquired a coffin in exchange for two goats, a pig, two logs of sycamore wood and a quantity of copper.

The system put a value on labour as well as materials. In one transaction, making a wooden bed 'cost' five sacks of grain, decorating it cost one and a half sacks and stringing it cost one sack. The wood itself 'cost' three *deben*, meaning the finished article had a total value of seven and a half sacks of grain and three *deben* of copper, or ten and a half *deben*. It is interesting to compare the relative values of different commodities. A wooden bed, despite the workmanship involved, was worth only one-fifth of an ox, while a coffin was more expensive. Even in a society without money, prices reflected the laws of supply and demand. During the reign of Ramesses XI at the end of the New Kingdom, the mismanagement of state resources and attacks by marauding Libyans throughout the Theban area sent grain prices rocketing. The cost of a sack quickly doubled from one or two *deben* to four *deben*.

Deir el-Medina, despite being a closed community established and provisioned by the state, was as economically active as any society. The favoured location for this activity was not the village itself but the riverbank, a good hour's walk away. Two Theban tombs illustrate the scene on market day. In one, workmen unload sacks of grain from a barge and exchange them for fish, loaves of bread and vegetables provided by women sitting on the riverbank with baskets of produce. The woman selling bread has brought an awning to shade a pair of amphorae: she seems to have been selling beer as well as bread. We can imagine the women of Deir el-Medina trudging down to the Nile with their bags and baskets to set up their stalls ready for the arrival of a ship.

A second tomb depicts a more structured form of economic activity, as Syrian merchants unload their wares and conduct deals with men in booths. The latter are clearly professional traders, though it is not clear whether they are acting on their own account or as agents of a temple or government institution. One of them is shown sitting on a low stool, gesticulating towards a foreign purchaser and holding a pair of scales. Above him hang a number of fringed linen shawls and a pair of sandals. Another trader also holds a pair of scales and has a pair of sandals on a table in front of him, with another pair hanging above his head.

There were two reasons why traders had sandals as part of their stock. First, they were items that everyone used and hence a common currency that could be used in just about any trans-action. Second, over a period of 150 years, the price of a pair of sandals remained remarkably stable – it was dictated by the negligible cost of materials, the standard amount of labour required to make a pair and tradition – making them a reliable form of currency. *The Satire of the Trades* mocked the lowly sandal maker:

> The sandal maker is sorely afflicted
> among his vats of oil.

He prospers, if one prospers among corpses,
for he chews leather.⁵

However, everyone needed his products. Finds from the work-men's village at Amarna included a wooden pattern for cutting the shape of a sole from a sheet of leather, and a sandal with red and green decoration.

Carter recorded no fewer than ninety-three fragments of sandals from Tutankhamun's tomb, ranging from a pair in sheet gold adorning the king's mummy to thirty-two simple rushwork pairs scattered throughout the Annexe. There are examples decorated with wood and marquetry designs, and others with needlework representations of Nubian and Asiatic prisoners, so that each time the king took a step he would symbolically crush his enemies underfoot. He also had several elegant pairs of leather sandals that were embellished with gold or multicoloured beads. As *The Times* reported during the clearance of the tomb:

When these sandals have been restored, they will be among the most wonderful articles in all the mass of extraordinary works of art, and I fully expect that in a few years' time we shall see our smartest ladies wearing footgear more or less resembling and absolutely inspired by these wonderful things.⁶

⊲◦▷

Sandals also featured on a decorated block from Hermopolis that came from a temple at Amarna. It depicts a pair of houses on the riverbank; in one of them, a bedroom is identified by a pair of sandals next to a bed. As we have seen, larger dwell-ings in ancient Egypt often had a dedicated bedroom. Archaeologically, they are identifiable by the fact that they contain an alcove for a single bed – there is no evidence of double beds in ancient Egypt. Examples of actual beds have survived from tombs of all periods. Like chairs, they seem to have been status symbols; in both cases, furniture indicated that its owner had risen to new social heights.

When Tutankhamun's grandfather, Amenhotep III, wished to cement diplomatic relations with the Babylonian king Kadashman-Enlil, he sent gifts of furniture for the king's new palace that included

One bed of ebony, overlaid with ivory and gold; three beds of ebony, overlaid with gold.[7]

Egyptian furniture was evidently highly prized throughout the ancient world. Two generations later, Tutankhamun's tomb was provided with nine beds. Three of them are ritual couches that were used in funeral ceremonies, made of gilded wood with sides in the form of protective animal deities. The other six are designed for daily use, with short legs and a footboard. One of the beds was covered with stucco and gold leaf and may have been made for the tomb, but Carter believed that the other five had been used during the king's lifetime. One of them was an ingenious folding model, the only example of a travelling bed to survive from ancient Egypt.

Made of a lightweight wood, the 179-centimetre-long bed folds twice for ease of transport and storage, emphasizing the pharaohs' peripatetic lifestyle. All the legs – including four in the middle that provide added rigidity – are shaped like lion's feet, and the footboard is panelled. The bed, like all examples from ancient Egypt, is higher at the head than at the foot. It stands just thirty centimetres above the ground – Egyptian beds, like chairs and stools, seem to have been considerably lower than their modern counterparts. They were generally placed on small stone mounts, which would have provided

Fig. 23. Folding bed.

extra height and helped to deter termites. For added protection from these wood-eating insects, Tutankhamun's travelling bed was originally painted with limewash.

While kings and high officials slept in their favourite bed with pillows and fine linen sheets, their lowlier compatriots generally slept on mats on the floor, huddled around the hearth in the central living room – in an Egyptian winter, night-time temperatures can drop close to freezing. Although sheep and goats were common in the Nile Valley, it is not known to what extent the Egyptians made woollen textiles. A few examples have survived, including from the workmen's village at Amarna, but more often, it seems, people made do with linen sheets reinforced with extra strips of cloth. In the summer months, by contrast, an entire family sleeping together in the same room would have been uncomfortably hot; people would therefore have slept on the roof, reached by a narrow staircase from the back of the house.

Of course, beds and bedrooms were not just for sleeping: the confined spaces and densely packed houses of ancient

Egyptian settlements brought families and neighbours into close proximity and provided abundant opportunities for love and sex – both within and outside marriage. At the romantic end of the spectrum, a number of love songs have survived from the community of Deir el-Medina. Written from both a female and a male perspective, they are characterized by the use of yearning language and colourful imagery:

> My sister has come!
> My heart thrills, my arms stretch out to embrace her.
> My heart is carefree in its place,
> Like a goldfish in its pond.
> Oh night, you are mine for ever,
> Since (my) mistress has come to me.[8]

But alongside love and romance, baser human instincts also enjoyed free rein. Adultery does not seem to have been a punishable offence under ancient Egyptian law, but it was certainly disapproved of. As a popular work of moral instruction urged its listeners:

> If you wish a friendship to last,
> when you enter a house,
> as master, brother or friend,
> whatever place you enter,
> beware of approaching the women! [. . .]
> He who is undone through lust,
> none of his plans will succeed.[9]

Moreover, adultery was often associated with criminality. The chief workman Paneb, who lived in Deir el-Medina at the end of the nineteenth dynasty, had affairs with at least three married women and was also involved in theft, tomb robbing and desecration. Eventually his crimes caught up with him, and his own son testified against him with accusations of adultery and fornication.

The full range of sexual misdemeanours is listed in the work known as the 'Negative Confession' in Chapter 125 of the *Book of the Dead*, in which the deceased lists a range of sins he claims never to have committed. Alongside slander, fraud and murder, they include fornication and, specifically, penetrative sex with a passive male partner. Indeed, homosexuality was evidently regarded by the ancient Egyptians as being on a par with adultery. The moralistic teaching quoted above goes into some detail:

> Do not have sex with a boy
> when you know that what is condemned will satisfy
>   his desire.
> There is no cooling his lust.
> Let him not spend the night doing what is
>   condemned:
> he will cool down (only) after he has mastered his
>   desire.[10]

A popular fable about an Old Kingdom ruler called Neferkara and his army commander Sasenet centred on the illicit affair between the king and the general, 'in whose entire house there was no wife'. The story describes how the king

> arrived at the house of General Sasenet. Then he threw a brick, and kicked (the wall), so that a [ladder?] was let down for him . . . Later, after His Majesty had done what he desired with him, he returned to his palace.[11]

The textual evidence for sex outside marriage is complemented by artistic sources. Alongside the officially sanctioned
art in tomb chapels, graffiti from Deir el-Medina and other
sites in Egypt include graphic illustrations of sexual intercourse; the most famous images are to be found on the
so-called 'Turin Erotic Papyrus', depicting a man with an
outsize erection copulating in a range of different positions.
A broadly contemporary medical papyrus includes among its
treatments the earliest known oral contraceptive, using celery
as the main pharmaceutical ingredient. All in all, the evidence
suggests that sex was not always practised with a view to
procreation, and that the lack of a dedicated bedroom in the
average ancient Egyptian home did not prevent opportunistic
couplings.

⋖•▭•⟩

The interpretation of dreams is associated in Western thought
with ancient Egypt through the biblical story of Joseph, with
his dream of seven lean and seven fat years. In fact, attempts
to explain subconscious narratives were long established in the
Nile Valley by the time the Old Testament was written.

According to legend, the kings of the late eighteenth dynasty
owed their position on the throne to a dream. In the middle
of the dynasty, the pharaoh Amenhotep II – known for his
feats of horsemanship – was blessed with a number of children,
including several sons. After his death, sibling rivalry seems to
have become internecine, and it was one of the younger sons,
Thutmose, who succeeded his father. But according to Thutmose,
the explanation for his unexpected ascendancy lay in a dream.
Like his father before him, Thutmose was a keen rider and
liked to exercise on the Giza Plateau, where there was a royal
rest house near the Great Sphinx. According to the inscription:

One of these days it happened that Prince Thutmose came travelling at the time of midday. He rested in the shadow of this great god. A wave of sleep seized him at the moment the sun was at its zenith. And he found the majesty of this noble god speaking from his own mouth like a father speaks to his son, saying: 'Look at me, see me, Thutmose my son. I am your father Horemakhet-Khepri-Ra-Atum. I shall give you the kingship on earth before the living . . . Behold, my condition is suffering; all my limbs are ruined. The sand of the desert, which I used to dominate, (now) overwhelms me. I have waited so that you might carry out what is in my heart.'[12]

On waking, Thutmose did what he had been asked and cleared the sand from around the Sphinx, building a retaining wall to keep the dunes at bay. According to the text, the statue was the embodiment of the triune creator god, uniting the sun at its rising, zenith and setting. In return for Thutmose's good deed, the Sphinx granted him the right to succeed his father as the next pharaoh. Thutmose IV had the story of his elevation to the kingship carved on a great stone slab between the Sphinx's paws. Thereafter, subsequent kings of the eighteenth dynasty, beginning with his son Amenhotep III, seem to have made a pilgrimage to the Sphinx in the first year of their reign, in order to legitimize their rule.

Another, more mundane text deals with the interpretation of everyday dreams. The dream book of Qenherkhepeshef, preserved in a papyrus from the nineteenth dynasty, is likely to have been composed nearly a thousand years earlier, if the style of its language is a reliable guide. It lists a series of different dreams, with the word 'good' or 'bad' alongside each, plus an interpretation of the meaning. So, for example, 'If a man sees himself in a dream sitting in a garden in the sun – good: it means pleasure,' but 'If a man sees himself in a dream shod with white sandals – bad: it means roaming the earth.'[13] The dream book takes the same form as 'calendars of lucky and unlucky days', or horoscopes, which also date back to the twelfth dynasty. It should be seen alongside references to seers and oracles as indicative of a rich body of superstition. For the ancient Egyptians, oracles, letters to the dead, protective spells and other occult practices played a central role in people's lives, helping them to feel in control in the face of an unpredictable environment.

The perceived ubiquity of malign forces led to a range of cultural practices, from naming conventions to 'birthing beds', where pregnant women could undergo labour and childbirth in a ritually cleansed, protected space. But perhaps the most widespread custom to fend off evil spirits was the wearing of amulets, which took a dizzying range of forms, depending on the threat to be countered or the protection to be desired. A snake's head amulet would protect against snake bites and a scorpion against scorpion stings. An image of the god Imhotep would provide healing power and the knot of Isis protection. A set square would ensure rectitude, while the sign for 'million' would mean a long life. Most numerous of all are the amulets associated with fecundity and childbirth: the emblem of the fertility god Min and images of the household deities Bes and Taweret, a tilapia fish, the goddess Hathor and the infant god Harpocrates.

If birth was attended by a whole host of dangers, rebirth into the afterlife was believed to be an equally fraught process. When the priests embalmed Tutankhamun, they included an iron amulet in the form of a miniature headrest at the back of the king's golden mask. Its function was to prevent the deceased from losing his head, in accordance with a spell in the *Book of the Dead*:

Your head shall not be taken from you afterwards; your
head shall never be taken from you.[14]

In an early-nineteenth-dynasty funerary papyrus, a headrest is
listed alongside the heart, the knot of Isis and the pillar of
Osiris as crucial elements to assist the dead in the next world.

In daily life, a headrest was used instead of a pillow, its
concave upper surface padded with linen to support the head.
The most common material for everyday headrests was wood,
but more fragile materials could be employed for the afterlife.
Among the eight examples buried with Tutankhamun, one is
made of tinted ivory, with legs shaped like duck's heads; another
takes the form of the air god Shu, squatting between two lions
representing the horizon, thus emphasizing a symbolic connection between the head of the deceased and the rising sun. But
by far the most beautiful headrests are two of glass. One is
turquoise blue, with a band of gold leaf around the shaft;
another, in a rich lapis lazuli colour, is decorated with the king's
names and titles in gold leaf on the shaft and a gold foil edging.
In both cases, blue recalls the colour of the sky; to travel forever
across the heavens in the company of the sun god was the
dream of every pharaoh.

⊲◦⊳

The aforementioned dream book of Qenherkhepeshef is
written from an entirely male perspective. Some of the interpretations illustrate men's particular anxieties (for example,
of being cuckolded) and aspirations (succeeding one's father
and inheriting his offices), reflecting a gender bias in ancient
Egyptian sources. Indeed, maleness was the default gender
in pharaonic culture; the vast majority of surviving texts and
images were produced by men, for men.

Egyptian art reflected and reinforced the roles that the genders were expected to fulfil. It was assumed that men would marry, beget children and support a family. Decorated tomb chapels, prepared for male officials, depicted the ideal state of affairs from the man's perspective: the tomb owner is dominant, while his female relatives occupy minor supporting roles. In pair statues, the man is usually placed in the dominant position on the woman's right. Men are usually shown in an active pose, striding with their legs apart, while women are more often depicted standing passively with their feet together. Men are customarily rendered with reddish-brown skin that emphasizes their outdoor lifestyle, whereas women are shown with yellow or light brown skin, befitting people who spent their lives looking after the household. The fact that ancient Egyptian women engaged in many activities outside the home did not detract from the deeply held ideals of male and female roles. For the Egyptians, the epitome of an ordered civilization was one in which fathers handed down their jobs and positions to their sons, and this heavily gendered perspective started at the very top.

The institution of kingship was inherently male: there was no word in ancient Egyptian for 'queen'. Senior female members of the royal family were identified instead by reference to the male monarch – as 'king's mother' or 'king's wife' – even if, in reality, they exercised considerable political influence on their own account. This gender stereotyping determined every aspect of royal ideology. The king was the *son* of Ra, the *lord* of the Two Lands, the incarnation of the god Horus, the heir and champion of Osiris. So thoroughly masculine was every aspect of kingship that the accession of a female sovereign presented significant challenges to language and costume as well as theology. In the middle of the eighteenth dynasty, the female ruler Hatshepsut vacillated between using male and female titles, between depicting herself as a man and a woman, between calling herself 'son of Ra' and 'daughter of Amun'. Perhaps it was to overcome this inherent tension between her gender and her office that the circumlocution 'pharaoh' (*per-aa*, meaning 'great house' or 'palace') was invented to refer to the monarch.

One essential aspect of royal iconography that Hatshepsut could not wish away was the divine beard. As the gods' representative on earth, the king was often depicted wearing a long, curled beard that was the marker of divinity. The pharaoh may have even donned a false beard for certain important rituals. Statues of Hatshepsut often show her wearing a false beard strapped to a face that looks distinctly feminine. The contradiction must have jarred with her contemporaries, and it perhaps helps to explain why her posthumous memory was proscribed: the reign of a female king was too much of a departure from centuries of hallowed tradition.

The divine beard is a reminder that hair played a key role in reinforcing gender identity in ancient Egyptian culture and also had a religious dimension. As part of a priest's ritual purification, he would shave his head and probably his whole body before entering the temple. In a sacred context, facial and body hair were deemed unclean, and most men were clean-shaven in secular life, too. There was a brief fashion for thin moustaches in the third and early fourth dynasties, and high officials might grow a short goatee, but anything longer that might stray into divine territory was unconscionable.

The clean-shaven image was one of wholesome vitality and cleanliness, a counterpart to the idealized male physique that emphasized youth, virility and muscularity. The two come together in an eighteenth-dynasty Theban tomb scene of military conscription, which shows young men lining up to have their hair cut – short back and sides, like new recruits throughout history. Medical texts, written by and for the small literate elite, preserve several recipes for hair removal.

So important was the king's appearance that royal hairdressers formed part of the palace entourage from an early period. Their access, proximity and intimacy with the monarch gave them a high status in royal circles. One of the most elaborate and beautifully decorated Old Kingdom tombs at Saqqara was built for a man called Ty, a fifth-dynasty chief of the palace hairdressers. Another splendid monument of the same period was commissioned by the royal manicurists (and twin brothers), Niankhkhnum and Khnumhotep. While workmen were not infrequently shown with unkempt hair, their bosses and the king were always shown carefully coiffed.

The importance in ancient Egyptian elite culture of maintaining one's personal appearance is emphasized by the discovery of Tutankhamun's shaving set among his tomb equipment. A white-painted box, according to an ink inscription written on the lid, had once contained 'The equipment of His Majesty – life, prosperity, health! – when he was a child. Contents: copper-handled razors, knife razors, ewers, linen.' Much of the royal shaving gear had been carried off by tomb robbers, leaving behind just two cloth pads, a bundle of linen and the box's clay sealing. Carter recovered a knife razor from the Annexe floor and a further group of razors from the fill of the tomb's entrance corridor, perhaps dropped by the thieves as they made their escape.

Fig. 24. Razor.

Egyptians of both sexes generally kept their hair short, perhaps for comfort in a hot climate, but no doubt also to control against infestations of lice. This was particularly pertinent for children, whose heads were usually shaved, save for a single tress of hair hanging down one side, known as the 'sidelock of youth'. Short hair did not, however, prevent adults from sporting elaborate coiffures, thanks to the age-old custom of wearing wigs. Fashions came and went, ranging from short curled wigs to long straight ones; tripartite wigs were popular for a time, while in the eighteenth dynasty, the 'Nubian' style of tapering rows of tightly curled ringlets was all the rage. This variation in preference over time can be reliably used to date uninscribed reliefs and statues.

Although Tutankhamun is depicted on objects from his tomb wearing a variety of wigs and headpieces, none was discovered in the burial. However, when his mummy was unwrapped, his head had short hair and his face was clean-shaven. Even in death, a pharaoh had to look his best.

⋘○⋙

Just as both sexes sported wigs, ancient Egyptian men and women alike wore make-up. The adornment of the face with mineral pigments was a tradition that stretched back into prehistory and continued until the end of pharaonic civilization. No self-respecting upper- or middle-class Egyptian would have wished to be seen in public without at least some dark powder to emphasize the eyes and protect against the glare of the sun. The essential item of any make-up kit was a container and applicator for eye paint. Made from malachite or galena mixed with water or gum, kohl was kept in small tubes that were made from a range of materials, depending on the taste and wealth of the owner. Tutankhamun was buried with a sumptuous double kohl tube, twelve centimetres long and made of wood, glass and ivory. He also had a tiny tube, barely four centimetres long, bound together with two gold kohl sticks. They are likely to have been essential items on his royal dressing table.

Since the wearing of make-up was ubiquitous in ancient Egypt, it cannot be assumed that an unidentified grave containing a wealth of cosmetic equipment and jewellery necessarily belonged to a woman. Nevertheless, there are some gender differences between burials, with women's graves tending to contain fewer items than men's. In the time of Tutankhamun, the husband normally had a richer set of funerary equipment than his wife, often including an extra coffin. Where items were shared, the man was identified as the principal owner. This disparity is seen in the joint tomb of Tutankhamun's great-grandparents, Yuya and Tjuyu. They were both interred with a wealth of fine objects, but Yuya's were markedly richer and more numerous than his wife's.

In other ways, the late eighteenth dynasty must have been an exhilarating time to be a female member of Egypt's royal family. For much of the previous fifteen centuries of pharaonic civilization, women had been all but invisible in the official record and kept well away from any levers of power. The wives of the great pyramid-builders of the fourth dynasty, Khufu and Khafra, are ephemeral and poorly attested, and their successors of the twelfth dynasty are almost invisible. However, all that changed during the battles of liberation against the Hyksos at the start of the New Kingdom. In a time of national emergency, the womenfolk of the insurgent Theban royal family seem to have taken day-to-day charge of the administration while their husbands were fighting to regain Egyptian independence. A succession of queens from this period – Tetisheri, Ahhotep, Ahmose-Nefertari – loom large in the monuments and the pattern, once established, seems to have become part of the eighteenth dynasty's modus operandi.

Even the contested reign of Hatshepsut in the middle of the dynasty did not prevent succeeding generations of royal women from occupying positions of influence and power.

Amenhotep III granted his chief wife Tiye exceptional status. He even had a temple built for her at Sedeinga in Nubia, a counterpart to his edifice at nearby Soleb. The lavish burial provided for her parents in the Valley of the Kings further underscored her standing at court.

The model of a royal couple jointly exercising power was taken to a new level in the following reign. On monuments from Amarna, Nefertiti is shown at the same scale as her husband Akhenaten; in some reliefs, the outlines of husband and wife, sitting side by side, almost merge into one, suggesting that the couple are ruling as joint monarchs. Contemporary scenes of the wider royal family emphasize femininity: Akhenaten and Nefertiti's daughters are given great prominence, while royal sons (including Prince Tutankhaten) are entirely absent. So dominant were the women around Akhenaten that it can be plausibly argued that Tutankhaten's claim to the throne was based more on his marriage to his half-sister (one of Akhenaten and Nefertiti's daughters) than on his own descent in the male line from previous pharaohs.

Compared with other ancient Middle Eastern and Mediterranean societies, women in ancient Egypt had a uniquely visible and autonomous position. At the beginning of the eighteenth dynasty, a new office was created in the cult of the supreme state deity, to be held by one of the monarch's close female relatives. The post of 'God's Wife of Amun' ensured royal leverage over an increasingly wealthy and influential priesthood, but it also brought a feminine aspect to the religious life of the nation. Although women were not otherwise allowed to serve as priests, many wives of high officials held roles as temple singers or musicians. And the prominence in the New Kingdom of the cult of Hathor brought a more nurturing aspect to pharaonic religion than is apparent in earlier periods.

Perhaps the most striking indication of women's status in

ancient Egypt is seen in the realm of law. Uniquely for the ancient world, Egyptian women enjoyed equal legal status to men. Wives could testify against their husbands, divorce seems to have been relatively easy and common, and women maintained control over their own property, even after marrying. They were also free to dispose of their wealth as they wished. The legal autonomy of Egyptian women is highlighted in the will of Naunakht, from the twentieth dynasty. The woman in question describes herself as 'a free woman of the land of Pharaoh'. When it came to drawing up her testamentary wishes, she was determined to reward only those of her children who had been dutiful and supported her in her old age. She instructed the scribe to record her instructions unambiguously:

> I brought up these eight servants of yours and gave them
> a household – everything as is customarily done for those
> of their standing. But, look, I am grown old and, look,
> they do not care for me in turn. Whichever of them has
> given me a hand, to him will I give of my property;
> whichever has not, to him will I not give of my property.[15]

This picture of Egyptian women exercising control over their households is supported by evidence from the workers' village of Deir el-Medina that shows women occupying a variety of roles. They produced manufactured goods, bought and sold property, and transacted business. Love songs portray women as equal partners in relationships; some are written in women's voices and speak of women's desires. And in a community where the menfolk stayed away during the working week, it fell to women to run the household. As an eighteenth-dynasty instructional text warned its male listeners:

Do not control your wife in her house if you know she is efficient.[16]

Despite all this, ancient Egypt was still a patriarchal society. It was theologically impossible for a woman to be pharaoh. Only men could become government officials. And though women could exercise influence, they were constrained by a social order that was created largely by and for men. In the instructional text quoted above, the next section re-exerts a more stereotypical male perspective, portraying women as bad influences:

Do not go after a woman. Do not let her steal your heart.[17]

Elsewhere in the text, the same theme is developed at greater length:

Guard against a woman who is an outsider, who is not known in her town. Do not look at her when she passes by. Do not have carnal knowledge of her. A deep stretch of water of unknown course is a woman away from her husband! 'I am fair,' she says to you every day when there are no witnesses. She is ready to ambush you. It is a great and mortal vice when it is reported.[18]

Legal records from Deir el-Medina show that women were subject to violence and rape. That women were objectified by men is illustrated in a popular folk story, written in the Middle Kingdom but set in the Old Kingdom court of King Sneferu. In the *Tales of Wonder*, Sneferu plans a boating party but wishes the boats to be rowed by young women from the palace. As he instructs his staff:

> Let there be brought to me twenty women with beautiful
> bodies, deep-bosomed with braided hair, who still have
> their virgin bloom. Let there be brought to me twenty
> nets and give these nets to the women in place of their
> clothes.[19]

Ancient Egyptian women may have been better off than their
counterparts in other contemporary societies, but ingrained
attitudes and societal norms continued to favour men. In the
end, despite the prominent role played by female members of
the royal family throughout the eighteenth dynasty, it was
Tutankhamun and not his wife who gained the throne.

⊲○▷

The layout of ancient Egyptian houses – the front room for
receiving guests and producing handicrafts, the central room
for eating and sleeping, the back room for preparing food and
the roof for warm summer nights – tells us something about
the pattern of daily life. The surviving texts from Egyptian
settlements record transactions and disputes, shedding light on
aspects of the law, economy and society, while laundry lists and
love songs provide glimpses into the private lives of the Nile
Valley's inhabitants. But it is the material culture – the objects
made and handled by the ancient Egyptians – that provides
the richest and most tangible evidence, directly illustrating the
manufacture and processing of commodities, customs of dress
and appearance.

It is all too easy, when looking back on a society as distant
from our own as ancient Egypt, to highlight the exotic and the
unusual and draw the conclusion that the people were not the same
as us. Yet the objects of daily life that have survived the inter-
vening millennia speak of a society where people's hopes and
fears, loves and loathings, triumphs and tragedies were much the

Fig. 25. Game box and stand.

same as those of any human culture. The material remains of the Egyptians' leisure pursuits, diversions and pastimes provide a good illustration of this common ground. When the ancient citizens of Deir el-Medina, Amarna, Memphis or Thebes were not toiling in the fields or workshops, cooking or eating meals, looking after children or elderly relatives, praying or sleeping, they found time for enjoyment.

Although tomb decoration is usually rather serious in its depiction of an idealized state of affairs, a few jokes can be found in the accompanying inscriptions – even if they do not always translate well. The Turin Erotic Papyrus may be either pornographic or satirical; either way, it shows that the ancient Egyptians were not always serious or decorous. Another, more clearly satirical, papyrus shows animals carrying out a range of human activities, including playing board games. This was not an accidental choice, for such games were an integral part of pharaonic culture. In the late fourth millennium BC, when the hieroglyphic writing system was being formalized, individual signs representing familiar objects were adopted to stand for sounds or combinations of sounds. One such sign was a game board, which was chosen to stand for the combination of the letters m and n. The sign appears on a small label dating to the beginning of the first dynasty, and was thereafter one of the most common hieroglyphs. It was used, in combination with other signs, to write the name of the god Amun, and so became one of the most frequent signs in royal names – including that of Tutankhamun.

Scenes of men and women playing board games appear in Egyptian art from all periods, from the chapel of Mereruka in the fifth dynasty to the mortuary temple of Ramesses III in the twentieth. Tutankhamun was buried with at least four complete game boards and portions of two more. One of the finest objects from the entire tomb is an inlaid game box and stand, found in the Annexe. The whole piece is forty-four centimetres long and a masterpiece of the cabinet maker's craft. The box is made from a relatively poor-quality wood but is veneered in Nubian ebony. It sits on a four-legged ebony stand, with each leg shaped like a lion's foot with ivory claws. The stand, in turn, rests on a sledge. The sides and ends of the box are inscribed with hieroglyphs giving the king's name and titles, while the upper and lower surfaces are veneered with ivory, onto which raised strips of wood have been glued to mark out the board. Ingeniously, the box provides for two different games: one surface is marked out for the game of *djau* ('walls'), also known as 'twenty squares', and the other for a game called *senet* ('passing'). The box has an integral drawer – found empty when it was discovered – that would originally have contained ivory 'knuckle bones' and casting sticks of ebony and ivory. These were used, in the manner of modern dice, to determine the number of places a player would advance on each turn.

The game of *djau* was of Asiatic origin and seems to have

reached the Nile Valley as a result of imperial expansion in the eighteenth dynasty. The board was marked out with three rows of squares: four squares in each of the outer rows and twelve in the middle one. Three of the squares were marked with special symbols and were unlucky. Each player was allotted five pieces and the aim was to remove them all from the board while avoiding the unlucky squares and one's opponent's pieces.

Senet was a much older game, possibly dating back to the dawn of Egyptian history. It was played with pieces shaped like cotton reels; one player had white pieces, the other red. No full account of the rules has survived, but it is clear that a player could block or capture an opponent's pieces. Pieces were moved in a backwards S-shape from the top-right to the bottom-left of the board, towards the final five squares that were marked with either the sign for 'good' or the sign for 'water'. If landed on, these brought the player advantage or disadvantage, for example, by requiring them to miss a turn. The aim of the game was, like backgammon, to remove one's pieces from the board before one's opponent.

The inclusion of board games in a tomb was not merely an indication of their popularity in ancient Egypt; like all aspects of mortuary provision, there was also a religious connotation. *Senet*, with its characteristics of trials, pitfalls and the hope of ultimate victory, was an appropriate metaphor for the journey to the afterlife and the last judgement. A spell from the *Book of the Dead*, if properly incanted, allowed the deceased to leave the tomb in order to play *senet*, but only if he answered a series of trick questions and identified himself with the gods. Tutankhamun's board games were interred with him not just to provide a pleasant diversion in the next world, but to ensure that he got there at all.

Whether king, courtier or commoner, there is no doubting the sense of belonging felt by most ancient Egyptians to their family and community. For the majority of peasant farmers, their local neighbourhood was the only place they knew well. There might have been the occasional trip to a nearby village to barter for supplies, or to the provincial capital to pay taxes or petition the governor, but the overwhelming proportion of their lives would have been spent within half a day's walk from home. For wealthier individuals, like the traders depicted in New Kingdom tomb scenes or government officials, trips further afield may have been more frequent. And for those courtiers in the king's service, frequent travel was part of the job. But for all Egyptians, great or poor, there was no place like home.

The inhabitants of Deir el-Medina took pride in their community's history and status. They honoured its founders, King Amenhotep I and Queen Ahmose-Nefertari, observed their festivals and felt privileged to be part of a continuing tradition of royal service. In the nineteenth and twentieth dynasties, an entire genre of literature known as 'Praise of Cities' grew up extolling the major settlements of the land, Thebes included:

> See, I do not wish to leave Thebes;
> I have been taken against my will.
> I will dance again when I sail north,
> When Thebes is with me again,
> And the domain of Amun is all around me.[20]

The *Book of the Dead* also reflected the importance of local identity and the bonds that connected an individual, his home town and his local god, in this case with a paean of praise to the capital city, Memphis:

I have come today from the city of my god: Memphis.
It is truly the most beautiful of all the provinces in this
land. Its god is the lord of truth, the lord of food, rich
in costly things. All lands come to it: Upper Egypt sails
downstream to it, Lower Egypt with sail and oar, to
make it festive every day, as its god has commanded. No
one who dwells in it says, 'Would that I had!'[21]

This sentiment was also given practical expression. During the
civil war of the First Intermediate Period, provincial governors
up and down the Nile Valley strove to protect their own patch
from attack and from the effects of civil strife and famine. Men
such as Iti of Imyotru and Ankhtifi of Moalla claimed to have
fed their communities when the surrounding regions were
starving. Fifteen centuries later, during the invasion of Egypt
by the Persians, a man named Wedjahorresnet from Sais – a
delta city in the front line of the Persian advance – was able
to use his diplomatic skills to prevent the desecration of his
local temple. In his autobiographical inscription, he proudly
recounts how

The Great King of every foreign land, Cambyses, came
to Egypt, the foreigners of every foreign land with him.
He conquered this land in its entirety; and they settled
themselves in it . . . I caused His Majesty to understand
the greatness of Sais . . . and the greatness of the temple
of Neith . . . I petitioned the Majesty of the Dual King
Cambyses concerning all the foreigners who had settled
in the temple of Neith, to have them expelled from it
and thus restore the temple of Neith to its former effectiveness . . . His Majesty did this because I had caused
His Majesty to appreciate the greatness of Sais. For it is
the city of all the gods.[22]

When Egypt was invaded by a Persian army for a second time, in the fourth century BC, followed swiftly by its conquest by Alexander the Great, the high priest of Hermopolis, Padiusir, was similarly moved to protect his local community and its holy places. He wished to be remembered as having been 'loyal to the lord of Hermopolis from the moment of my birth' and 'a follower of his god unto death!'[23]

There were sound, pragmatic reasons for making such a boast. Texts of moral instruction repeatedly stressed the importance of behaving properly 'in a town you know well'.[24] Moreover, charity began at home, and in a close-knit community, everyone depended on their neighbours:

> If praiseworthy acts are performed,
> friends will say, 'Welcome'.
> Supplies are not brought to a town,
> but friends are fetched in a time of grief.[25]

Alongside a duty towards family and friends and a sense of belonging to the local community, there is also evidence of regional identities in ancient Egypt. This is hardly surprising, given the geographic extent of the country and the cultural differences between the Mediterranean north and the African south. In the most perennially popular of all ancient Egyptian stories, *The Tale of Sinuhe*, the eponymous hero's confusion is described as being 'like a delta-dweller seeing himself in Elephantine, (or) a man of the marshes in Nubia'.[26] Regional dialects, apparent in the Coptic phase of the Egyptian language, are harder to discern in the hieroglyphic script, but there are occasional references to the difficulties in understanding someone from a different part of the Nile Valley. In one New Kingdom letter, the writer lambasts his correspondent's musings as being 'so confused when heard that no interpreter can understand them. They are like a delta man's conversation with a man of Elephantine.'[27]

Trumping both local and regional affiliations, however, was the question of national identity. By comparison with other ancient civilizations, the Egyptians had a particularly well developed sense of their own distinctiveness, which they believed was god-given. As Akhenaten's *Great Hymn to the Orb* addressed the creator:

You put every man in his place . . .
Their tongues differ in speech, their characters likewise.
Their skins are different, because you made the
        foreigners distinct.[28]

This is remarkably even-handed for a royal text – pharaonic ideology generally contrasted the blessed state of the Egyptians with the unfortunate predicament of all other peoples. Xenophobia was part of the official discourse, even if, in reality, people from elsewhere were able to settle and succeed in the Nile Valley. In the reign of Akhenaten, a man of Asiatic ancestry called Aper-El rose to become vizier while retaining his Canaanite name. Another high official of the New Kingdom, Maiherpri, achieved success despite his Nubian ethnicity. He is shown with black skin and curly hair on his funerary papyrus, but in all other respects he is depicted as the quintessential Egyptian courtier. Fundamentally, to adopt Egyptian cultural norms was to be accepted as an Egyptian, whatever one's ethnic background or skin colour.

What did an ancient Egyptian see when he or she looked in the mirror? Tutankhamun's treasures included two elaborate mirror cases of gilded wood; the mirrors themselves, presumably made of polished gold or silver, had been carried off by tomb robbers in antiquity. The first case, found in the cartouche-shaped box, is shaped like an *ankh*, the sign for 'life' but also the word for 'mirror'. The interior is lined with silver and the lid is decorated with the king's throne name, picked out in coloured glass and semi-precious stones, with further bands of hieroglyphs in raised relief. The second case presents an even more elaborate set of symbols: lined with gold, it has a handle fashioned to resemble the god Heh (the symbol for 'million'), holding palm branches ('years') resting on gilded tadpoles ('100,000') and the ring sign ('eternity'). The whole object thus wished the king an eternity of years when he looked at his reflection. By contrast, when one of Tutankhamun's subjects looked in the mirror, the ideal reflection would have been rather more down to earth, if no less heartfelt: a family man or woman and a valued member of the community, respected by their fellows and happy with their lot – a picture of contented domesticity.

SEVEN

Humanity

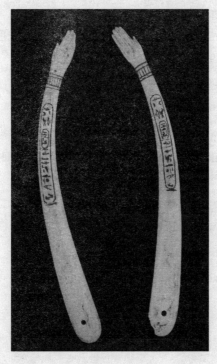

Fig. 26. Ivory clappers.

Just as the domestic surroundings of all ancient Egyptians had much in common, life in the ancient Nile Valley was full of dangers and challenges for everyone, from the pharaoh to his lowliest subject. Despite its cultural sophistication, pharaonic civilization was a pre-modern society, with all the poverty, hunger and disease that entailed. Because of its high infant mortality rate, ancient Egypt surrounded childbirth with a host of rituals and superstitions, yet many mothers and babies did not survive the ordeal. Average life expectancy was low, so childhood was comparatively short. Formal education was the preserve of a tiny elite; most sons would learn a trade from their father, most daughters the skills of household management from their mother. After reaching puberty, marriage was the next significant rite of passage. The ancient Egyptians seem to have had a surprisingly 'modern' attitude to cohabitation, but they valued relationships as much as any society; living in extended families, the bonds between grandparents and grandchildren were often particularly strong. Despite the best efforts of medics and magicians, illness, deformity and death were constant companions, and few ancient Egyptians survived into old age. The objects from the tomb of Tutankhamun, though amassed for a young man in his teens, reflect every stage of life from infancy to maturity; though made for a god king, they are infused with humanity.

The first trial of life that faced every Egyptian was simply being born. The death of a child, during or shortly after its birth, was an all too common experience for families throughout the land. Because of the dangers of childbirth – for the mother as well as the baby – the process was attended by a host of special ceremonies and rituals with the aim of giving the woman and her unborn child the best chance of survival.

While religious ideology demanded a mythological explanation of how babies were made – typically involving the ram-headed god Khnum forming a baby from clay on his potter's wheel – even the accounts of 'divine birth' promulgated by Hatshepsut and Amenhotep III referenced the act of procreation; in both cases, the god Amun is said to have assumed the form of the pharaoh's biological father while paying a night-time visit to the mother. The New Kingdom text known as *The Tale of the Doomed Prince* is more explicit; when the gods grant a childless king his wish for a son, nature takes its course:

> That night he slept with his wife, and she [became] pregnant. When she had completed the months of child-bearing, a son was born.[1]

The surviving medical texts include a specialist gynaecological papyrus and a raft of pregnancy tests. Some of these are fanciful but others are rooted in common sense and everyday observation: taking a woman's pulse, observing the colour of her skin and eyes, testing her propensity to vomit. If they could afford to do so, pregnant women were advised to massage their bellies with oil, both to prevent stretch marks and to ease labour. During the eighteenth dynasty, oil intended for this purpose was sometimes stored in special travertine containers shaped like naked pregnant women.

Some of the vessels have features redolent of Taweret, the goddess of fertility and childbirth, who was generally depicted as a pregnant hippopotamus.

There is no known reference in any ancient Egyptian text to a nine-month gestation period, but the usual length of a pregnancy would have been common knowledge. When a mother was about to go into labour, she and a small number of close female attendants would withdraw into a special confinement pavilion. Some of the workers' houses in the village of Deir el-Medina had a permanent 'birthing bed' in their front room; hung with sheets, this would have constituted an appropriate space for the mother's confinement. In wealthier households, a temporary pavilion of wooden poles and linen shrouds would have been erected on the roof or in the court-yard. Scenes from Deir el-Medina and its counterpart at Amarna, the workmen's village, suggest that the pavilion may have been draped with convolvulus and grape vines – symbols of fertility and abundance – and hung with garlands of flowers for decoration and perfume.

The most extensive description of childbirth from ancient Egypt is a fictional account in the *Tales of Wonder*. In one of the tales, a woman called Ruddjedet gives birth to three sons who are destined to reign as kings of the fifth dynasty. The opening lines of the story describe her confinement:

> One of those days, Ruddjedet was suffering the pains of childbirth. And the Majesty of Ra, lord of Sakhbu, said to Isis, Nephthys, Meskhenet, Heqet and Khnum, 'Go forth and let Ruddjedet give birth to three children who are in her womb' . . . Then they arrived at the house of Rauser . . . Then he said to them, 'My ladies, look: the woman is suffering the pains of childbirth.' Then they said, 'Let us see her! Look, we know about childbirth.'

Then he said to them, 'Go in,' and they entered in before
Ruddjedet. Then they sealed the room with her and them
inside.[2]

In this story, Ruddjedet is accompanied by a series of deities
disguised as travelling musicians. The choice of gods and
goddesses is no accident: Isis was revered as the mother of
Horus, whose earthly incarnation every Egyptian king claimed
to be; Nephthys was Isis's sister, and ideally suited to support
her in her motherly duties; Meskhenet was the personification
of the birth brick (see below), and was customarily depicted
as a woman wearing the uterus of a cow on her head; Heqet
was a frog goddess particularly associated with fertility and
childbirth. And Khnum, as we have already seen, was a
craftsman god who fashioned people – and especially kings
– on his potter's wheel.

In real life, an expectant mother's confinement was accompanied by a host of rites to 'cleanse' the pavilion and keep
out malign forces. Some of the strangest artefacts to survive
from these contexts are curved ivory wands, incised with
images of Taweret, Bes and various mythical beasts. The mother's attendants, as well as sweeping the area with wands and
uttering protective spells, may have sung and made loud noises
to scare away any evil spirits. Sacred rattles or sistra were a
favourite percussion instrument on such occasions, as were
ivory clappers. A pair of the latter, similar to castanets, was
found in Tutankhamun's tomb, perhaps signifying the close
connection in ancient Egyptian thought between birth and
rebirth. Each clapper is shaped like a human arm and fifteen
centimetres in length. A hole at the shoulder end would have
allowed the pair to be strung together and shaken to produce
a rhythmic sound. Tutankhamun's clappers bear the names of
his grandmother Tiye and his half-sister Meritaten, empha-

sizing the association with womenfolk and women's concerns. They may have been used by or for Tutankhamun's female relatives.

A private house at Amarna yielded a more down-to-earth collection of objects related to childbirth. In a cupboard under the stairs, four items were found that had clearly been put away for safe keeping, to be brought out when a birth was expected. The collection comprised a small stela showing a woman and girl worshipping Taweret, a terracotta figurine of a naked woman with prominent breasts and hair bound in two tight tresses, and a pair of painted pottery beds. Other sources confirm that an expectant mother's hair would be tightly bound; releasing it at the time of birth was thought to ease the labour.

Once all the magical rites had been performed, everything was ready for the birth itself. The *Tales of Wonder* describe the culmination of Ruddjedet's labour:

> Then Isis took up position in front of her, Nephthys behind her, while Heqet hastened the birth . . . And this child slipped out into her arms, a child of one cubit, with strong bones . . . And they washed him, when his umbilical cord had been cut, and placed him on a pillow of cloth.[3]

Other textual and artistic evidence shows that Egyptian women gave birth squatting on a pair of birth bricks, as is still the case in some developing countries. The only surviving example of such a brick was discovered in the ruins of a thirteenth-dynasty mayor's house at south Abydos. Measuring thirty-five centimetres long by seventeen centimetres wide, it was originally decorated on all six sides. The decoration on the base shows a scene that chimes perfectly with the description in the *Tales of Wonder*, albeit with the various stages of childbirth merged into a single tableau: the mother cradles a newborn baby; a female attendant stands behind her, touching the back of her head; another attendant kneels in front of the mother, holding out her arms ready to catch the newborn child. Behind each attendant stands an emblem of Hathor; and the goddess's sacred colour, turquoise blue, is used for the hair of all three female figures. The edges of the brick are decorated with magical motifs, including a serval cat, a cobra, a baboon, lions and a human enemy being decapitated. The upper face of the brick has crumbled away, but it is even possible to identify the woman to whom it may have belonged: a king's daughter named Reniseneb, who lived in the mayor's house and was presumably married to a mayor.

Once a woman's child had been delivered, her confinement lasted a further fourteen days. With another round of ritual purification completed, she was ready to re-emerge into the world, after which the equally challenging business of parent-hood began.

⊂⚬⊃

In the streets of south Abydos around the house where the birth brick was found, many of the dwellings harboured the tragic secret of an infant buried beneath the floor of a back room, while houses in the contemporary settlement of Kahun sometimes yielded two or three infant burials to a box. In the Theban hills above the village of Deir el-Medina, a New Kingdom cemetery contained over a hundred children buried in everything from pottery jars and baskets to chests and coffins, depending on the resources of their grieving family. The poorest graves were generally those of newborn babies, such as that of a little boy named Iryky whose deformities – an abnormally large head and torso, and stunted limbs – mean that he is unlikely to have survived many hours after being born.

Fig. 27. Mummified bodies of Tutankhamun's stillborn daughters.

At least little Iryky received a name. Even more unfortunate were the two infant daughters of Tutankhamun and Ankhesenamun, neither of whom lived to see the light of day. As Carter was clearing the Treasury, he came across a simple, undecorated wooden box, with no docket or inscription. Inside were two tiny coffins, and each held a second coffin. Inside each of the inner coffins was a tiny mummified body. Both were simply labelled as 'Osiris' (meaning 'deceased'), suggesting that the babies were stillborn. Modern examination of the mummies using a CT scanner has revealed details of their short, tragic lives. One baby had been seven months in the womb and still had its umbilical cord attached. Its sex could not be established with certainty, but it is likely to have been female. Though the little girl was not a full-term birth, she had been provided with a funerary mask of gilded cartonnage. The second baby was definitely a girl, and nearly full-term; a short length of umbilical cord remained, suggesting she died during or immediately after birth. The two stillborn daughters of the boy pharaoh and his young wife marked the end of the eighteenth-dynasty royal line. As Carter remarked, 'had one of those babes lived, there might never have been a Rameses'.[4]

Such tragedies were all too common in Tutankhamun's Egypt. One of his older sisters, Meketaten, seems to have died in childbirth: a scene in her tomb chamber at Amarna shows her lying on her deathbed, mourned by her parents, while a lady-in-waiting holds a babe in her arms. As a contemporary instructional text warned:

When death comes, he takes the child in its mother's arms as well as the old.[5]

If a baby survived birth and its first few hours of life, it would be breastfed for as long as three years. The aforementioned text urged its male listener to be thankful to his mother:

Double the food your mother gave you; support her as she supported you. She had a heavy burden in you, but she did not abandon you. When you were born at your due time, she was still yoked (to you). Her breast was in your mouth for three years as you grew and your excrement disgusted (her).[6]

The large number of surviving scenes of mothers suckling their infants shows how important the practice was. Breastfeeding may have been seen as a form of birth control, and it certainly provided a baby with safer, more reliable nutrition than anything else that was available. Special pottery vessels, shaped and decorated to resemble a nursing mother, were made to store breast milk; their capacity, at around one-tenth of a litre, would have accommodated roughly the amount produced by one breast at one feed.

One notable feature of ancient Egyptian family life was the frequent use of a wet nurse to suckle a newborn baby, leaving the mother free to undertake other duties. Wet nurses seem to have been employed at all strata of society. An economic text from Deir el-Medina records the payment made by a community scribe to both a doctor and a wet nurse following his wife's confinement. Interestingly, the wet nurse received thirty and a half *deben*, compared to twenty-two *deben* for the doctor. It is possible that the wet nurse was being remunerated for suckling all three of the family's children; but the amount nevertheless indicates that it was a respected and lucrative occupation.

Royal babies were invariably looked after by wet nurses. Notwithstanding the myth that the king was suckled by a goddess, the royal wet nurses who carried out the task could achieve renown for their efforts, in addition to advancement for their own children, who grew up alongside the future monarch. A scene in the tomb of the eighteenth-dynasty high official Qenamun shows his mother nursing the future Amenhotep II, who is depicted sitting on her lap in full royal regalia. Qenamun's glittering career owed much to his mother's nursing duties. In a similar vein, Tutankhamun's successor Ay seems to have gained prominence because his wife Teye had been wet nurse to the future queen Nefertiti. Indeed Ay sported the title 'God's father', to indicate that he was, through his wife's efforts, effectively the king's father-in-law.

One of the most important archaeological discoveries of the 1990s was the tomb of Tutankhamun's wet nurse, the lady Maia.

A relief shows her with the young Tutankhamun on her lap, his pet dog beneath her chair. She bore the titles 'royal nurse' and 'the one who fed the god's body', and she is referred to as 'beloved of the Lord of the Two Lands', emphasizing the bond between nurse and infant. Interestingly, Maia was buried at Saqqara, the necropolis that served the administrative capital at Memphis, which may indicate that Tutankhamun spent some of his childhood away from his father's residence at Amarna.

When not being fed, babies were carried by their mothers or nurses in linen slings, worn at the front, side or back of the body. Nubians, by contrast, apparently employed baskets, carried on the back. In ancient Egypt, as in the modern Nile Valley, motherhood gave a woman a role and status in society that was universally admired. As the instructional text put it:

> When, as a young man, you take a wife and settle down
> in your (own) house, pay attention to your child. Educate
> him in every respect as your mother did. Do not give
> her cause to blame you, lest she raise her hands to god
> and he hears her cries.[7]

Fathers also achieved social status as a result of having children. The ancient Egyptian ideal was for a man to pass on his office to his son, and many surviving inscriptions refer to the blessings and challenges of fatherhood:

> If you are a man of virtue
> and produce a son by god's grace;
> if he is upright and takes after you,
> looks after your possessions in their proper place:
> do for him every good thing,
> for he is your son, your spirit fathered him.[8]

If a man's son takes heed of what his father says,
no plan of his will go wrong.
So teach your son to be a (good) listener.[9]

While every Egyptian father wished for a son, there is evidence that daughters were also much loved. A text from Deir el-Medina records the absence of one of the workmen who was attending the 'feast of his daughter', suggesting that children's birthdays were marked as family occasions. Had Tutankhamun's daughters survived, no doubt he would have shown them the same affection.

⟨ː⟩

If a baby in ancient Egypt survived its first few weeks of life, it was doing well. And if a boy or girl made it through childhood without succumbing to accident or disease, they could count themselves fortunate. Children of all ages were so vulnerable that they were surrounded by magic and religion from birth. Very often, the name given to a child sought to afford it divine protection. Amuletic charms would be placed around babies' necks to ward off malign forces. Sometimes they took the form of cylindrical tubes containing rolled-up scraps of papyrus; parents would ask their local oracle for a decree granting the child a long and healthy life, which would be recorded on papyrus and worn as a good luck charm.

Once a child was no longer a toddler, they became a useful extra pair of hands for many families. In a society where the overwhelming majority of the population were subsistence farmers or craftspeople, families relied on their children to carry out simple tasks in the fields, in the workshop and around the house. Scenes in private Pyramid Age tombs show young boys watching over flocks of sheep or tending cattle, as Egyptian children in rural villages do today. Boys could also help out by chasing birds away during the grain harvest, collecting firewood for fuel, carrying drinking vessels for herdsmen or passing on messages for their brothers and parents. In a provincial sixth-dynasty tomb, a kitchen scene shows a cook stirring the pot while his assistant eats. The latter asks a young boy to run an errand, and the boy answers, 'I'll do it!'

While boys were out in the fields, girls would generally stay at home and help their mothers and older sisters with household chores. In one of the Tombs of the Nobles at Thebes, boys and girls are shown gleaning, picking up missed ears of grain once the reapers have passed, and putting them in baskets. In two other tombs of the same period, girls – probably the daughters of household servants – are shown making up beds for the master and mistress of the house. Boys and girls alike would have been expected to pull their weight from a young age.

However much work children in ancient Egypt were tasked with, there was plenty of time for play. There were places to explore, friends to meet and opportunities to get into scrapes. An eighteenth-dynasty painting shows a boy and a girl being admonished by a doorkeeper whom they have been teasing, while their exhausted nanny drinks from a jar of beer. To keep children out of mischief, they were given simple toys to play with. The earliest examples have been found in predynastic graves. A child's burial at Nagada, north of Thebes, contained a set of stone skittles, four stone balls and a 'gate' of stone bars through which the balls had to be rolled. The set, which employed a variety of costly materials – travertine, breccia, porphyry and marble – must have belonged to the child of a wealthy family.

Ball games seem to have been popular throughout pharaonic history. Middle Kingdom tombs show girls juggling with balls, while a satirical sketch from Deir el-Medina shows a mouse engaging in the same activity. In the ruins of Kahun, balls were found made from wood and from pieces of leather sewn together and stuffed with dried grass or barley husks. One such ball had been restitched, indicating that it was a treasured toy. Kahun also produced a series of wooden spinning tops, ranging in height from barely two centimetres to more than seven centimetres, as well as 'tipcats', wooden sticks pointed at both ends that were thrown into the air and hit as far as possible with a stick or club. The excavator of Kahun found a dwelling containing painted wooden puppets and a large stock of doll's hair made from fine linen fibres; he dubbed it 'the toymaker's shop'.

The most intricate children's toys preserved from ancient Egypt are wooden models of various kinds. Girls' graves from sites close to Kahun have yielded remarkable examples, including a doll with moveable arms and a set of dancing dwarfs to which strings would have been attached to move their limbs like marionettes. A crocodile with a moveable lower jaw is known from elsewhere in Egypt, as is a lion with a moveable jaw, eyes of rock crystal and bronze teeth. Since Tutankhamun was around nine or ten years old when he came to the throne and little more than eighteen when he died, it seems appropriate that one of the many boxes buried with him should have been his toy chest. Its internal compartments and drawers contained a random selection of objects, including a game board, a pair of slings and a fire-making set. In these few simple toys, we seem to come closer to the real-life Tutankhamun.

For children whose families could not afford toys, there were always games. Ancient Egyptian paintings generally show boys and girls playing separately, as is still the case in school playgrounds the world over. A particularly rich source of evidence is the decorated tomb of Ptahhotep, a high official of the fifth dynasty buried at Saqqara. The walls of his chapel depict boys playing a range of games, some of which are still played in the Nile Valley some four and a half thousand years later. There is the 'star game', which involves two boys standing in the centre of a group and stretching out their arms to hold two (or sometimes four) other boys, who lean back and are spun round as quickly as possible. There is a game akin to modern cheer-leading, where three boys carry a fourth on their shoulders. And there is the game known in modern Egypt as *khazza lawizza* ('jumping over the goose'), whereby two boys sit face to face and stretch out their arms and legs to form a hurdle over which another boy has to jump. A fifth-dynasty statue from Giza shows a game of leapfrog – played, unusually, by a boy and girl; also from Giza comes an illustration of what has been dubbed 'the hut game', where children have to escape from an imaginary enclosure without being caught.

For ancient Egyptian children, the moment soon arrived when it was time to put away childish things and undergo the rite of passage to adulthood. Until puberty, boys and girls are generally depicted naked and wearing their hair in the 'sidelock of youth'. However, their nudity seems to be an artistic convention serving to identify them as 'not-yet-adults'. After puberty, decorum required men and women alike to be fully clothed.

While there is little evidence for any rite of passage under-gone by girls, boys' transition to adulthood seems to have been marked by circumcision. The earliest depiction of this procedure is found in a sixth-dynasty tomb at Saqqara, where a man carries out the operation with a sharp stone knife, while the boy is held by an attendant. But there are other references scattered through the sources. Wooden models of naked young men from the end of the Pyramid Age routinely show them as circumcised. An inscription of the First Intermediate Period recounts how one young lad was 'circumcised together with 120 men', suggesting a mass ceremony. From the eighteenth dynasty, a relief at Karnak seems to show the circumcision of royal princes, and there is a reference to the operation being carried out on a future vizier, Useramun. Thereafter, there are no direct references to circumcision until the twenty-fifth-dynasty victory inscription of Piankhi, a Nubian pharaoh who conquered Egypt. He prided himself on being a pious follower of the god Amun-Ra, and refused to receive the submission of four local delta rulers in person because they were 'uncircumcised and ate fish'. This inscription equates being circumcised with ritual purity, but that might have been a later interpretation.

Being circumcised meant gaining admission to a world of adults, a traumatic experience, but necessary to achieve social recognition. However, if an Egyptian youth thought that an easier life would follow the removal of his foreskin, he would have been sorely mistaken.

◄○►

A boy's ear is upon his back: he hears when he is beaten.

So ran an Egyptian proverb; for a boy lucky enough to receive a formal education, strict discipline was the norm. Girls and boys would most often have been trained for adult duties by their mothers and fathers respectively. As we have seen, the Egyptian ideal was for a son to succeed his father in the same office, and for most of the population this would have been the only training on offer. For a privileged few, however, a formal education provided a passport into the world of the literate bureaucrat and the prospect of material success.

The earliest mention of a specific 'house of instruction' is found in an inscription from the Middle Kingdom tomb of a provincial governor called Kheti. When speaking of the people he hopes will visit his tomb in the future, he refers to 'every scribe and every scholar . . . who has been to the house of instruction'. Though schools are likely to have existed in earlier

times, his reference is almost certainly to the prestigious institution located at the royal residence near Memphis. From the
twelfth dynasty onwards, this establishment seems to have
attracted boys of ability and potential from all backgrounds
from throughout the Nile Valley, and not just the sons of the
nobility.

A contemporary instructional text known as *The Teaching of
Kheti* is framed as an extended lecture by the eponymous author
to his son, as they travel to the school from their home in
Tjaru on Egypt's far north-eastern frontier:

> Beginning of the teaching
> made by the man from Tjaru,
> whose name is Khety, son of Duauf,
> for his son named Pepy,
> as he fared south to the Residence
> to put him in the school for scribes,
> surrounded by the children of officials,
> among the upper echelons of the Residence.[10]

Kheti is determined that his son will succeed at his studies; as
he points out, being able to read and write is a passport to
success:

> I shall make you love writing more than your mother.
> I will make you appreciate its benefits.
> It is greater, indeed, than all other offices:
> there is nothing (like it) in this (whole) land.
> When he has (only just) begun to grow and is still a
>   child,
> he is greeted and sent to carry out commissions,
> before he has even arrived at (the age of) wearing a
>   loincloth![11]

Kheti's instructions take the form of a series of satirical caricatures of other occupations and are designed to convince his son of the benefits of being a scribe, the training that equipped a boy to join the ranks of the bureaucracy and become a member of the ruling class. What is remarkable is that social mobility seems to have flourished in ancient Egypt. There are instances from every period of pharaonic history of low-born men reaching high office through their own efforts and talents. The fact that – even in a fictional account – a man from a remote border town was able to send his son to the elite Residence school demonstrates that such an occurrence was not particularly unusual.

Schooling seems to have included arithmetic, but it was the arts of literacy that took centre stage. The classic instructional text, studied by generations of ancient Egyptian schoolboys, was *Kemit* ('compendium'), an anthology comprising a series of model letters, an example of narrative storytelling and short sentences such as occur in typical autobiographies. Pupils

Fig. 28. Ebony and ivory child's chair.

learned the text by heart, reproducing its contents to hone their writing and composition skills. Thereafter, their instruction would have taken the form of learning and copying a range of other classic texts. In the eighteenth dynasty, such primers included *The Tale of Sinuhe* and *The Teaching of Kheti*. It is thanks to the frequent copies made by scribal trainees that these texts have survived to the present day. Rather than expensive papyrus, pupils generally employed reusable writing tablets, several of which have been discovered in archaeological contexts; in an eighteenth-dynasty Theban tomb, a high official is shown being followed by his apprentice son, who carries both a writing tablet and a scroll of papyrus.

Most boys are likely to have studied while sitting cross-legged on the floor, in emulation of the scribe's quintessential pose. For a privileged few, such as royal princes, a chair may have been part of the school furniture. A child's armchair, made from ebony with ivory inlays and panels embossed with gold foil, was included among Tutankhamun's tomb equipment. Its concave seat was designed to accommodate a cushion, but its upright back would have kept its occupant alert.

Not much is known about the format of a typical lesson, although *The Teaching of Kheti* provides some information about the school day. Kheti warns his son:

If you go out of the schoolhouse
when midday (break) is announced,
and go walking in the streets,
everyone will dispute with you in the end.[12]

It seems likely from this that lessons took place in the morning when the temperature was a little cooler, leaving the afternoon free for self-study and other activities. A New Kingdom literary work, *Truth and Falsehood*, refers to a boy who was sent to school and learned to write well. He practised all the arts of war and surpassed his older companions who were at school with him.[13]

This indicates that physical exercise was part of the curriculum, at least during the militaristic eighteenth, nineteenth and twentieth dynasties.

Indeed, by the New Kingdom, going to school seems to have been the expectation for the sons of reasonably prosperous middle-class families. Another instructional text from the period reminds a son that his mother

sent you to school and you were taught to write. She kept a look out for you every day with bread and beer at home.[14]

Not every boy could attend the prestigious Residence school, so there must have been educational establishments in all the principal towns of Egypt. A high priest of Amun named Bekenkhons describes spending four years at a school at Karnak, and recent excavations have revealed a series of small offices and storage rooms at the back of the Ramesseum, complete with fragments of school texts. While school provided the essential foundations, further training was required before entering a profession. After four years at school, Bekenkhons spent eleven years as an apprentice in the royal stables before commencing his career in the temple priesthood. Fifteen years of formal education more or less equates to the combination of primary, secondary and tertiary education in modern Western society.

High priest or royal steward, architect or vizier, every position of note in pharaonic Egypt depended on the ability to read and write. Gaining these fundamental skills – mastered by perhaps only 5 per cent of the population – was hard, but worth it. As *The Teaching of Kheti* put it:

> A day in the classroom is good for you:
> though difficult, its works last for ever.[15]

⊲◦▷

By the time of Tutankhamun, the sons of lower- and middle-ranking officials, as well as those of the ruling elite, could expect to receive some formal education. For those with talent and ability, this would be at the prestigious Residence school. But there was a yet more privileged education that was reserved for the sons of the king's closest advisers and of Egypt's vassal rulers: an upbringing alongside the pharaoh's own children within the royal household. Even at the height of the Pyramid Age, when royal authority was at its zenith, such an upbringing could be the passport to wealth and high office for men of non-royal birth. One of the grandest tombs at Saqqara was built for a fifth-dynasty official named Ptahshepses, who seems to have owed his position to the fact that he had been educated in the palace, where 'the king valued him above all the children'; he later married a princess, further cementing his royal ties. Five centuries later, Kheti, a provincial governor of Asyut, was brought up at court and boasted that the king 'had me instructed in swimming, together with the royal children'. Also in the twelfth dynasty, an official named Ikhernofret gained advancement through his education as a foster child of the king and went on to be entrusted with royal missions of a sensitive nature, the monarch having recognized him as 'wise and articulate, (with) born intelligence'.[16]

It is not known for certain how such individuals were able to gain admission to the king's inner circle, but one likely route was through their parents. The children of royal wet nurses would grow up in the company of their mothers' royal charges, as would the sons of royal tutors. In ancient Egypt, as in monarchies down the ages, the king's sons were educated by tutors within the confines of the palace. Several such tutors are known from pharaonic history. The early-eighteenth-dynasty mayor of Elkab, Paheri, was tutor to a son of Thutmose I; the prince is depicted in Paheri's tomb, sitting on his teacher's lap. A little later in the dynasty, the owner of a Theban tomb, Hekareshu, boasted of having been tutor to four royal princes; again, they were shown sitting on his lap, celebrating his close association with the ruling family. In Hekareshu's case, his son Hekaerneheh grew up alongside the princes. This would stand him in good stead and enable him to serve as tutor to the next generation of royal children. What is particularly interesting about this family of tutors is that both Hekareshu and Hekaerneheh were of Nubian ancestry, their adopted 'loyalist' names (meaning 'the ruler is joyful' and 'the ruler forever', respectively) signalling their devotion to the monarch.

Hekaerneheh gloried in the title 'child of the nursery', a designation shared by over sixty individuals from the eighteenth dynasty, many of whom rose to high office. To be a child of the nursery was to rub shoulders with the offspring of Egypt's great and good, in an atmosphere of privilege and power. The country's future leaders were trained from infancy for the responsibilities they would later assume, receiving an education that was practical and vocational rather than narrowly academic. There was also an overtly political dimension. The inhabitants of the nursery – where children lived as well as learned – included the sons of foreign vassals, brought to court for indoctrination into the Egyptian way of life, in the hope that it would inculcate a lifelong loyalty to the pharaoh.

In the eighteenth dynasty, the most important royal nursery was at Gurob, where kings since the dawn of history had built their pleasure palaces. The abundance of birdlife made for excellent hunting, while the royal women who lived in the adjoining harem palace busied themselves with the manufacture of textiles. Gurob was hence a place of women and children, relaxation and laughter. Royal princesses and the daughters of the elite could expect to learn from their mothers the accomplishments expected of them: weaving, singing, dancing and perhaps a smattering of reading and writing.

By contrast, a harsher discipline was enforced when it came to the education of princes and their male contemporaries. Reading and writing were central elements in the curriculum, under the guidance of the scribe in the House of the Royal Children. For, as *The Teaching of Kheti* noted:

> Whatever position a scribe may occupy in the
>   Residence,
> he will not suffer in it.[17]

Once the young princes and their schoolmates had mastered the Egyptian language, they were introduced to Babylonian, the diplomatic lingua franca of the age. The curriculum also included mathematics and music, for an appreciation of singing and instrumental music went hand in hand with membership of polite society. Energetic and physical pursuits also played an important part in the education of future leaders – in the militaristic culture of the eighteenth dynasty, training the body was as important as educating the mind. Running, jumping, swimming, rowing and wrestling were all part of the weekly routine, designed to develop strength, stamina and team spirit. The future Amenhotep II – keener than most of his contemporaries on sport and feats of physical endurance – was taught archery by a provincial mayor named Min, who proudly recorded the episode in his Theban tomb.

Fig. 29. Box lid with Princess Neferneferura as an infant.

Such was the upbringing and education of a royal prince and his chosen playmates. The nursery was designed to train future leaders and to provide the king with a close-knit group of lifelong friends whom he could count on to implement his policies and support the status quo. As for the female relatives of this privileged elite, their options were more circumscribed. There is no evidence that girls from any stratum of society attended school – even daughters of high officials might only expect to be adopted into the court as 'royal ornaments' to lend beauty and glamour to the king's retinue. Hatshepsut's daughter, the princess Neferura, was provided with her own tutor, but his role was probably that of guardian rather than teacher.

Tutankhamun's six sisters played a prominent role in court life, accompanying their parents on great state occasions, but it is unlikely that they received any formal education. One of the objects from Tutankhamun's tomb, a box-lid found in the Antechamber, is decorated with inlays depicting his second-youngest sister Neferneferura sucking her thumb. Hers was a life which, though pampered, was prescribed from the outset. For princess and peasant alike, the destiny of every Egyptian girl was to marry and have children.

Take a wife while you are young, so that she may bear you a son. She should bear (children) for you while you are (still) a youth. It is right to make offspring! Happy is the man whose offspring are many: he is respected on account of his children.[18]

The advice given to boys in ancient Egypt underscores the importance of children and the status of parenthood in pharaonic society. Having children outside wedlock was not unknown, but marriage was regarded as the proper state in which to raise a family. Indeed, much of the surviving evidence for marriage is inextricably bound up with the matter of childbearing. An instructional text from the Middle Kingdom seems to encourage marital harmony for its own sake, but with an ulterior motive:

If you are successful and establish your household,
love your wife passionately,
fill her belly, clothe her back.
Ointment is the (proper) prescription for her body.
Bring her joy as long as you live,
for she is a fertile field for her master.[19]

The final phrase delivers the punchline: since a wife's principal duty was to bear children, treating her well would maximize the chances of a large family.

That is not to say that marriages were merely convenient domestic arrangements designed for optimal child-rearing. The text quoted above also includes an encouragement of long-term marital happiness as the path to satisfaction for husband and wife alike:

If you marry a woman who is plump
and jolly and well known by her townsfolk,
if she is faithful and time is kind to her,
do not be driven apart, but let her eat,
for her jollity brings contentment.[20]

In reliefs and statues, wives are generally shown with their arms around their husband's waist or shoulder in a loving embrace. The pair statue – the depiction of a married couple, side by side – first made its appearance in the early fourth dynasty, and remained a popular form of statuary. Two-dimensional art also includes scenes of husbands and wives sharing meals, playing *senet* and taking part in other leisure pursuits together. Some of the most beautiful examples of the genre are found on the Little Golden Shrine from the tomb of Tutankhamun. Measuring fifty centimetres high, twenty-six centimetres wide and thirty-two centimetres deep, and carved to resemble the ancestral shrine of Upper Egypt, the wooden shrine is mounted on a silver-covered sledge and overlaid with thick gold foil. Its sides and twin doors are decorated with eighteen embossed and chased scenes, many of which depict the young king and his wife Ankhesenamun. The couple are shown together, hunting and fowling in the marshes; they hold hands, and Ankhesenamun presents her husband with bouquets of fresh flowers. In one of the most intimate scenes, Ankhesenamun fastens a broad collar around her husband's neck. A contemporary painted relief from their childhood home of Amarna depicts the pair taking a stroll in a garden. Though executed within the formal canon of Egyptian art, these scenes nonetheless betray a genuine tenderness.

Given the importance of marriage, it seems odd that there is no evidence that it was marked by any sort of special cere-mony. There is no ancient Egyptian word for 'wedding'; the most oft-used terms referred simply to 'establishing a house-hold', 'entering the household' or 'living together'. Amenhotep III celebrated the arrival of his Mittanian spouse by issuing a commemorative scarab, but it does not refer to any kind of ceremony to cement the union. Later in the New Kingdom, Ramesses II welcomed a Hittite princess to Egypt as his bride. His commemorative inscription recounts his pleasure at the match, the princess's installation in the royal palace and her adoption of an Egyptian name – but no wedding celebrations.

Ancient Egyptian had a word for 'wife', but more often a married woman was designated 'mistress of the house', empha-sizing her role in running the household. Just as there was no ritual accompanying the act of marriage, so there was no reli-gious dimension. Cohabitation seems to have been the only significant act, and there was not much difference in the way married and unmarried households were treated. Social recog-nition apparently derived from the stability and longevity of a relationship rather than its legal status. Given this lack of underpinning law, some brides' fathers took the precaution of insisting that their future son-in-law swear an oath in front of witnesses. An inscription from Deir el-Medina, written in the reign of Ramesses III, records how a member of the commu-nity named Telmont demanded such a concession from his daughter's suitor, Nekhemmut:

> Let Nekhemmut swear an oath to the Lord that he will not desert my daughter.

Nekhemmut did as he was asked, swearing:

> As Amun lives and the Ruler lives, if I ever in the future desert the daughter of Telmont, may I be liable to a hundred lashes and lose all that I have acquired while with her.[21]

One consequence of the lack of any legal status for marriage is that divorce may have been relatively common. Other documents from the workmen's village suggest that measures could be put in place to protect women from the financial consequences of divorce, including formal assurances about the their property rights. The absence of laws around marriage also meant that polygamy was not expressly forbidden, although ancient Egyptians were generally monogamous: for most people, economic and personal considerations limited them to a single spouse. A ninth-dynasty official named Meryaa, who was proudly shown in his tomb with six wives, was very much the exception.

One of the most curious features of Egyptian society in Tutankhamun's time is the apparent preponderance of consanguineous marriage. Kings often married their half-sisters, both for political reasons – to maintain control of the levers of power – and in conscious emulation of the gods. Amenhotep I's parents were brother and sister, as were his grandparents. Tutankhamun himself married his own sister or half-sister, while recent DNA analysis suggests that his parents were also closely related. The narrowing of the gene pool and its negative health impact may explain the premature death of the boy king and his two stillborn daughters. The pharaoh was to be feared and respected, but not necessarily emulated: outside the royal family, there is one incontrovertible case of close-kin marriage, and two other cases where circumstantial evidence makes it likely. In all three instances, the husband and wife may have been half-siblings rather than full brother and sister. Keeping it in the family had its limits.

◁◇▷

The average ancient Egyptian family may not have been incestuous, but it was certainly close-knit and – from time to time

– fractious. In the stereotypical image of a family, as represented
in the decoration of countless tomb chapels throughout
pharaonic history, the invariably male tomb owner is accompanied by his wife, children and servants. Often they are
depicted at a smaller scale than him, to emphasize their subor-
dinate position. The head of the family might also be shown
presenting offerings to his parents, in keeping with society's
expectations:

> Pour libations for your father and mother who are at
> peace in the necropolis. When the gods witness your
> action, they will say, 'Accepted!'[22]

But this age-old ideal of the nuclear family headed by a
successful man was just that: an ideal. Documentary evidence
shows that the reality was often much more complicated. The
letters of Hekanakht reveal not just an ambitious, canny busi-
nessman but a hectoring, jealous and irascible husband, whose
family relationships were far from harmonious.

Hekanakht lived in an extended household. In addition to
his wife and children, there were at least three more relatives
living under the same roof: Hekanakht's mother, his older
sister (or aunt – the ancient Egyptian language did not distin-
guish between older female relatives) and his younger brother.
This reflects the essential pattern of village life in the Nile
Valley: widowed and unmarried female relatives, as well as
men who had not yet married and established their own
household, tended to live with the head of the family.
Hekanakht's household also included the steward of his estate,
a scribe and field-hand, and a housemaid. As if those were
not enough combustible ingredients, matters seem to have
been complicated further by the fact that he had been married
previously – and there are indications that his older children

(presumably from his first marriage) did not get on particularly well with his new wife. Neither did the housemaid, whom Hekanakht accused of plotting against her. Three, possibly four, generations under one roof, plus an assortment of servants, certainly made for a lively atmosphere.

From about the same period as Hekanakht's letters, the census lists from the town of Kahun are another remarkable set of surviving documents. These texts allow us to chart the evolving composition of a household over time. When it first appears in the census, a modest townhouse belonged to a soldier named Hori, his wife Shepset and their baby son Sneferu. Some years later, they have been joined by five daughters and Hori's widowed mother, Harekhni. Later still, presumably after Hori's death, Sneferu is named head of the household. Living with him are his widowed mother and grandmother, and two aunts. We can see a similar set-up nearly a thousand years later, in the twentieth-dynasty tomb of the chief workman Inherkhau at Deir el-Medina, where scenes show him and his wife with their four granddaughters. In many large Egyptian families, live-in grandmothers would have helped out with childcare and domestic chores, sharing with the mother some of the burden of running the household.

In such circumstances, it is not surprising that children often formed close bonds with their grandmothers, whom they may have seen more often than their parents. This was true not just in peasant households but at the very apex of society. Following the death of Amenhotep III, his beloved chief wife Tiye seems to have moved, at least for a time, to her son Akhenaten's new capital. She is depicted in a number of reliefs from Amarna and had her own steward in the city, whose lavishly decorated tomb marked him out as a member of the innermost circle at court. With Akhenaten and Nefertiti busy overseeing affairs of state and taking part in religious ceremonies, it is tempting to imagine their children spending their lives with an array of wet nurses and maids, and perhaps their grandmother, in the North Palace at Amarna – a building that seems to have been a special residence for the royal women, concubines and children.

Tutankhamun's special affection for his grandmother is confirmed by one of the most poignant objects found in his tomb. A miniature coffin made from gilded and resin-coated wood was found to contain a coffinette of gilded wood; nested inside these two protective layers was a third miniature coffin of painted wood and a tightly wrapped linen bundle. When unwrapped, the bundle contained a solid gold pendant of a squatting king. The innermost miniature coffin held a fourth tiny coffin-shaped box, wrapped in linen, smeared with unguents and inscribed with Tiye's name. Inside it was a lock of plaited hair. Recent DNA analysis has confirmed that it

Fig. 30. Lock of Queen Tiye's hair.

belonged to Tiye: a treasured memento of a much-loved grand-mother. She ceased to be mentioned in inscriptions from around the fifteenth year of Akhenaten's reign, suggesting that she died when Prince Tutankhaten was around five or six years old. The boy king evidently remembered her as a reassuring presence during his early life.

The almost total absence of the young prince from the official record seems to indicate his deliberate exclusion from court life. Only a single mention has survived from his father's reign: a passing reference in a caption to a now-lost scene from a dismantled building. Akhenaten's revolutionary brand of king-ship seems to have had no room for any male relative; to have recognized a prince and heir would have been to acknowledge a future beyond his own reign, unthinkable for a pharaoh who saw himself as having reset the clock of time to the moment of creation.

By contrast with Tutankhamun's invisibility at Amarna, his sisters – Meritaten, Meketaten, Ankhesenpaaten, Neferneferuaten-tasherit, Neferneferura and Setepenra – feature prominently in reliefs, paintings, sculptures and inscriptions. Moreover, for the first time in Egyptian art, the little princesses are shown in realistic poses, acting as children might. In one painting, Neferneferuaten-tasherit and Neferneferura sit together, one princess touching her sister under the chin. A famous stela shows Akhenaten, Nefertiti and their three oldest daughters in a family scene. Akhenaten lifts up Meritaten to kiss her, his hand gently cradling her tiny head; Meketaten sits on her mother's lap, holding her hand while turning her head towards her and pointing to her father and older sister; Ankhesenpaaten rests against Nefertiti's shoulder and plays with a pendant from her crown. Although the royal couple sit on thrones and wear crowns, the focus of the painting is on their daughters.

The depiction of affection within a family was a further break with the past, and for the royal family to be depicted thus was nothing short of revolutionary. A second stela shows Akhenaten touching Nefertiti under the chin as they sit side by side. A further example depicts the couple face to face, their noses almost touching as she secures a broad collar around his neck. A fourth stela features Nefertiti sitting on Akhenaten's lap with two of their daughters. while an unfinished statue depicted Akhenaten kissing one of his daughters. In all cases, the iconography of Akhenaten's reign underscores the rise in the ideological importance of the royal family.

Interestingly, the most intimate scenes are found on private stelae rather than public monuments, stone slabs set up in the homes of high officials as a focus for worship. In Akhenaten's brave new world, the royal family was not just the first family of Egypt but a holy family, supplanting the traditional deities as figures of devotion.

⋖○▷

Akhenaten promoted praying to the royal family as the path to divine blessing, but there were dangers that even the pharaoh could not deflect. The ancient Egyptians had to contend with disease and its devastating effects every day.

The evidence for affliction in pharaonic times is both archaeological and textual. Mummies and other ancient human remains often bear the tell-tale signs of disease. Parasitic infections – spread by dirty water and contaminated food – were rife, ranging from bilharzia and malaria to a depressing range of parasitic infestations. There was also onchocerciasis ('river blindness'), a parasitic disease spread by flies that was a major cause of eye infections. Mummies of all periods have revealed traces of malarial infection as well as a range of tumours, both benign and malignant, while bodies from the New Kingdom betray the classic symptoms of pulmonary tuberculosis and sand pneumoconiosis, and the features associated with an increased risk of cardiovascular disease.

As well as these life-threatening conditions, ancient Egyptians were also prone to less serious afflictions caused by poor hygiene. Fleas and lice seem to have been widespread, and they may have been one reason why people generally wore their natural hair cropped short and covered by elaborate wigs. Skin complaints were common, as was toothache. The lack of sugar in the ancient Egyptian diet meant that dental caries was rare, but the coarse plant material and sand that found their way into flour and bread wore away the teeth, resulting in tooth decay and infection. Perhaps it is no accident that one of the earliest attested medical professionals, a high official of the early third dynasty who was buried alongside the step pyramid of King Djoser, was a 'chief of dentists' – the royal court, like the general population, certainly required oral care. The mummies of two of the greatest pharaohs, Amenhotep III and Ramesses II, showed that they both suffered from dental abscesses.

Supplementing the physical evidence from bodies, surviving papyri name a wide range of diseases that include a variety of eye conditions, from reduced vision to cataracts. On a stela from Deir el-Medina, one blind man attributed his affliction to supernatural causes:

> I am a man who swore falsely by Ptah, lord of truth,
> And he made me see darkness by day.
> I will declare his might to the one who ignores him as
>   well as the one who knows him,
> To the small and the great:
> Beware Ptah, lord of truth![23]

The specialist literature displays a more scientific understanding of disease. Many different types of intestinal worms are mentioned in medical papyri, demonstrating that the ancient Egyptians were keen observers of parasitic agents. A papyrus dealing with the diagnosis and treatment of external traumas describes the symptoms of tetanus and the neurological consequences of spinal injury, while another text deals with heart failure:

> As to: 'the heart weakens', it means the heart does not
> speak, or it means the vessels of the heart are dumb.[24]

Gynaecological complications – prolapse of the uterus and ovarian cysts, in particular – were a major concern in a society where mother and infant mortality were high and where families depended on the next generation. The widespread prevalence of gastro-intestinal conditions is also suggested by frequent references in medical texts.

Most devastating of all were the periodic epidemics of highly contagious infectious diseases. Here the texts are largely silent – the experience being too traumatic to be committed to permanent record – but inscriptions from neighbouring lands and circumstantial evidence combine to suggest that ancient Egypt suffered from outbreaks of plague. Diplomatic correspondence from Burnaburiash, king of Babylon, to Akhenaten refers to the death from plague of one of Amenhotep III's secondary wives. Plague also seems to have ravaged other parts of the eastern Mediterranean. It claimed one of the wives of the ruler of Alashiya (Cyprus), who wrote ominously, 'the hand of Nergal [the goddess of pestilence] is in my country and in my own house'.[25] The ruler of one of the Levantine city-states took measures to protect his people, declaring, 'I will not permit men from Sumur to enter my city. There is a pestilence in

Sumur.'[26] It may be no coincidence that Amenhotep III commissioned over 700 statues of the Egyptian goddess of pestilence, the lion-headed Sekhmet, for monuments on the east and west bank of Thebes – the biggest single statuary programme in pharaonic history. In the reign of Akhenaten, an epidemic of infectious disease may have claimed members of the royal family – including the queen mother Tiye and Akhenaten's two youngest daughters – in the final years of his reign; this may also account for the fact that the bodies buried in the South Tombs Cemetery at Amarna were mostly children and young adults. In a series of desperate 'plague prayers', the Hittite ruler Mursili blamed the plague ravaging his country on Egyptian prisoners of war who had been brought to Hatti during or shortly after the reign of Tutankhamun.

Those who were lucky enough to survive such scourges might still be scarred for life. Deformity is not often depicted in ancient Egyptian sculpture and painting – the purpose of art being to portray an ideal state of affairs – but skeletons and mummified remains tell a different story. Several bear the tell-tale signs of hernias and spinal tuberculosis, which left sufferers with hunchbacks and twisted spines. In the predynastic cemetery of Adaima in Upper Egypt, two skeletons with the latter disease were uncovered, in each case accompanied by pottery representations of the deformity. These seem to be rare examples of sufferers celebrating their disability. In a similar vein, the stela of a doorman from the late eighteenth dynasty shows him with a wasted right leg and a deformed foot, supporting himself on a long stick.

Also notable is the special status accorded to dwarfs throughout pharaonic history. Incidences of chondrodystrophic dwarfism are abundant, and frequently depicted in art. In the Pyramid Age, the dwarfs Seneb and Perniankhu held important offices in the royal court. Dwarfs were often employed as dancers, singers, attendants and wardrobe officials in the king's private apartments. Perhaps for this reason, the god Bes, protector of hearth and home, was depicted as a cheeky-faced dwarf. But the effects of dwarfism could also be tragic, as illustrated by the skeleton of a woman who died in childbirth because the head of her baby could not pass through her small and deformed birth canal.

Like disease, deformity touched not just members of the royal court but royalty itself. The famous depiction of the Queen of Punt from the mortuary temple of Hatshepsut in western Thebes shows a woman suffering from elephantiasis. Examination of the royal mummies from the New Kingdom has revealed that King Siptah had a withered left foot, the result of poliomyelitis or a spinal defect, while Ramesses V seems to have suffered from both smallpox and a scrotal hernia. And Tutankhamun, hailed in modern times as 'Egypt's golden boy', presented a complex and debilitating series of pathologies. CT scans, X-rays and DNA analysis of his mummy have revealed an overbite and misalignment of the lower teeth, a cleft palate, an elongated skull, scoliosis, a withered leg, a club foot and repeated bouts of malaria. As the archaeologist of Amarna has noted:

> Tutankhamun, weak in health . . . and dying young, looks like a representative of his people rather than a tragic product of an anomalous family.[27]

⊲—⊳

Faced with a barrage of debilitating, deforming and deadly diseases, the Egyptians were not entirely helpless. Though prayers to the gods, magic spells and protective amulets all played a part in their attempts to deflect illness and calamity, medicine also had a place – and in a recognizably modern form. The ancient Egyptian word for doctor (*sunu*) is attested from the formative period of pharaonic civilization. Indeed, the medical profession seems to have been stratified from very early on, with doctors, overseers of doctors, inspectors of doctors and chief doctors all attested. While most doctors seem to have been men, with women generally serving as midwives and wet nurses, an overseer of female doctors is known from the Old Kingdom. Alongside general physicians, there were also specialists: priests of Selqet, the scorpion goddess mentioned in texts from the first dynasty onwards, may have had particular expertise in treating stings and bites. Two high officials, Imhotep from the early third dynasty and Amenhotep, son of Hapu, from the late eighteenth, were later revered as physicians and healers.

Human remains from ancient Egypt sometimes bear traces of medical intervention, with identifiable procedures including trepanning, splints and sutures. Circumcision is attested in mummies as well as in art; although clearly a rite of passage, it may also have been carried out for reasons of hygiene. The full range and sophistication of ancient medicine is revealed by the surviving papyri. The oldest example of a specialist medical text comes from Kahun; covering a range of gynae- cological and veterinary treatments, it suggested that doctors and vets belonged to the same profession. A slightly later text, discovered in the Ramesseum, has sections on gynaecology and paediatrics – underlining the Egyptians' preoccupation with reproduction, childbirth and child mortality – as well as ophthalmology and the vascular system.

The two most important surviving treatises on medicine both date from the early eighteenth dynasty and may have been penned by the same scribe, perhaps himself a doctor. One deals with external traumas, the other with internal conditions. The former, known today as the 'Edwin Smith Surgical Papyrus', may represent a later copy of a much earlier text, since the style and grammar of the language suggest an Old Kingdom original. It is remarkably modern in its approach, dealing systematically with trauma injuries, starting at the top of the head and working down to the spinal vertebrae. In total, forty-eight cases are considered. Each one begins with the words 'If you examine a man who has . . .', followed by a description of the symptoms, using visual, olfactory and other sensory information. There then follows a diagnosis, in one of three forms: 'An ailment which I will treat', 'An ailment with which I will contend' or 'An ailment not to be treated'. If treatment of the condition is considered feasible, a description of the appropriate procedure follows. Favoured treatments for trauma injuries include bandaging, splints, poultices, manipulation, the application of honey and salts to open wounds and the use of a heated knife to lance a tumour. Alongside these medical interventions, a common recommendation is to leave the patient 'at his mooring post' – in other words, enforced bed rest – indicating a common-sense approach and an appreciation of the body's capacity to heal itself. Rather less insightful are later additions that include recipes for a suppository and an anti-ageing remedy, the latter described as a 'recipe for transforming an old man into a youth'.

The second significant medical text, known as the 'Ebers Papyrus', focuses on internal diseases, displaying a level of medical knowledge on a par with that of pre-modern Europe. For example, there is some evidence that the properties of opium were known and applied. The ancient Egyptians also appear to have had a rudimentary understanding of the circulatory system, which they envisaged – not wholly erroneously – as a network of vessels centred on the heart and extending to the organs and other parts of the body. Alongside blood, water and air, the circulatory system was believed to transport a corruptive waste substance (termed *wehedu*) that was thought to be the root cause of many ailments, with purges and enemas prescribed to flush it out. This belief survived down into Hellenistic times and has echoes in the medieval concept of the bodily humours. Many of the sections of the Ebers Papyrus were copied, verbatim, in a later medical text, showing that it was considered a standard reference work.

One of the most remarkable paragraphs, the true significance of which has only recently been recognized, concerns the treatment of migraine. Our very word for the condition, from the Greek for 'half-head', is a direct translation of the ancient Egyptian term (*ges-tep*). Not only did the Egyptians name the affliction, they also seem to have had an advanced notion of how to alleviate its symptoms. The relevant paragraph in the Ebers Papyrus runs as follows:

> Another [remedy] for migraine pain: The head of a
> catfish, applied with oil. Apply to the [sufferer's] head.[28]

When first translated, it was assumed that this curious-sounding remedy referred to the eating of deep-fried fish. However, closer inspection of the text suggests that the catfish was to be treated with oil rather than cooked in it. Nile catfish discharge electricity through their heads, which they use to stun their prey. A thin coating of oil on the fish's head, before it was applied it to the head of the migraine sufferer, would have helped both to conduct the electric current and salve the area of application. If this interpretation of the text is correct, it indicates that the ancient Egyptians had discovered that a mild electric shock could be an effective treatment for migraine. Western medicine would have to wait another three and a half thousand years to gain the same insight.

By comparison with the Edwin Smith and Ebers papyri, some of the Egyptians' other medical remedies belong to a

pre-scientific age. As we have seen, prayers and acts of propiti-
ation towards the goddess Sekhmet were believed to be effective
in warding off pestilence. In the Late Period, a special type of
stela known as a *cippus* was erected in temple courtyards and other
public places. It bore a figure of the god Harpocrates standing on
a crocodile and grasping dangerous creatures such as snakes and
scorpions. It was believed that water poured over the inscription
would absorb healing properties and could be drunk to treat bites
and stings – and perhaps the placebo effect worked.

Somewhere between these extremes of medical insight and
wishful thinking is the first aid kit from the tomb of
Tutankhamun. A rounded box of ebony and cedar, it was found
to contain several bandages of various sizes, a finger stall (akin
to a thimble), a protective linen gauntlet and a crystalline
limestone armlet of unknown use. This odd assortment of items
would have been good for preventing and treating cuts and
bruises, but not much more.

⊲⊙⊳

Given the vicissitudes that lay in store for an Egyptian baby
from the moment of its birth, it is a wonder that anyone in
the ancient Nile Valley managed to reach old age. But, against
all the odds, a few lucky souls did. Skeletons of individuals
aged over sixty are rare, but the surviving texts and inscriptions
point to a few remarkably long lives. At least two kings,
Pepi II of the sixth dynasty and Ramesses II of the nineteenth,
are known to have reigned for at least sixty years, which suggests
they lived into their eighties. In a society where the average
life expectancy was between thirty and thirty-six, these rulers
must have appeared truly god-like to their subjects. A few
commoners also reached notable milestones: Amenhotep, son
of Hapu, a high official at the court of Amenhotep III, claimed
on a statue to have lived to the age of eighty, before declaring

'I will complete 110 years' (this being the ideal lifetime). A few generations later, the autobiographical inscription of Bekenkhons, the high priest of Amun under Ramesses II, suggests that he was at least ninety when he died.

For ordinary Egyptians outside the charmed royal circle, reaching 'a good old age' was a commonly expressed wish, not that being elderly was regarded with particular envy or respect. Wisdom was thought to be the preserve of ancestors, while the state of old age was widely associated with physical frailty, aches and pains:

Old age has come about, advanced years have
 descended,
feebleness has arrived, weakness has come anew.
One sleeps like a child all day.
Eyes are weak, ears are deaf,
strength perishes: for the heart is weary,
the silent mouth does not speak,
the failing mind does nor remember yesterday,
the bones suffer from old age,
good has turned to bad,
all sense of taste has gone!
What old age does to people
is bad in every way.
The blocked nose does not breathe;
standing and sitting are (both) painful.[29]

So powerful was this stereotype that, in the *Tales of Wonder*, the narrator greets an aged magician by expressing amazement at his physical youthfulness:

You seem much younger than your years – old age is
(usually) the time of dying, the time of burial, the time

of rejoining the earth – sleeping until day-break, free from illness, without a rattling cough![30]

Egyptian art likewise emphasized youth and physical perfection: toned muscularity for men, nubile slimness for women. When old age is explicitly depicted, it tends to be linked with the material success that came with a long and successful career. In the tomb of the sixth-dynasty official Khentika at Saqqara, the owner is shown on one side of the doorway as a younger man, full of vim and vigour, and on the other side as an older man with breasts and a rounded belly. In ancient Egyptian society, rolls of fat on the torso and abdomen were signifiers of wealth and privilege, since they implied an abundance of food and a sedentary lifestyle. A seated statue of Hemiunu, the overseer of the Great Pyramid of Khufu, displays these features prominently, as does the wooden statue of an anonymous high official of the fifth dynasty. The latter was nicknamed Sheikh el-Beled, or 'village elder', by the nineteenth-century Egyptian workmen who discovered it, since it reminded them of their own portly community leader. Further examples of the same artistic convention can be seen a millennium later in the tomb of Sennefer at Thebes and on the statues of Amenhotep, son of Hapu, which depict him as a revered elder.

As well as idealized images of longevity, a few more realistic portrayals aim neither to laud nor to laugh at the changes associated with ageing. A painted limestone relief from the reign of Tutankhamun shows an aged official with a double chin, protruding collarbones, skinny wrists, bony fingers and a serene, wise face. It is perhaps the most striking image of old age in ancient Egyptian art. Seven centuries later, statues of the mayor of Thebes, Montuemhat, show him with sagging facial muscles but a distinct air of nobility. Most unusual of all are the depictions of grey hair in the tombs of sculptors and painters. In a tomb at Deir el-Medina, a nineteenth-dynasty workman showed himself with his extended family, at various stages of ageing: his aunt has a black wig with grey ends, his father-in-law has greying hair, his mother-in-law has grey hair and his father's hair is completely white. Grey hair is also shown on certain minor figures in the tomb of Huy, viceroy of Kush under Tutankhamun.

Alongside these respectful images of old age among the upper and middle classes, there are occasional instances of caricature among the peasantry. In an eighteenth-dynasty tomb at Thebes, a naked labourer with a pot belly, receding hairline and stubble is shown carrying bundles of papyrus. In a slightly earlier tomb at Elkab, an elderly farmer – also naked, pot-bellied and balding – is taunted by a younger workmate with the words, 'Hurry up, don't chatter so much, you bald old peasant!'[31] A scene in a twelfth-dynasty tomb at Meir in Middle Egypt depicts an old man, again naked and pot-bellied, chatting to a shipwright. A further indication of his age is the stick he holds to support himself.

Indeed, the hieroglyphic sign for 'old' in ancient Egyptian was the image of a man, bent over and leaning on a stick. If a man were fortunate enough to reach advanced years, he might petition the authorities to appoint his son as his deputy and future successor. The youth appointed to such a position was referred to as a 'staff of old age', a reference to the support he would provide for his elderly relative.

A walking stick was synonymous with advanced years, so it is ironic that the largest surviving collection of sticks from ancient Egypt – 130 in total – should have been found in the tomb of a teenager. Tutankhamun, who died before he reached his twentieth year, walked with a stick due to deformity rather than longevity. On the Little Golden Shrine, his young wife is shown supporting him, one hand on his upper arm and the other holding his hand. A famous painted limestone relief from Amarna, nicknamed 'the walk in the garden', shows a young royal couple – unnamed, though surely Tutankhamun and Ankhesenamun – strolling together, she holding flowers, he propped up on a long stick.

In the end, the Egyptians believed that old age, like kingship, was a gift of the gods. Tutankhamun's great Restoration Stela began and ended with the confident words 'Tutankhamun-ruler-of-Thebes, given life like Ra forever and ever'. It would prove to be a vain hope.

Fig. 31. Painted relief from Amarna showing Tutankhamun and his wife; the young king leans on a stick for support.

EIGHT

Piety

Fig. 32. Sistrum (sacred rattle).

In an attempt to ward off harm and make sense of the world around them, the ancient Egyptians had recourse to a wide variety of beliefs and rituals. Magic, religion and medicine were regarded as complementary and overlapping. Wearing an amulet, casting a spell, saying a prayer, dedicating a votive offering or consulting an oracle were all believed to conjure supernatural assistance, whether alone or in combination.

Pharaonic religion is a vast topic, reflecting the different traditions that were woven together into a complex web of belief. At one end of the spectrum were the sophisticated theologies dreamed up by professional priesthoods: creation accounts and groups of deities, esoteric rites and abstruse myths. At the other end was the realm of private religious observance: protective charms and simple prayers, household deities and ancestor worship. Somewhere between these two poles lay the daily observance of temple cults performed by professional and lay priests, ostensibly on behalf of the king but rooted in their local communities. Festivals and pilgrimages brought state religion within reach of the masses, helping to knit the whole tapestry together. Cultic and magical objects from the tomb of Tutankhamun, though intended to facilitate the elite experience of religion, nonetheless draw on a wider spectrum of belief. The picture that emerges is of a civilization steeped in piety, as a practical means of navigating life and preparing for death.

⊂▥⊃

At the heart of every religious tradition is a myth of origins, from the Rainbow Serpent of indigenous Australia to the seven-day creation story of the Old Testament. It is a measure of the intellectual sophistication of pharaonic civilization that the ancient Egyptians did not content themselves with a single creation myth but had at least three. It is also characteristic of the Egyptian way of thinking that the existence of distinct traditions, far from being considered problematic, served to emphasize the complexity and ineffability of the divine. Moreover, the web of creation stories served to knit together diverse strands of regional tradition into a national fabric of belief. Whereas some civilizations have depended upon a single, undiluted myth, pharaonic culture drew strength from the multi-layered character of its religious traditions.

As a leading scholar of ancient Egyptian religion has noted:

> When speculating about the beginning of life, the Egyptians used the models of creativity they saw around them: the sexual acts that produced people and animals, the seed-sowing that produced crops, and the powers of the mind and the hand that produced objects.[1]

The Egyptians were also heavily influenced by their natural environment, in particular the annual inundation of the Nile Valley, after which the land would re-emerge fertilized and revitalized. This yearly cycle of regeneration was complemented and strengthened by the daily promise of renewal inherent in the sunrise. The twin images of a mound of earth arising from the floodwaters and the solar disc rising from the eastern horizon burned themselves deeply into the Egyptian subconscious. The primeval mound and the sun are the twin leitmotifs of pharaonic mythology that symbolize the mystery and creative power of nature.

The most abstract of the three main creation myths was developed at Hermopolis in Middle Egypt. The town's ancient name was Khemnu, or 'eight', referring to the number of central characters in its creation story, a group of primeval beings that inhabited and personified the waters of chaos. The group comprised four pairs of male and female attributes, which could be depicted as frogs and snakes, respectively: Amun and Amaunet represented hiddenness, Heh and Hauhet formlessness, Kek and Kauket darkness, and Nun and Naunet the watery abyss itself. These primeval elements interacted to create a burst of energy that brought forth the sun and, with it, the start of the creative process. In one version of the myth, the sun god was born on a primeval mound known as the Isle of Flames; according to a later interpretation, the god Thoth placed an egg on the mound and it hatched to reveal the sun god. In an example of the ancient Egyptians' penchant for theological elaboration, the group could also be reimagined as eight baboons, because of these primates' habit of sitting on their haunches to greet the rising sun.

It is the sun that takes centre stage in the most enduringly popular creation myth, the one that was closely associated with the cult centre of the sun god Ra at Heliopolis. Whereas the Hermopolitan myth is first attested in the Coffin Texts from the end of third millennium BC, the Heliopolitan myth is referenced in the oldest surviving body of religious writings, the Pyramid Texts. In the story's most basic form, the solar creator god Atum is alone among the primeval waters that once covered the world. To provide company for himself, he miraculously uses his own bodily fluids to brings forth twin children: a son Shu (dry sunlight) and a daughter Tefnut (moisture). According to one of the Pyramid Texts, Atum 'sneezed out Shu and spat out Tefnut'. This is a clever play on words – the term for 'sneeze' is *yshsh*, close to the sound of the name Shu, while 'spit' is *tef*, the beginning of the name Tefnut. In a similar vein, based on the similarity between the words for 'tear' (*remyt*) and 'people' (*remetj*), Atum sends one of his eyes to find his children in the watery abyss in a later version of the myth. His eye (personified as a female goddess) returns to find that Atum has grown a new eye; distraught at this usurpation, she weeps and her tears become humanity.

Another of the Pyramid Texts provides an earthier description of Shu and Tefnut's birth, recognizing the sexual act as the driving force of natural creation. In this account, Atum takes his penis in his hand, masturbates and ejaculates his twins into existence. One of the most curious titles borne by priestesses in the later periods of pharaonic civilization was 'god's hand', referring to the means by which the creator god started the creative process. The two accounts of masturbating and spitting were sometimes brought together by Atum taking his semen into his mouth and spitting out his children; this was evidently based on close observation of the tilapia fish, which takes both semen and eggs into its mouth before spitting out live young.

Shu and Tefnut not only embodied the essential ingredients for further growth (light and moisture), but the two aspects of eternity, cyclical and linear time. It is no coincidence that in the reign of Akhenaten, the king and his queen deliberately adopted the iconography of Shu and Tefnut and associated themselves with their creator god, the solar orb Aten: Akhenaten's purpose was to take the world back to the moment of creation, when the original perfect triad ruled the earth.

The Heliopolitan myth did not end with the appearance of

Shu and Tefnut. The forces of creation, once unleashed by Atum, were unstoppable. Sexual union, now able to take its natural course, resulted in the birth of another set of twins, Geb (the earth) and Nut (the sky) – in the process providing a divine precedent for the brother–sister unions of the eighteenth-dynasty royal family. Indeed, according to the creation story, this second brother–sister pair was so passionately attracted to each other that their father, Shu, separated them by raising Nut above her brother, but not before she had given birth to two sets of twins, Osiris and Isis and Seth and Nephthys. This brought the number of deities to nine, which as three times three, meant a plurality of pluralities in Egyptian thought, and hence totality. Each of the group of nine gods had a particular role in the creation story; together they set the scene for the formation and elaboration of the world and the perfection of created order by the kings of Egypt. The coda to the Heliopolitan creation myth involves Osiris and Isis joining in union and bringing forth a son, Horus, who would rule over Egypt, bridging 'the time of the gods' and the era of human kings.

When Carter was clearing the tomb of Tutankhamun, he came upon a series of twenty-two wooden chests lined up in the Treasury, each about ninety centimetres tall, covered with black resin and designed to resemble a simple shrine. The chests' double doors had been firmly sealed but tomb robbers had forced them open. Instead of precious metals, the robbers – and Carter – found that each shrine contained a gilded wooden figure of a deity standing on a resin-coated wooden pedestal. Their eyes are outlined in copper alloy, their irises and pupils made of calcite and obsidian. Some of the deities are recognizable by their specific attributes and most of the others are identified by the name written on the base. One of the ritual statues, a standing male figure, is named as Geb. The earth god

was a natural choice to accompany a royal burial, for he represented Egypt, the pharaoh's domain; he stood for fertility and
the earth's productive potential; and he was a central character
in the primary creation myth, the resonance of which assured
it a central place in Egyptian religion until the end of pharaonic
civilization.

⊲◦⊳

By comparison with the Hermopolitan and Heliopolitan
accounts, the third major creation myth is the most theologically sophisticated. It was composed, probably in the nineteenth
dynasty – so a generation or two after Tutankhamun – by
priests in Memphis, Egypt's traditional administrative capital.
From the beginning of history, the principal god of Memphis
had been a craftsman god called Ptah, so it is no surprise that
he is at the centre of the so-called Memphite Theology. In the
sole surviving version of the text, carved in the twenty-fifth
dynasty when pharaonic culture was looking back to earlier
periods for inspiration and affirmation, Ptah is said to have
created the world through his thought and word. First he
devised all deities, people and living creatures in his heart – a
process known as *sia* or 'insight'. Then he gave them form
through his 'authoritative utterance', *hu*. The echoes in the
account of creation in St John's Gospel – 'In the beginning
was the Word, and the Word was with God, and the Word
was God' – are striking. As for Ptah himself, like the god of
the Judaeo-Christian tradition, he was self-engendered, the
'father of the gods from whom all life emerged'.

In order to link the Memphite Theology with the other
creation myths while maintaining the primacy of their city's
principal deity, the theologians of Memphis associated Ptah
with the primeval mound (personified as Ta-tenen, 'the land
which becomes distinct') and cast him as having created Atum

as the agent of his thought and word. It was by such means that the edifice of Egyptian religion was built over many centuries, with regional traditions systematically incorporated into a country-wide mythology. This enabled local allegiances to be maintained while forging a national religion, and the cult of Ptah provides an instructive illustration of this process.

The earliest known representation of the god of Memphis in his characteristic form (mummiform, wearing a close-fitting skullcap and holding a sceptre) is on a bowl from the city's main cemetery at Saqqara that dates from the middle of the first dynasty. It is therefore likely that the cult of Ptah came into being at, or before, the beginning of dynastic civilization. Herodotus, who drew much of his information from the Memphite priesthood, claimed that the temple of Ptah had been founded by Menes, the first king of Egypt. In origin, as well as being a local city god, Ptah seems to have been closely linked with craftsmanship. His name may derive from a root meaning 'to sculpt', and the high priest of his cult in the Pyramid Age was known as 'the great leader of craftsmen'. From this association, casting him as a creator deity who brought the world into being, fashioned the gods, sculpted the earth and shaped humanity was a small step.

Ptah's syncretization with Ta-tenen gave him a role in the afterlife – the primeval mound being one of the most potent symbols of regeneration – and he soon absorbed the cult of an ancient falcon-headed mortuary god, Sokar. In due course, Ptah-Sokar came to be associated with the supreme underworld god, Osiris, to form a tripartite deity, Ptah-Sokar-Osiris. It was as a chthonic deity that Ptah was represented in the sanctuary of Ramesses II's great rock-cut temple at Abu Simbel, alongside the other major gods of the nineteenth dynasty. While the temple was oriented so that the rising sun would illuminate the sanctuary on two days each year (one of them, it is assumed, being Ramesses II's birthday), the figure of Ptah remained in the shadows. A shadowy presence or not, Ptah's prominence in the state religion of the time is confirmed by his inclusion in the names of two of its pharaohs: Ramesses II's successor, Merenptah ('beloved of Ptah') and the last king of the dynasty, Siptah ('man of Ptah').

A rather different aspect of Ptah was his approachability. At some point in history, he absorbed the powers of a sacred tree that grew in the precincts of Memphis. The cult of 'Ptah under his moringa tree' became popular with ordinary citizens who, denied access to the inner sanctum of the city's main temple, could petition their god in the open air. This notion of direct access developed into 'Ptah the hearing ear': votive stelae outside the walls of the Ptah temple in Memphis were often carved with images of human ears, in the belief that the god would hear the prayers of his faithful supplicants. By the time of the Middle Kingdom, he bore the moniker 'Lord of Ankhtawy', signalling his elevation to god of the whole Memphite region; and in the nineteenth dynasty, his popularity as a god spread to other parts of Egypt, including Thebes. A stela from Deir el-Medina shows him surrounded by ears; 'chapels of the hearing ear' were erected beyond the perimeters of major temples, including at nearby Medinet Habu. He also had his own chapel within the great temple of Amun-Ra at Karnak. It must have seemed entirely natural to the composers of the Memphite Theology to ascribe to him the creation not just of the other gods and goddesses, but also of all the towns and shrines throughout Egypt.

Despite a growing national popularity, the pre-eminent cult centre of Ptah remained in his home city of Memphis. Today, the site is a jumble of scattered stones and tumbledown ruins, overgrown with vegetation. But in its heyday, the temple of Ptah was one of the grandest, most imposing centres of worship in the Nile Valley. It was located to the south of the royal citadel, and an ancient model of the temple of 'Ptah south of his wall' shows a high enclosure with crenellations and buttressed towers. Indeed, from the outside, it resembled a fortress as much as a place of worship. The architecture was designed not only to overawe but to exclude: Egyptian temples were the preserve of the king and his closest circle, out of bounds to the general population. As one of the most venerable and important deities of Egypt, Ptah was the regular recipient of royal largesse. One of Tutankhamun's first acts on succeeding to the throne was to restore the temples of the gods that had fallen into ruin during the preceding reign, and the god of Egypt's capital city was a major focus of his patronage:

> He fashioned (the image of) Ptah south of his wall, lord of Memphis . . . his sacred image of electrum, lapis lazuli, turquoise and every precious stone.[2]

Perhaps it was to recall this benefaction that a gilded figure of Ptah was included among the ritual statuettes buried in the boy king's tomb. Like its companion deities, it is made of wood, coated with gesso and covered in gold foil. Embossed decoration depicts the god's broad collar and his tightly fitting feathered cloak. In his protruding hands, he holds his distinctive staff that combines the symbols for 'power' (*user*), 'stability' (*djed*) and 'life' (*ankh*), fashioned from gilded bronze. He is also characterized by a straight beard and a smooth, shiny skullcap, formed from blue faience. To reinforce his identity as the god of craftsman, he stands on a wooden pedestal shaped like a measuring rod – although it could just as easily represent the mound of creation or the hieroglyph for truth, such are his myriad associations.

While the patron deity of Memphis is not the best-known

ancient Egyptian god – that accolade surely belongs to the sun god Ra or the Theban god Amun – he is, perhaps, the most multi-faceted member of the pharaonic pantheon. Craftsman, creator, underworld power, royal protector and hearer of prayers; immanent in a holy tree, the all-hearing ear and accessible in a community shrine – thanks to the ingenuity of his priesthood and the desire of the Egyptian people for divine succour, Ptah cornered the market in every sphere of Egyptian religion. He even gave his name to the country itself: when the Greeks conquered Egypt, they were so impressed by the 'temple of the spirit of Ptah' (*Hikuptah*) at Memphis that they applied its moniker, suitably Graecisized, to the whole land – *Aigyptos*. Hence, in the last two letters of the word 'Egypt', the name of the god Ptah lives on, 5,000 years after his cult began.

⬥

From the earliest recorded beginnings of Egyptian religion, worship of the gods and maintenance of their cults co-existed alongside an even more esoteric and mysterious set of practices: magic. Indeed, in pharaonic culture, magic and religion were intertwined strands of belief and ritual that were impossible to disentangle.

The Pyramid Texts are full of magical spells. Many seem to hark back to older, oral traditions; some may have been passed down from prehistoric times. Despite the royal, funerary setting in which the Pyramid Texts were inscribed, they include everyday incantations against snake bites and scorpion stings, alongside loftier spells to assist resurrection and transcendence in the afterlife. The Egyptians believed that magic was involved in all of creation, good and evil, from the highest to the lowest. It had existed from the beginning of time – in some texts, it is said to have pre-dated the gods – and was inherent in every living creature.

Deities were thought to possess magical powers, and the

gods could be propitiated, co-opted and coerced just as effectively by magic as by 'orthodox' religious rites. One of the most famous of all ancient Egyptian religious writings is a section of the Pyramid Texts dubbed the 'Cannibal Hymn'. Though first attested in the pyramid of Unas, the last king of the fifth dynasty, it may already have been ancient by the time it was written down. Certainly, its imagery is strikingly primitive:

For Unas eats people, lives on the gods . . .

For Unas eats their magic, swallows their spirits.
Their great ones are for his morning meal,
Their middle ones are for his dinner,
Their little ones for his night meal.
Their old males and females are for his fuel.
It is the great ones of the northern sky who lay a fire
    for him,
For the contents of the cauldrons – the legs of their
    elders.
For those who are in heaven serve Unas.
They scrape out the pots for him with their women's
    legs . . .

Unas feeds on the lungs of the wise
And satisfies himself by living on (their) hearts and
    their magic.[3]

The language of the Cannibal Hymn is replete with metaphor, its wordplay resonant of esoteric knowledge. It is best understood as a mythologization of butchery ritual, in which the gods are butchered, cooked and eaten by the king so that he may absorb and deploy their powers to assist him in his resurrection and apotheosis after death.

There is an echo of the same sphere of belief in a pair of the strangest objects buried in Tutankhamun's tomb. Made of gilded wood and some 167 centimetres high, each comprises a model of a stylized animal skin, headless and stuffed, hung on a pole and set in a travertine pot. Though the pots are incised with the king's titles, the objects (called *imiut*) have their roots deep in Egypt's prehistoric past. They are attested in inscriptions from the early first dynasty, but are likely to have been older still. At the dawn of history, an *imiut* was planted in the ground next to the king's throne as a symbol of protection. The headless, impaled animal corpse probably stood for the king's enemies: decapitated and thus incapacitated. In time, it came to be identified with Anubis, the god of mummification – *imiut* means 'that which is in the (place of) embalming'. There was, perhaps, a certain ill-defined logic to the association; but it reflects, above all, the skill with which Egypt's 'intellectual systematizers' absorbed every kind of superstitious belief and practice from every village, town and province into a single national system of religion. The result was a brilliant means of unifying a disparate country with strong local traditions, but it is also why Egyptian religion appears so complex and contradictory. As one scholar has put it, 'We demand consistency in religious thought; they did not . . . We have a canon of scripture; they did not. We reject magic; they did not.'[4]

By Tutankhamun's time, the *imiut* had become firmly identified with Anubis, yet its inclusion in a royal tomb had as much to do with its ancient atavistic power as its more recent association with the preservation of the body. Indeed, the placement of Tutankhamun's two *imiut*s, in the north-west and south-west corners of the burial chamber, seems to have been designed to form a protective shield around his sarcophagus.

According to a literary text of the late Middle Kingdom, magic was given to humanity by the creator 'as a weapon to ward off what may befall'.⁵ People of all ranks routinely turned to magic when other interventions proved ineffective. Amulets and *cippi* straddled the worlds of magic and religion, while medical papyri (see Chapter 7) unselfconsciously included magical spells alongside pharmacological prescriptions. A cult temple might conceal within its foundations broken pots inscribed with the names of enemies and even the skeleton of a mutilated victim. The clergy of every major temple included a type of celebrant called a lector priest – nominally responsible for reading sacred texts, they were more popularly associated with the understanding and performance of magical spells, rituals and prescriptions. The burial of one such individual in western Thebes, close to the Ramesseum, included a group of magical papyri, an ivory wand and a wooden statuette of a woman wearing an animal mask and holding serpents in her hands. This is the paraphernalia of a powerful magician, yet it was not thought incongruous for him to have been buried in some of the most hallowed ground in Egypt.

The blurring and blending of magic and religion gave the ancient Egyptians a wide range of possible interventions with which they might navigate the trials of life, while also allowing them to try different 'layers' of supernatural practice. The gods and the forces of creation were there to be worshipped and appeased, but they were fully expected to deliver their side of the bargain.

⊲○⊳

Perhaps the most important deity in the sprawling Egyptian pantheon, across the vast span of pharaonic history, was the sun god, Ra. To understand why, one has only to visit the Nile Valley; although the river is the defining geographical feature and the bringer of life, the sun is the most visible and tangible natural phenomenon. Sunrise and sunset are swift and dramatic;

the transition from bright daylight to the darkness of night is abrupt, with the absence of the sun felt as sharply as its presence. During daylight hours, the Egyptian sun burns brightly, in winter and summer alike. And last but not least, the sun rises every twenty-four hours, offering the daily promise of rebirth and renewal – whereas the Nile floods only once a year. For these reasons, the sun was an object of awe and reverence for the Egyptians from time immemorial.

Unlike Ptah lurking in the shadows or Amun, 'the hidden one', there was no mystery about Ra. His name means 'sun' and his power was there for all to see and feel, with no need for priestly mediation or interpretation. It was this directness of experience that so appealed to Akhenaten and led him to promote the shining orb of the visible sun as his sole deity. Ra's incontrovertible position as supreme creator – as expressed in the creation myth developed by his priests at Heliopolis – led him to absorb the attributes of countless other deities while retaining his own identity. For example, from an early period, the cult of Ra was associated with that of the sky god Horus to produce the two-fold deity Ra-Horakhty ('Ra-Horus of the two horizons'), closely identified with the morning and midday sun. At the beginning of the Middle Kingdom, when a line of rulers from Thebes came to the throne, they sought to identify their local god, Amun, with the cult of the sun to boost his – and their – national legitimacy. The result was Amun-Ra, who as 'lord of the thrones of the Two Lands' would retain his position as chief god of Egypt until near the end of pharaonic civilization. All the major temples of Thebes were dedicated to aspects of him as patron deity of Thebes and of kingship. In return for his blessing and protection, countless generations of pharaohs showered his cult with donations of land, gold, livestock and precious objects, making it the wealthiest and most powerful institution in the land after the monarchy. Amun-Ra, 'king of the gods', was thus also the god of kings.

The elevation of Amun-Ra to state god in the eleventh dynasty was not the first time that the cult of the sun had been harnessed to royal ideology and political expediency. As early as the second dynasty, theologians explicitly identified the ruler with the power of the sun. One of Egypt's early kings bore the name Nebra ('lord of the sun'), and from the fourth dynasty onwards most throne names included the element 'Ra', thus expressing the king's mandate from the sun god. The builders of the second and third pyramids at Giza were Khafra ('Ra, he rises') and Menkaura ('The spirits of Ra endure'), while Tutankhamun's throne name was Nebkheperura ('Ra is lord of forms'). In addition to these increasingly complex theological formulations, kings of Egypt expressed their close personal relationship with the sun god through the boldly explicit title 'son of Ra'.

The sun's tangible daytime presence was a powerful metaphor for the king ruling over his people. The other aspect of the sun that fascinated the Egyptians was its daily movement across the sky – and, they believed, its corresponding nightly passage through the underworld. As a riverine civilization, when the Egyptians contemplated a long journey, they naturally thought of a boat as the obvious means of transport. From the very beginning of dynastic history, they conceived of Ra travelling by boat across the vault of heaven. They called his 'morning barque' *mandjet* and his 'evening barque' (for the journey throughout the underworld) *mesketet*. To join him in his cosmic journey was the dying wish of every king of the Pyramid Age; the purpose of many of the Pyramid Texts (and indeed of the pyramids them-selves) was to assist his ascension to that end. Participating in the crew of *mandjet* and *mesketet* was both a royal prerogative and a royal duty, and creation depended on it. A literary text of

the Middle Kingdom explicitly connected the proper performance of the king's duties with this greater cosmic purpose:

> Jubilation is in the barque of Ra;
> kingship has become what it was in the past.[6]

To enable the monarch to participate in the voyage of creation for all eternity, royal burials were frequently equipped with
one or more model boats. An early instance is the flotilla of
twelve life-sized, narrow-hulled cedar wood craft (one for each
hour of the day) that were symbolically 'moored' alongside the
funerary palace of a first-dynasty king at Abydos. The two
perfectly preserved solar boats (one for the day journey, the
other for the night) buried in pits next to the Great Pyramid
at Giza served a similar purpose. Such was the durability of
royal ideology that Tutankhamun's grave goods over a millennium later included four model solar barques. Each has the
indented stern post and vertical, lotus-shaped prow characteristic of *mandjet* and *mesketet*; each is fitted with a pair of steering
oars astern and a gilded throne amidships. The distinctive shape
of the barques recalls the images of divine boats scratched into
the rocks of the Eastern Desert in predynastic times.

Fig. 33. Model solar barque.

The sun god's cosmic journey was recalled – and recreated – in the water-borne processions that formed the centrepiece of the great religious festivals of the eighteenth dynasty – especially the Festival of the Sanctuary that took Amun-Ra from Karnak to Luxor, and the Beautiful Festival of the Valley that saw him cross the Nile to western Thebes. At the heart of these events were the barque shrines that housed the gods' divine images. Renewing and beautifying these sacred objects was another royal duty, and one in which Tutankhamun took great pride:

> His Majesty . . . hewed their river barques from new pine from the hilltops . . . worked with the best gold from the hill countries so that they lit up the river.[7]

In so doing, the boy king was following a family tradition. The most glittering of all solar barques, and the most dazzling boat processions ever staged in Egypt, were the product of his grandfather's reign. Amenhotep III was not only a devotee of the sun god: as his long reign went on, he increasingly identified himself with the solar deity. He built solar courts and temples, commissioned larger-than-life statues of himself in quartzite and red granite (stones with strong solar connotations) and, for the *pièce de résistance*, conceived an extraordinary set of solar rituals as the centrepiece of his jubilee celebrations. Harking back to the earliest days of pharaonic culture, he retained certain core elements of the *sed* festival: his appearance in a special robe and the erection of a dedicated jubilee palace. But Amenhotep re-imagined the age-old ceremony of 'territorial claim', which earlier monarchs had celebrated by striding between two sets of cairns, as a great water-borne pageant. He had two huge, artificial basins excavated on either bank of the Nile; their purpose, and the sequence of events on jubilee day itself, is described in the first-hand account from the tomb of Kheruef, one of the king's high officials:

> The king's appearance at the great gates inside his palace, 'The House of Rejoicing'. Ushering in the nobles, the royal companions, the chamberlain, the doormen, the royal acquaintances, the crew of the barge, the comptrollers and the royal dignitaries. They were rewarded with the Gold of Honour and with ducks and fish of gold, and they received ribbons of green linen, every man being made to stand according to his rank. They were supplied with food from the royal breakfast: bread, beer, oxen and fowl. They were commanded to His Majesty's lake to row in the royal barge. They took the ropes of the Evening Barque and the prow-rope of the Morning Barque, and they towed upon 'The Great Place' until they stopped at the steps of the throne. It was His Majesty who did these (things) in accordance with the writings of old. Generations of people since the time of the ancestors had not celebrated such jubilee rites.[8]

Through these lavish celebrations, Amenhotep III was announcing his oneness with the sun god. No longer merely the 'son of Ra', Amenhotep had become Ra on earth. The moment must have had a profound effect on the king's advisers and on the wider populace watching from the banks. Indeed, so deeply embedded in the Egyptian consciousness was the primacy of the solar cult that early Christian texts from the Nile Valley occasionally appealed to 'Jesus, the Holy Spirit and Ra'.

The great barque processions that came to dominate religious life at Thebes during the eighteenth dynasty had an impact not just on the people who observed them, but on the very fabric of ancient Egyptian temples. The earliest sacred buildings in the Nile Valley were – as far as can be discerned from the fragmentary contemporary depictions and scant archaeological remains – flimsy, lightweight structures of wooden posts, wicker-work fences and matting walls. Their architecture suggests that they were intended for temporary use – although one notable example, a predynastic shrine at Hierakonpolis, seems to have remained a focus for cult activities for many generations. Indeed, this particular building may have come to be regarded as the archetypal shrine for all of Upper Egypt, the so-called 'great house' (*per-wer*). At the other end of Egypt, in the north-western delta settlement of Buto, a series of reed huts on either side of a watercourse was revered throughout Lower Egypt and came to represent the region as a whole in sacred archi-tecture; its name, 'the house of anointing' (*per-nezer*), may indicate a role in early coronation rituals.

These early tent shrines, built when the institution of divine kingship was in its infancy, established themselves in the Egyptian consciousness and in royal ideology as the ideal type for all sacred architecture. Even when stone became widely used for cult buildings in the Pyramid Age, the monumental, durable edifices erected by the state consciously harked back to their flimsy, impermanent predecessors. This is seen most strikingly in the Step Pyramid complex, built at the beginning of the third dynasty, where the structures in the festival court along the enclosure's southern side replicate the architecture of posts and matting in hard limestone.

A number of building styles are already evident in this early period. The first, an open-sided, rectangular tent with a curved roof, standing on a pedestal and reached by a small flight of steps, became the quintessential booth in which the king appeared during important ceremonies. A similar design, with a half-height screen along its front, lent its form to a range of ritual buildings, while the knotted ends of the matting screen became a decorative motif used widely in Egyptian art. A third type of building consisted of a rectangular tent with solid walls – of matting or wood – giving a plain external appearance; bound bundles of reed at the tops of the walls and in the building's corners provided stability. This architectural style, which screened the interior entirely from view, was adopted as the ideal type for temple exteriors, including each section of the monumental entrance gateway ('pylon') that characterized temples from the eighteenth dynasty onwards. The longevity and potency of this architectural form are illustrated by the pectorals from Tutankhamun's tomb, four of which are shaped like a classic tent shrine. One fine example, inlaid with carnelian, turquoise and lapis lazuli, is decorated with figures inside the shrine: the king is seated between the goddess Sekhmet and the god Ptah.

Not only did pharaonic temples consciously imitate the post-and-matting structures of distant ages, they also sought to recreate the moment of creation in their construction. The first act of a temple foundation ceremony was to lay out the plan of the building on the ground. The 'stretching the cord' ceremony was generally undertaken by the king, in his capacity as high priest of every cult. Once the plan had been pegged out, a pit was dug beneath the foundations, into which ritual deposits of a magical nature were placed, to protect the building from malign forces. The third element of the ceremony, 'pouring the sand', served to seal the foundation pit and purify the site, while recreating the primeval mound of creation myth at the heart of the new sacred structure. The inner sanctum, which housed the god's shrine, was located at the highest point, atop the mound of sand. This meant that priests approaching the sanctuary would do so from below; the upward slope of the floor was often enhanced by a downward-sloping roof, features that combined to heighten the sense of mystery as the god's dwelling place was neared. The sanctuary appeared cave-like, perhaps recalling some of the earliest sacred places identified by the inhabitants of the Nile Valley.

But a deity could not hide from view for ever: in order to be believed, a god or goddess also had to be seen – or at least experienced. This tension between invisibility and visibility was exploited in Egyptian shrines and temples, often to dramatic effect. A small shrine on the island of Elephantine is a rare example of a sacred building that seems to have been created by and for its local community. Dating to the late predynastic or early dynastic period, it consists of a couple of small mudbrick chambers nestled between two gigantic natural granite boulders. The cave-like sanctuary would have been where the image of the deity was kept, hidden from view; in front of it, an open courtyard provided an arena where the image was revealed to worshippers. From contemporary depictions, it seems that the image itself would have been carried in a small tent shrine or carrying chair; a pedestal would have been required wherever this portable shrine was set down, and the forecourt of the Elephantine building is equipped with such an altar.

Over the centuries, these primitive carrying shrines evolved into the barque shrines that played a starring role in the great festivals of New Kingdom Thebes. The avenue of sphinxes linking Karnak and Luxor temples was furnished at regular intervals with sacred 'way stations' where the shrine could rest as it was carried on the shoulders of priests. The temples at either end were laid out with ceremonial axes that passed through successive courts and pylons to provide a suitably impressive route for religious processions. In this way, subtly and with a nod to ancient precedent, the architecture of Egyptian temples underwent evolution and transformation, to accommodate new forms and rites of worship.

━◁ΙΟΙ▷━

Most Egyptian temples were positioned deliberately in the landscape. The Small Aten Temple at Amarna was aligned with the dry valley that housed the royal tomb, while Karnak temple was positioned facing the Nile, so that river-borne processions – and, more prosaically, the cargo ships that kept the temple supplied with provisions – could moor at a specially constructed quay for ease of access. Priests and officials entered the temple along an avenue of ram-headed sphinxes, which blended an ancient symbol of the sun god Ra (the sphinx) with the sacred animal of Amun (the ram), thus announcing Karnak as the abode of Amun-Ra.

The main gateway formed an imposing entrance, its twin towers resembling the hieroglyph for 'horizon' and identifying the temple as the place of creation and rebirth. All around the temple, a high enclosure wall served to keep the forces of chaos – and the general populace – at a safe distance. Sometimes, as at Luxor Temple, the bricks in these enclosure walls were laid in wavy patterns, to recall the waters of creation. From the entrance, the main axis led through further pylons and courts to the sanctuary, while to either side were a myriad of ancillary spaces: offering chambers, chapels for subsidiary deities, store-rooms for temple equipment, vestries for the clergy, halls for royal ceremonies and the temple treasury.

Each area of the temple had a particular role in the celebration of the daily ritual by which the resident deity was propitiated. The temple was, at heart, the house of the god, and the cult image was tended as if it were the god's physical body: every day, it was fed and watered, washed, clothed and anointed. In this way, it was revivified daily as the vessel for the god's spirit. The morning ritual saw the priests preparing offerings in the offering room, consecrating them by pouring libations of wine and fumigating with incense, before presenting them to the god in the temple sanctuary. An abbreviated version of the same ritual would be carried out at midday and in the evening. At some major temples, an hourly ritual was observed throughout the day and night. The food and drink presented to the god's image were brought from a temple's land holdings and by the faithful as pious donations; after the deity had 'consumed' them, they were distributed to the priesthood. The presentation of food and drink was so fundamental to religious observance that the hieroglyph for both 'offering' and 'satisfied' (*hetep*) depicts a loaf of bread on an offering slab.

Ancient Egyptian religion had no single canonical set of scriptures; instead, the vast accumulation of sacred writings, handed down from generation to generation, provided a rich source for interpretation and practice. Theological exegesis took place in one of the most important and mysterious of all sacred structures: the House of Life. First attested at the end of the Pyramid Age, it was, first and foremost, the temple scriptorium, in which religious texts and ritual incantations were compiled and studied. From an early period, it was closely identified with esoteric knowledge and magic. In the Middle Kingdom, for example, one high official was called 'master of the secrets of the House of Life', while another bore the title 'overseer of writings in the House of Life, to whom all private matters are revealed'.

In the New Kingdom, there were numerous 'scribes of the House of Life', and a man named Amenwahsu, buried at Thebes in the reign of Ramesses II, gloried in the designation 'the scribe who wrote the annals of the gods and goddesses in the House of Life'. The only archaeological evidence for a temple scriptorium comes from Amarna: next to 'the Place of

Correspondence of Pharaoh', a hundred metres east of the Small Aten Temple, two buildings were excavated, their bricks stamped with the words 'House of Life'. One of them yielded a fragmentary funerary papyrus, but otherwise they were found empty: their sacred texts must have been removed when Amarna was abandoned, early in the reign of Tutankhamun.

Scribes of the House of Life would have been the most learned men in pharaonic Egypt, steeped in ancient wisdom and expert in the cults of the gods, the interpretation of oracles and the conduct of religious rites and festivals. For this reason, in the Late Period of Egyptian civilization, priests of the House of Life were known as 'masters of magic'. The deity who presided over the institution, and over the art of writing itself, was Thoth, the scribe of the gods. When, in the twentieth dynasty, Ramesses IV sought to understand the achievements of earlier reigns, he described himself as 'excellent of understanding like Thoth' who 'delved into the annals like their maker, having examined the writings of the House of Life'.[9]

The cult of Thoth was an ancient one. His two sacred animals, the baboon and the ibis, were worshipped from the beginning of Egyptian history. In the Pyramid Texts, he is cast as the advocate of the deceased king; in the myth of Horus and Seth, he supports Horus's cause against his scheming uncle; and in the *Book of the Dead*, he is identified as a god of protection who also records and announces the verdict of the last judgement. Because of all these roles, Thoth became an important figure in funerary beliefs and practices. One of the amulets found suspended around the neck of Tutankhamun's mummy depicts Thoth as an ibis-headed man; five centimetres high and made of gold, its inlay of greenish-blue feldspar recalls the colour of the Nile, vegetation and rejuvenation. In the complex way of ancient Egyptian religion, this symbolism linked Thoth with his role in the Hermopolitan creation myth.

Towards the end of pharaonic civilization, when hieroglyphs were used only for religious texts, the cult of Thoth achieved particular prominence. At a time when the Nile Valley was under threat from outside forces, worshipping an ancient god of writing and creation gave the Egyptians a way of expressing and celebrating their own indigenous traditions. In the thirty-first dynasty, a high priest of Thoth from Hermopolis named Padiusir took great comfort in his local cult and in preserving its temple from destruction and decay, 'while the ruler of foreign lands was protector of Egypt and nothing was in its former place'. His autobiographical inscription provides a perfect summary of the functioning of an ancient Egyptian temple and the sense of devotion the priesthood felt to their ancient places of worship:

> After I became controller for Thoth, lord of Hermopolis . . .
> I caused everything to be as before, every priest in his (proper) time. I promoted his pure priests and advanced the roster priests of his temple. I detailed all of his serv-ants and gave orders to his staff. I did not reduce the offerings in his temple but (rather) filled his granaries with barley and emmer and his treasury with all good things . . . I presented gold, silver and genuine precious stones . . . I caused to rise again what was found ruined. I restored what had decayed long ago and was no longer in place . . . May he who comes after say, 'A follower of his god unto death!'[10]

⬤

As Padiusir's inscription illustrates, the cults of Egypt's old gods experienced a final flourishing during the centuries of Persian domination that preceded Alexander the Great's conquest of the Nile Valley in 332 BC. In these twilight years of pharaonic civilization, the outward expression of religion adopted a peculiar, and quintessentially Egyptian, form: sacred animal cults. The worship of animals had a long history in the Nile Valley. Predynastic rulers of Hierakonpolis had been interred with a veritable menagerie of animals – dogs, lions, elephants – and the sacred Apis bull had been worshipped at Memphis since the foundation of the Egyptian state. But these were largely local traditions, reflecting specific traditions of belief.

By contrast, in the Late Period, animal cults were ubiquitous. There were sacred cats at Bubastis, sacred dogs and gazelles at Thebes, sacred crocodiles in the Fayum and even sacred fish at Busiris in the delta. At Padiusir's home town of Hermopolis, a vast area of the temple enclosure was devoted to rearing flocks of sacred ibis, worshipped as incarnations of Thoth. When they died, even the tiniest parts of them – individual feathers, nest material, fragments of eggshell – were carefully gathered for sale and burial.

One of the greatest concentrations of animal cults was at Saqqara. Most impressive of all the catacombs was the Serapeum, where generations of Apis bulls were interred with great ceremony. Nearby stood a further complex dedicated to the 'Mother of Apis', a sacred cow worshipped as the incarnation of the goddess Isis. After its death, each cow was purified, embalmed, wrapped in linen bandages and adorned with amulets before being interred in a subterranean vault that had taken up to two years to excavate from the living rock. The huge stone sarcophagus carved for every Mother of Apis was so heavy that a team of thirty men was required to haul it into place.

The most extensive of the animal cemeteries at Saqqara were the ibis galleries, housing over 2 million mummified birds. Each gallery measured thirty feet by thirty feet and was filled from floor to ceiling with neat stacks of pottery jars containing a mummified body part or corpse of a sacred ibis. To keep pace with demand, ibises were bred on an industrial scale on the shores of nearby Lake Abusir and at farms throughout Egypt. In addition to ibises, baboons were also worshipped at Saqqara as manifestations of Thoth. Brought by river or sea from sub-Saharan Africa, the apes were kept in a compound inside the temple of Ptah at Memphis. Pilgrims came to Saqqara from far and wide, seeking advice, insight into the future, cures for sickness, even success in court cases – all in the hope that the holy baboons would carry their supplication to the gods.

In pursuit of divine favour, the Late Period saw worshippers travel in large numbers to important cult centres throughout the Nile Valley. One site in particular held a special mystique: Abydos, burial place of Egypt's first kings and the cult centre of Osiris. Thousands of devotees left millions of offering vessels around the tomb of the first-dynasty king Djer, which was believed to be the tomb of Osiris himself. As early as the Middle Kingdom, making the journey to Abydos was the ambition of every pious Egyptian – the pharaonic equivalent of making the *hajj* to Mecca for Muslims. From the eleventh dynasty onwards, burials throughout Egypt were often furnished with a model boat, to enable the deceased to travel up or downstream to Abydos in fulfilment of a lifelong ambition.

Kings also shared the desire to visit Abydos. Among the many model craft found in Tutankhamun's tomb were three large sailing boats. In one of them, the rigging and the linen sails, dyed red with madder, were preserved intact. Their hulls are made either from a single block of wood or several pieces joined together, their smooth exterior resembling the surface of the carvel-built ships that plied the Nile in the eighteenth dynasty. Carter had no hesitation in identifying these craft as 'vessels for the holy pilgrimage to and from Abydos'.[11]

As for what awaited a pilgrim on their arrival at Abydos, whether king or commoner, an inscription from the late twelfth dynasty provides a first-hand account of the holiest day in the town's calendar, when a passion play called 'the mysteries of Osiris' was performed before crowds of worshippers. The drama re-enacted the murder, death, burial and rebirth of Osiris; at its core was a procession, in which the god's image was carried in a barque shrine from the temple to the royal necropolis and back again, with dramatic tableaux unfolding along the way. In the fullest surviving description, a royal envoy who had been entrusted with ensuring that everything went according to plan described the scene:

> I masterminded the great procession that follows in the god's footsteps . . . Wearing his beautiful regalia, (Osiris) proceeded to the vicinity of Peqer. I cleared the god's path to his tomb in front of Peqer. I protected Wennefer on that day of great battle. I slew all his enemies on the shore of Nedyt.[12]

For pilgrims who could not attend the mysteries of Osiris in person, the next best thing was to erect a commemorative stela along the processional route so that they might participate vicariously. The surviving memorials, which number in their hundreds, show that worshippers came from far and wide to leave their mark. One was erected by a washerman from Memphis, who included his wife, mother, two brothers, five sisters, a brother-in-law, son, nephew and three friends on his monument; another was set up by a pilgrim from Athribis in the delta. Such was the attraction of the great god Osiris, lord of Abydos, who offered his followers the promise of eternal life.

Spectacles like the mysteries of Osiris attracted mass participation. So did the festivals of eighteenth-dynasty Thebes, which were developed as part of a strategy to reshape Egyptian society and bolster royal authority, following the expulsion of the Hyksos. From the beginning of the New Kingdom onwards, the scale, professionalism and sheer visual drama of state religion touched a wider section of the population than ever before. The inhabitants of Thebes and other major cult centres not only enjoyed the spectacle, the sense of occasion and the feasting that accompanied such major events, but were able to place prayers along the processional route in the hope that the passing deity might grant their requests.

In earlier periods, by contrast, state religion was the preserve of the ruling elite. In the Old and Middle Kingdoms, ordinary people had little opportunity to interact with major deities. Instead, for the majority of Egyptians, religious life was conducted in private, away from the formal temple setting. Early community shrines – built in informal style, without state involvement – have been excavated at a range of sites, from the island of Elephantine at the First Nile Cataract to Tell Ibrahim Awad in the north-eastern delta. All are characterized by irregular, mudbrick architecture and deposits of crude votive offerings. The peculiar forms of these artefacts sometimes show local or regional preferences – curious plaques with hedgehog heads seem to have been favoured at Elephantine, scorpions at Hierakonpolis, baboons and tent shrines at Abydos – but in most cases they belong outside the realm of official religion. Objects associated with fertility – female figurines and suggestively shaped stones – are common, underlining the central preoccupation with childbirth and the survival of the next generation. In all cases, the votive offerings are small items of little intrinsic value but huge symbolic importance; they illustrate a stratum of belief and practice that is largely invisible in the written record, but which must have been the norm for the vast majority of the pharaoh's subjects.

As the Egyptian state came to exert an increasing influence over every aspect of its citizens' lives, informal community shrines gave way to more formal buildings referencing the king and ruling elite. At Elephantine, for example, a respected local governor towards the end of the Pyramid Age achieved such renown that he was worshipped as a sort of saint. Where people would previously have placed votive offerings in a sacred cave, they now said their prayers in a state-sanctioned monument to a deified official. Similar cults were established in other towns. At Edfu, the shrine of a regional governor remained a focus of popular worship for 600 years after his death. In the New Kingdom, these local saints were displaced by popular manifestations of the principal gods, while statues of the king and his high officials were set up in temples like Karnak to act as intermediaries between ordinary people and the gods.

Alongside this thoroughgoing state usurpation of religion, the surviving written evidence gives the sense that ordinary Egyptians of the New Kingdom lived largely secular lives. Instructional texts instead place an emphasis on 'getting on', on adhering to social norms in order to achieve worldly success. Of the fifty-three maxims in *The Teaching of Ani*, only two deal with religious observance:

> Observe the festival of your god and repeat it in due season. God is angry if it is neglected ...

> Make offerings to your god and beware lest you offend him.[13]

This rather contrasts with Herodotus's description of the ancient Egyptians as 'beyond measure religious, more than any other nation',[14] a view that was coloured by an outpouring of native religious sentiment at a time of foreign domination.

A more accurate picture may be revealed by the surviving settlements. Workers' dwellings at Deir el-Medina often contained small shrines, where household deities like Taweret and Bes would have been worshipped alongside revered family members. Ancestor busts and stelae dedicated to recently deceased relatives provide further evidence of this practice. In the city of Amarna, some houses were furnished with a mudbrick altar in the central living room, possibly used for displaying votive objects on special occasions. At other times, such objects would have been kept in a wooden chest. A collection from the house of an overseer of works included faience models of a human ear, a bull's head and figures of Bes, and model cobras. In an indication of how widespread such practices were, even the house of the high priest Panehsy, whose day job was officiating in the Great Aten Temple, yielded a range of votive objects, including a bowl with a rearing cobra rising from the base, a cow-shaped vessel and finger rings decorated with the 'sacred eye' (*wedjat*).

This last category is among the most common of all finds at Amarna. Rings were easily made at a household level – many clay ring moulds have been discovered – and the 'sacred eye' motif brought together two of the most important strands of Egyptian religion: the solar cult and the Osiris myth. The design, which combines elements of a human eye with the markings found around the eye of a falcon, was identified both as the 'eye of Ra', with connotations of power and protection, and the 'eye of Horus' or 'lunar eye', which stood for healing and wholeness. As a result, the sacred eye was among the most powerful amuletic symbols in the whole of

Fig. 34. *Wedjat* eye bracelet.

Egyptian religion, worn by the living and placed on the bodies of the dead. The incision wound on mummies was often covered with a metal plate bearing a sacred eye, and kings were buried wearing pairs of sacred eye bracelet. In Tutankhamun's tomb, several sacred eye rings were found on the floor of the Annexe, while his left arm was adorned with a sacred eye bracelet made from gold with inlays of obsidian and lapis lazuli. This small item, more than the statues of gods and other cultic paraphernalia included among Tutankhamun's grave goods, connected him in death with the religious lives of his subjects.

<hr />

If the myriad members of Egypt's vast pantheon were largely removed from the lives of ordinary citizens, there was one notable exception – a deity whose accessibility was famed and whose cult was correspondingly popular. Hathor, like all ancient Egyptian gods and goddesses, was multi-faceted: divine cow; protector of the king; daughter and avenging eye of the sun god; mistress of foreign lands and protector of travellers; goddess of music and dancing. But at the core of her identity was her role as the archetypal mother goddess.

The veneration of cattle in Egypt began in distant prehistory, when the early inhabitants of the Nile Valley were semi-nomadic herders. Not only were cows a principal source of sustenance, their needs determined the pattern of their herders' lives, requiring them to move from pasture to pasture depending on the seasons. This may lie behind a deep-rooted connection made between cows and the stars, for the precession of the constellations, like the movements of a herd, marked the turning of the year. A predynastic cosmetic palette is decorated with the image of a cow's head, with stars attached to the tips of the horns, on the top of the head and in place of the ears. When this celestial cow goddess was first named, she was called Bat ('female power'). She appears twice at the top of the Narmer Palette, gazing down protectively on the first king of the first dynasty as he ritually unifies the land of Egypt; and again on his belt, a symbol of monarchical authority. As late as the twelfth dynasty, Bat retained a position in royal ideology, and was depicted reconciling Horus and Seth. But as the Middle Kingdom unfolded, Bat's role and most of her distinctive iconography were absorbed into the cult of another cow goddess, Hathor.

The name Hathor means 'mansion of Horus', alluding both to the sky (the 'house' in which the falcon god Horus lived) and the womb in which the king (Horus's earthly incarnation) was nurtured. It was entirely appropriate for a cow to be identified as the monarch's mother and protector, for was the ruler not the strong bull who defended Egypt? And what better embodiment of the nurturing maternal instinct than a milch cow? Hathor was first identified by name in the early first dynasty, by which time she was already associated with the king. This role was formalized at the start of the Pyramid Age, when it became customary for the chief queen to act as a priestess of Hathor: the masterful sculptures of Menkaura from his pyramid temple at Giza show Hathor standing next to the king, taking the place of his wife. At the same time, as the sun started to replace the stars as the dominant theme of royal funerary beliefs, Hathor dropped the stars of Bat in favour of a solar disc between her horns.

Unlike other royal patron deities, the great cow goddess

remained accessible to ordinary people. The dominance of bovine imagery in ancient Egyptian thought and iconography, combined with the central importance of reproduction and motherhood in Egyptian society, guaranteed Hathor a universal role. People dreamed of Hathor in their sleep, and shrines to her were the focus of popular veneration throughout the Nile Valley. One prominent example, at Deir el-Bahri in the hills of western Thebes, was frequented by local women seeking a child or protection for themselves and their babies. At Amarna, a shrine outside the walls of the Great Palace was dedicated to Hathor, and a large pottery bowl found among the ruins of the city bore the face of the cow goddess moulded into its side.

Another key aspect of Hathor was her relationship with happiness, singing and dancing. In ancient Egypt, music was regarded as an integral part of worship; for, as the instructional literature noted, 'Singing, dancing and incense are [god's] daily bread, receiving obeisance his wealth'.[15] The sistrum or sacred rattle was especially associated with Hathor. An eleventh-dynasty hymn to the goddess emphasizes this connection:

> My body speaks, my lips repeat: 'Pure sistrum-playing
>   for Hathor.
> Sistrum-playing a million times, because you love the
>   sistrum;
> A million of sistrum-playing, for your spirit in every
>   place.
> I am the one who makes the worshipper waken the
>   sistrum for Hathor
> Every day and at every hour she wishes,
> May your heart be content with the sistrum,
> May you proceed in perfect satisfaction,
> May you rejoice in life and joy.'[16]

On the Little Golden Shrine from Tutankhamun's tomb, the king's young wife Ankhesenamun is shown in the guise of a priestess of Hathor, shaking a sistrum in front of her husband as she presents him with a broad collar. A pair of actual sistra, fifty-two centimetres tall and made from gilded wood and copper alloy, were found among the objects in the tomb. Rare survivors from a world of lost ritual music, each is relatively simple in form: a wooden grip, octagonal in cross section and covered with gold leaf, is surmounted by a cube into which an arched metal loop is slotted. The loop has three snake-shaped metal rods slotted through it, each mounted with three sets of square jangles. Signs of wear on the inside of the arches show that both instruments were played; they may have been used in the king's funeral ceremonies.

The last of Hathor's many aspects was her role as a funerary goddess. Protector of the unborn, the newborn and the living, she was also worshipped as protector of the dead. As 'lady of the sycamore', she was worshipped in the Memphite region as a goddess who supplied food and drink to the deceased. As 'lady of the west', she was believed to dwell in the western mountain at Thebes – the very massif into which the royal tombs were carved – and receive the dying sun each evening. The first major royal monument to be built at Thebes, the mortuary temple of Mentuhotep II, has at its heart a shrine to Hathor. The adjacent monument, built into the same embayment by Hatshepsut, also features a shrine to her. In the *Book of the Dead*, the goddess appears in multiple forms known as the 'seven Hathors', which find later echoes in the biblical story of Joseph. And in Tutankhamun's tomb, one of the three ritual couches used at the king's funeral was carved with the heads of a cow wearing a sun disc between her horns. In this case, star-shaped blotches on her skin identify her as Mehet-weret ('great flood'), who embodied the star-spangled waterway of heaven on which the sun god sailed in his barque during the day. This remarkable object thus unites the iconographies and roles of the three great cow goddesses: Bat of the starry sky, Hathor, protector of the king and lady of the west, and Mehet-weret, who offered the promise of resurrection. From birth to death and rebirth, Hathor was there for every Egyptian, every step of the way.

⊰◉⊱

> Death is in my sight today
> like a man's longing to see home
> after spending many years in captivity.[17]

Ancient Egyptians took great pains to prepare for the next world. The above quote, taken from an extraordinary literary work of the twelfth dynasty dubbed by modern scholars *The Dialogue of a Man and His Soul*, reflects the idealized view of the hereafter as a blessed state, free from the cares of the world. But for most Egyptians, experience of death would have been an unwelcome everyday occurrence. As we have seen, infant mortality was high, death in childbirth not uncommon and average life expectancy only thirty-five years or so. Only a minority of children born in ancient Egypt survived into adulthood. In times of famine, pestilence or civil disorder, death stalked the land like a grim reaper. Even in times of relative peace and plenty, death from accident or disease was so common as to pass almost without comment. In the reign of Ramesses II, arguably the most glorious of all pharaohs, gold-mining expeditions to Nubia would routinely lose half of their workforce and half their transport donkeys from thirst. A few generations later, in the reign of Ramesses IV, an expedition was sent to the Wadi Hammamat to bring back siltstone for the royal workshops. In a commemorative inscription, the king lauded the unprecedented scale of the achievement. After listing the 9,000 or so members of the expedition who survived the ordeal, the inscription adds, almost as an afterthought, 'and those who are dead and omitted from this list: 900 men'.[18] The statistic is chilling: a workman on state corvée work had a one in ten chance of dying, and such loss was considered neither disastrous nor unusual.

In ancient Egypt, the living and the recently dead remained part of the same community. During the Beautiful Festival of the Valley, people would visit family cemeteries to commemorate and commune with their dead relatives. The dead could also be petitioned, for they were believed to have the power to intervene in the lives of the living. Some twenty or so 'letters to the dead' survive, probably the small written tip of a largely oral phenomenon. In one early example from the Old Kingdom, a widow and her son write to her deceased husband seeking his help. After the husband's death, his relatives had removed both property and servants from the marital home. The widow takes the opportunity to remind him of his frequent pronouncements on the importance of solidarity between generations, in order to embarrass him into supporting her cause. Letters to the dead seem to have been written soon after a person's death, however, and the memory of a deceased person rarely survived beyond a generation or so. Tombs were often built over, usurped or even robbed within a few years of a burial, suggesting that any power the dead were believed to wield over the living was of short duration.

For those who forged successful careers as members of the ruling class, as well as those whose position in society left them no option but 'to grunt and sweat under a weary life', the next world offered the hope of something better:

> . . . the land of eternity,
> Which is right and correct and without terror?[19]

Whatever one's means, it was essential to make appropriate preparations for death, burial and resurrection. As a song promised:

> One says, 'Welcome, safe and sound!'
> To him who reaches the Beyond.[20]

Yet these optimistic sentiments were by no means universal. Other texts present a more pessimistic view of death, urging readers to make the most of their life on earth:

> Do as your heart commands while you are upon the
>   earth!
> When that day of wailing comes for you,
> The weary-hearted hears not their wailing,
> Their mourning rescues no man from the
>   netherworld![21]

Instead of a magical portal into another, eternal realm, death could be presented as a benighted state, 'the undiscovered country from whose bourn no traveller returns':

> None returns from there
> To tell of their condition,
> To tell of their ruin,
> To cease our heartache
> Until we hasten to the place where they have gone![22]

This ambivalence towards death is most powerfully expressed in *The Dialogue of a Man and His Soul*. The premise of the text is a dispute between a man who is tired of life and his eternal soul. While the man longs for death, his soul tries to persuade him to make the most of life. For the world-weary human:

> Yonder is a place of alighting, of security for the mind.
> The West is a harbour to which the alert are (safely)
>   rowed;[23]

but, from his soul's perspective:

> If you think about burial, it is heart-breaking, tearful,
>   miserable!
> It is taking a man away from his home
> And casting him upon the high ground!
> You will not go out again and see the sun.[24]

After many rounds of argument and counter-argument, the soul prevails and the man puts thoughts of death out of his mind, deciding to concentrate on living life to the full. Even for a society steeped in mortuary ideology and funerary ritual, death was still something to be put off for as long as possible.

Beliefs about death underwent considerable change throughout pharaonic history. By Tutankhamun's time, a complex web of concepts had evolved to describe the altered state into which a person would be transformed. The deceased was believed to live on in three distinct aspects, each of which had to be provided for in the tomb, its contents or the mortuary cult. First, and most important, was the *ka* or vital force, which could survive death but required sustenance and a body in which to live – hence the importance of mummification. Second, there was the *ba*, or soul. This was depicted as a bird with a human face, and it was believed to fly between the tomb and the outside world. The *ba* seems to have been equated with a person's moral essence, which explains its role in dissuading a world-weary man from taking his own life; making provision for its needs would enable the deceased to be free in the next world. The third aspect was the *akh*, or shining spirit. This is perhaps the hardest concept to explain but represented the transfigured, quasi-divine state that the righteous dead hoped to attain.

If all three aspects were to be given life and force, a proper burial was key. The thousands of artefacts interred alongside Tutankhamun had but one objective: to enable him to live forever through the sustenance and well-being of his *ka*, *ba* and *akh*. Every object was an insurance policy. Perhaps the most telling are four bronze lamps found in the Antechamber. Each measures twenty-three centimetres tall and is shaped like an *ankh* – the sign of life – with human hands holding a length of twisted flax set in a gilded bronze torch holder, mounted on a base of black-varnished wood. Carter declared them

Fig. 35. Ritual torch with *ankh*.

'absolutely new in type'.[25] They may have been used in the final stages of the king's interment. In the darkness of the tomb, the torches would have produced a low, flickering light – scarcely bright enough to see by, but enough to give a hint of rebirth, magnified by the sign of life that held each flame.

NINE

Mortality

Fig. 36. Floral collar placed on Tutankhamun's coffin.

All the prayers in the world could only hope to postpone the inevitability of death. When the end came, it often did so swiftly and unexpectedly – for kings and commoners alike. The death of a pharaoh was a particularly dangerous moment, politically and ideologically. The stability of the state was threatened, as was the continuation of the cosmos. As a result, the preparations made for the proper burial and successful resurrection of the monarch were especially careful, and nowhere is this better attested than in the elaborate sepulchres carved for the pharaohs in the Valley of the Kings. But everyone in ancient Egypt, whatever their status and means, aspired to be ready for the hereafter; as a result, pharaonic civilization can appear to us today as a society obsessed with death. Pyramids, mummies and tombs, sarcophagi, grave goods and afterlife books: the most distinctive elements of ancient Egyptian culture belong to the mortuary sphere. However, in making elaborate preparations for burial, the inhabitants of the ancient Nile Valley were focusing not on leaving this world, but on entering the next. Their motivation was a love of life, not a death wish. The objects from the tomb of Tutankhamun comprise the most extensive and complete funerary assemblage ever discovered in Egypt. From his simple funerary garland to his elaborate shrines and coffins, the material remains of one young man's untimely demise reveal a wealth of information about an entire civilization.

⊲◦▷

Any death was a cause for grief and mourning. The death of a king – the gods' representative on earth and defender of creation – would have provoked fear and trepidation, too; for the passing of an absolute monarch represented a time of supreme psychological and political vulnerability for the whole of ancient Egyptian society. Not surprisingly, written accounts of a pharaoh's demise are rare. Texts usually skirt over the details and simply record the transition from one reign to the next as if nothing untoward had occurred:

> The Dual King, Son of Ra, Intef, who lives like Ra forever . . . departed in peace to his horizon. Now when his son had descended in his place . . . I followed him.[1]

This approach – 'the king is dead, long live the king' – downplayed any hiatus and emphasized the continuity of kingship. But the reality must have been much more fraught, especially if the ruler had died unexpectedly or – worse – in suspicious or violent circumstances.

Such incidents may well have been more common than the ancient texts would like us to think. The best-known example of regicide in ancient Egypt is the death of Amenemhat I, the first king of the twelfth dynasty, in a palace coup. This period of Egyptian history was one of unprecedented literary creativity, and a remarkable text composed after the murder features the dead king recalling the manner of his assassination to his son and successor:

> It was after supper and night had fallen. I was taking an hour of rest, lying on my bed, for I was weary. My mind

was beginning to drift off, when weapons (meant) for defence were turned against me. I was like a snake of the desert. I awoke at the fighting . . . and found it was the guard about to strike me. If I had seized weapons there and then, I would have made the buggers retreat . . . But no one is brave in the night, no one can fight alone.[2]

As for the impact of such news, another literary work of the period vividly conjures up the reaction of members of the royal court on being told about the dreadful events of the night before:

The Residence was silent,
hearts in mourning,
the great double doors sealed,
the entourage with heads in laps,
the elite in grief.[3]

When the hero of this particular story hears the news, even though he is far away from the Residence, he is overcome:

my heart was distraught, my arms (thrown) open,
every limb trembling.[4]

Such must have been the reaction of Tutankhamun's inner circle when the king died suddenly, still a teenager.[5] Recent scientific examination of his mummified body has dispelled many of the theories surrounding his untimely demise, but a fracture of his left femur, together with signs of an open wound behind the knee, seems to have occurred shortly before his death, and may have contributed to it. The Egyptologist who supervised the autopsy has speculated that the pharaoh may have died as a result of a chariot accident. Alternatively, he

Fig. 37. The king's mummified body.

may have succumbed to the combined effects of malaria and plague, exacerbating congenital weakness.

Not only would the suddenness of Tutankhamun's death have alarmed his courtiers – work had barely started on his tomb in the Valley of the Kings – but there was also the highly sensitive matter of the royal succession. The ideal in ancient Egypt was for a father to pass his position on to his eldest son. In the context of the royal family, patrilineal succession was the norm, and the heir apparent was usually the king's eldest son by his chief queen. But when the king had no son, the husband of the chief queen's daughter might be adopted as heir (as seems to have been the case with Thutmose I); or the chief queen herself might act as regent until the succession could be secured (as happened with Hatshepsut during the minority of Thutmose III, and perhaps with Nefertiti after the death of Akhenaten). When Tutankhamun died without any children – his two daughters having been stillborn – the last remaining member of the eighteenth-dynasty royal line was his young widow, Ankhesenamun, but she was too young and too weak to rule alone. She and her supporters must have known that if she were to secure her continued position, she needed a new husband – and before the funeral rites of Tutankhamun were over. For another pharaonic tradition held that the person who carried out the burial of a deceased king secured legitimacy as the next ruler.

This dangerous state of affairs prompted one of the most intriguing episodes in ancient Egyptian history. The bizarre series of events that followed Tutankhamun's death are recounted not in any Egyptian text but in the royal annals of Egypt's imperial rival, the kingdom of the Hittites. According to these records, the newly widowed Egyptian queen wrote to the Hittite ruler, Shuppiluliuma, with an extraordinary request:

> My husband has died and I have no sons. They say that you have many sons. If you would give me one of your sons, he would become my husband. Never shall I take one of my servants and make him my husband! . . . I am afraid![16]

Shuppiluliuma could scarcely believe what he was reading, telling his courtiers, 'Nothing like this has ever happened to me in my entire life!'[17] Instead of sending one of his sons to Egypt, he decided to send an envoy, to investigate and report back. Some months later, the envoy returned with his Egyptian counterpart and confirmed that the matter was as had been reported:

> Nibhururiya [the Hittite rendering of Nebkheperura, Tutankhamun's throne name], who was our lord, died.

He has no son . . . We are seeking a son of our Lord
for the kingship in Egypt.[8]

Shuppiluliuma was persuaded to send his son to Egypt, but
the prince died on the journey – and the Hittite king held the
Egyptians responsible. Eventually, he launched a retaliatory
attack on the Egyptian-held province of Syria, but Egyptian
prisoners of war spread plague throughout the Hittite
population.

The Hittite account of the events following Tutankhamun's
death may explain a curious anomaly in the king's burial.
Tradition held that a king should be buried seventy days after
his death. However, historical evidence suggests that
Tutankhamun died in late summer, while the botanical remains
from his tomb indicate that his burial took place in late spring
– the interval seems to have been three times longer than
custom dictated. Having failed to secure a foreign prince as
her husband, Ankhesenamun seems to have had no option but
to marry a superannuated courtier, the 'god's father' Ay, who
may have been distantly related to the royal family and had
first achieved high office during the reign of Akhenaten. He
would go on to usurp the tomb being prepared for Tutankhamun
and have himself depicted officiating at his predecessor's burial,
in order to legitimize his own accession. What became of
Ankhesenamun thereafter is not known: following her marriage
to Ay, she disappears from the historical record without a trace.

⊲◦⊳

Ay's elevation from courtier to king illustrates an aspect of
ancient Egyptian civilization that otherwise remains largely
hidden in the official record: the office of pharaoh was, at its
heart, a political position, and one to which ambitious men
could aspire. In normal times, the rules of succession and royal

protocol limited the possibilities of advancement for commoners. But on rare occasions, when royal authority broke down or the dynastic line faltered, it was those closest to power who were best placed to take advantage. Those who stood behind the throne were in a unique position to claim it for themselves.

The structure of government in ancient Egypt was a quintessentially pharaonic combination of tradition and innovation. Some of the basic elements – the office of vizier, the political division of the country into provinces, the central role of the treasury – were put in place at the beginning of dynastic history, in order to cement the unification of the country. Other aspects evolved over time to suit changing circumstances. For example, in the first two dynasties, most high officials were members of the extended royal clan. By contrast, from the third dynasty onwards, talented men from relatively humble backgrounds were able to rise up the ranks of the administration, sometimes to the very top. The promotion of commoners gained traction over the succeeding centuries and by the beginning of the New Kingdom, most members of the royal family were excluded from major political or military office, to prevent them forming rival centres of power. Only the crown prince, who often controlled the army in the king's name, and the chief royal wife were allowed access to the levers of power. Akhenaten, who wished to bolster his own authority and minimize any possible opposition, went even further, deliberately promoting self-made men who owed everything to the monarch's patronage.

In the eighteenth dynasty, the period for which we have the most evidence, pharaonic government was divided into two major sections. The first was concerned with the administration of Egypt itself. Its areas of primary focus were crop production, tax collection, the administration of justice and maintaining internal security. Each department was controlled by a small group of trusted senior officials, who together constituted the king's inner circle. The royal household was headed by a chancellor and a chamberlain, and the king's personal estates by a chief steward. National economic matters were the responsibility of the treasury, which was headed by two overseers – one for the Delta, one for the Valley – alongside an overseer of granaries and a chief taxation master. Together, they ensured the regular collection of taxes, maintenance of the state's stocks of grain and the smooth functioning of the agricultural economy that underpinned Egypt's prosperity and security. The most senior position in the civil administration was held by the vizier. The title is an approximation of the Egyptian term, *taity zab tjaty* ('courtier, judge and deputy'), which conveyed the scope of the office. In Tutankhamun's time there was a northern and a southern vizier, reflecting the extent of the Egyptian realm and the practical advantages of a division of responsibilities. Under the viziers were tiers of local officials – regional governors, town mayors and village chiefs – as well as the police, the judiciary and the courts. Low-level civil disputes concerning property rights were decided by village councils, while the most serious criminal cases were considered by the vizier himself. The final two branches of the home administration were the military – overseen by a great army general, assisted by chief deputies of the northern and southern corps, and below them the usual hierarchy of officers – and the temples. Religious affairs were supervised by an overseer of priests of Upper and Lower Egypt (sometimes the vizier), under whom the various high priests controlled the major temples and their extensive economic interests.

The second section of government concerned the administration of Egypt's foreign conquests in Nubia and the Levant. The northern territories, comprising a series of city-states, lent themselves to a dispersed model of Egyptian governors and battalion commanders, and vassal princes. Nubia, by contrast, had a more centralized form of government, modelled on that of the Egyptian Nile Valley: a viceroy of Kush, assisted by two deputies and a single battalion commander. Under them, the mayors of Egyptian colonial towns and the chiefs of indigenous tribes held strictly limited authority.

The viceroy of Kush during Tutankhamun's reign was Amenhotep-Huy; the scenes and inscriptions in his Theban tomb provide a glimpse into the lives of the king's closest advisers at the height of pharaonic civilization. His formal appointment took place at the royal palace, in the king's presence, but due to Tutankhamun's tender age, the proclamation was read out by the overseer of the treasury. The speech was short and to the point: 'Thus speaks Pharaoh: there is handed over to you from Nekhen to Nesut-tawy,' confirming Huy's jurisdiction over a vast stretch of the Nile Valley, extending from Hierakonpolis in Upper Egypt to Napata in Upper Nubia. Huy's reply was equally laconic: 'May Amun, Lord of Nesut-tawy, do according to all that you have commanded, O sovereign, my lord.'[9] He then received his insignia of office – a rolled-up scarf and a gold signet ring – and was welcomed by his officials as he marched off in procession, preceded by a contingent of the viceroy's marines. Only after giving thanks in the temple of Amun did Huy don his ceremonial robes, gold armlets and gold collar, signifying his new quasi-royal status. He then journeyed from the royal residence to Nubia aboard the viceregal boat to take up his office at the Egyptian seat of government.

Other members of Tutankhamun's inner circle included the northern and southern viziers, the chief steward and the commander-in-chief of the army, but two individuals seem to have exercised particular influence over domestic affairs during his reign, and both secured a presence in his tomb. The first was the man who manoeuvred to succeed him as king following Tutankhamun's untimely death and Ankhesenamun's fruitless appeal to the Hittites. Ay was a commoner, but with close connections to the royal family. He may have been Tiye's brother, and his wife was Nefertiti's wet nurse. When Akhenaten came to the throne, Ay was both foster father to the king's great wife and probable uncle to the king. He expressed his loyalty by having two copies of Akhenaten's *Great Hymn to the Orb* carved on the walls of his tomb at Amarna, and his reward was a string of high offices, including commander of chariotry and royal scribe (private secretary to the king). Ay would have used his connections to ensure the succession of the boy king Tutankhamun, who was too young to rule in his own right, and, a decade later, to secure his own succession. However, his triumph was short-lived: after reigning for just three years, he followed his forebears to the grave. His hope of founding his own dynasty was dashed when his son and crown prince, Nakhtmin, was shunted aside by the general Horemheb. In short order, Ay was expunged from history by the new military regime.

The second of Tutankhamun's closest lieutenants presents a very different picture. Maya was a self-made man from a humble background. His career, like Ay's, began under Akhenaten, and the two officials must have known each other well – both served as fan-bearer on the king's right hand, and while Ay commanded the chariotry, Maya was overseer of the army. But following the accession of Tutankhamun and Horemheb's promotion to great army commander, Maya decided to concentrate on civilian affairs. He was overseer of the treasury and also held the office of overseer of works, supervising a number of royal building projects including the excavation and preparation of the royal tomb in the Valley of

Ankhesenamun and Tutankhamun (Little Golden Shrine) (66)

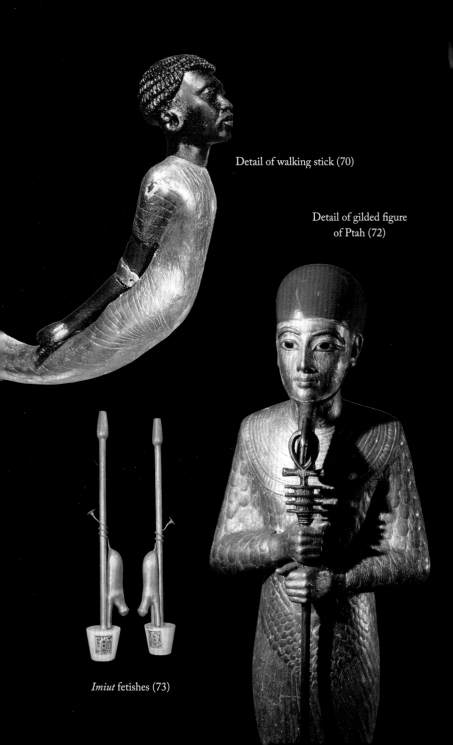

Detail of walking stick (70)

Detail of gilded figure
of Ptah (72)

Imiut fetishes (73)

Anubis carrying shrine (83) at the time of discovery

Canopic chest (84)

Funeral procession (east wall of burial chamber) (85)

Opening of the mouth (north wall of burial chamber) (86)

Wooden statue of
Tutankhamun as Nefertem (94)

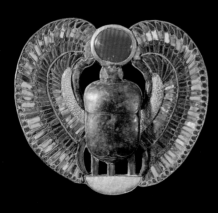

Scarab pectoral (96)

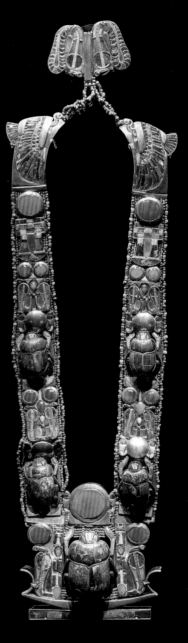

Pectoral, chain and counterpoise
with lapis lazuli scarabs (95)

Black resin scarab (90) at the time of discovery,
in situ on the third (innermost) coffin

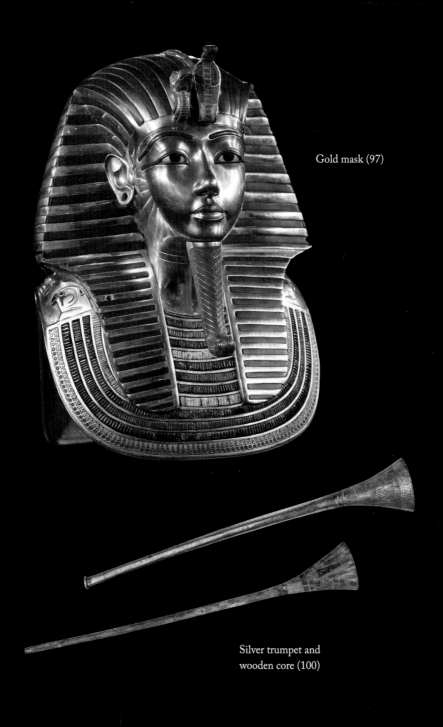

Gold mask (97)

Silver trumpet and
wooden core (100)

the Kings. When Tutankhamun died, his tomb far from complete, Maya was responsible for the hurried preparation and provisioning of a smaller burial in the floor of the valley. Among the objects he assembled for the tomb was a fine wooden figure of the mummified king, lying on a lion-headed funerary couch. The natural grain of the wood was used to great effect as part of the decoration, while the royal uraeus on the pharaoh's brow was picked out in gold leaf. Along each long side of the artefact, an incised band of hieroglyphs records its presentation by Maya:

> Made by the servant who is beneficial to His Majesty, who seeks what is good and finds what is fine, and does it thoroughly for his lord, who makes excellent things in the Splendid Place, overseer of building works in the Place of Eternity, the royal scribe, overseer of the treasury, Maya.[10]

Fig. 38. Bier figure.

Maya would later supervise the resealing of Tutankhamun's tomb after robbers had entered it. Ever loyal to the reigning monarch, he would also oversee the construction of a tomb for his old colleague, Horemheb, and restore the tomb of an earlier eighteenth-dynasty pharaoh, Thutmose IV. As for his own final resting place in the Memphite necropolis at Saqqara, Maya built a tomb that, above ground, deferred to the monument prepared for Horemheb; but below ground, the burial chambers recall those of a royal sepulchre with reliefs in golden yellow, the royal colour of resurrection.

The contrasting fates of Ay and Maya illustrate the opportunities and risks of high office in ancient Egypt. Making a bid for the ultimate prize could all too easily end in ignominy and proscription, but keeping one's head down and serving loyally could bring worldly success and immortality.

⊲◦⊳

A tomb was of no use unless the body itself was preserved. Fundamental to ancient Egyptian beliefs about the afterlife was the notion that the continuation of a person's existence depended upon the proper treatment of their corpse. In prehistoric times, the inhabitants of the Nile Valley buried their dead in pits dug into the desert floor, away from settlements and fields and beyond the reach of the annual inundation. The hot, dry sand would have drawn out all the fluids and moisture from the body in a matter of days, arresting the process of decay and leaving the corpse dry, leathery and preserved. The accidental unearthing of such 'natural mummies' may have led the Egyptians to experiment with artificial methods of achieving the same effect. The earliest attempts at embalming date to the middle of the fourth millennium BC: a woman buried at Hierakonpolis had bandages wrapped around her head, hands and arms, while in another burial the upper body had been stuffed with linen bundles. Traces of resin found on the skin suggest that the bodies were treated with unguents before being placed in the grave. In these early examples, the focus of preservation seems to have been the head, the part of the body that most clearly expressed an individual's identity.

Over the following centuries, the elaboration of funeral rites prolonged the period between death and burial, while the introduction of coffins – intended to provide the body with extra protection – unwittingly promoted decay by shielding it from direct contact with the surrounding sand. To outwit the natural processes of decomposition, artificial mummification was swiftly perfected; the first mummified bodies are from graves of the first dynasty, and the basic elements of the technique remained largely unchanged for the next 3,000 years. Because of the religious and ritual sensitivities surrounding mummification, there are very few written sources that describe the process. The fullest accounts are found in the writings of Greek and Roman authors, who were fascinated and horrified by the Egyptians' obsessive attention to the bodies of their dead. The fourth-century BC historian Herodotus, for example, described how Egyptian embalmers

first draw out part of the brain through the nostrils with an iron hook, and inject certain drugs into the rest. Then, making a cut near the flank with a sharp knife of Ethiopian stone (flint or obsidian), they take out all the intestines and clean the belly, rinsing it with palm wine and bruised spices; and presently, filling the belly with pure ground myrrh and cassia and any other spices, save only frankincense, they sew up the anus. Having done this, they conceal the body for seventy days, embalmed in saltpetre; no longer time is allowed for the embalming; and when the seventy days are past they wash the body

and wrap the whole of it in bandages of fine linen cloth,
anointed with gum . . . which done, they give the dead
man back to his friends.[II]

While this description may have been deliberately titillating
for a Greek readership, its accuracy has been confirmed by the
examination of mummies. Once a body had been washed to
clean and purify it, a sharp, hooked bronze tool was inserted
up the nose and into the cranium. By waggling the instrument
around, the brain could be mashed into a gooey pulp that could
then be extracted via the nose, leaving the head as intact as
possible. (The embalmers who carried out the mummification
of Tutankhamun seem to have been amateurs, for they removed
not only his nose but also the back of his head.) The Egyptians
had no understanding of brain function: for them, the heart
was the seat of intelligence and emotion; the brain was simply
an internal organ that needed to be removed as completely as
possible to prevent the decomposition of the entire body. To
that same end, the next step was the removal of the viscera, via
an incision in the side of the abdomen. Only the heart was left
in the body, as it would play a vital role in the last judgement.

Once eviscerated, the body was filled with lumps of resin
and resin-soaked bandages to preserve its shape, before being
packed and covered with natron – a naturally occurring mixture
of sodium carbonate and sodium bicarbonate – for forty days,
to dehydrate the flesh. The seventy days mentioned by
Herodotus was, in fact, the duration of the entire mummification process, including the time taken to 'rebuild' the body
after dehydration. This involved filling it with bandages,
sawdust, dried lichen and even soil, and inserting linen bundles
into the eye sockets to restore the shrunken features.

Molten resin, oils and unguents were then poured over the
body, to act as preservatives and to disguise the aroma of dried

flesh. The end goal was to refashion the deceased into a perfect divine image, a vehicle for resurrection and an eternal home for the soul. However, the unfortunate result in some cases (including Tutankhamun), was a thick, black layer of congealed resin that obliterated the features and gave the preserved bodies their modern name, the word 'mummy' being derived from the Arabic *mummiya*, 'tar'.

Following the cleansing, preservation and anointing of the body, the corpse was wrapped in linen bandages, with amulets and other magical objects inserted between the layers. Priests are shown wrapping a mummy in a nineteenth-dynasty Theban tomb, while a mid-eighteenth-dynasty funerary papyrus from the Memphite area depicts a body laid out on a bed, with a priest adjusting its position. Similar scenes from the burial chambers of Theban tombs show the mummy on a lion-headed embalming bed (an example survives from Tutankhamun's tomb), while a priest leans over the body and chants prayers.

In most of these depictions, the chief officiant wears the jackal mask of Anubis, god of mummification. The association of jackals with the necropolis was an ancient one. The animals are denizens of the low desert and can often be seen prowling among graves, and Anubis came to be regarded as the guardian of the dead. In the Pyramid Texts, he appears frequently in connection with the royal tomb; and when Carter and Carnarvon broke through the wall separating Tutankhamun's burial chamber from the adjoining Treasury, they were confronted with a life-sized statue of Anubis, recumbent on a shrine, mounted on a sledge. With gaunt, powerful features, the jackal is carved from wood and painted black. His eyes are inlaid with calcite and obsidian, his claws are fashioned from silver, and his ears and the scarf around his neck are picked out in gold. The shrine upon which he lies resembles an ancestral tent shrine, its golden side panels decorated with the signs for stability and protection. This magnificent, haunting object, nearly a metre long, would have been borne aloft on the shoulders of priests during the funeral procession and set down in the rearmost chamber of the tomb to watch over the king in the afterlife.

⊰○⊱

The ancient Egyptian belief in life after death required that a tomb be furnished with the essentials for continued existence. The most basic grave goods were supplies of food and drink: the daily staples of bread and beer and, for higher-status tomb owners, more prestigious comestibles such as wine, dates and olive oil. Ancient Egyptian graves of every period were provided with sustenance for the deceased. In most cases, only the pottery containers have survived; but in a few instances, like the tomb of Tutankhamun, the contents have also been preserved, allowing us an insight into the Egyptians' eating habits.

To enable the tomb owner to enjoy a blessed afterlife, food and drink were necessary but not sufficient. Egyptian society was acutely conscious of social status. Maintaining one's rank in the hereafter was almost as important as having enough to eat; to this end, graves were conceived not simply as mechanisms to guarantee resurrection but as expressions of the owner's social and economic standing. Throughout pharaonic history, people were as unequal in death as in life. Objects denoting a person's position – from the flint knives and stone maceheads of predynastic chieftains to the royal regalia of New Kingdom pharaohs – were important in any funerary assemblage. A lavish, richly equipped tomb was the ultimate status symbol.

Status was likewise reflected in the investment of time and resource involved in a tomb's construction. Scraping a simple pit in the sand was the work of a couple of hours, but building a mudbrick or stone tomb chapel, not to mention decorating it with richly painted scenes, was an altogether more time-consuming and costly undertaking. It required an element of sacrifice, by individuals and the wider community, but society's expectations around mortuary provision were so powerful that tomb-building was a sport in which every ancient Egyptian sought to compete. The urge to prepare the best possible funerary monument is an ever-present theme in Egyptian writings:

> Embellish your place in the necropolis, the tomb that will conceal your corpse. Set it before you as your mission, as something that counts in your eyes. Emulate the great ones of old who are at peace in their tombs. No blame attaches to the one who does this.[12]

Economic records from Deir el-Medina show that the workers used their skills and access to specialist materials to build and furnish tombs that were far grander than their social and economic status would normally permit. Some of these work-men's tombs in the hillside above the village are almost as elaborate as the tombs of grand viziers.

The construction of a king's tomb was an undertaking on a different scale entirely. Recent excavations in the town of the pyramid-builders at Giza have revealed the administrative effort required to erect the largest of all mortuary monuments. The royal tombs of the New Kingdom, cut into the hills at Amarna and Thebes, may not have required so vast a workforce, but they certainly needed architects and masons, plasterers and painters. The foundation and long-term maintenance of specialist workmen's villages underscores the economic and bureaucratic investment made by the Egyptian state in providing for the pharaohs' afterlife. At Deir el-Medina, gener-ation upon generation of tomb workers and their families enjoyed a privileged existence in a gated community, deep in the Theban hills, their every need supplied by the government. The importance of their top-secret project also gave them economic leverage: when, in the reign of Ramesses III, the government was late paying the workers, they withdrew their labour – the first recorded strike in history – and the state had to back down.

Despite all the time and effort spent preparing a pharaoh's tomb, the death of a king must have caused a feverish bout of activity. Very often, the intended monument might be a work in progress. A judgement would have had to be made as to whether it could be quickly finished to an acceptable degree (as happened with the royal tomb of Horemheb), or whether an alternative tomb would need to be pressed into service (as was the case for Tutankhamun). Alongside the preparation of the tomb and the mummification of the body, there was the considerable task of amassing the grave goods, a mixture of everyday items and ritual objects prepared specially for the tomb. Getting hold of the right equipment in sufficient quantities would have meant leaning on officials to contribute and raiding the palace storerooms to supplement the pharaoh's own treasured possessions.

As early as the third dynasty, it seems to have been commonplace for kings to commandeer artefacts made for their predecessors. In Tutankhamun's case, surplus equipment made for the Theban burials of his two royal predecessors, Akhenaten and Neferneferuaten, was hurriedly pressed into service. Some items were left unaltered: objects bearing Akhenaten's name include a box, a fan, a faience bangle and the linen shawl that clothed the statue of Anubis, while Neferneferuaten's cartouches appear on a set of gold sequins, two more bangles and a further linen shawl. A few of the more sensitive artefacts – the second coffin, gold mummy bands and the 'bow of honour' – were reinscribed for their new owner. The scale of reused material in Tutankhamun's tomb – including much of his jewellery and one of his *shabti* figures – conveys a sense of the hurry that must have surrounded the preparation of his burial.

Nowhere in the tomb is this haste more apparent than in one of the most sensitive pieces of funerary equipment for any ancient Egyptian: the canopic chest. According to long-standing tradition, a person's intestines, stomach, liver and lungs were removed from the corpse, embalmed individually and placed in containers known to archaeologists as canopic jars. There, safe from putrefaction, they could continue to serve their purpose in the afterlife. Tutankhamun's canopic equipment was lavish: each of the viscera was placed in a miniature gold coffin, with carnelian and glass inlays; the four coffinettes were inserted into cylindrical compartments carved into a solid block of calcite, with a stone stopper carved to resemble the pharaoh's head sealing each compartment. The canopic box was mounted on a sledge, draped with a linen shawl and placed inside a gilded wooden shrine with a decorative canopy. Finally, this shrine was nested inside a second, larger shrine, which was guarded by four exquisitely carved figurines of the four protector goddesses, Neith, Nephthys, Selket and Isis. The whole assemblage constitutes the finest, most elaborate set of canopic equipment ever found, yet much of it was appropriated: the coffinettes were originally made for Neferneferuaten, while the calcite stoppers do not resemble the face of Tutankhamun as depicted on other objects from the tomb. Even pharaohs, it seems, had to beg, borrow and steal to furnish their eternal resting place.

Burials and their associated equipment are the material manifestation of the way a society lays its dead to rest, but an invisible realm of funerary practice carries no less significance. In modern Western cultures, the funeral is perhaps more significant, both to the relatives of the deceased and wider society, than the grave and its accoutrements. Because the architectural and artefactual remains of the ancient Egyptian way of death are so abundant and impressive, we might conclude that the ritual aspects were less important, but nothing could be further from the truth.

Scenes depicting funeral ceremonies are a common element in the decoration of elite, non-royal tombs in western Thebes. The most complete example belongs to the burial of the vizier Rekhmira, but even relatively minor officials like Pairy, a priest of Amun in the reign of Amenhotep III, have mortuary vignettes painted on the walls of their tomb. In Pairy's case, they comprise the pilgrimage by boat to Abydos, the funeral procession itself, the opening of the mouth ceremony and the arrival of the deceased and his wife in the realm of Osiris, god of the dead. Such scenes allow us to recreate the various stages of a high-status eighteenth-dynasty Egyptian funeral.

The sequence of events began with mummification, but the spiritual preparation of the body for the afterlife was just as important as its physical preservation. The pilgrimage to Abydos served to acquaint and associate the deceased with Osiris, and to prepare them to enter his kingdom. On the day of the funeral itself, the mummy was received from the embalmers, placed in a coffin, set on a boat-like bier (recalling the barque shrines of the gods) and borne to the tomb. If, as seems likely, the embalming workshops of Thebes were located on the east bank of the Nile, adjacent to the main town, the ferrying of the body across the river to the land of the dead would have taken on an additional symbolic significance.

The funeral procession, from the quayside to the cemetery, lay at the heart of the proceedings, and would have been a colourful – and noisy – spectacle. A twelfth-dynasty description of a private funeral sets the scene:

> The funeral cortège is made for you on the day of
>   interment,
> the mummy case of gold, (its) head of lapis lazuli,
> the sky above you as you lie on the bier,
> oxen pulling you, musicians in front of you.
> Dances of the dead are performed for you at the
>   mouth of your tomb,
> the offering formula is recited for you,
> a sacrifice is made at your offering tables.[13]

As this account indicates, while a single coffin could have been carried by pallbearers (usually the male friends and relatives of the deceased), a heavier set of burial equipment would have required a team of oxen to drag it on a sledge or in a wheeled cart. A mid-eighteenth-dynasty tomb shows a catafalque on a sledge being pulled by teams of oxen driven by stick-wielding ox-hands; priests and family members precede the coffin, while offering bearers walk behind it carrying chests, furniture and other grave goods.

A couple of generations later, the tomb of Tutankhamun contains a rare depiction of a royal funeral cortège, painted on the east wall of the burial chamber. The details suggest that a king's funeral was not too different from those of his high officials, differing in scale and opulence rather than substance. Tutankhamun's catafalque is pulled by twelve men, including two figures with shaved heads (who may be the northern and southern viziers, Usermont and Pentu). As they process, the men chant, 'O Nebkheperura, come in peace! O god who protects the land!'

In addition to the main catafalque bearing the coffinned mummy, high-status funeral processions might also feature a second sledge carrying a mysterious object called a *tekenu*. Artistic sources generally depict a pear-shaped bundle wrapped in an animal skin, sometimes with a human head poking out of the top. In other instances, it seems to show a man lying in the foetal position. It is likely that the *tekenu* represents material left over from the process of mummification; regarded as sacred, these odds and ends would be bundled up and interred in a pit separate from the main burial. Alternatively, the *tekenu* may have been the placenta, saved from birth and preserved throughout a person's life as their magical 'twin'. Its presence at the funeral would have emphasized the ritual connection between birth and rebirth.

Another, equally mysterious aspect of ancient Egyptian funerals was a group of dancers called the *muu*. Wearing tall wicker headdresses, they would join a funeral procession as it reached the edge of the necropolis, emerging from 'the Hall of the *Muu*' to greet the mummy and accompany it to the grave. One interpretation is that they represented the gate-keepers and ferrymen of the underworld, but in truth, their significance is unknown.

When an ancient Egyptian cortège reached the mouth of the tomb, the funeral proper could begin. Crowds of female mourners, led by the widow of the deceased, threw dust over their heads, raised their hands to the sky and ululated. Then a complex series of rites prepared the dead for burial. Like much of ancient Egyptian religious practice, the elements of funerary ritual seem to have appeared first in the royal sphere, after which they were gradually adopted more widely. The person presiding over the funeral, known as the *sem* priest, was originally the king's eldest son and heir. (At Tutankhamun's funeral, the aged courtier Ay acted the role.) The chief celebrant was another key figure, identified in scenes by his distinctive kilt, a wide sash worn over the shoulder and by the scroll that he carried. This was the lector priest – the Egyptian term meaning 'he who carries the scroll'. Originally reserved for senior members of the royal family, the office was opened up to a wider section of society in the Middle Kingdom and quickly evolved into one of the most important of all priestly roles. At funerals, the lector priest was responsible for reciting the offering formula and for performing the all-important spells and rites to transform the deceased into a transfigured spirit.

As the mourners' wailing died down, a bull might be sacrificed and its choice cuts offered to the deceased, libations poured and incense burned to conjure the presence of the divine. The mummy in its coffin was set upright on a patch of sand, recalling the primeval mound of creation, and a cone of scented unguent was placed on its head. The stage was set for the most important ceremony of all.

⊲○▷

> My mouth is opened by Ptah and the bonds in my mouth
> have been loosened by my local god. Thoth comes indeed,
> full and ready with magic. The bonds of Seth which
> constricted my mouth have been loosened . . . My mouth
> is opened, my mouth is forced apart by Shu with that
> iron knife of his, with which he forced apart the mouths
> of the gods.[14]

In order for a mummified body to be transformed into an immortal home for the soul of the deceased, the ancient Egyptians believed it had to be able to breathe. This required a special ritual. As well as being performed at funerals, the opening of the mouth ceremony featured at the dedication of cult images and even at the consecration of temples. Whatever the object – mummy, statue or temple – the purpose of the ritual was to animate the recipient. At a funeral, it could be carried out by the *sem* priest (as illustrated on the north wall of Tutankhamun's burial chamber), by the lector priest or by a priest wearing the jackal mask of Anubis.

As befits one of the most ritually charged of all religious ceremonies, the origins of the opening of the mouth are ancient. The earliest textual reference is found in a private tomb of the early fourth dynasty, and the royal annals record the ceremony as having been practised on cult statues in the reigns of the earliest kings. However, its origins may go back further still. Special sets of opening of the mouth equipment – comprising models of the tools used in the ritual – were commonly included among the grave goods of Old Kingdom private tombs. They generally consist of a limestone slab carved with recesses for each of the elements: two narrow-necked bottles (one black and one white); four, or occasionally five, straight-sided beakers (two black and two white); a pair of finger-shaped blades of dark stone; and, in pride of place, a fishtail-shaped knife.

Fishtail flint knives are attested in burials from the early predynastic period, and there is some evidence that an implement of this form was used to cut a baby's umbilical cord. The possible associations of the opening of the mouth ritual with childbirth are strengthened by the two finger-shaped blades found in model sets, which recall the way in which a doctor or midwife checks a newborn baby's mouth for obstructions with their little fingers. The bottles and beakers may have symbolized the various liquid and solid foods with which babies were weaned. According to this interpretation, the opening of the mouth ceremony may have begun as a ritual sequence of actions symbolizing a baby's birth and growth, and, by extension, the steps needed to enable a cult statue or dead person to be reborn. In ancient Egyptian, the verb 'to fashion' and 'to bear' is the same word; it would have been natural to apply the same rituals to a divine image or mummified corpse as to a human baby.

The ancient Egyptians loved to weave different strands of belief into a dense tapestry of ideology. The more ancient the myth or practice, the greater the tendency to elaboration. The evolution of the opening of the mouth ceremony provides a striking illustration of this phenomenon. Between the Old and New Kingdoms, the key instrument used in the ritual shifted from a pair of finger-shaped blades to an adze; both were tools with an otherworldly connection. The finger blades were made of meteoric iron, a material that was believed to come from the stars, and in the Pyramid Texts, two iron blades, called 'two stars', are said to open the mouth of the king. It did not escape the Egyptians' notice that the adze used to make wooden statues resembled the shape of the constellation Ursa Major. Both items were hence deemed suitable for performing the opening of the mouth, since they carried the same extraterrestrial connotations.

At a funeral, the key rite of touching the lips of the mummy with the adze and other special tools took place at the mouth of the tomb, prior to interment. The specific liturgy of the opening of the mouth is first attested in the Pyramid Texts; by the New Kingdom, it had been codified into seventy-five distinct verses. These make reference to the knife, fingers and adze and give a starring role to Ptah, underworld deity and divine craftsman. The most widely attested description of the ceremony, quoted above, is found in Chapter 23 of the *Book of the Dead*. At the same time as the opening of the mouth was being performed, the *tekenu* might be pulled back and forth on its sledge, accompanied by ritual prayers.

These ceremonies completed, priests carried out a final anointing of the mummy with oils and unguents, and presented additional food and drink offerings. Then came the moment of burial: the body, laid inside its nest of coffins and shrines, was installed in the burial chamber, with the canopic chest and other equipment placed around it. Finally, after the burial chamber had been sealed, the mourners held a wake at the tomb, sending the deceased off on the journey into the world beyond.

⊲◌⊳

Once the lid of Tutankhamun's outermost coffin had been set in place, the royal insignia of cobra and vulture on its brow were garlanded with a wreath of olive leaves and cornflowers, a final act of reverence for the dead king. As Carter recounted after the discovery:

> Laid on that golden outer lid was a tiny wreath of flowers – as it pleased us to think, the last farewell offering of the widowed girl queen to her husband. Among all that regal splendour there was nothing so beautiful as those few withered flowers.[15]

The olive leaves had been arranged so that they alternately showed their green upper and silvery lower surfaces. They and the flowers had been painstakingly sewn onto narrow strips of papyrus pith. In addition to this final love token, a second, larger garland had been placed on the chest of the king's innermost coffin and several other items of burial equipment – notably the portable statue of Anubis and some gilded statues of gods – had likewise been adorned with floral wreaths. Artistic evidence from contemporary private tombs indicates that garlands were carried by mourners in the funeral procession and placed near the mummy during the last rites. Six floral collars were found in the pit that contained the leftover embalming materials from Tutankhamun's burial. The custom of dedicating wreaths to honour the dead is an ancient one.

The garlands of flowers and fruit discovered on mummies

provide valuable information about the flora of ancient Egypt. Then, as now, the components of a funerary wreath were selected for their scent, colour and symbolism. Favourite elements included the fruits of the persea and mandrake – auspicious as well as decorative – and field bindweed, with its connotations of sexuality and fertility. The wreaths placed around Tutankhamun's divine statuettes contained sprouting grains of barley (symbolizing rebirth), leaves from the olive and pomegranate (food and abundance), willow (for the winding waterways of the underworld) and cornflowers (pale blue, connoting regeneration). In the nineteenth dynasty, the mummy of Ramesses II had narcissus bulbs placed around its neck; the appearance of the flowers each spring provided a floral metaphor for the king's rebirth.

Ancient Egypt had a diverse flora, reflecting the country's climatic range, from Mediterranean to sub-tropical, and its diverse habitats, from the marshy banks of the Nile and well-watered fields to the arid desert edge. The riverbanks supported thick beds of reed and sedge, dominated by the stately papyrus; in gardens, the Egyptians cultivated a range of native species including willow herb, narcissus and chrysanthemum. Species introduced from the Levant in the early eighteenth dynasty offered new colours and forms; as well as pomegranates and cornflowers, these introductions included poppies, delphiniums, hollyhocks, lilies and safflowers, the red and yellow dyes of which were used to colour linen. The 'Botanical Garden' reliefs of Thutmose III at Karnak depict further exotica: iris, dragonwort and arum.

From this wide selection of plants, the Egyptians chose a select few for religious settings. In the first and second dynasties, coffins and sacred brooms were created from the branches of *Ceruana pratensis*; its scent was believed to ward off evil spirits. Papyrus was regarded as the symbolic plant of Lower

Egypt, and a metaphor for the Nile Valley as a whole. When depicted intertwined with lilies (representing Upper Egypt), it formed an artistic motif known as *sema-tawy*, 'joining the Two Lands'. For cultic purposes, the most important flowers were the blooms of the white and blue waterlily that grew in great abundance on the Nile in ancient times. Both species were used in funerary wreaths; entire blooms, still attached to their long stems, could also be included among mummy wrappings.

There were three main reasons why waterlilies were favoured for the burials of the dead and the cults of the gods. First, blue waterlily flowers have an intense perfume, which for the Egyptians was an indication of divine presence: in the scene of Amenhotep III's 'divine birth' in Luxor Temple, the accompanying text describes how the king's mother, on being visited in the night by the god Amun-Ra, 'awoke because of the god's scent'.[16] On a more practical level, sweet-smelling blooms were a boon in a hot country with rudimentary sanitation; guests at banquets would routinely wear lotus blossoms in their hair or carry them as nosegays. Second, because waterlilies open at sunrise and close at sunset, they were associated with the sun god and with rebirth. And third, *Nymphaea caerulea* contains powerful alkaloids which, when dissolved in alcohol and imbibed, have a narcotic effect. Like many societies, the ancient Egyptians believed that the altered state of consciousness produced by intoxication brought a person into proximity with the divine realm.

In secular settings, too, flowers were valued for their decorative and sweet-smelling properties. The Egyptian word for 'flower' (*setji-she*) meant 'garden scent', indicating that fragrance was highly prized. Garlands of fresh flowers were handed out at banquets, and servant girls would tie them around guests' necks. Individual flowers were sewn onto a collar of papyrus lined with linen and thin strips of palm leaf. Popular materials for garlands included persea, olive, willow and pomegranate leaves, blue waterlilies, cornflowers and bitterweed, and red berries from withania nightshade, perhaps enhanced with blue faience beads. A floral collar was discovered in the ruins of a house at Amarna, possibly discarded after a banquet. And in the nineteenth-dynasty Theban tomb of an 'overseer of the garden of the Ramesseum', the owner is shown making garlands. Jewellery also took its cue from these natural forms: in the eighteenth dynasty, it became fashionable to wear large beaded collars with elements fashioned from coloured glass to resemble leaves, flowers and fruits.

Lastly, flowers were presented by the ancient Egyptians as love tokens. Fragrance is an age-old metaphor for the sweetness of love, and one New Kingdom love poem has a young woman say to her lover:

I belong to you like this plot of ground
That I planted with flowers
And sweet-smelling herbs.[17]

The young Ankhesenamun might well have expressed such sentiments as she bid a final farewell to her dead husband and wished him godspeed in the next life.

◁◦▷

Tutankhamun's mummified body was surrounded by the most elaborate set of protective layers ever found in an ancient Egyptian burial. The face of the mummy was covered by the famous gold funeral mask and the whole body was laid in a beautifully fashioned anthropoid coffin, also wrought from solid gold. This coffin was placed inside a second one, made from wood and decorated with sheet gold and coloured glass inlays. In turn, this second coffin was nested inside an anthropoid coffin of gilded wood. Such a set of coffins would have been considered more than adequate to protect the body of a deceased commoner and to aid its magical rebirth. However, kings had long exercised their royal prerogative to be buried in the ultimate timeproof container: a stone sarcophagus.

Stone's durability made it the material of choice for any structure in ancient Egypt that aspired to permanence; invariably, these were royal commissions. Because of the practical challenges in quarrying and transporting large blocks of stone, only a large-scale expedition could carry out such work. As a result, the architectural and sculptural use of stone was a state monopoly for much of pharaonic history. Building stone was generally quarried as close to the construction site as possible. The limestone blocks used to build the pyramids of Giza were quarried at Giza, with only the fine casing blocks brought across the river from Tura. Sandstone for the great temples of Upper Egypt was mainly extracted from the Nile-side quarries at Gebel el-Silsila, from where it could be transported

Fig. 39. The royal sarcophagus.

by barge to its final destination. By contrast, the finest-quality sculptural stone – from which royal statues and sarcophagi were carved – was often brought considerable distances. Two especially favoured types of stone, red granite and translucent calcite, were only found in sufficient quantity and quality at Aswan and Hatnub, respectively. The former lay at Egypt's southernmost border, at the foot of the First Nile Cataract, while the latter was located in the desert, some distance from the river. Yet great blocks were extracted from these quarries and ferried hundreds of miles to the royal workshops at Memphis, where they were carved to furnish the tombs of Egypt's Pyramid Age rulers.

The effort expended in securing an appropriate block for the king's funerary chest is illustrated by a series of inscriptions carved in the siltstone quarries of the Black Mountains, a remote and desolate region of the Eastern Desert. Here – and only here – Egypt's geological riches include seams of fine-grained, greenish-black stone that can be carved with the sharpest of detail and was used to create some of the master-pieces of ancient Egyptian art. Usually, such sculptures were relatively small-scale, reflecting the difficulties inherent in obtaining and transporting large blocks of siltstone. But Mentuhotep IV, an otherwise ephemeral king of the eleventh dynasty, wanted to outdo his predecessors by securing a block large enough for the royal sarcophagus. His gruelling expedition recorded every step of its mammoth task in beautifully executed hieroglyphs, cut into the quarry face for posterity:

Second month of the inundation season, day twenty-three. Setting to work on this mountain, on the block set aside for the sarcophagus . . . Day twenty-seven: descent of the lid of this sarcophagus, being a block four cubits by eight cubits by two cubits, as it came from the works. Calves were slaughtered, goats sacrificed and incense burned. Lo, an expedition of 3,000 sailors from the districts of Lower Egypt conducted it safely to the Nile Valley.[18]

At the conclusion of the expedition, its leader, the vizier Amenemhat, summed up his monumental achievement:

I brought back for him a sarcophagus which conjures up everlasting life and is beneficent for ever.[19]

Mentuhotep IV's siltstone sarcophagus has not survived. But Tutankhamun's great chest – in Carter's words, 'an immense yellow quartzite sarcophagus, intact, with the lid still firmly fixed in its place, just as the pious hands had left it'[20] – is one of the finest examples from pharaonic times. Carved from a single block of stone, it was supported at each corner on a block of calcite, while the lid was of red granite. The ensemble thus brought together the three most auspicious types of stone that had been used for royal burials since the dawn of history.

The word 'sarcophagus' is derived from the Greek meaning 'flesh-eater', but in ancient Egyptian the terminology was altogether more optimistic: their word was *neb-ankh*, 'lord of life', which expressed the hope that, with the aid of the sarcophagus, the dead might be reborn to eternal life. A stone chest was no mere container for a corpse: it was a resurrection machine, and the decoration of royal sarcophagi underscores this belief. Early examples from the Old and Middle Kingdoms are generally very plain, apart from recessed panels of so-called 'palace façade decoration' that recalled the external appearance of the royal compound at Memphis. This emphasized the afterlife as a continuation of earthly life; private coffins provided homes for the deceased, while the royal sarcophagus afforded an eternal palace for the dead king. In the New Kingdom, by contrast, royal sarcophagi are characterized by more elaborate decoration, reflecting new strands of belief.

Tutankhamun's chest is carved at the corners with figures of four funerary goddesses (Isis, Nephthys, Selket and Neith), their wings spreading out to envelop it. Further magical protection is afforded by a frieze of Isis knots and Osiris pillars around the base and an incised *wedjat* eye at the western end. Much of this decoration pertains to the Osiris myth, but an earlier, solar version of the royal afterlife is reflected in the winged sun disc depicted at the head end of the sarcophagus lid and in the materials used for its construction – red granite and golden yellow quartzite having strong solar connotations.

Coffins and sarcophagi comprise one of the richest sources of information for changing conceptions of the ancient Egyptian afterlife. Towards the end of the Old Kingdom, scenes previously confined to tomb walls began to be included on the inside of coffins. The sky goddess Nut was often depicted on the underside of the lid, spreading herself over the deceased just as she was believed to spread her body over the earth; the coffin effectively became a tomb in miniature. At the same time, religious spells and incantations that had previously been reserved for royalty and inscribed inside pyramids were now adapted for use inside private coffins. The Pyramid Texts were expanded and became the Coffin Texts, often written in closely crowded vertical columns of cursive hieroglyphs or hieratic script. Whereas the Pyramid Texts had reflected astral or solar visions of the afterlife – the king joining the circumpolar stars or journeying with Ra across the heavens – these were joined in the Coffin Texts by a new emphasis on the role of Osiris, who, as lord of the underworld, offered the prospect of eternal life to all the righteous dead. The result was a dizzying combination of religious traditions. One spell, for example, associates the deceased with the circumpolar stars, while another hedges its bets, offering an afterlife with Ra or Osiris:

> Hey, N [name of the deceased]! You are a god and you shall be a god. You shall have no enemies or hangers-on, (either) with Ra who is in heaven or with Osiris the great god who is in Abydos.[21]

For those pinning their hopes on Osiris, the Coffin Texts introduced a new concept: an afterlife with the god in the Field of Reeds. It is not difficult to see why this belief swiftly gained ground: an idyllic existence in a rural setting was infinitely preferable to a dangerous journey on Ra's barque, fighting off the enemies of creation. Even the agricultural tasks required in the Elysian Fields could be delegated, thanks to the introduction of *shabti* figurines, leaving the deceased to enjoy a leisurely and bucolic existence for all eternity. The only problem was getting to the Field of Reeds, for an afterlife with Osiris was not guaranteed. Standing in the way was the last judgement, a concept developed by the ancient Egyptians that would endure in the Judaeo-Christian tradition until the present day.

◁○▷

When Osiris first appears in pharaonic religion, it is as a dead king and one of a host of chthonic deities who peopled the afterlife of the Egyptian imagination. But in the Coffin Texts he takes on a new role as judge and lord of the underworld. As the Egyptians faced the uncertainty of death, they responded by multiplying the imagined barriers that stood between the deceased and a blessed hereafter. The preservation of the body, the provisioning of the tomb, the correct spells and incantations, maps of the underworld, servant statuettes, magical objects: all these things were deemed necessary if the dead were to be reborn. A last judgement before Osiris simply took this tendency to its logical conclusion. A spell in the Coffin Texts provides a concise description of judgement day:

> Hey, N! Take your staff, your loincloth and your sandals, and go down to the court, so that you may be true of voice against your enemies, against those who would act against you, male or female, and those who would cast judgement before you on this happy day in the court![22]

To be declared 'true of voice' was to pass the test for entering into the realm of Osiris; the expression came to be used as a circumlocution for 'deceased', so devoutly did the Egyptians wish to be justified in the last judgement.

From the beginning of the eighteenth dynasty, funerary literature underwent its second major transformation. Texts ceased to be inscribed inside coffins and instead were written on rolls of papyrus, to be interred alongside the deceased as part of the burial equipment. The Coffin Texts were thus transformed into what the Egyptians called the *Book of Going Forth by Day*, since their purpose was to enable the soul of the deceased to leave the tomb during the day and enjoy a free-spirited afterlife. Modern scholars have dubbed these magico-religious compositions the *Book of the Dead*; by whichever name, they were to remain the principal collection of funerary literature until the early Roman Period.

One hundred and ninety-two separate spells are attested from different anthologies of the *Book of the Dead*. Among the stranger ones are formulae 'for repelling a beetle', 'for not eating faeces or drinking urine in the realm of the dead', 'for being transformed into any shape one may wish to take' and 'for escaping from the catcher of fish'. These and many others could be brought together in different compilations, according to an individual's wishes and means. The wealthier the tomb owner, the longer and more beautifully decorated the anthology. One of the most impressive surviving examples was made for the daughter of a high priest of Amun-Ra in the twenty-first dynasty; almost all its chapters are illustrated with colourful vignettes. No version of the *Book of the Dead* contained all 192 spells, although certain incantations were considered essential. Among these were the *shabti* formula (Chapter 6), a description of the Field of Reeds (Chapter 110) and a spell for not walking upside-down in the land of the dead (Chapter 189), apparently one of the greatest fears associated with the afterlife. All three of these were borrowed from the Coffin Texts. But a new spell, composed at the beginning of the New Kingdom and drawing on earlier strands of belief, came to enjoy pre-eminence.

Chapter 125 concerned the last judgement, and was often illustrated by a vignette depicting the central drama in the process: the weighing of the heart. The Egyptians believed that a person's heart would bear witness to their past behaviour, on 'that dreadful day of judgement when the secrets of all hearts shall be disclosed'.[23] Weighing the heart of the deceased against the feather of truth would reveal whether or not they had led a blameless life. If a person was guiltless, they would be 'light-hearted' and would pass the test. If, on the other hand they approached the judgement with a 'heavy heart', they would be found out. Illustrations of the ritual show a giant set of scales with the heart on one balance and the feather of truth on the other. The deceased looks on while Anubis carries out the weighing and Thoth records the result. Lurking in the wings is the hideous creature known as Ammut, 'devourer of the dead'. Part-crocodile, part-hippopotamus and part-lion, it would eat those who were found guilty.

Lined up in rows, observing the process attentively, are the forty-two members of the divine tribunal. According to Chapter 125, not only did the deceased have to undergo the weighing of the heart, they also had to declare twice, before Osiris and the tribunal, that they had not committed a long list of specific sins. Known as the 'negative confession', this declaration of innocence provides vivid insights into the seamier side of daily life in ancient Egypt. It is worth quoting in full:

I have not done people wrong.

I have not impoverished my fellows.

I have not done wrong in the Place of Truth.

I have not learned false things.

I have not done evil.

I have not, on any day, made extra work beyond what was due to be done for me.

I have not caused my name to become tainted as a slave master.

I have not deprived a poor man of his property.

I have not done what the gods abhor.

I have not slandered a servant to his master.

I have not caused pain.

I have not created hunger.

I have not caused tears.

I have not killed.

I have not given orders to kill.

I have not created suffering for anyone.

I have not diminished the food offerings in the local temples.

I have not destroyed the gods' loaves.

I have not taken away the spirits' food.

I have not committed buggery.

I have not fornicated.

I have not reduced provisions.

I have not committed fraud.

I have not encroached upon (others') fields.

I have not interfered with the weights of the hand scales.

I have not disturbed the plummet of the standing scales.

I have not taken milk from the mouths of children.

I have not deprived herds of their pastures.

I have not snared the birds in the gods' reserves.

I have not caught the fish in their marshlands.

I have not diverted water in its due season.

I have not dammed fast-flowing water.

I have not extinguished the flame.

I have not neglected the (proper) dates for (offering) choice cuts (of meat).

I have not held back cattle from the god's offerings.

I have not opposed a god in his procession.[24]

Once a person had declared their innocence and passed the weighing of the heart, they could enter the realm of Osiris as a justified, transfigured spirit. This was the ultimate goal of every Egyptian, and scenes of the deceased in the company of Osiris were generally given prominence in the decoration of the burial chamber – as if depicting the desired outcome would guarantee it. On the north wall of Tutankhamun's burial chamber, after Ay has performed the opening of the mouth ritual on the king's mummy, the reborn king is shown being welcomed by Nut to the realm of the gods and then, accompanied by his *ka*, being embraced by Osiris. On the south wall, Tutankhamun is shown enjoying the afterlife in the company of three other funerary deities, Hathor, Anubis and Isis.

The belief that the righteous dead would be assimilated with the lord of the underworld dominated ancient Egyptian funerary religion for half of its 3,000-year history. In the scene of Tutankhamun's funeral procession, he is referred to as 'the Osiris king, the lord of the Two Lands'. In the decoration of his sumptuous coffins, the hands crossed on the breast and the curled, divine beard are elements taken from the iconography of Osiris. In the security and darkness of the tomb, with all the proper rites accomplished, the dead king became one with the king of the dead.

<◦>

To the casual observer, pharaonic civilization seems to have been preserved in aspic for 3,000 years. The stiff poses of its art, the monumentality of its architecture, the plethora of strange animal-headed deities, the centrality of the pharaoh and the apparent obsession with death: these outward manifestations of ancient Egyptian culture were there at the beginning and at the end, hallmarks of an apparently unchanging society. Yet look carefully, and the civilization of the ancient Nile Valley can be seen to have undergone continuous change throughout the three millennia of pharaonic rule. Fashions came and went, beliefs waxed and waned, the power of the court ebbed and flowed.

The web of beliefs about the afterlife represented in Tutankhamun's tomb exemplifies an Egyptian tendency to add to, rather than replace, outdated cultural baggage. The Pyramid Texts were adapted and embellished to form the Coffin Texts, which formed the basis of the *Book of the Dead*. Earthly, astral, solar and Osirian conceptions of the afterlife each had its moment of supremacy, but none was ever fully discarded. The king's two *imiut* fetishes harked back to the earliest days of Egyptian state religion, while the golden shrines from the burial chamber bear sacred inscriptions that appear for the first time and which would only subsequently be codified into new afterlife texts. Tradition and innovation were equally respected.

In the same vein, while the east wall of Tutankhamun's burial chamber depicts the funeral procession, and the north and south walls give prominence to the opening of the mouth and the assimilation with Osiris, the west wall – the culmination of the entire decorative scheme – features the opening section of an afterlife book that had been composed just a few generations earlier, at the beginning of the eighteenth dynasty. The Egyptians called this text *Amduat*, literally 'what is in the underworld'. If the *Book of the Dead* helped the deceased to be reborn in the next life, the *Amduat* served as a guide when they got there. Eighteenth-dynasty royal tombs, with their descending passages and maze of corridors, were designed to reflect the geography of the underworld, and scenes from the *Amduat* were painted on the tomb walls to help the king navigate through the next life. The earliest surviving example, painted in the burial chamber of Thutmose III's tomb, resembles a huge papyrus map, unrolled around the walls. The *Amduat* also cleverly amalgamated diverse earlier strands of funerary belief to create a new, unified mythology.

The guidebook to the netherworld was divided into twelve chapters, corresponding to the twelve hours of night. The first hour, illustrated in Tutankhamun's tomb, marked the transition between day and night, when the sun god and his followers entered the night realm aboard the evening barque. As they did so, they had to fend off an attack by the serpent of chaos, Apep. In the second and third hours, having survived this attack unscathed, the solar barque travelled through fertile fields along the winding waterways of the underworld, but this rural idyll was a cruel deception. For in the fourth and fifth hours, the barque had to navigate a serpent-infested land called

Rosetau, home to the ancient Memphite underworld god Sokar. This was the precursor to the deepest and darkest part of the underworld, reached in the sixth hour – the dead of night. Here Ra encountered the grave of Osiris, watched over by his sister goddesses, Isis and Nephthys. The light of the sun brought Osiris back to life; indeed, Ra was revealed as the soul of Osiris which, when reunited with his body, made the god of the dead live again. Watching over this joyous reunion were the souls of Egypt's dead kings, granted the privilege of a ringside seat at Osiris's resurrection.

Once again, however, the joy was short-lived. In the seventh hour, Ra and his allies were attacked for a second time by the forces of chaos; a further battle ensued against the foes of Osiris, and all were overcome. In the eighth hour, the souls of the dead rose from their slumber, were reclothed and joined together to rejoice at Ra's arrival. Further dangers awaited the sun god's barque in the ninth hour, but it emerged unscathed to rescue the souls of the drowned in the tenth hour, giving them, too, the benefit of an afterlife. The healing theme of the tenth hour gives a prominent role to the sacred *wedjat* eye. At the eleventh hour, a fiery fate was dealt to the last of the rebels, while Isis and Nephthys delivered crowns to Neith, a funerary goddess closely connected with divine kingship – the whole of creation was seen to affirm the sacred institution of monarchy. Finally, in the twelfth hour, the solar barque sailed from the underworld at dawn; Shu, god of light and air, raised it into the eastern horizon, from where it would begin its daytime journey across the heavens. Osiris and his fellow dead, meanwhile, returned to their slumber in the underworld, until they were reawakened and revivified once again by Ra.

The theologians behind the *Amduat* explained the apparent contradiction between the solar and Osirian views of the after-life, while also including Sokar, finding a special place for dead monarchs and reinforcing the god-given authority of the pharaoh. It was little wonder that the new afterlife book was enthusiastically embraced by the kings of the eighteenth dynasty (on the walls of their tombs) and by their loyal officials (on papyrus copies). Royal burials in the Valley of the Kings gave pride of place to scenes from the *Amduat* until the end of the New Kingdom and the abandonment of the necropolis.

At the start of the *Amduat*, the sun god was generally depicted as his ram-headed alter ego, Atum. At the end of the underworld journey, he was depicted as the scarab beetle, Khepri. Although Tutankhamun's extract from *Amduat*, painted on the west wall of his burial chamber, represents the first hour of night, it shows Ra as a scarab: in my end is my beginning. An identical beetle, made from black resin, was found on the king's upper body, nestling between hands of sheet gold that had been sewn onto the mummy wrappings. This small, inconspicuous object was perhaps the most powerful of all talismans.

Fig. 40. Black resin scarab.

TEN

Legacy

Fig. 41. Hussein Abdel Rassul wearing the pectoral
and chain with scarabs.

Tutankhamun wished his body to rest for eternity in the Valley of the Kings, while his eternal soul would be reborn into the afterlife. Against all the odds, the boy king's tomb remained largely undisturbed, while those of pharaohs before and after him were robbed and desecrated. As he lay in his great stone sarcophagus, aeons passed. Ancient Egyptian civilization was extinguished after 3,000 years; ancient Greece and Rome came and went, and the inhabitants of the Nile Valley saw their religion replaced by Christianity and then Islam. Pharaonic Egypt passed from history into myth. And then, with the advent of antiquarianism and archaeology, the secrets of the pharaohs began to be recovered. The golden age of Egyptology, which began with the decipherment of hieroglyphics in 1822, culminated in the rediscovery of Tutankhamun's tomb a century later. Overnight, thanks to Howard Carter and his patron Lord Carnarvon, a minor ruler became the most famous pharaoh of them all. The West's long fascination with ancient Egypt turned into something of an obsession. Tutankhamun's name and image have become global brands, and exhibitions of his treasures have attracted millions of visitors. But the rediscovery of his tomb and its treasures has also prompted complex questions: about modern Egypt's relationship with its ancient past and with the West; about the ownership and custodianship of antiquities; and about the tensions between scientific enquiry and the popular imagination. Tutankhamun's legacy is as contested as it is enduring.

⋖◦⋗

The kings of ancient Egypt bore a plethora of titles and epithets, but among the most common was the phrase *di ankh djet*, 'given life forever', or *di ankh mi Ra djet*, 'given life like Ra forever'. It formed part of the titulary of Djoser, first king of the third dynasty and builder of the first pyramid, in around 2650 BC, and it was still being used under Ptolemy XV Caesarion, son of Cleopatra and Julius Caesar, more than twenty-six centuries later. The lasting appeal of the phrase lay in its simplicity and potency, for it expressed the essence of the ideology of kingship: the pharaoh was immortal. As we have seen, theologians made this essential truth more nuanced by declaring that true immortality belonged to the royal *ka* rather than to its host, but the message to the king's subjects down the centuries was clear and unchanging: their monarch was one of the gods and had been granted eternal life.

The truth, of course, was that not only did every king die, most were soon forgotten. Every king expected to be remembered forever, but few were granted their wish. And those who did live on in popular memory were, to a large extent, great builders or successful military leaders.

Although the ancient Egyptians seem never to have developed an objective sense of history, they had a keen appreciation of the past. Monuments erected by earlier kings were all around them, and some already belonged to remote antiquity: a greater span of time separated the Great Pyramid from Cleopatra than separates her from our own age. The pyramid-builders of the fourth dynasty must already have become semi-mythical figures by the height of the Middle Kingdom some five centuries later, but there was no escaping the architectural accomplishment or physical imprint of earlier kings, and memories of them lived on as part of ancient Egyptian folklore.

Not that commissioning a spectacular monument was a guarantee of immortality. Djoser, while dimly remembered, was by no means as famous as his chief architect, Imhotep, who belonged to a select group of individuals who gained long-lasting fame on account of their wisdom and learning. As a New Kingdom instructional text put it:

> Is there one here like Hordedef? Is there another like Imhotep? . . . Those wise men who foretold what was to come: what they said came into being . . . They are gone, their names forgotten; but writings cause them to be remembered.[1]

The written word was supposed to confer immortality – hence the Egyptian obsession with carving names and titles in stone – but the scribes were not fools: they and their royal masters knew that inscriptions could be effaced and that history was selective.

Other than fleeting references in literary works, the best guide to which Egyptian kings were remembered by posterity is the category of inscriptions known as king lists. Carved in stone or inscribed on papyrus to honour illustrious royal ancestors – and to grant the reigning king legitimacy by association – a handful of examples have survived. The earliest, a series of annals carved on a slab of granite known today as the Palermo Stone, lists the kings – and their principal achievements – as far back as the beginning of the first dynasty, and beyond. The top of the stone originally gave the names of the mythical rulers who presided over Egypt between the time of the gods and the unification of the country. In this way, the monarchs who came later were seen to be part of a god-given order. The surviving fragments make it difficult to reconstruct the original, but there seems to have been no attempt at censorship: every reign up to the time the stone was commissioned appears to have been recorded.

The same cannot be said for the three great rolls of honour drawn up in the nineteenth dynasty – the Abydos king lists of Seti I and Ramesses II and the so-called Turin Canon – which all took a selective approach to the past. Kings who were regarded as founder figures – Menes, the first king to unify Egypt; Mentuhotep II, who reunited the country after a period of civil war; and Ahmose, victor over the Hyksos and founder of the eighteenth dynasty – were all given prominence. By contrast, monarchs who had reigned during periods of turmoil or whose authority had been otherwise disputed were generally omitted, as were sovereigns whose existence transgressed the bounds of decorum: Hatshepsut, the female pharaoh, is absent, as are the 'Amarna pharaohs' – Akhenaten, Neferneferuaten, Tutankhamun and Ay – because of their association with the break from orthodox religion.

Deliberately omitting 'problematic' rulers from a roll call of esteemed forebears was straightforward, but erasing their monuments required a more concerted effort. From Djoser onwards, every king who had the time and the means made it a priority to build a mortuary temple, in addition to a tomb. Here, he hoped, his cult would be celebrated for all eternity. In fact, despite the elaborate preparations, which extended to the construction of whole new settlements for the mortuary priests and their families, most of these royal foundations lapsed within a few generations. Once a dynasty passed from power, the impetus to maintain a king's cult waned. Djoser's survived in some form until the nineteenth dynasty, a period of some 1,400 years, but it was the exception. The mortuary cults of all the other great rulers, from pyramid-builders to military leaders,

fizzled out, either through benign neglect or deliberate seques-
tration of their resources.

Tutankhamun had the double misfortune of being tainted
by his association with Akhenaten's revolution and of leaving
no heirs to safeguard his memory. As a consequence, both the
tomb and mortuary temple he had been preparing for himself
were usurped by his successor, Ay, and most of his other monuments – the processional colonnade at Luxor Temple, a set of
colossal statues at Karnak and even his grand 'Restoration Stela'
– were reinscribed by the next king, Horemheb. Indeed, once
he was established on the throne, Tutankhamun's one-time
general went about rewriting history with military efficiency.
He dismantled Akhenaten's Theban temples and used the blocks
as fill for his own constructions at Karnak. He began the
official proscription of the same king's memory: a legal text
from his reign refers obliquely to an incident having occurred
in 'the time of the enemy belonging to Akhetaten'. Moreover,
Horemheb dated his accession from the death of Amenhotep III,
thus airbrushing Akhenaten and his three successors from
history. Horemheb's successors did the same, and Ramesses II
delivered the coup de grâce by systematically plundering the
site of Amarna, reducing its buildings to their foundations. By
royal command, all traces of Akhenaten, his wife and his son
were erased.

All the while, Tutankhamun lay at rest in his tomb, his
mummified body enveloped in nine layers of magical protection.
On the floor of the Antechamber, just inside the entrance to
the tomb, Carter found a calcite cup carved to resemble the
flowers and buds of the white and blue waterlilies. Each handle
is topped by a figure of the god Heh ('million') holding palm
fronds ('years') resting on tadpoles ('hundreds of thousands'),
with *ankh*s ('life') on either side. The wish that the king be
granted eternal life is clear. It is a message reinforced by the

Fig. 42. Tutankhamun's 'wishing cup'.

inscribed panel on the bowl, which gives the king's names and titles, including the epithet 'given life forever'. Most poignant of all is the longer inscription carved around the rim of his 'wishing cup':

> May your *ka* live, and may you pass a million years, one who loves Thebes and dwells in it, your face toward the north wind; may your eyes see the good place.[2]

Even if the boy pharaoh did not expect to be remembered forever, he hoped at least to be left in peace for all eternity.

⊲◦▷

Although royal burials in the Valley of the Kings were attended by great ritual and ceremony, many ordinary ancient Egyptians – including some of those who laboured to build the tombs – saw them for what they were: stores of treasure, waiting to be robbed. There were, in every generation, individuals for whom the desire for self-enrichment outweighed any worries about breaking the law or committing sacrilege. Tomb robbery was a heinous crime in ancient Egypt, for it transgressed some of the most fundamental tenets of society and religion: the sanctity of the necropolis and the reverence for the dead. Despoiling a king's burial was even worse. Yet theft in the Theban royal necropolis was a reasonably frequent occurrence.

One of the most celebrated cases of ancient tomb robbery is known thanks to the chance preservation of the records of the ensuing investigation. The crime in question was part of a pattern of activity, the roots of which can be traced back to the strike of the necropolis workmen under Ramesses III. The failure of the state to pay the wages of its most sensitive group of employees led to a long-term breakdown in trust between the community of workmen and the government. In the following decades, as the Egyptian economy began to falter and central control to weaken, some of the workmen decided to enrich themselves at the state's expense.

The first serious incident took place early in the reign of Ramesses IX, when robbers broke into the tomb of Ramesses VI, sealed only a decade earlier. This act of sacrilege was followed a few years later by the vandalism of two of the greatest monuments on the west bank of Thebes, the mortuary temples of Ramesses II and Ramesses III. On both occasions, the culprits did relatively little damage. A formal investigation was launched, but to little effect. Within a short time, the robbers struck again, targeting the less well-guarded tombs of the seventeenth-dynasty kings, dug into an easily accessible hillside. One night, a stonemason called Amunpanefer set out with a band of accomplices. Entering the royal burials,

> We opened their coffins and their mummy wrappings . . .
> We brought back the gold we found on the noble mummy
> of this god, together with his pectorals and other jewellery which were around his neck.[3]

Having thoroughly pillaged one tomb of all its portable wealth (amounting to thirty-two pounds of gold), the robbers set fire to the royal coffins, reducing them to ashes. When the robbery finally came to light four years later, the government punished the ringleaders and set up a royal commission to investigate what had happened. The findings were even worse than feared: of the ten royal tombs that were inspected, only one was still intact. Some had been partly robbed, others completely ransacked. But corruption was by now endemic at every level of government, and the culprits went unpunished.

Three decades later, following further tomb robberies and acts of desecration, a second royal commission was established. This time, the inquiry was led by the vizier, assisted by the royal treasurer and two members of the king's inner circle. Once again, the investigation served to highlight the scale of the problem: although most of the robbers came from the workmen's village, they had not acted alone. The commission found evidence of widespread negligence and complicity among state and temple officials. Some had turned a blind eye to crimes carried out under their noses, while others had been active collaborators. A theft from the great temple of Amun-Ra at Karnak, arguably the most sacred place in the whole of Egypt, had been particularly audacious. On investigation, the chief guard of the temple was found to have been behind the robbery.

While such systematic corruption and criminality may reflect the general sclerosis in Egyptian society in the dying days of the twentieth dynasty, the robbery of royal tombs was likely a feature of all periods of pharaonic history. At the end of the eighteenth dynasty, a period characterized by strong central government, the tomb of Tutankhamun was robbed at least twice within a short time of his burial. In the first attempt, thieves broke through the outer and inner walls of the entrance corridor to penetrate the Antechamber. After they had ransacked the contents, presumably in the search for small, portable items of intrinsic value, the break-in was evidently discovered. The blocking walls were restored, the corridor filled with limestone chippings and the tomb resealed by officials. A short time later, however, robbers tunnelled through the fill of the corridor to gain access to the entire tomb – not once, but twice. Carter estimated that they succeeded in carrying off perhaps 60 per cent of the king's jewellery from the Treasury. In the burial chamber, they managed to open the outermost shrine, but they never got as far as the sarcophagus and its precious contents. Indeed, during the final break-in, the thieves must have been caught: a knotted scarf filled with eight gold rings must have been recovered by the necropolis guards and tossed back into one of the boxes in the Antechamber, to be found by Carter and his team thirty-two centuries later.

The burial chamber was closed off, the corridor refilled and the blocking walls at either end resealed. One of the individuals involved in this process was the scribe Djehutymose, who worked for the high official Maya. He scribbled his name on the underside of a jar stand, as his team hurriedly put the objects displaced by the robbers back in random boxes. Maya would subsequently supervise the restoration of another nearby royal tomb, that of Thutmose IV, following yet another robbery.

It was geological accident rather than official protection that saved Tutankhamun's tomb from the wholesale plunder suffered by other royal sepulchres at the end of the New Kingdom. Some 180 years after the boy king's burial, the tomb of Ramesses VI was cut directly above it into the side of the Valley of the Kings. The mass of limestone spoil excavated from this later tomb was dumped outside its entrance, spilling down to the valley floor and covering Tutankhamun's final resting place. So when tomb robbery became a way of life among the Theban hills at the end of the twentieth dynasty, Tutankhamun's tomb was invisible, its existence forgotten. It was just as well, for the military strongman in charge during the final years of Ramesses XI's reign, General Paiankh, issued an order to the scribe of the necropolis to

> uncover a tomb among the tombs of the ancestors and preserve its seal until I return.[4]

This instruction marked the beginning of a policy to strip royal tombs of their gold, in order to finance Paiankh's wider ambitions. The initial targets were those that were the easiest to pilfer: the tombs of the seventeenth dynasty, the burials of royal relatives in the Valley of the Queens and the kings' mortuary temples at the edge of the cultivation. Then, on the pretext of safeguarding the integrity of all royal tombs, the authorities switched their focus to the Valley of the Kings. Over little more than a decade, the tombs of the New Kingdom pharaohs were systematically emptied. Gold and precious objects were removed and taken directly to the state treasury, while the mummies were taken to an office in western Thebes for unwrapping and basic repackaging. The necropolis scribe in charge of the whole operation called himself, without a hint of irony, 'overseer of the treasuries of the kings'. The high priest of Amun-Ra was even bolder, reusing coffins taken from the tomb of the great warrior pharaoh Thutmose I for his own burial.

With ancient Egypt busy cannibalizing its own past, there would soon be little left to show for the glories of its golden age. The Valley of the Kings, largely bereft of its treasures, was neglected and soon forgotten, to be covered by the sands of time.

After the Valley of the Kings was abandoned, Egypt descended into chaos and division as the apparatus of the state frayed and fell apart. The Third Intermediate Period, as the centuries following the collapse of the New Kingdom are known, was characterized by competing dynasties in the north and south of the country, with families of Libyan as well as of Egyptian descent vying for power. Even when some semblance of order and unity was restored, Egypt was a changed place. For while the hallmarks of pharaonic culture were still present, the country was perennially insecure, buffeted by a series of foreign invasions from Nubians, Assyrians, Persians and Macedonians, who sought to absorb the productive Nile Valley into their own emerging empires. For the final millennium of pharaonic history, Egypt was no longer the supreme power in the ancient world but merely one of a number of states jostling for hegemony in the eastern Mediterranean and Near East. The golden age of Tutankhamun and his eighteenth-dynasty forebears must have seemed a very distant memory.

In time, even hieroglyphic writing, that quintessential feature of ancient Egyptian civilization, fell victim to external pressures and internal forces. Egypt's highly distinctive writing system had been developed in the late fourth millennium BC, in the years leading up to the unification of the Nile Valley, and was still a characteristic of pharaonic rule under the Ptolemies and Romans nearly four millennia later. But the unstoppable dominance of the Greek language, combined with the advent of Christianity, eventually dealt ancient Egyptian culture and its writing system a terminal blow. The last text written in Egyptian hieroglyphics was a simple prayer, carved by a priest of Isis into the Philae temple on 24 August in AD 394. Over the following sixty years, a series of inscriptions by members of a single family charts the last gasps of pagan religion and the end of pharaonic culture. On 2 December 452, two brothers carved the last inscription in Egypt's native language, written in the demotic script. Four years later, the same two brothers carved their final testaments, this time in Greek. Thereafter, knowledge of the ancient script was lost, and Egypt began to recede from history into myth.

Nevertheless, the presence of ancient Egypt in the Western imagination – and the subtle influence of pharaonic culture on Western civilization – endured. Beginning with Augustus, Roman emperors brought Egyptian obelisks to Rome, to add a touch of the exotic and to symbolize the subjugation of the Nile Valley. In reality, Rome was as much in Egypt's thrall: the cults of Isis and Serapis spread throughout the empire, bringing with them an Egyptianization of sculpture and architecture. The fashion for Egyptian and Egypt-inspired objects reached its zenith in the reign of Hadrian, whose journey up the Nile in AD 130 was one of the defining events of his life. The gardens of his villa at Tivoli were decorated with pharaonic sculpture, while his deceased lover Antinous, who had drowned in the Nile during that fateful visit to Egypt, was worshipped in the form of an Egyptian deity. A pair of granite lions, created under one of the last native Egyptian pharaohs, adorned the Pantheon in the heart of Rome. And it was not only Roman imperial religion that found itself drawn to ancient Egyptian precedents: early Christianity also borrowed heavily from the cult of Isis.

In the early Renaissance, the continued presence of numerous Egyptian and Egyptianizing objects in and around Rome spurred a growing interest in pharaonic civilization. The Nile Valley gained a reputation as an inaccessible and mystical land whose secrets looked set to remain hidden. The fact that Egypt was also the setting for many of the most famous biblical stories gave it further potency. An antiquarian interest in the physical relics of the past was complemented by a rekindled fascination in the forgotten knowledge of the ancients. At the heart of this phenomenon lay two texts that were to shape Western engagement with ancient Egypt until the Enlightenment.

In the early centuries AD, a community of Greek writers in Egypt, probably based at Alexandria, had composed a body of texts. The writings comprised religion and philosophy, magic and alchemy, and reflected the diverse cultural influences that were alive in Alexandria at the time – Platonism, Stoicism and popular philosophy, spiced up with some Jewish and Near Eastern elements. Writing under the collective pseudonym 'Hermes Trismegistus', the writers claimed great antiquity for their work. When the corpus reached the hands of the early church fathers, Hermes Trismegistus was acknowledged as a real person and credited with the invention of hieroglyphs; the writings became known as the *Corpus Hermeticum*. European theologians saw in them prefigurations of the essential truths of Christianity. The *Corpus* gained a hallowed status and was translated from Greek into Latin, and subsequently into many European languages. Another hugely influential work was the *Hieroglyphika* by the fifth-century author Horapollo. When it was rediscovered by scholars in fifteenth-century Florence, it strongly reinforced the theory – bolstered by Greek and Roman authors like Herodotus, Strabo and Diodorus Siculus – that ancient Egyptian writing encoded deeper mystical truths.

Encouraged by these two texts, Renaissance humanists were attracted by the notion that an unbroken thread of wisdom could be traced all the way back to the ancient Egyptians. As for hieroglyphs, the theories put forward for their decipherment were wildly speculative. One of the first collections of hieroglyphic inscriptions was published in Basel in 1556, followed by another book, *Thesaurus hieroglyphicorum*, in 1608, which treated them as mere decoration. One man who vehemently disagreed with this interpretation was a German Jesuit priest called Athanasius Kircher. While living in Rome, he was able to study the surviving pharaonic monuments first-hand. He established a museum of Egyptian antiquities and took pains to learn the Coptic language, recognizing it as related to ancient Egyptian. He felt certain that the hieroglyphs must express profound truths and gave his imagination full rein when producing interpretations of ancient Egyptian inscriptions. In his influential work of 1652, *Oedipus Aegyptiacus*, he drew on the writings of Pythagoreans and Plato, as well as the Hermetic philosophers, to propose a convoluted explanation of hieroglyphics and the cosmos.

Despite growing evidence that it was profoundly mistaken, Hermeticism remained influential throughout the seventeenth and eighteenth centuries – the belief that Egypt was the source of occult wisdom was too enticing to abandon. A late manifestation of this tradition is seen in the libretto of Mozart's 1791 work, *The Magic Flute*, which references the rites of Isis and Osiris. Just seven years after the work was composed, however, Napoleon's expedition to Egypt launched the modern, scientific study of the ancient Nile Valley. The published account of the expedition, the *Description de l'Egypte*, sought to present an accurate picture of the civilization's antiquities, shorn of the superstition and fanciful interpretation of earlier accounts. Of even greater significance was the Rosetta Stone, discovered by Napoleon's soldiers but subsequently surrendered to the British and taken to the British Museum; its bilingual inscription, in ancient Egyptian and Greek, provided the key that led to the decipherment of hieroglyphics by Jean-François Champollion in 1822.

Once scholars were able to read pharaonic writing – for the first time in over fourteen centuries – some of them were rather disappointed by what they found. For instead of mystical secrets, most pharaonic inscriptions turned out to be rather pedestrian: bureaucratic records, formulaic descriptions of kings' activities and endless royal titularies. The famed sophistication of ancient Egypt looked like an illusion. And yet what the written record failed to demonstrate, archaeology triumphantly asserted. The material remains of ancient Egypt, epitomized by the objects from Tutankhamun's tomb, display a level of design and craftmanship that, arguably, has never been surpassed. Pharaonic jewellers, goldsmiths, cabinet makers and stonemasons achieved unprecedented levels of artistry and perfection, ten or twenty centuries before the glories of ancient Greece and thirty or forty before the European Renaissance.

One small illustration of this prowess is the collection of gloves buried with Tutankhamun. Gloves are intricate items to make and were highly prized in ancient Egypt – the diplomatic gifts from the King of Mittani to Amenhotep III included

Fig. 43. Linen glove.

'a pair of gloves trimmed with red wool',[5] while the courtier Ay had himself depicted in his Amarna tomb wearing a pair of red leather gloves, a gift from his king. As befitted a royal burial, Tutankhamun was interred with multiple pairs. One of the finest was found, neatly folded, in a box in the Annexe. Made from fine linen, they are decorated on both sides with a tapestry feather pattern, and they have tapes for securing them around the wearer's wrists. Rather modern in design, they feature a type of stitch unknown in modern glove-making until the eighteenth century. The pharaoh's glove makers got there 3,000 years earlier.

While the decipherment of hieroglyphics allowed the ancient Egyptians to speak for themselves once again, it was the discovery of Tutankhamun's tomb that revealed the true glories of pharaonic culture.

⊲ΙΟΙ⊳

From the very start of antiquarian interest in Egypt, visitors picked up where the Romans had left off, collecting Egyptian antiquities to furnish the homes and gardens of the European elite. Benoît de Maillet, French consul general in Egypt during the reign of Louis XV, was the first of many European diplomats who used their influence to amass collections of Egyptian antiquities for royal and aristocratic patrons. The Napoleonic expedition of 1798 provided a further spur to the rediscovery of pharaonic civilization and stimulated an orgy of acquisition. By the mid-1810s, collecting ancient art and artefacts seems to have been the primary concern of the French representative in Egypt, Bernardino Drovetti, who exercised a virtual monopoly on collecting throughout the Nile Valley. This did not go unnoticed in London, and in 1815, buoyed by Wellington's victory over Napoleon at Waterloo, the British Foreign Office urged its diplomats to start collecting for the British Museum.

Henry Salt was appointed Britain's first consul general in Egypt, and his main task was to amass antiquities. The ensuing rivalry between Drovetti and Salt dominated the exploration – or, rather, the ransacking – of Egypt's ancient sites throughout the second and third decades of the nineteenth century. As a later observer put it, 'the archaeological field became a battle plain for two armies of Dragomans and Fellah-navvies. One was headed by the redoubtable Salt; the other owned the command of Drovetti.'[6] Rather more wistful was a popular saying in early-nineteenth-century Cairo: 'The riches of Egypt are for the foreigners therein.'[7]

Drovetti and Salt merely directed the business of acquisition; the actual work of removing paintings and sculpture from the ruins of Egyptian temples and tombs fell to their agents. Perhaps the most famous of all these treasure hunters was Giovanni Battista Belzoni, an Italian circus strongman-turned-archaeologist who worked in Egypt, both for Salt and on his own account, between 1815 and 1818. He masterminded the removal of a gigantic head of Ramesses II from the king's mortuary temple in western Thebes; the bust's subsequent journey from the banks of the Nile to the Thames may have inspired the composition of Shelley's sonnet 'Ozymandias'. Two centuries on, the sculpture remains the focal point of the British Museum's Egyptian galleries. In 1817, Belzoni discovered the tomb of Seti I in the Valley of the Kings and immediately set about removing its great calcite sarcophagus; refused by the British Museum, it was acquired by Sir John Soane as the centrepiece of a 'sepulchral chamber' in his private museum.

Not to be outdone, the French sent an expedition to Egypt in 1821 with the express purpose of removing an even more famous antiquity: the zodiac from the ceiling of the temple of Hathor at Dendera. The mission's patron lauded the permissive Egyptian policy that facilitated such activities:

Among other means employed, by the government of
Egypt, to allure Europeans thither, is the permission
granted to all comers to search for and carry away antiquities, whether on the surface or under-ground.[8]

When the zodiac was unveiled at the Louvre, it caused even
more of a stir than the arrival of the Rosetta Stone in London
twenty years earlier. But not everyone was impressed by this
orgy of treasure-seeking. A British visitor lamented:

The whole of ancient Thebes is the private property of
the English and French consuls; a line of demarcation
is drawn through every temple, and these buildings that
have hitherto withstood the attacks of *Barbarians*, will
not resist the speculation of civilized cupidity, virtuosi,
and antiquarians.[9]

Despite such protestations, the stripping of ancient sites
continued unabated. In the early 1840s, the Prussian scholar
Richard Lepsius set new standards of observation and recording,
establishing Egyptology as an independent academic discipline,
but his three-year expedition to the Nile Valley brought back
some 15,000 antiquities and casts, including entire buildings
from Giza and Saqqara. Even before an export licence had
been granted, workers were sent in secret to dismantle three
chapels. Only when the blocks had been taken down and
packed did the Prussian authorities seek official permission to
ship them to Berlin.

The unholy race to acquire Egypt's past is epitomized by the
tussle over one particular antiquity: the king list from Karnak
temple. Lepsius, recognizing its importance as a source of
pharaonic history, wanted it for the Berlin Museum, but the
French had their eyes on it for the Louvre. In the summer of

1843, as Lepsius was making his way upstream, a French adventurer cut the block from the temple, having worked secretly at night, and loaded it onto his boat to take down the Nile and onwards to Paris. As the two men passed on the river, the Frenchman invited Lepsius aboard and sat him down on a crate which, unbeknownst to the Prussian, contained the priceless relic.

Throughout the nineteenth and early twentieth centuries, successive 'archaeological' missions to Egypt combined scientific enquiry with the acquisition of antiquities. The Frenchman Auguste Mariette, revered today as the founder of the Egyptian Antiquities Service and the first director of the Egyptian Museum, began his career by searching the sands of Saqqara for objects to send back to the Louvre. To avoid detection, he dug secretly at night and even had one of his assistants produce fake antiquities to fob off the Egyptian government inspectors, hiding the real finds in an underground shaft before smuggling them out in grain sacks.

Even more egregious were the actions in the 1880s of the Englishman Ernest Wallis Budge. On his first trip to Egypt, having discovered that he had a natural flair for acquiring antiquities, he soon 'made the acquaintance and somehow gained the good will of two natives' who would supply him with 'many valuable objects' in the years to come.[10] During one collecting trip to Thebes, he acquired a remarkable series of funerary papyri – no doubt illicitly excavated from a nearby tomb – and smuggled them back to his storeroom in Luxor. The director of the Antiquities Service, having got wind of his activities, sent police to arrest him, but Budge managed to buy them off. Antiquities Service guards were then posted around Budge's storeroom to stop him removing his ill-gotten gains, but the Englishman had learned a lesson or two from his dealer friends. First he arranged for the guards to be sent a hearty meal. Then, under the cover of darkness, he had an underground tunnel dug from the storeroom to the adjoining garden of the Luxor Hotel. While he and the hotel manager watched anxiously, and while the guards were busy eating:

> man after man went into the sardâb of the house and brought out, piece by piece and box by box, everything which was of the slightest value commercially . . . In this way we saved the Papyrus of Ani, and all the rest of my acquisitions from the officials of the Service of Antiquities, and all Luxor rejoiced.[11]

Budge used all sorts of ruses to smuggle the antiquities out of Egypt. His reward was to be appointed the first keeper of Egyptian antiquities at the British Museum.

The passing of new antiquities laws eventually made such acts of outright theft harder to pull off, but even the most dedicated of archaeologists seems to have found it hard to resist the temptation. In the spring of 1924, when Howard Carter and his team were temporarily locked out of the tomb of Tutankhamun – following a spat with the Egyptian authorities – the Antiquities Service took the opportunity to carry out a thorough survey of the tomb and the associated spaces used by the expedition. When searching the space used by Carter and his associates for dining (the tomb of Ramesses XI), officials found a remarkable bust of the young Tutankhamun neatly packed inside a Fortnum & Mason wine crate. Made from wood, covered with gesso and painted, the sculpture represents the king as the sun god Nefertem, emerging on a waterlily flower. In the late eighteenth dynasty, a popular version of the creation myth of Heliopolis focused on the metaphor of the lotus flower rising to the surface of the waters of chaos, its petals opening to reveal the newborn sun as a golden child.

The three-dimensional portrayal of this act of creation, made for Tutankhamun's tomb, is perhaps the most sensitive of all the portraits of the boy pharaoh. On discovering it secreted in a box, the Antiquities Service took the view that Carter was intending to smuggle it out of Egypt. He strenuously denied any wrongdoing, claiming that it had been found in the fill of the tomb's entrance corridor and taken to the dining tomb for conservation and storage. However, Carter's 1923 account of the clearance of the corridor makes no mention of the bust's discovery. Back in London, he openly displayed Egyptian antiquities in his home. And his collection, bequeathed on his death to his niece, included at least nineteen objects from Tutankhamun's tomb, with no indication of how he acquired them.

Reflecting on the responsibilities of an archaeologist, Carter took the moral high ground, asserting:

> In his research work his one and sole idea is to rescue remains of the past from destruction, and that when in the course of his work he passes inviolate thresholds, he feels not only an awe and wonder distilled from their tremendous past, but the sense of a sacred obligation.[12]

Perhaps.

◁─▷

Throughout the excavation and clearance of Tutankhamun's tomb, Carter kept a detailed digging diary and journal; preserved in the Griffith Institute at the University of Oxford, these precious documents provide a wealth of first-hand information about the greatest archaeological discovery in history. However, even a man as meticulous as Carter was not immune to gilding his narrative when it suited him. The

hazy circumstances surrounding the discovery of the bust of
Tutankhamun as the god Nefertem are a case in point, and
Carter's account of the discovery of the tomb itself is even
more striking.

The published version is well known, with its reference to
'wonderful things'. (That famous phrase actually seems to have
been an embellishment; Carter's journal from the day of the
discovery is more prosaic: 'when Lord Carnarvon said to me
"Can you see anything?" I replied to him, "Yes, it is wonderful."'[13]) Nowhere, however, does Carter give credit to the
Egyptian labourers who carried out the back-breaking clearance
– over six long seasons – of the 200,000 tons of rubble and
limestone chippings that overlay the tomb. Instead, in his
account of 'years and years of dull and unprofitable work', the
first-person plural is used, without further comment:

> We had now dug in The Valley for several seasons, with
> extremely scanty results.[14]

In the same vein, Carter recounts the breakthrough that
indicated the presence of a previously undiscovered tomb:

> Hardly had I arrived on the work next morning
> (November 4th) than the unusual silence, due to the
> stoppage of the work, made me realize that something
> out of the ordinary had happened, and I was greeted by
> the announcement that a step cut in the rock had been
> discovered.[15]

On closer reading, this description reveals an aspect of the dig
that is generally overlooked: it was the habit of Carter's Egyptian
workmen, headed by a trusted foreman, to begin work as soon
as the sun had risen, before the archaeologist arrived to oversee

operations. The discovery of that crucial first step was made by one of the workers, not by Carter. Thanks to recent work in the archives, we can identify that unsung hero.

One of the reasons why the discovery of Tutankhamun's tomb created such a stir around the world was the series of stunning black and white photographs taken by Harry Burton, the staff photographer of the Metropolitan Museum of Art in New York. Burton's images are striking for their large format, fine detail and dramatic lighting. Among the hundreds of images from the time of the discovery is one of a young Egyptian boy, aged between nine and twelve, wearing a plain white linen galabeya and headcloth. Suspended around his neck is one of the most lavish and dramatic pieces of jewellery from Tutankhamun's tomb: a heavy pectoral, chain and counterpoise featuring a series of large scarab beetles carved from lapis lazuli. The pectoral's centrepiece is a representation of the solar barque, with a large scarab pushing the sun disc above the hieroglyph for 'horizon', flanked by two serpents each supporting a sun disc. The chain is composed of baskets (*neb*), scarabs (*kheperu*) and sun discs (*ra*) in gold, lapis lazuli, carnelian and green feldspar, which together spell out Tutankhamun's throne name, Nebkheperura. Why should such an important object from the tomb have been given to a young Egyptian boy to model? The answer, omitted from Carter's account, is that the boy in question, Hussein Abdel Rassul, had discovered the tomb.

The Abdel Rassul family were longstanding and somewhat notorious residents of western Thebes. In the 1870s, one of their number had discovered the cache of royal mummies at Deir el-Bahri, when a stray goat disappeared down a partially concealed tomb shaft. Fifty years later, young Hussein Abdel Rassul was employed by Carter as a water boy, responsible for bringing water by donkey from the Nile to the dig site in the Valley of the Kings. The water jars had pointed bases, so shallow holes had to be dug in the ground to support them. It was while he was digging such a hole, on the early morning of 4 November 1922, that Hussein revealed a flat stone step in the floor of the valley. And the rest is history.

The whitewashing of an Egyptian water boy from the account of the discovery exemplifies the invisibility of the Nile Valley's inhabitants from the annals of Egyptology. As early as the 1820s, in the aftermath of the Napoleonic expedition, forty-four Egyptian students were sent from Al-Azhar to Paris to learn modern skills; they were led by an imam named Rifa'a Rafi el-Tahtawi, who went on to become a major figure in his country's nineteenth-century renaissance. In 1868, he published the first account of ancient Egyptian history in Arabic. Today, he is all but forgotten.

In the 1880s, the British archaeologist Flinders Petrie began work at the site of Qift in Upper Egypt and made a surprising discovery:

> Among this rather untoward people we found however, as in every place, a small percentage of excellent men; some half-dozen were of the very best type of native, faithful, friendly, and laborious, and from among these workmen we have drawn about forty to sixty for our work . . . They have formed the backbone of my upper Egyptian staff, and I hope that I may keep these good friends so long as I work anywhere within reach of them.[16]

The men from Qift whom Petrie trained passed their skills to their descendants, some of whom are still employed as professional diggers by archaeologists working in Egypt; 'Qifti' is common parlance among Egyptologists for a skilled site foreman.

Following the British invasion and occupation of Egypt in

1882, the authorities allowed an Egyptian called Ahmed Kamal to establish a school of Egyptology for Egyptians, but this pioneering move lasted only three years. Kamal was later promoted to assistant curator at the Egyptian Museum, becoming the first Egyptian to be employed in a substantive position there. His appointment was followed shortly afterwards by that of Ahmed Najib as chief inspector of antiquities, but these were token gestures. Generation after generation of Western archaeologists were happy to take the credit for a succession of great discoveries, while barely acknowledging the indigenous labourers who made it possible.

Early on in his archaeological career, before he teamed up with Lord Carnarvon, Howard Carter worked for the American philanthropist Theodore Davis. Together, they found the longest and deepest tomb in the Valley of the Kings, created for the female pharaoh Hatshepsut. The whole tomb, from entrance to burial chamber, was filled with stone chippings, rubbish and bat droppings. Clearing it was hot, dirty and dangerous work, carried out by an army of poorly paid Egyptian workmen, but Davis barely acknowledged them in his publication, other than to reassure readers that 'Happily the work was so well watched and conducted that no accidents occurred, though many of the men and boys were temporarily overcome by the heat and bad air.'[17] In the later discovery of Tutankhamun's tomb, Carter was thus only the latest in a long line of Egyptologists to downplay the role of his workers.

Writing in the year of Hussein Abdel Rassul's chance find, another Egyptologist, Arthur Weigall, epitomized the unselfconscious superiority towards other peoples alongside a grudging acceptance of their right to self-determination that characterized colonial attitudes towards Egypt in the years after the First World War:

> In Egypt, where scientific excavations are conducted entirely by Europeans and Americans, one has to consider . . . one's duty to the Egyptians, who care not one jot for their history, but who, nevertheless, as the living descendants of the Pharaohs should be the nominal stewards of their ancient possessions.[18]

It is hardly surprising that the discovery of Tutankhamun's tomb should have fed a growing sense of Egyptian nationalism: after 1922, the people of the Nile Valley wished to be masters of their future, as well as of their past.

⊲⊙⊳

The distinctive art and architecture of ancient Egypt have been a source of inspiration for Western civilization since the days of the pharaohs themselves. One of the earliest types of human statuary from ancient Greece, the standing figures of naked youths termed *kouroi*, was heavily influenced by Egyptian prototypes, which Greek traders would have encountered in the great pharaonic cities of the Nile Delta. Doric columns were likewise developed by Egyptian architects centuries before they appeared in Greek buildings. Alexander the Great was moved by his encounters with pharaonic monuments, and in particular by his visit to the oracle of Amun in the Siwa Oasis, to regard himself as a divine monarch and to adopt an increasingly 'oriental' mode of kingship. And as we have seen, when the Roman emperor Hadrian sought inspiration for the decoration of his estate and the posthumous deification of his lover Antinous, it was to pharaonic Egypt that he turned.

The classical interest in ancient Egypt and the preponderance of pharaonic monuments, especially in and around Rome, had a profound effect on European taste from the time of the

Renaissance. In the late sixteenth century, Pope Sixtus V enacted a new masterplan for Rome, with Egyptian obelisks re-erected at the focal points. While his aim was to conscript these monuments of ancient paganism to celebrate the triumph of Christianity, others looked to ancient Egypt as the source of an older universal truth. Egyptian iconography was enthusiastically embraced by Freemasonry, which helped to boost the Egyptian revival in seventeenth- and eighteenth-century Europe. In the years before the Napoleonic expedition, Egyptian motifs were being used in a variety of settings, from interior design to mausolea.

But it was Bonaparte's adventures in the Nile Valley between 1798 and 1801 that sparked the first real bout of 'Egyptomania' in the West. The publication of two accounts of the expedition, Vivant Denon's *Voyage dans la Basse et la Haute Egypte* (1802) and the official *Description de l'Egypte* (from 1809 onwards), brought accurate drawings of ancient Egyptian art and architecture to the attention of a wide and discerning European audience. Suddenly, decoration in the Egyptian style became all the rage. Napoleon commissioned a Sèvres porcelain service, decorated with elements copied from Philae, Luxor, Karnak and Edfu. Not to be outdone, the Prince Regent commissioned an 'Egyptian gallery' for his Royal Pavilion at Brighton, together with furniture in the Egyptian style. One such piece is a couch in the form of a papyrus skiff, painted green and with gilded crocodile's feet. Sphinxes and obelisks – both genuine antiquities and modern reproductions – sprang up along the boulevards of Paris and in the gardens of England's stately homes. Nelson's victory over Napoleon at the Battle of the Nile in August 1798 gave the Egyptian revival in England an added patriotic dimension. The results included a design for a greenhouse at Trentham Hall in Staffordshire modelled on the temple of Esna; and the Egyptian Hall on Piccadilly, which served as an appropriate venue for Belzoni's Egyptian exhibition in 1821.

In the 1830s and 1840s, the watercolours of David Roberts and the accounts of early Egyptologists like Champollion and John Gardner Wilkinson implanted exotic images of the Nile Valley firmly in the public imagination. Egyptian motifs found their way into a bewildering array of domestic and commercial settings, from a house in Penzance and a shop-front in Hertford to a public library in Plymouth, a flax mill in Leeds and a terrace of lighthouse keepers' cottages in the far north of Scotland. The Crystal Palace at Sydenham in London in 1854 had an Egyptian Court, dominated by a pair of gigantic seated statues modelled on the façade of the temple of Abu Simbel. This, in turn, inspired the creation of an Egyptian garden in Staffordshire, an Egyptian temple at Antwerp Zoo and even an obelisk-shaped sewer vent in Sydney. By the end of the nineteenth century, Egyptianizing design elements were ubiquitous. Only the convulsions of the Great War could halt Europe's fascination for all things Egyptian.

The stage was thus set for the discovery of Tutankhamun's tomb in 1922, which unleashed a second wave of Egyptomania around the world. The exoticism of pharaonic art offered an escape from recent horrors, while the sumptuousness of Tutankhamun's grave goods provided an antidote to late Victorian and Edwardian austerity. Women's fashion enthusiastically embraced pharaonic designs; one 1923 advertisement proclaimed that

The decorative splendors of the Tut-ankh-amen period are reflected in the rich embroidery motif of this distinguished Wrap-Over Coat with its aristocratic collar of bisque squirrel.[19]

Jewellers also found inspiration in the treasure trove unearthed by Carter and Carnarvon. In January 1924, the *Illustrated London News* devoted a full page to 'The "Tutankhamen" influence on modern jewellery', showcasing pieces 'incorporating Egyptian trinkets from 1,500 to 3,000 years ago'.[20] In addition to ancient gems in modern settings (for 'women interested in Egyptology, who desire to be in the Tutankhamen fashion'), Cartier issued a series of pieces inspired by the discovery: a diamond, emerald and ruby pendant in the shape of the king's funerary mask; a brooch in the form of a winged scarab; and a cloisonné enamel pendant. The last of these was copied directly from a scarab pectoral of gold, lapis lazuli, carnelian and green feldspar found in the Treasury of Tutankhamun's tomb. The pectoral, which originally hung on a cord, would have been worn around the king's neck; like other pieces of his jewellery, its design elements form a rebus of the pharaoh's throne name. Among a wealth of precious gems, it must rank as one of the finest, most perfectly conceived and executed gems from the whole of pharaonic civilization.

For 1920s customers who could not stretch to a piece of Cartier jewellery, manufacturers of household goods provided plenty of opportunities to indulge in the latest craze: everything from porcelain vases to biscuit tins were produced with Egyptianizing motifs. Indeed, the popular appetite for Tutankhamun-inspired objects seemed insatiable. Just three years after the discovery of the tomb, as Carter and his assistants were starting to clear the burial chamber, the Exposition Internationale des Arts Décoratifs et Industriels Modernes in Paris showcased a new, democratic, forward-looking style ('Art-Deco') that found inspiration in motifs from a three-and-a-half-thousand-year-old burial. Fashion, like antiquarianism, had once been the preserve of the wealthy elite;

now, the world of design and the world of the pharaohs were accessible to everyone.

⊲⊙⊳

The discovery of Tutankhamun's tomb

> broke upon a world sated with post-First World War conferences, with nothing proved and nothing achieved, after a summer journalistically so dull that an English farmer's report of a gooseberry the size of a crab-apple achieved the main news page of the London metropolitan dailies. It was hardly surprising therefore that the Tutenkhamun discovery should have received a volume of world-wide publicity exceeding anything in the entire history of science.[21]

Interest in the treasures of the boy pharaoh reached fever pitch the following year, with the official opening of the burial chamber. As the *New York Times* reported:

> There is only one topic of conversation . . . One cannot escape the name of Tut-Ankh-Amen anywhere. It is shouted in the streets, whispered in the hotels, while the local shops advertise Tut-Ankh-Amen art, Tut-Ankh-Amen hats, Tut-Ankh-Amen curios, Tut-Ankh-Amen photographs, and tomorrow probably genuine Tut-Ankh-Amen antiquities. Every hotel in Luxor today had something à la Tut-Ankh-Amen . . . There is a Tut-Ankh-Amen dance tonight at which the piece is to be a Tut-Ankh-Amen rag.[22]

As with all new crazes, enterprising corporations and individuals saw an opportunity to make money from 'Tutmania'.

1923 saw the publication of two romantic novels that imagined the love life of Tutankhamun; and two popular records, with lyrics about 'Old King Tut' (at that stage, nobody was aware that the king had only been a teenager when he died). A Californian grower of citrus fruit marketed 'King Tut Lemons', and US president Herbert Hoover even called one of his dogs 'King Tut'. An obscure Egyptian king of the late eighteenth dynasty had become a global phenomenon.

Cashing in on the popularity of ancient Egypt, while also basking in the reflected glory that the discovery had been made by an Englishman (albeit with some Egyptian help), the British Empire Exhibition of 1924–5 featured full-scale replicas of many of the objects recovered from the Antechamber. Foremost among them were the two black-skinned guardian figures that were pictured on cigarette cards and penknives and were, for a time, the most famous artefacts from the tomb. But once the gilded shrines had been dismantled, the sarcophagus and the nest of three coffins opened and the mass of congealed unguents carefully removed, Carter – and the rest of the world – came face to face with Tutankhamun's funerary mask of beaten gold. Overnight, it became the tomb's defining artefact and the iconic image of ancient Egypt.

According to pharaonic belief, the flesh of the gods was made of gold, effulgent and untarnishing. Each of Tutankhamun's three anthropoid coffins was created as an image of the deceased, deified king, with shining golden skin. The funerary mask was the final layer of protection for his fragile body; it was designed to function as both portrait and homing beacon, helping the king's wandering *ba* to recognize the mummy as its eternal dwelling place. One of Tutankhamun's inscriptions speaks of 'his sacred image of electrum, lapis lazuli, turquoise and every precious stone';[23] the mask is indeed made of these materials, with inlays of carnelian, green feldspar, quartz, obsidian, faience and glass. The skill and sophistication of pharaonic goldsmiths is attested in the three different grades of gold used to make the mask. The underlying body is made from 23-carat gold and the headdress from 22.5-carat gold, while the surface of the face is finished with a thin layer of 18.4-carat gold with a high silver content, imparting a distinctive radiance. Texts on the back of the mask from the *Book of the Dead* associate parts of it – and parts of the king's mummified body – with different deities.

Despite its status as the *ne plus ultra* of pharaonic craftsmanship, the gold mask has had a chequered history since its discovery. When Carter and his assistants first opened Tutankhamun's coffins, they were met with a thick layer of unguents, which had congealed and set, gluing the mask and coffins to each other. The solution was as dangerous as it was ingenious:

As heat was the only practical means of melting this material and rendering it amenable, in order to apply a temperature sufficiently high for the purpose, without causing damage to those wonderful specimens of ancient Egyptian arts and crafts, the interior of the golden coffin had to be completely lined with thick plates of zinc, which would not melt under a temperature of 968° Fahrenheit (520° C) . . . Our next procedure was to place under the hollow of the gold coffin several Primus paraffin lamps burning at full blast . . . Although the temperature arrived at was some 932° Fahrenheit (500° C), it took several hours before any real effect was noticeable . . . This mask had also been protected by being bound with a folded wet blanket continually fed with water, its face padded with wet wadding. As it had necessarily been subjected to the full power of the heat collected in the interior of the coffin, it was freed and lifted away with comparative ease.[24]

In the process, the curved divine beard, which identified Tutankhamun as a god, became detached. The mask is shown without its beard in Carter's 1927 publication,[25] and the missing element was only reattached some years later.[26] Following a series of worldwide exhibitions of objects from the tomb between 1961 and 1981 – including the London exhibition on the fiftieth anniversary of the discovery – the mask no longer leaves Egypt. It is simply too fragile and too precious.

The sheer quantity and variety of objects in Tutankhamun's tomb necessitated an unprecedented array of specialists to carry out the analysis and conservation. The team brought together by Carter marked a departure in Egyptian archaeology. The expedition was the first to have its own chemist, alongside a photographer, engineer, philologist, epigrapher and amateur archaeobotanist, in addition to draughtsmen and experienced excavators. The large number of specialisms required signalled the end of the heroic age of gentleman amateurs, and gone were the days when a single scholar could hope to encompass the whole of Egyptology. The result was that the study of ancient Egypt was transformed from a popular pastime into an academic discipline. In the process, it lost some of its panache and grew increasingly remote from the wider public. Writing in 1923, one scholar warned, 'It is the business of the archaeologist to wake the dreaming dead: not to send the living to sleep';[27] but his words went unheeded. Egyptology after Tutankhamun grew as dusty and desiccated as the Valley of the Kings. And with a gulf opening up between popular interest in ancient Egypt and academic scholarship, it was perhaps inevitable that unscrupulous elements would aim to fill the gap.

The association of ancient Egypt with occult knowledge, having been a central feature of the Hermetic tradition from the sixteenth to the eighteenth century, was largely sidelined by the nineteenth-century scientific exploration of the Nile Valley. However, like a mummy awaiting resurrection, the belief in the otherworldliness of pharaonic civilization was poised for rebirth when the circumstances were favourable. The unearthing of Tutankhamun's tomb in 1922 provided the opportunity the mystics and pseudo-scientists had been waiting for.

For the proponents of alternative theories, the discovery fell like a seed onto fertile ground. Stories based on Egyptian mummies coming back to life had been a familiar genre of anglophone literature for the best part of a century, attracting authors as respected as Louisa May Alcott, Bram Stoker, H. Rider Haggard and Arthur Conan Doyle. A second crucial element in the development of the 'curse of Tutankhamun' narrative was the deal signed between Lord Carnarvon and *The Times* of London for exclusive coverage of the discovery and access to the tomb. While this made Carnarvon a good deal of money, it infuriated journalists working for other papers, who felt excluded from the biggest story of the decade. In the absence of real events to report, some decided to make up their own.

Stories of an ancient curse, awakened when the tomb was entered and affecting anyone connected to the excavations, began to circulate when Carnarvon fell ill in March 1923, four months after the discovery. When he died of blood poisoning the following month, there was no stopping the torrent of wild speculation. Before long, the curse was said to have claimed the lives of a host of other high-profile victims, ranging from a princely visitor to the tomb and Carnarvon's two half-brothers to the head of antiquities at the Louvre and two Egyptologists at the Metropolitan Museum of Art. Carter felt compelled to rebuff such 'ridiculous' stories, but he had, perhaps unwittingly, contributed to the theory himself in the preface to his official account of the discovery.

The first six pages of Volume One of *The Tomb of Tut.ankh. Amen* are dedicated to an account, by Carter and his novelist friend Percy White, of 'a true incident connected with the discovery of the tomb of Tutankhamen'.[28] The story tells how 'at the moment Mr Carter was about to open the tomb's sealed entrance, a cobra made its way into his house and killed the much-cherished canary'[29] – Carter's caged bird being regarded by his Egyptian workmen as a good luck charm. This might have been thought no more than an unfortunate accident, had it not been for the sight that first met Carter on entering the tomb:

> for the ray of light from our candle revealed the contents
> of the ante-chamber to the tomb, and shone on the head
> of the King bearing on his forehead the Uraeus – the
> symbol of royalty and protection – the cobra![30]

The king in question was one of the twin guardian statues that stood against the bricked-up wall between the Antechamber and the burial chamber, protecting the body of the king that lay beyond. In Percy White's colourful prose:

> Standing out impressively against the almost spectral back-
> ground were those twin effigies of the King, guarding,
> with mace and staff of office, the then untouched tomb,
> the royal cobra rising from the pleading brows.[31]

The coincidence of the cobra on the statues' brows and the death of Carter's canary was not lost on his Egyptian foremen:

The *Reises* were awed; before them was the image of the serpent that had killed the lucky bird![32]

With such a story circulating in the Valley of the Kings in early 1923, frustrated journalists looking for a sensational scoop had the perfect material. They were soon asserting that an inscription inside the tomb warned that 'Death comes on swift wings to him that toucheth the tomb of the pharaoh.' The fact that no such inscription existed, or that, of the twenty-six people present at the opening of the tomb, just six died over the following decade, did nothing to quell the story. For, as Carter himself acknowledged:

> however superstitious the Egyptian *fellaheen* may be, they are less credulous than our own willing victims of occult romanticism, who haunt psychic tea-parties, and when-

Fig. 44. Black guardian statues.

ever a tomb is opened, persuade themselves that forces long dormant have been let loose on an intruding world.[33]

Once all of those most closely connected with the discovery of Tutankhamun's tomb had died, the bandwagon of Egypt-related sensationalism rolled on. There have been a few eighteenth-dynasty 'revelations' over the years, ranging from the just-about plausible to the downright preposterous. Akhenaten remains the focus of a bewildering array of theories and movements, from Black Power to gay liberation. However, since the mid-twentieth century, the focus has largely shifted from the mummies of long-dead kings to the most enduring symbols of ancient Egypt: the pyramids and the Great Sphinx of Giza.

Fantastical explanations of the pyramids have a long history. No less a figure than Flinders Petrie, the founding father of Egyptian archaeology, first visited Egypt because of his interest in the notion of the 'pyramid inch'. Based on the writings of Charles Piazzi Smyth, this theory asserted that the dimensions of the Great Pyramid encoded lost knowledge. Petrie's accurate measurements disproved the theory and set him on the course of scientific archaeology. However, not to be deflected by the results of modern science, various New Age writers have come up with a host of alternative 'explanations' for the greatest monuments of the Old Kingdom:

The Great Pyramid serves as a model of planet Earth, the human brain, the hydrogen atom, a volcano. Now dormant, it once served as an energy capacitor, a huge hydraulic pump or an astronomical observatory. The pyramid stands on an upside-down pyramid of pure crystal and equal size. . .[34]

No amount of evidence for the actual construction of the pyramids and the Sphinx in the fourth dynasty makes a jot of difference, for 'people will believe what they want'.[35] One notable exception is the archaeologist who has led the excavation of the pyramid workers' settlement over recent decades. Arriving at Giza on a New Age quest, his 'encounters with bedrock reality . . . transformed him through the cognitive dissonance of a paradigm shift'.[36]

One of the central assertions of these unorthodox theories is that the Giza monuments were built thousands of years before the Old Kingdom by visitors from another world. Petrie himself was not immune to a similar train of thought, stubbornly insisting – against accumulating evidence to the contrary – that Egyptian civilization had been brought to the Nile Valley by a 'new race' of people from some unidentified land to the east. Such interpretations share a common stance that seeks to deny the indigenous origins of pharaonic culture. For most New Age writers, ancient Egypt was too sophisticated a civilization to have been developed by the Egyptians themselves. This colonial mindset, rather than any malevolent spirit awakened from a dusty tomb, is the real curse of the pharaohs.

◄□►

History is deeply political. How a nation interprets its past speaks volumes about how it sees itself in the present. From the very beginning of Egyptology, the modern inhabitants of the Nile Valley have harboured contradictory views of their ancient culture, regarding it variously as a diplomatic bargaining chip, an economic resource and as a token of once and future greatness. The relationship between Western archaeologists, pharaonic remains and the Egyptian authorities has been correspondingly fraught.

The Napoleonic invasion of Egypt in 1798 had profound consequences for modern Egypt and its ancient remains. While the legacy of the pharaohs was brought into the spotlight of scientific enquiry, the political fall-out from the French occupation and withdrawal led to the rise to power of Muhammad Ali, a new ruler who was utterly focused on modernization. As he sought to industrialize and urbanize the country, its ancient remains bore the brunt. As early as 1829, just seven years after the decipherment of hieroglyphics, Champollion felt compelled to appeal to Muhammad Ali to protect his country's patrimony. Six years later, the Egyptian government passed its first piece of antiquities legislation. It blamed Europeans for the destruction of Egypt's monuments but cited European precedents for the introduction of an export ban on antiquities and the establishment of a national collection. However, within a few years, Egypt's first museum was in a parlous condition:

> nothing but a confused mass of broken mummies and cases, some imperfect tablets, and various fragments, which, had they been capable of being spoilt, would have been rendered valueless by the damp of the place.[37]

Just two decades after its establishment, the collection had disappeared entirely, through a combination of neglect and indifference; the final pieces were presented to Archduke Maximilian of Austria as a diplomatic gift in 1855.

The thoughtless neglect and wanton destruction of Egypt's pharaonic inheritance provoked despair and anger among Western observers. It also provided a justification for the continued export of antiquities to European collections. The French claimed the moral high ground, asserting that:

France, snatching an obelisk from the ever heightening mud of the Nile, or the savage ignorance of the Turks . . . earns a right to the thanks of the learned of Europe, to whom belong all the monuments of antiquity, because they know how to appreciate them. Antiquity is a garden that belongs by natural right to those who cultivate and harvest its fruits.[38]

The American consul in Cairo, George Gliddon, was even more outspoken, claiming that 'in destroying the Ancient Monuments of Egypt, the present government of that country has been influenced by avarice, wantonness and negligence'.[39] He praised Champollion for delivering antiquities 'out of the house of bondage'[40] to the safety of European museums.

This defence would continue to be used by collectors and treasure hunters throughout the nineteenth century, but not every Egyptologist agreed with such sentiments. As early as 1821, Champollion had expressed misgivings about the removal of the Dendera zodiac and its transport to the Louvre:

We applaud the patriotic sentiments which guided this, our two compatriots' bold project, carried out so skilfully and successfully . . . But in congratulating Messrs Saulnier and Lelorrain on having, so carefully, transported the circular zodiac of Dendera from the banks of the Nile to those of the Seine, and not the Thames, we cannot, however, refrain from expressing a certain regret that this magnificent temple has been deprived of one of its finest monuments . . . Should we, in France, follow the example of Lord Elgin? Certainly not.[41]

Eventually, Egypt gained a national museum that was worthy of the name. It opened in 1863, in a series of disused warehouses at Bulaq, pending a more permanent home. Its French director, Auguste Mariette, ensured that each of the artefacts on display had an accompanying description and that the provenance of every object was recorded. It soon became a major tourist attraction, but Mariette wanted it to serve the Egyptians themselves. In his guide to the collection, he wrote:

> The Museum of Cairo is not only intended for European travellers. It is the Viceroy's intention that it should be above all accessible to the natives, to whom the Museum is entrusted in order to teach them the history of their country . . . Not long ago, Egypt destroyed its monuments; today, it respects them; tomorrow it shall love them.[42]

As the collection continued to expand, fuelled by excavations the length and breadth of the Nile Valley, the museum outgrew its premises and moved first to a converted palace at Giza and eventually, in 1902, to a purpose-built edifice in central Cairo. Tellingly, this repository for Egypt's national collection of antiquities was designed by a Frenchman, and the inscriptions on its grand, neo-classical façade gave pride of place to the Western heroes of Egyptology: six Frenchmen, five Britons, four Germans, three Italians, a Dutchman, a Dane and a Swede. The only Egyptian to be celebrated was the reigning khedive, Abbas II – a puppet ruler propped up by the British – and his name was written in Latin. Europe's implicit claim to ancient Egypt was further reinforced when Mariette's sarcophagus was installed in the front garden of the museum.

The Egyptian Museum was designed with plenty of space to accommodate the growing national collection of antiquities, but nobody could have foreseen that it would one day have to find room for the vast number of objects from Tutankhamun's tomb. As a result of this unexpected influx of artefacts, by the mid-1920s the museum was overcrowded and in a bad state of disrepair. The American Egyptologist James Henry Breasted persuaded his benefactor, John D. Rockefeller, to fund a brand new museum, but there was one condition: Western scholars would be guaranteed control of the museum and its associated research institute for a period of thirty-three years. The Egyptian government refused.

The discovery of Tutankhamun's treasure, coming just eight months after Egypt's declaration of independence, had a profound impact on Egyptian domestic sentiment and nationalist politics. Interest in Egypt's past was propelled into the mainstream of Egyptian cultural and political thought. The teaching of pharaonic history was introduced in government schools, a state university was founded, programmes were

Fig. 45. Statuette of a deity carrying the king.

introduced to train Egyptian Egyptologists, and the Antiquities Service and museum – for so long bastions of Western influence – were steadily Egyptianized.

Perhaps most significantly, the system of dividing finds between the archaeologist and the state came to an end. To coincide with Egypt's declaration of independence, the director of the Antiquities Service announced that all finds would henceforth be claimed for the state, with only duplicates given to the excavators at the service's discretion. Carnarvon's original permit to excavate in the Valley of the Kings, signed in 1914, had specified an even distribution of finds, except in the event of an unrobbed tomb being found. The Egyptian authorities now invoked that exception, and successfully sought to retain the entire contents of the tomb. Eventually, in the officers' revolution of 1952, European influence over the Egyptian Museum was brought to an end; since then, Egypt's antiquities have been curated by the Egyptians themselves.

But the entanglement of ancient history and modern politics did not end there. In the Arab Spring uprising of 2011, sixty-three items were looted from the Egyptian Museum, which unwittingly found itself at the epicentre of the violence. Among the stolen objects were five from the treasure of Tutankhamun, of which the most important was a gilded statuette of the boy king being carried on the head of a deity. Unique in the surviving corpus of ancient Egyptian art, it must have had a powerful symbolic significance and is paralleled only in a two-dimensional relief in the late-nineteenth-dynasty tomb of Seti II. Several weeks after the theft, fragments of the mutilated statuette were recovered; with the pedestal, the arms and face of the god, and the miniature figure of Tutankhamun all missing, the piece is damaged beyond recognition.

As Egypt's national collection moves for the third time, into the state-of-the-art Grand Egyptian Museum in the shadow of the Giza pyramids, the authorities have once again called for the repatriation of antiquities exported to the West in the nineteenth and early twentieth centuries. Top of their list is the Rosetta Stone, but in 2020 the museum's director of archaeological affairs acknowledged that it would never leave London, conceding that Egyptian artefacts in museums around the world 'will instead inspire people to travel to Egypt to see where they originated'.[43] This is unlikely to be the last word in a centuries-long struggle for the custodianship of pharaonic antiquities. Egypt's past will continue to shape its future.

Another of the artefacts from Tutankhamun's tomb stolen from the Egyptian Museum in 2011 was a trumpet of gilded bronze with a painted wooden core. It was one of two such instruments interred with the king, the only examples to have survived from pharaonic Egypt. The larger trumpet was made of silver. It, too, had a core of gessoed and painted wood, designed to fit snugly inside the instrument, to help it retain its shape when not in use and to protect the thin metal from damage. The silver trumpet, a masterpiece of metalworking, is fifty-eight centimetres long and is made from two pieces of hammered sheet metal, folded over and soldered together. The bell, shaped like an open waterlily, is delicately chased with decoration resembling sepals, each containing the royal cartouche. A larger, rectangular panel, shows the three principal deities of the Egyptian pantheon, Amun-Ra, Ra-Horakhty and Ptah. Around the rim of the bell is a band of gold chased to resemble the petals of the flower. A corresponding band of gold at the other end of the instrument forms the mouthpiece.

Tutankhamun's trumpets complement the pictorial and

textual evidence for music in ancient Egypt. The repertoire of instruments attested in pharaonic times also includes percussion, woodwind and strings. Music was evidently a feature at banquets and religious festivals, but also in more mundane settings: farm workers and wine makers carried out their tasks to the accompaniment of rhythmic songs. While harps, lutes and lyres were favoured in intimate family settings, and sistra were shaken at religious festivals to stimulate the presence of a deity, trumpets seem to have been used primarily in military and ceremonial settings.

In the hills of Amarna, the rock-cut tomb prepared for Huya, the steward of Tutankhamun's beloved grandmother Tiye, includes a wealth of scenes depicting life at the royal court. One tableau, commemorating Tiye's visit to her 'sunshade', shows a trumpeter holding his instrument and its wooden core as he stands in front of a group of royal attendants. At Thebes, fragments from a battle scene dating to the reign of Tutankhamun include a depiction of bound Nubian captives, their ropes held by the king. Behind them, a trumpeter turns towards the infantrymen and standard-bearers and blasts a note of triumph. The aftermath of the same campaign may be shown in a rock-cut shrine at Gebel el-Silsila; a trumpeter plays while Egyptian and Nubian troops perform a leaping dance and the Nubians sing:

Greetings to you, King of Egypt,
Light for the Nine Bows!
Your great name is in the land of Kush,
Your war-cry in all their places!
It is your might, o good ruler,
Which has made the foreign lands into piles of
     corpses.
Pharaoh is the Light![44]

Finally, a similar scene of Nubian troops dancing to the strains of a trumpet was carved in the reign of Tutankhamun on the walls of the colonnade hall at Luxor Temple.

Such scenes conjure up a lost world of sound. Music was clearly important in the lives of all ancient Egyptians: a limestone stela from the workmen's village at Amarna depicts members of a modest family that include a daughter playing the harp. Yet in the absence of any musical notation, the nature of pharaonic music remains unknown. Tutankhamun's trumpets produce just three notes, of which the upper and lower were so difficult to play that it is likely that only the middle note would have been used in practice. The sound is harsh to the modern Western ear, 'rather the timbre of a medieval trombone or primitive horn than that of a trumpet or cornet'.[45] The tunes the ancient Egyptians played remain elusive, a salutary reminder that, even after more than two centuries of excavation in the Nile Valley, many details of pharaonic civilization escape us. As the archaeologist of Amarna Barry Kemp has put it, 'beyond the limits of academic research is a whole range of lost experiences'.[46] Study of the material remains left by the ancient Egyptians – epitomized most spectacularly by the objects from the tomb of Tutankhamun – reveals much about their daily lives, their geography and history, government and religion, but the human experience of living in the pharaonic Nile Valley can never be recovered.

In another rock-cut tomb at Amarna, carved for Akhenaten's steward, a large scene over five registers depicts units of the palace guard. Each of the top and bottom two registers shows a detachment of ten soldiers, their different nationalities – Egyptian and Nubian, Libyan and Asiatic – illustrating the multicultural character of Tutankhamun's Egypt. The middle register is blank but for the single figure of a trumpeter, on the far left of the scene, holding his instrument to his lips. We imagine the empty space before him being occupied by the sound of his trumpet call. It is a remarkable tableau, unique in pharaonic art, indicating both that sound exerted a powerful grip on the Egyptian consciousness and that we can only dimly discern the contours of the past.

In 1939, the year of Howard Carter's death, it was suggested that Tutankhamun's silver trumpet might be played again, for the first time in nearly three and a half thousand years. In a live BBC broadcast, the instrument was handed to a British army trumpeter, who was standing in front of a microphone. Bandsman James Tappern inserted a modern mouthpiece, brought the trumpet to his lips and began to play, producing three haunting notes from the thin, delicate instrument.

Like Tutankhamun himself, the music that once surrounded him has vanished, and all that remains are echoes of the past. The objects buried with him provide glimpses into his world and into the civilization of which he remains the ultimate symbol, but it is left to our imagination to fill in the gaps.

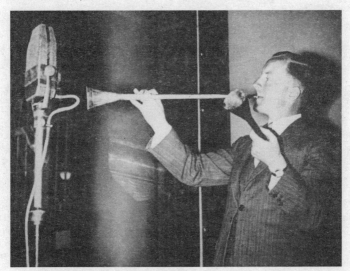

Fig. 46. Bandsman Tappern playing Tutankhamun's trumpet.

List of Objects
(with Carter's catalogue numbers)

1. Galena, malachite, lead and tin oxide, orpiment, yellow ochre (456b, 620(79–81), 620(82–83), 620(85–86))

2. Pectoral with green glass (267d)

3. Chisels of meteoric iron (316a–p)

4. Ostrich-feather fan (242)

5. Throw sticks (370l–m, 370p, 370t)

6. Scene of bird-hunting (Little Golden Shrine) (108)

7. Rush and papyrus sandals (21a–b)

8. Model papyrus skiff (313)

9. Osiris bed (288a)

10. Ceremonial sickle (561)

11. Flint knives (620(62–63))

12. Gilded Hathor head (264)

13. Fire drill (585aa)

14. Crook and flail (269h, 269e)

15. Scribal palettes (271b, 271e(2))

16. Model barge (309)

17. Fighting sticks (582c–h)

18. Cubit measuring rods (50dd)

19. Ebony and ivory casting sticks (associated with 345, 383 and 580)

20. Ivory bracelet with running horse (585q)

21. Chariot (122)

22. Composite bow and arrows (370)

23. Leather scale armour (587a)

24. Calcite jar of Thutmose III (404)

25. Silver pomegranate-shaped vase (469)

26. Bronze scimitars (582a, 620(52))

27. Small indigo glass cups (32k, 32l)

28. Gold and iron daggers (256dd, 256k)

29. Painted Box (21)

30. Gold pendant of a king (320c)

31. Loaves of bread (620(112), 620(117))

32. Model granary (277)

33. Bulbs of garlic (32x)

34. Basket of fruit (97)

35. Chickpeas and lentils (277, 614f)

36. Box of beef (the foreleg of an ox) (62h)

37. Dish of stoned dates (154)

38. Wine jars (11, 180, 195, 206, 362, 392, 409, 411, 413, 431, 434, 486, 489, 490, 500, 508, 509, 516, 523, 536, 539, 541, 549, 560, 563, 568, 570, 571)

39. Duck breasts (Pit 54)

40. Jars of honey (614j–k)

41. Leopard-skin cloak (44q)

42. Falcon pectoral (267m(1))

43. Statuette of the king harpooning (275c(a))

44. Footrest with enemies (378)

45. *Shabti*s with different crowns (110, 318a, 330a, 605a)

46. Faience *hes* and *nemset* vases (461r, 461b)

47. Gold and silver coronation staffs (235a, 235b)

48. Cartouche-shaped box (269)

49. Bow-fronted travelling box (79, 574)

50. Golden throne (91)

51. Folding stools (140)

52. Linen loincloth (50b)

53. Large portable chest (32)

54. Leather and beadwork sandals (85a)

55. Folding bed (586)

56. Headrests (403b)

57. Shaving equipment (68, 12g, 620(53))

58. Kohl tube (from boxes 44, 46)

59. Game box and stand (345, 383, 580)

60. Mirror case (269b)

61. Ivory clappers (620(13))

62. Mummified bodies of Tutankhamun's stillborn daughters (317a(2), 317b(2))

63. Wooden toy chest (585)

64. Ebony and ivory child's chair (39)

65. Box lid with Princess Neferneferura as an infant (54hh)

66. Ankhesenamun and Tutankhamun (Little Golden Shrine) (108)

67. Lock of hair (320e)

68. DNA analysis (256)

69. First aid kit (79i–q, 79t–u)

70. Walking sticks (48a-d, 50v–cc, 50kk–qq, 50uu–xx)

71. Gilded figure of Geb (299a)

72. Gilded figure of Ptah (291a)

73. *Imiut* fetishes (194, 202)

74. Model solar barque (311)

75. Shrine-shaped pectoral (267q)

76. Feldspar amulet of Thoth (256,4,a)

77. Model sailing boat (276)

78. *Wedjat* eye bracelet (256zz)

79. Sistra (76(a))

80. Ritual torch with *ankh* (41a)

81. The royal mummy (256)

82. Bier figure (331, 331a)

Acknowledgements

I thank my agents, Jon Wood and Veronica Goldstein, and the editorial team at Picador; all those who support, curate and staff the libraries I use for my research, especially the Cambridge University Library and the Haddon Library; the scholars, past and present, upon whose research I have drawn; Professor Clayton MacKenzie, formerly of Hong Kong Baptist University, for giving me an early opportunity to present some of the ideas in this book before a live audience; and, as always, Michael Bailey for his unwavering support, particularly during the challenging times of 2020 and 2021.

Notes

Introduction

1 Carter and Mace (1923): 79.
2 Quoted in Collins and McNamara (2014): 28–32.
3 Carter and Mace (1923): 86.
4 Carter and Mace (1923): 86.

CHAPTER 1: Geography

1 Herodotus (2004): 279–81.
2 Strabo (1949): 1.4.
3 Quoted in Manley and Abdel-Hakim (eds) (2004): 9.
4 Quoted in Vivian (2000): 376.
5 Pliny, *Natural History*, Book 5, quoted in Wilkinson (2014): 6.
6 Letter from Hekanakht to his steward Merisu, translated in Wilkinson (2016): 145.

CHAPTER 2: History

1 Threatened by modern development, the Nabta Playa stone circle was removed in the early 2000s and re-erected in the grounds of the Nubia Museum in Aswan.
2 This object is also displayed in the Nubia Museum.
3 Griffith Institute, Carter Archive, Tutankhamun, notes on objects, quoted in Reeves (1990): 196.
4 Frederick the Great of Prussia famously remarked that 'a crown is just a hat that lets the rain in'.
5 Lehner and Hawass (2017): 30.
6 Kemp (2006): 195 fig. 67 (3).
7 Kemp (2006): 217.
8 Semna inscription of Senusret III, translated in Wilkinson (2016): 186–7.

9 Kamose Stela, translated in Wilkinson (2016): 51.

10 Skeletal evidence suggests that the domesticated horse had reached Nubia before the New Kingdom: a further indication, perhaps, of close links between the Hyksos and the Kingdom of Kush. The earliest depictions of horses in ancient Egyptian art are pairs of horses bridled for attachment to chariots, from the complex of Ahmose at Abydos: see Harvey (1994): 5, top left.

11 Amenhotep II, Great Sphinx Stela, translated in Wilkinson (2010): 257.

CHAPTER 3: Supremacy

1 Boundary stela of Akhenaten, translated in Wilkinson (2016): 203.

2 Cycle of Hymns to Senusret III, translated in Wilkinson (2016): 97.

3 Amenhotep II, Medamud inscription, translated in Wilkinson (2010): 257.

4 *Daily Telegraph*, 17 January 1923, quoted in Reeves (1990): 174.

5 Carter and Mace (1923): 104.

6 Inscription of Ahmose, son of Abana, translated in Wilkinson (2016): 19.

7 Kemp (2006): 37.

8 Roaf (1990): 136–7.

9 Carter (1933): 100.

10 The Battle of Megiddo, translated in Wilkinson (2016): 58.

11 The Battle of Megiddo, translated in Wilkinson (2016): 59.

12 The Battle of Megiddo, translated in Wilkinson (2016): 56.

13 The Battle of Megiddo, translated in Wilkinson (2016): 59.

14 The Battle of Megiddo, translated in Wilkinson (2016): 60.

15 Thutmose III obelisk inscription, right side, translated in Wilkinson (2010): 242.

16 The Battle of Megiddo, translated in Wilkinson (2016): 61.

17 Kemp (2005): 30, fig. 7.

18 Kemp (2005): 31.

19 Archaeologists prefer the term 'Chalcolithic' ('Copper-Stone Age'), reflecting the period's transitional nature.

20 A source of cobaltiferous alum has been located in Egypt, but whether or not it was exploited in antiquity remains to be established: see Kaczmarczyk (1986 and 1991).

21 *Daily Telegraph*, 1 December 1923, quoted in Reeves (1990): 200.

22 Carter (1933): 60.

23 Tomb of Huya, west wall, author's translation; illustrated in Davies (1905): pl. XIII.

24 Marriage scarab of Amenhotep III, translated in Wilkinson (2016): 199.

25 Amarna Letter EA17, from Tushratta to Amenhotep III, translated in Moran (1992): 41.

26 EA17, translated in Moran (1992): 42.

27 EA22, inventory of gifts from Tushratta to Amenhotep III, translated in Moran (1992): 53.

28 EA22, translated in Moran (1992): 54.

29 EA22, translated in Moran (1992): 51.

30 Carter (1927): 97.

31 EA22, translated in Moran (1992): 51.

32 Quoted in Reeves (1990): 191.

33 Amenhotep III, bull hunt scarab, translated in Wilkinson (2010): 262.

34 EA17, translated in Moran (1992): 44.

35 Greaves and Little (1929): 123–7, quoted in Ogden (2000): 161.

36 EA17, translated in Moran (1992): 44.

37 EA4, Kadashman-Enlil to Amenhotep III, translated in Moran (1992): 9.

38 EA16, Ashuruballit to Akhenaten (?), translated in Moran (1992): 39.

CHAPTER 4: Bounty

1 Kemp (2012): 219.

2 EA22, translated in Moran (1992): 55.

3 *The Teaching of Khety* (also known as *The Satire of the Trades*), translated in Wilkinson (2016): 298.

4 *The Teaching of Ani*, thirteenth maxim, translated in Wilkinson (2016): 303.

5 *Shabti* spell (*Book of the Dead*, Chapter 6), author's translation.

6 Carter (1933): 45.

7 Wente (1990): 126.

8 *The Teaching of Ani*, twenty-fifth maxim, translated in Wilkinson (2016): 305.

9 *The Teaching of Khety*, translated in Wilkinson (2016): 293.

10 Carter (1933): 104.

11 From *The Great Hymn to the Orb*, translated in Wilkinson (2016): 103–4.

12 Papyrus BM10052, quoted in Kemp (1989): 243.

13 *Daily Mail*, 20 January 1923, quoted in Reeves (1990): 205.

14 Kemp (2012): 111.

15 *The Teaching of Ani*, forty-seventh maxim, translated in Wilkinson (2016): 309.

16 It is possible that the sign in question actually represents an oil press.

17 D'Auria *et al.* (1988): 142, quoted in Ikram (2000): 669.

18 In the medieval period, a similar quality was imputed to snails, because they seemed to dwell both in water and on land.

CHAPTER 5: Monarchy

1 William Shakespeare, *Hamlet*, Act IV, Scene 5.

2 Inscription of Ahmose, son of Abana, translated in Wilkinson (2016): 20.

3 Inscription of Harkhuf, translated in Wilkinson (2016): 10.

4 Restoration Decree of Tutankhamun, translated in Wilkinson (2016): 108–9.

5 Cycle of Hymns to Senusret III, translated in Wilkinson (2016): 97.

6 *The Teaching of King Amenemhat I for His Son*, translated in Wilkinson (2016): 277.

7 Restoration Decree of Tutankhamun, translated in Wilkinson (2016): 209.

8 Goebs (2007): 290.

9 Adoption Stela of Nitiqret, translated in Wilkinson (2016): 214.

10 Boundary Stela of Akhenaten, translated in Wilkinson (2016): 205.

11 *The Great Hymn to the Orb*, translated in Wilkinson (2016): 105.

CHAPTER 6: Domesticity

1 Kemp (2012): 199.

2 Harpist's Song from the Tomb of King Intef, translated in Wilkinson (2016): 226.

3 Vogelsang-Eastwood (2000): 286.

4 Kemp (2006): 323.

5 *The Teaching of Khety*, translated in Wilkinson (2016): 295.

6 *The Times*, 1 February 1923, quoted in Reeves (1990): 157.

7 EA5, Amenhotep III to Kadashman-Enlil, translated in Moran (1992): 11.

8 Translation after McDowell (1999): 154.

9 *The Teaching of Ptahhotep*, seventeenth maxim, translated in Wilkinson (2016): 264.

10 *The Teaching of Ptahhotep*, thirty-first maxim, translated in Wilkinson (2016): 269.

11 *King Neferkara and the General*, translated in Parkinson (1991): 55–6.

12 Sphinx Stela of Thutmose IV, author's translation; published in Helck (1957): 1542–3.

13 Papyrus Chester Beatty III, translated in McDowell (1999): 115.

14 *Book of the Dead*, Chapter 166, author's translation.

15 Will of Naunakht, translated in Wilkinson (2016): 135.

16 *The Teaching of Ani*, fiftieth maxim, translated in Wilkinson (2016): 310.

17 *The Teaching of Ani*, fifty-first maxim, translated in Wilkinson (2016): 310.

18 *The Teaching of Ani*, ninth maxim, translated in Wilkinson (2016): 302–3.

19 *Tales of Wonder*, translated in Wilkinson (2016): 237.

20 Hagen (2007): 249.

21 *Book of the Dead*, Chapter 183, quoted in Hagen (2007): 244.

22 Inscription of Wedjahorresnet, translated in Wilkinson (2016): 31–2.

23 Inscription of Padiusir, translated in Wilkinson (2016): 37–9.

24 *The Teaching of Ptahhotep*, twenty-ninth maxim, translated in Wilkinson (2016): 268.

25 *The Teaching of Ptahhotep*, twenty-first maxim, translated in Wilkinson (2016): 266.

26 *The Tale of Sinuhe*, R65–6, author's translation; published in Allen (2015): 55–154.

27 Wente (1990): 109, quoted in Hagen (2007): 250.

28 *The Great Hymn to the Orb*, translated in Wilkinson (2016): 104.

CHAPTER 7: Humanity

1 *The Tale of the Doomed Prince*, quoted in Janssen and Janssen (2007): 1.

2 *Tales of Wonder*, translated in Wilkinson (2016): 241.

3 *Tales of Wonder*, translated in Wilkinson (2016): 241.

4 Carter (1933): 19.

5 *The Teaching of Ani*, fourteenth maxim, translated in Wilkinson (2016): 304.

6 *The Teaching of Ani*, thirty-eighth maxim, translated in Wilkinson (2016): 308.

7 *The Teaching of Ani*, thirty-ninth maxim, translated in Wilkinson (2016): 308.

8 *The Teaching of Ptahhotep*, eleventh maxim, translated in Wilkinson (2016): 262.

9 *The Teaching of Ptahhotep*, epilogue, translated in Wilkinson (2016): 272.

10 *The Teaching of Kheti*, prologue, translated in Wilkinson (2016): 290.

11 *The Teaching of Kheti*, prologue, translated in Wilkinson (2016): 290–1.

12 *The Teaching of Kheti*, translated in Wilkinson (2016): 297.

13 *Truth and Falsehood*, quoted in Janssen and Janssen (2007): 71.

14 *The Teaching of Ani*, thirty-eighth maxim, translated in Wilkinson (2016): 308.

15 *The Teaching of Kheti*, epilogue, translated in Wilkinson (2016): 296.

16 Stela of Ikhernofret, translated in Wilkinson (2016): 14.

17 *The Teaching of Kheti*, prologue, translated in Wilkinson (2016): 290.

18 *The Teaching of Ani*, sixth maxim, translated in Wilkinson (2016): 302.

19 *The Teaching of Ptahhotep*, twentieth maxim, translated in Wilkinson (2016): 265.

20 *The Teaching of Ptahhotep*, thirty-sixth (last) maxim, translated in Wilkinson (2016): 271.

21 Janssen and Janssen (2007): 93.

22 *The Teaching of Ani*, twelfth maxim, translated in Wilkinson (2016): 303.

23 Stela of Neferabu, author's translation after Lichtheim (1976): 110.

24 Ebers Papyrus, paragraph 855e, quoted in Nunn (2001): 399.

25 EA35, from the king of Alashiya (Cyprus) to the king of Egypt, translated in Moran (1992): 108.

26 EA96, to Rib-Hadda, translated in Moran (1992): 170.

27 Kemp (2012): 229.

28 Ebers Papyrus, paragraph 250, author's translation after Nunn (2001): 400.

29 *The Teaching of Ptahhotep*, preamble, translated in Wilkinson (2016): 256–7.

30 *Tales of Wonder*, translated in Wilkinson (2016): 239.

31 Tomb of Paheri, author's translation; illustrated in Janssen and Janssen (2007): 147 fig. 55.

CHAPTER 8: Piety

1 Pinch (2004): 48.

2 Restoration Decree of Tutankhamun, translated in Wilkinson (2016): 209.

3 The 'Cannibal Hymn', translated in Wilkinson (2016): 90–1.

4 Schafer (1991): 3.

5 *The Teaching for King Merikara*, lines 137–8, author's translation.

6 *The Teaching of King Amenemhat I for His Son*, translated in Wilkinson (2016): 279.

7 Restoration Decree of Tutankhamun, translated in Wilkinson (2016): 210.

8 Tomb of Kheruef, author's translation; published in Helck (1958): 1867.
9 Wadi Hammamat inscription of Ramesses IV, translated in Peden (1994): 84–5.
10 Autobiographical inscription of Padiusir, translated in Wilkinson (2016): 38–9.
11 Carter (1933): 40.
12 Stela of Ikhernofret, translated in Wilkinson (2016): 14–15.
13 *The Teaching of Ani*, seventh and thirty-seventh maxims, translated in Wilkinson (2016): 302, 308.
14 Herodotus (2004): 319.
15 *The Teaching of Ani*, seventh maxim, translated in Wilkinson (2016): 302.
16 Hymn to Hathor, translated in Wilkinson (2016): 94–5.
17 *The Dialogue of a Man and His Soul*, translated in Wilkinson (2016): 122.
18 Wadi Hammamat inscription of Ramesses IV, quoted in Wilkinson (2010): 368.
19 Harpist's Song from the Tomb of Neferhotep, translated in Wilkinson (2016): 229.
20 Harpist's Song from the Tomb of Neferhotep, translated in Wilkinson (2016): 229.
21 Harpist's Song from the Tomb of King Intef, translated in Wilkinson (2016): 226–7.
22 Harpist's Song from the Tomb of King Intef, translated in Wilkinson (2016): 226.
23 *The Dialogue of a Man and His Soul*, translated in Wilkinson (2016): 117.
24 *The Dialogue of a Man and His Soul*, translated in Wilkinson (2016): 118.
25 Carter and Mace (1923): 104.

CHAPTER 9: Mortality

1 Stela of Tjetji, translated in Wilkinson (2010): 134.
2 *The Teaching of King Amenemhat I for His Son*, translated in Wilkinson (2010): 167.
3 *The Tale of Sinuhe*, R8–11, author's translation.
4 *The Tale of Sinuhe*, B2–3, author's translation.
5 The growth of the wisdom teeth and the fusion of cartilage in the long bones showed that Tutankhamun had been aged about nineteen when he died.

6 *The Deeds of Shuppiluliuma*, translation after Güterbock (1956): 94.
7 *The Deeds of Shuppiluliuma*, translation after Güterbock (1956): 94.
8 *The Deeds of Shuppiluliuma* (Güterbock (1956): 98), quoted in Bryce (1990): 102.
9 From the tomb of Huy, quoted in Wilkinson (2007): 211.
10 Funerary statuette of Tutankhamun, quoted in Martin (1991): 148–9.
11 Herodotus (2004): 371.
12 *The Teaching of Ani*, fourteenth maxim, translated in Wilkinson (2016): 303–4.
13 *The Tale of Sinuhe*, B190–6, author's translation.
14 *Book of the Dead*, Chapter 23, translated in Wilkinson (2016): 169.
15 Howard Carter speaking in a BBC broadcast.
16 Amenhotep III, divine birth inscription, translated in Wilkinson (2010): 271.
17 Papyrus Harris 500, translated in Lichtheim (1976): 192.
18 Quarrying inscription of Mentuhotep IV, translated in Wilkinson (2016): 183–4.
19 Quarrying inscription of Mentuhotep IV, translated in Wilkinson (2016): 183.
20 Carter (1927): 31.
21 Coffin Texts, Spell 19, translated in Wilkinson (2016): 162.
22 Coffin Texts, Spell 3, translated in Wilkinson (2016): 162.
23 Marriage service, Anglican *Book of Common Prayer*.
24 *Book of the Dead*, Chapter 125, translated in Wilkinson (2016): 169–70.

CHAPTER 10: Legacy

1 *Be a Writer*, translated in Wilkinson (2016): 287.
2 A version of the same text is inscribed on Howard Carter's tombstone in Putney Vale Cemetery.
3 Papyrus Amherst, p. 2, lines 3–7, author's translation.
4 Late Ramesside Letter, translated in Davies and Friedman (1998): 149.
5 EA22, translated in Moran (1992): 52.
6 Burton (1880).
7 Reported to have been quoted by Burckhardt: see Sattin (1988): 59.
8 Saulnier (1822): 76.
9 Henniker (1823): 139.
10 Budge (1920), vol. 1: 80.
11 Budge (1920), vol. 1: 144.

12 Unpublished manuscript in the archives of the Griffith Institute, quoted in Tyldesley (2012): 248.

13 Collins and McNamara (2014): 28–32.

14 Carter and Mace (1923): 67.

15 Carter and Mace (1923): 72.

16 Petrie (1896): 2.

17 Davis (1906): xiii.

18 Weigall (1923): 98.

19 Collins and McNamara (2014): 73.

20 *Illustrated London News*, 26 January 1924: 143, illustrated in Collins and McNamara (2014): 75.

21 Breasted (1948): 325.

22 *New York Times*, 18 February 1923, quoted in Collins and McNamara (2014): 63.

23 Restoration Decree of Tutankhamun, translated in Wilkinson 2016: 209.

24 Carter (1927): 62–3.

25 Carter (1927): pl. LXXIII.

26 There is a fitting postscript to this story. In August 2014, an accident resulted in the beard becoming detached once again from the mask. As Egyptian conservators struggled to re-attach it using epoxy resin and to remove the visible traces of glue, they caused further damage. Eventually, the mask was repaired – and the beard re-attached – by a German conservator specializing in the treatment of ancient metalwork. He used beeswax, a substance well known to the ancient Egyptians. Ancient materials and modern scientific expertise thus came together to save Egypt's most iconic object.

27 Weigall (1923): 27.

28 Carter and White (1923): vii.

29 Carter and White (1923): viii.

30 Carter and White (1923): xii.

31 Carter and White (1923): vii.

32 Carter and White (1923): xii.

33 Carter and White (1923): viii.

34 Lehner and Hawass (2017): 27.

35 Lehner and Hawass (2017): 30.

36 Lehner and Hawass (2017): 13.

37 Wilkinson (1843), vol. 1: 264.

38 de Verninac Saint-Maur (1835), quoted in translation in Reid (2002): 1.

39 Quoted in Colla (2007): 111.

40 Gliddon (1841): 138.
41 Champollion to *Revue encyclopédique*, October 1821; see Champollion (1986): 154–5.
42 Mariette (1868): 10.
43 Quoted in Sleigh (2020).
44 Author's translation after Darnell and Manassa (2007): 124.
45 Hickmann (1946): 33, quoted in Reeves (1990): 165.
46 Kemp (2012): 195.

Sources

The most accessible and reliable discussions of the objects from Tutankhamun's tomb are Hawass (2018) and Reeves (1990), supplemented by the online archive of the Griffith Institute at the University of Oxford (www.griffith.ox.ac.uk). For Carter's first-hand account of the discovery and clearance of the tomb, see Carter and Mace (1923) and Carter (1927 and 1933). A wide selection of writings from ancient Egypt, illuminating many different aspects of pharaonic civilization, is anthologized and translated in Wilkinson (2016). For an authoritative and accessible history of ancient Egypt, from predynastic times to the death of Cleopatra, see Wilkinson (2010). Wilkinson (2007) provides convenient biographies of one hundred ancient Egyptians, including Tutankhamun and his queen, spanning a similar period of time. For original and fascinating insights into the development of Egyptian civilization throughout the pharaonic period, Kemp (1989 and 2006) are unsurpassed.

CHAPTER I

The contribution of the deserts to the rise and development of ancient Egyptian civilization is discussed from a variety of perspectives in Friedman (ed.) (2002). For the remote reaches of the Western Desert, Vivian (2000) is indispensable. The phenomenon of Libyan desert glass is examined in de Michele (ed.) (1997), de Michele (1999), Anonymous (2006), Kleinmann *et al.* (2001) and Berdik (2006), while meteoric iron is discussed in Roth (1993). For the now-vanished desert fauna of Egypt, see Wilkinson (1999b). The role and influence of Egypt's northern neighbours (Libyans and Asiatics) are discussed in Wilkinson (2002 and 2010). For ancient Egyptian birdlife, Houlihan (1986) is the standard work. Gaudet (2014) covers every conceivable aspect of papyrus, while Jones (1990 and 1995) are the definitive treatments of boats and navigation. The inundation and the agricultural cycle are discussed in most books on ancient Egypt; Butzer (1976) is a classic, and may still be consulted with confidence.

CHAPTER 2

For the earliest periods of Egyptian prehistory, see Hoffman (1980) (now a little out of date) and Midant-Reynes (2000). Huyge (2002) presents a provocative interpretation of motifs in prehistoric rock art. The lives of the prehistoric cattle herders are discussed in Wengrow (2001) and Wilkinson (2003a and 2010). The processes of social stratification and craft specialization that led to the formation of the Egyptian state are explored in Brewer (2005) and Wilkinson (1999a), while the archaeological evidence from Hierakonpolis is presented and analysed in Adams (1995), Baba (2005), Friedman (2004) and Smythe (2005). For the early development of writing, see Postgate *et al.* (1995) and Wilkinson (2003b). The evidence for the construction of the Old Kingdom pyramids is presented in Tallet (2017) and contextualized magisterially in Lehner and Hawass (2017). For Kushite incursions into Upper Egypt during the Second Intermediate Period, see Davies (2003).

CHAPTER 3

Tutankhamun's chariots are examined in Littauer and Crouwel (1985), his archery equipment in McLeod (1970 and 1982). For warfare and foreign relations in the reign of Tutankhamun, see Darnell and Manassa (2007). The kingdom of Mittani is explored in Astour (2001) and Roaf (1990). For foreign influences in eighteenth-dynasty Egypt, see Lilyquist (2005), Parkinson and Schofield (1993), and Roehrig (ed.) (2005). The fascinating topic of Bronze Age glass and trading contacts in the eastern Mediterranean is the subject of a number of works, popular and academic, including Bass (1987), Gregory (2019), Kaczmarczyk (1986 and 1991), Nicholson *et al.* (1997), Nicholson and Henderson (2000) and Roehrig (2005). For the diplomatic relations between Egypt and other Near Eastern powers in the eighteenth dynasty, Cohen and Westbrook (2000) is the standard work, with Moran (1992) providing translations of the crucial Amarna Letters; Fletcher (2000) and Freed *et al.* (1999) also contain useful discussions. Tutankhamun's Painted Box is examined in detail in Davies and

Gardiner (1962). For a comprehensive treatment of ancient bronze see Ogden (2000); and, for gold, Ogden (2000) and Greaves and Little (1929). For the inscriptions mentioning the Akuyati rebellion, see Smith (1976).

CHAPTER 4

The ancient Egyptian staples of bread and beer are discussed in detail in Samuel (2000, 2001a and 2001b) and Geller (1992); other foodstuffs are discussed in Emery (1962) and Murray (2000b). For studies of pharaonic agriculture, see Brewer *et al.* (1994), and Murray (2000a); and, for horticulture, Eyre (1994) and Bellinger (2008). Basketry and cordage are the subject of a magisterial study by Wendrich (2000). For the earliest evidence of cereal production, see Caton-Thompson and Gardner (1934), Wendrich and Cappers (2005), and Wilkinson (2014). The agricultural economy in the New Kingdom is discussed in O'Connor (1983), while aspects of diet and malnutrition in ancient Egypt are explored in Taylor and Antoine (2014) and Kemp (2012). The rearing of livestock and the production of meat products are the focus of Ikram (2000). For banqueting scenes in the Tombs of the Nobles at Thebes, see Hawass (2009). Ancient Egyptian viticulture has been the subject of several studies, notably McGovern *et al.* (1997), Murray *et al.* (2000), Poo (1995), Lesko (1977) and Tallet (1998). Gardiner (1957) is a reliable source for the identification of individual hieroglyphic signs, while the birdlife of the ancient Nile Valley is explored in Houlihan (1986). For honey badgers in ancient Egyptian art, see Churcher (1984), Keimer (1942) and Zeuner (1963); aspects of apiculture, honey (including its medicinal uses) and the symbolism of bees are examined in D'Auria *et al.* (1988), Nunn (1996), Otto (1960), Reeves (1992), Sagrillo (2001) and Serpico and White (2000).

CHAPTER 5

For comprehensive studies of ancient Egyptian kingship, Goebs (2007), and O'Connor and Silverman (eds) (1995) are among the best. The origins of royal ideology and iconography are explored in Davis (1989), and Wilkinson (1999 and 2000); and royal names in Leprohon (2013) and Quirke (1990). For the cult of the Aten under Akhenaten and the return to orthodox religion under Tutankhamun, see Redford (1999) and Murnane (1999), respectively; Eaton-Krauss (2016) is also insightful on these topics. Tutankhamun's gilded throne is featured in a detailed study of the king's chairs and footstools by Eaton-Krauss (2008).

CHAPTER 6

The best, and most thought-provoking, discussion of daily life in Tutankhamun's Amarna – and, by extension, in other ancient Egyptian towns and villages – is Kemp (2012). For pharaonic clothing see Vogelsang-Eastwood (2000); and for craft production, Stevens and Eccleston (2007). The classic study of the ancient Egyptian barter economy is Janssen (1975); other recommended studies include Bleiberg (2007). Aspects of sexuality in ancient Egypt are explored in Manniche (1987), McDowell (1999), Meskell (2002), Ockinga (2007), Parkinson (1991 and 1995) and Wilfong (2007). For dreams and related beliefs, see Andrews (1994), Bryan (2000), Helck (1978), Satzinger (1985) and Wells (2000). The study of gender roles in ancient Egypt is relatively recent; among the best treatments are Robins (2000) and Green (2000). Tutankhamun's game boxes have been examined in detail by Tait (1982). Ancient Egyptian identity is a little-studied subject, ripe for further exploration; among the best contributions are Hagen (2007) and Smith (2007).

CHAPTER 7

For all aspects of childhood and old age in ancient Egypt, Janssen and Janssen (2007) is indispensable. Further insights into childbirth and child-rearing are provided by Wegner (2002) and Zivie (1998). Ancient Egyptian marriage – and marital breakdown – are discussed in Allam (1981), Černý (1954) and Eyre (1984). For family life and relationships, see Feucht (2001) and Dodson and Hilton (2004). The topics of illness, disease and medicine in the ancient Nile Valley have spawned an extensive literature; illuminating studies include Filer (1995 and 2001), Kozloff (2006), Kuckens (2013), Norrie (2014), Nunn (1996 and 2001), Ritner (2001), Strouhal (2001) and Taylor and Antoine (2014); Metropolitan Museum of Art (1999) includes a discussion of dwarfism in the Old Kingdom.

CHAPTER 8

The literature on ancient Egyptian religion is vast and varied, ranging from the academic to the esoteric. Quirke (1992) and R. Wilkinson (2003) (with its extensive bibliography) are reliable and accessible starting points. Lurker (1980), Shafer (1991) and Silverman (1991) are also useful syntheses. Herodotus (2004) offers a near-contemporary, external perspective on the idiosyncrasies of pharaonic belief and practice. For the various creation myths, see Gahlin (2007), Lesko (1991) and Pinch (2004). Kemp (2006) includes a fascinating discussion of the origins of sacred architecture, and Wilkinson (1999) an examination of religion during the formative period of pharaonic history. For temples, see Friedman (1996), Gardiner (1938), Gundlach (2000) and R. Wilkinson (2000); for ritual, including the priesthood, Doxey (2000) and Englund (2000); and for pilgrimages, Yoyotte (1960) and Jones (1990). Popular religion and personal piety are explored in many works, notably Baines (1987 and 1991); Kemp (1989, 1995 and 2012); and Ockinga (2000).

CHAPTER 9

The theme of regicide is, uniquely, referenced in literary works of the twelfth dynasty: see Allen (2015). For the 'Hittite affair' following the death of Tutankhamun, Bryce (1990) and Güterbock (1956) are the standard sources. The government and administration of Egypt during the New Kingdom are explored in O'Connor (1983) and Wilkinson (2010). Reeves and Wilkinson (1996) presents a comprehensive and accessible overview of the tombs in the Valley of the Kings, Hawass (2009) the Tombs of the Nobles at Thebes, and Martin (1991) the New Kingdom tombs of Memphis. For the mummy of Tutankhamun and mummification in general, see Filce Leek (1972) and Taylor and Antoine (2014). Funerals are discussed in Roth (2001a), and the opening of the mouth ritual in Roth (1992, 1993 and 2001b). Flowers and their symbolism are analysed in Germer (2001a and 2001b), Harer (1985) and Manniche (1989). The literature on coffins and sarcophagi is extensive; Lapp and Niwiński (2001) and Taylor (1989) present convenient summaries. Eaton-Krauss (1993) is the definitive study of Tutankhamun's sarcophagus. The various ancient Egyptian 'afterlife' books, including the *Book of the Dead*, are examined in Faulkner (1985),

Lesko (2001) and Davies and Friedman (1998), and anthologized in Lichtheim (1976) and Wilkinson (2016).

CHAPTER 10

For the story of Western engagement with ancient Egypt, see Wilkinson (2020). The complex relationship between pharaonic civilization and modern Egypt is explored in Gliddon (1841), Colla (2007) and Reid (2002 and 2015). For the forgotten history of Egyptians in the science of Egyptology, Elshakry (2015) is a good introduction. Curl (2005) is the definitive study of the impact of pharaonic art and architecture on Western taste and fashion, while Collins and McNamara (2014) presents a useful summary. Ancient Egyptian curses, from the death of Lord Carnarvon to the exponents of New Age theories, are explored in Carter and White (1923), Lehner and Hawass (2017), Morrison (2014) and, notably, Tyldesley (2012). For the multiple afterlives of Akhenaten, Montserrat (2000) is fascinating; Osman (1990) is but one example of the 'unorthodox' school of historical reinterpretation. The theft of objects from the Egyptian Museum during the revolution of 2011 is covered in Bartholet (2011), Knell (2011) and McGreal (2011); and changing Egyptian attitudes to the repatriation of pharaonic artefacts in Anonymous (2018) and Sleigh (2020). For music in ancient Egypt, see Lawergren (2001) and Manniche (1991); and, for evidence pertaining to Tutankhamun's trumpets, Darnell and Manassa (2007), Davies (1905), Hickmann (1946), Manniche (1976) and Montagu (1978).

Bibliography

Abt, Jeffrey, *American Egyptologist: The Life of James Henry Breasted and the Creation of His Oriental Institute*. Chicago and London: University of Chicago Press, 2011

Adams, Barbara, *Ancient Nekhen: Garstang in the City of Hierakonpolis*. New Malden: SIA Publishing, 1995

Allam, S., 'Quelques aspects du mariage dans l'Égypte ancienne', *Journal of Egyptian Archaeology* 67 (1981), pp. 116–35

Allen, James P., *Middle Egyptian Literature: Eight Literary Works of the Middle Kingdom*. Cambridge: Cambridge University Press, 2015

Andrews, Carol, *Amulets of Ancient Egypt*. London: British Museum Press, 1994

Anonymous, 'Tut's gem hints at space impact', *BBC News*, 19 July 2006. http://news.bbc.co.uk/1/hi/sci/tech/5196362.stm, accessed 20 July 2020

Anonymous, 'Egyptian museum calls for Rosetta Stone to be returned from UK after 200 years', *Daily Telegraph*, 6 November 2018. http://www.telegraph.co.uk/news/2018/11/06/egyptian-museum-calls-rosetta-stone-returned-uk-200-years/, accessed 15 July 2020

Astour, Michael C., 'Mitanni', in D. B. Redford (ed.), *The Oxford Encyclopedia of Ancient Egypt*, vol. 2, pp. 422–4. New York: Oxford University Press, 2001

Baba, Masahiro, 'Understanding the HK Potters: Experimental Firings', *Nekhen News* 17 (2005), pp. 20–1

Baines, John, 'Practical religion and piety', *Journal of Egyptian Archaeology* 73 (1987), pp. 79–98

Baines, John, 'Society, morality, and religious practice', in Byron E. Shafer (ed.), *Religion in Ancient Egypt: Gods, Myths, and Personal Practice*, pp. 123–200. London: Routledge, 1991

Bartholet, Jeffrey, 'Recovered Loot: A Q&A about the Return of Stolen Egyptian Antiquities', *Scientific American*, 29 July 2011. http://www.scientificamerican.com/article/hawass-return-of-stolen-egyptian-antiquities/, accessed 15 July 2020

Bass, George F., 'Oldest Known Shipwreck Reveals Splendors of the Bronze Age', *National Geographic* 172/6 (December 1987), pp. 693–733

Bellinger, John, *Ancient Egyptian Gardens*. Sheffield: Amarna Publishing, 2008

Berdik, Chris, 'Sahara's Largest Crater Revealed', *BU Today*, 13 March 2006. https://www.bu.edu/articles/2006/saharas-largest-crater-revealed/, accessed 28 September 2021

Bleiberg, Edward, 'State and private enterprise', in Toby Wilkinson (ed.), *The Egyptian World*, pp. 175–84. Abingdon: Routledge, 2007

Breasted, Charles, *Pioneer to the Past. The Story of James Henry Breasted, Archaeologist*. London: Herbert Jenkins, 1948

Brewer, Douglas J., *Ancient Egypt: Foundations of a Civilization*. Harlow: Pearson, 2005

Brewer, Douglas J., Donald B. Redford and Susan Redford, *Domestic Plants and Animals: The Egyptian Origins*, pp. 125–9. Warminster: Aris and Phillips, 1994

Bryan, Betsy M., 'The 18th Dynasty before the Amarna Period (*c.* 1550–1352 BC)', in Ian Shaw (ed.), *The Oxford History of Ancient* Egypt, pp. 207–64. Oxford: Oxford University Press, 2000

Bryce, Trevor R., 'The death of Niphururiya and its aftermath', *Journal of Egyptian Archaeology* 76 (1990), pp. 97–105

Budge, Sir E. A. Wallis, *By Nile and Tigris. A Narrative of Journeys in Egypt and Mesopotamia on Behalf of the British Museum Between the Years 1886 and 1913*. 2 vols. London: John Murray, 1920

Burton, Sir Richard, 'Giovanni Battista Belzoni', *Cornhill Magazine* 42 (July 1880), pp. 39–40

Butzer, Karl W., *Early Hydraulic Civilization in Egypt*. Chicago: University of Chicago Press, 1976

Carter, Howard, *The Tomb of Tut.ankh.Amen*, volume 2. London: Cassell, 1927 (reissued by Bloomsbury, 2014)

Carter, Howard, *The Tomb of Tut.ankh.Amen*, volume 3. London: Cassell, 1933 (reissued by Bloomsbury, 2014)

Carter, Howard and A. C. Mace, *The Tomb of Tut.ankh.Amen*, volume 1. London: Cassell, 1923 (reissued by Bloomsbury, 2014)

Carter, Howard and Percy White, 'The Tomb of the Bird', in Howard Carter and A. C. Mace, *The Tomb of Tut.ankh.Amen*, volume 1. London: Cassell, 1923 (reissued by Bloomsbury, 2014), pp. vii–xii

Caton-Thompson, Gertrude and E. W. Gardner, *The Desert Fayum*. 2 vols. London: Royal Anthropological Institute of Great Britain and Ireland, 1934

Černý, Jaroslav, 'Consanguineous marriages in pharaonic Egypt', *Journal of Egyptian Archaeology* 40 (1954), pp. 23–9

Champollion, Jean-François, ed. H. Hartleben, *Lettres et journaux écrits pendant le voyage d'Égypte*. Paris: Christian Bourgois, 1986. English tr.

Martin Rynja, *The Code-Breaker's Secret Diaries. The Perilous Expedition through Plague-Ridden Egypt to Uncover the Ancient Mysteries of the Hieroglyphs*. London: Gibson Square, 2009

Churcher, C. S., 'Zoological study of the ivory knife handle from Abu Zaidan', in Winifred Needler, *Predynastic and Archaic Egypt in The Brooklyn Museum*, pp. 152–68. New York: The Brooklyn Museum, 1984

Cohen, Raymond and Raymond Westbrook, *Amarna Diplomacy*. Baltimore and London: The Johns Hopkins University Press, 2000

Colla, Elliott, *Conflicted Antiquities: Egyptology, Egyptomania, Egyptian Modernity*. Durham NC and London: Duke University Press, 2007

Collins, Paul and Liam McNamara, *Discovering Tutankhamun*. Oxford: Ashmolean Museum, 2014

Curl, James Stevens, *The Egyptian Revival*. London and New York: Routledge, 2005

D'Auria, S., P. Lacovara and C. H. Roehrig (eds), *Mummies and Magic*. Boston: Museum of Fine Arts, 1988

Darnell, John Coleman and Colleen Manassa, *Tutankhamun's Armies: Battle and Conquest During Ancient Egypt's Late Eighteenth Dynasty*. Hoboken, NJ: John Wiley & Sons, 2007

Davies, N. de G., *The Rock Tombs of El Amarna, Part III: The Tombs of Huya and Ahmes*. London: Egypt Exploration Fund, 1905

Davies, N. M. and A. H. Gardiner, *Tutankhamun's Painted Box*. Oxford: Griffith Institute, 1962

Davies, Vivian and Renée Friedman, *Egypt*. London: British Museum Press, 1998

Davies, W. Vivian, 'Sobeknakht of Elkab and the coming of Kush', *Egyptian Archaeology* 23 (2003), pp. 3–6

Davis, Theodore M., *The Tomb of Hâtshopsitû*. London: Constable & Co., 1906

Davis, Theodore M., *The Tombs of Harmhabi and Touatânkhamanou*. London: Constable & Co., 1912

Davis, Whitney, *The Canonical Tradition in Ancient Egyptian Art*. Cambridge: Cambridge University Press, 1989

de Michele, Vincenzo, 'The "Libyan Desert Glass" scarab in Tutankhamen's pectoral', *Sahara* 10 (1999), pp. 107–9

de Michele, Vincenzo (ed.), *SILICA '96: Meeting on Libyan Desert Glass and Related Desert Events*. Milan: Pyramids, Segrate, 1997

de Verninac Saint-Maur, E., *Voyage du Luxor en Égypte: enterpris par ordre du roi pour transporter, de Thèbes à Paris, l'un des obélisques de Sésostris*. Paris: Arthus Bertrand, 1835

Dodson, Aidan and Dyan Hilton, *The Complete Royal Families of Ancient Egypt*. London: Thames and Hudson, 2004

Doxey, Denise M., 'Priesthood', in Donald B. Redford (ed.), *The Oxford Encyclopedia of Ancient Egypt*, vol. 3, pp. 68–73. New York: Oxford University Press, 2000

Eaton-Krauss, Marianne, *The Sarcophagus in the Tomb of Tutankhamun*. Oxford: Griffith Institute, 1993

Eaton-Krauss, Marianne, *The Thrones, Chairs, Stools, and Footstools from the Tomb of Tutankhamun*. Oxford: Griffith Institute, 2008

Eaton-Krauss, Marianne, *The Unknown Tutankhamun*. London: Bloomsbury, 2016

Elshakry, Marwa, 'Histories of Egyptology in Egypt. Some Thoughts', in William Carruthers (ed.), *Histories of Egyptology. Interdisciplinary Measures*, pp. 185–97. New York and London: Routledge, 2015

Emery, W. B., *A Funerary Repast in an Egyptian Tomb of the Archaic Period*. Leiden: Nederlands Instituut voor het Nabije Oosten, 1962

Englund, Gertie, 'Offerings: an overview', in Donald B. Redford (ed.), *The Oxford Encyclopedia of Ancient Egypt*, vol. 2, pp. 564–9. New York: Oxford University Press, 2000

Eyre, C. J., 'Crime and adultery in ancient Egypt', *Journal of Egyptian Archaeology* 70 (1984), pp. 92–105

Eyre, C. J., 'The water regime for orchards and plantations in pharaonic Egypt', *Journal of Egyptian Archaeology* 80 (1994), pp. 57–80

Faulkner, Raymond O., ed. Carol Andrews, *The Ancient Egyptian Book of the Dead*. London: British Museum Publications, 1985

Feucht, Erika, 'Family', in Donald B. Redford (ed.), *The Oxford Encyclopedia of Ancient Egypt*, vol. 1, pp. 501–4. New York: Oxford University Press, 2001

Filce Leek, F., *The Human Remains from the Tomb of Tutankhamun*. Oxford: Griffith Institute, 1972

Filer, Joyce, *Disease*. London: British Museum Press, 1995

Filer, Joyce, 'Hygiene', in Donald B. Redford (ed.), *The Oxford Encyclopedia of Ancient Egypt*, vol. 2, pp. 133–6. New York: Oxford University Press, 2001

Fletcher, Joann, *Egypt's Sun King: Amenhotep III. An Intimate Chronicle of Ancient Egypt's Most Glorious Pharaoh*. London: Duncan Baird Publishers, 2000

Freed, Rita E., Yvonne J. Markowitz and Sue H. D'Auria (eds), *Pharaohs of the Sun: Akhenaten, Nefertiti, Tutankhamun*. London: Thames and Hudson, 1999

Friedman, Renée, 'The Ceremonial Centre at Hierakonpolis Locality HK29A', in Jeffrey Spencer (ed.), *Aspects of Early Egypt*, pp. 16–35. London: British Museum Press, 1996

Friedman, Renée, 'Predynastic Kilns at HK11C: One Side of the Story', *Nekhen News* 16 (2004), pp. 18–19

Friedman, Renée (ed.), *Egypt and Nubia: Gifts of the Desert*. London: British Museum Press, 2002

Gahlin, Lucia, 'Creation myths', in Toby Wilkinson (ed.), *The Egyptian World*, pp. 296–309. Abingdon: Routledge, 2007

Gardiner, Alan, *Egyptian Grammar*, third edition. Oxford: Griffith Institute, 1957

Gardiner, Alan H., 'The House of Life', *Journal of Egyptian Archaeology* 24 (1938), pp. 157–79

Gaudet, John, *Papyrus: The Plant that Changed the World – From Ancient Egypt to Today's Water Wars*. New York: Pegasus Books, 2014

Geller, Jeremy, 'From Prehistory to History: Beer in Egypt', in Renée Friedman and Barbara Adams (eds), *The Followers of Horus*, pp. 19–26. Oxford: Oxbow Books, 1992

Germer, Renate, 'Flora', in Donald B. Redford (ed.), *The Oxford Encyclopedia of Ancient Egypt*, vol. 1, pp. 535–41. New York: Oxford University Press, 2001a

Germer, Renate, 'Flowers', in Donald B. Redford (ed.), *The Oxford Encyclopedia of Ancient Egypt*, vol. 1, pp. 541–4. New York: Oxford University Press, 2001b

Gliddon, George, *An Appeal to the Antiquaries of Europe on the Destruction of the Monuments of Egypt*. London: James Madden, 1841

Goebs, Katja, 'Kingship', in Toby Wilkinson (ed.), *The Egyptian World*, pp. 275–95. Abingdon: Routledge, 2007

Greaves, R. H. and O. H. Little, 'The gold resources of Egypt', *Report of the Fifteenth International Geological Congress*, pp. 123–7. South Africa, 1929

Green, Lyn, 'Hairstyles', in Donald B. Redford (ed.), *The Oxford Encyclopedia of Ancient Egypt*, vol. 2, pp. 73–6. New York: Oxford University Press, 2000

Gregory, Andy, 'Ancient royal tombs dating back more than 3,000 years uncovered in Greece', *Independent*, 18 December 2019. http://www.independent.co.uk, accessed 2 January 2020

Gundlach, Rolf, 'Temples', in Donald B. Redford (ed.), *The Oxford Encyclopedia of Ancient Egypt*, vol. 3, pp. 363–79. New York: Oxford University Press, 2000

Güterbock, Hans G., 'The Deeds of Suppiluliumas as Told by his Son, Mursili II', *Journal of Cuneiform Studies* 10 (1956), pp. 41–68, 75–98, 107–30

Hagen, Fredrik, 'Local identities', in Toby Wilkinson (ed.), *The Egyptian World*, pp. 242–51. Abingdon: Routledge, 2007

Harer, W. B., 'Pharmacological and biological properties of the Egyptian lotus', *Journal of the American Research Center in Egypt* 22 (1985), pp. 49–54

Harvey, Stephen, 'Monuments of Ahmose at Abydos', *Egyptian Archaeology* 4 (1994), pp. 3–5

Hawass, Zahi, *Life in Paradise: The Noble Tombs of Thebes*. Cairo: The American University in Cairo Press, 2009

Hawass, Zahi, *Tutankhamun: Treasures of the Golden Pharaoh*. New York: Melcher Media, 2018

Helck, Wolfgang, *Urkunden des ägyptischen Altertums, Abteilung IV: Urkunden der 18. Dynastie. Heft 19: Historische Inschriften Thutmosis' IV. und biographische Inschriften zeiner Zeitgenossen*. Berlin: Akademie-Verlag, 1957

Helck, Wolfgang, *Urkunden des ägyptischen Altertums, Abteilung IV: Urkunden der 18. Dynastie. Heft 21: Inschriften von Zeitgenossen Amenophis' III*. Berlin: Akademie-Verlag, 1958

Helck, Wolfgang 'Die Weihinschrift Sesostris' I. am Satet-Tempel von Elephantine', *Mitteilungen des Deutschen Archäologischen Instituts Abteilung Kairo* 34 (1978), pp. 69–78

Henniker, Sir Frederick, Bt., *Notes During a Visit to Egypt, Nubia, the Oasis, Mount Sinai, and Jerusalem*. London: John Murray, 1823

Herodotus, tr. A. D. Godley, *The Persian Wars, Books I–II*. Cambridge, MA and London: Harvard University Press, 2004

Hickmann, Hans, *La trompette dans l'Egypte ancienne*. Cairo: Institut Français d'Archéologie Orientale, 1946

Hoffman, Michael A., *Egypt Before the Pharaohs*. London: ARK, 1980

Houlihan, Patrick H., *The Birds of Ancient Egypt*. Warminster: Aris & Phillips, 1986

Huyge, Dirk, 'Cosmology, Ideology and Personal Religious Practice in Ancient Egyptian Rock Art', in Renée Friedman (ed.), *Egypt and Nubia: Gifts of the Desert*, pp. 192–206. London: British Museum Press, 2002

Ikram, Salima, 'Meat Processing', in Paul T. Nicholson and Ian Shaw (eds), *Ancient Egyptian Materials and Technology*, pp. 656–71. Cambridge: Cambridge University Press, 2000

Janssen, Jac J., *Commodity Prices from the Ramesside Period*. Leiden: Brill, 1975

Janssen, Rosalind M. and Jac J. Janssen, *Growing Up and Getting Old in Ancient Egypt*. London: Golden House Publications, 2007

Jones, Dilwyn, *Model Boats from the Tomb of Tut'ankhamun*. Oxford: Griffith Institute, 1990

Jones, Dilwyn, *Boats*. London: British Museum Press, 1995

Kaczmarczyk, Alexander, 'The source of cobalt in ancient Egyptian pigments', in Jacqueline S. Olin and M. James Blackman (eds), *Proceedings of the 24th International Archaeometry Symposium*, pp. 369–76. Washington, DC: Smithsonian Institution Press, 1986

Kaczmarczyk, Alexander, 'The identity of wsbt alum', *Journal of Egyptian Archaeology* 77 (1991), 195

Keimer, L., *Quelques représentations rarissimes de Mustélides conservées sur des bas-reliefs de l'Ancien Empire*. Cairo: Institut Français d'Archéologie Orientale, 1942

Kemp, Barry, *The City of Akhenaten and Nefertiti: Amarna and its People*. London: Thames and Hudson, 2012

Kemp, Barry J., *Ancient Egypt: Anatomy of a Civilization*, first edition. London: Routledge, 1989

Kemp, Barry J., 'How Religious were the Ancient Egyptians?', *Cambridge Archaeological Journal* 5/1 (1995), pp. 25–54

Kemp, Barry J., *Ancient Egypt: Anatomy of a Civilization*, second edition. Abingdon: Routledge, 2006

Kleinmann, Barbara, Peter Horn and Falko Langenhorst, 'Evidence for shock metamorphism in sandstones from the Libyan Desert Glass strewn field', *Meteorics and Planetary Science* 36 (2001), pp. 1277–82

Knell, Yolande, 'Egyptian Museum: Cairo's looted treasure', *BBC News*, 13 February 2011. http://www.bbc.co.uk/news/world-middle-east-12442863, accessed 15 July 2020

Kozloff, Arielle, 'Bubonic plague during the reign of Amenhotep III?', *KMT* 17/3 (2006), pp. 36–46

Kuckens, Kathleen, *The Children of Amarna: Disease and Famine in the Time of Akhenaten*, Master of Arts thesis, University of Arkansas, Fayetteville, 2013

Lapp, Günther and Andrzej Niwiński, 'Coffins, sarcophagi, and cartonnages', in Donald B. Redford (ed.), *The Oxford Encyclopedia of Ancient Egypt*, vol. 1, pp. 279–87. New York: Oxford University Press, 2001

Lawergren, Bo, 'Music', in Donald B. Redford (ed.), *The Oxford Encyclopedia of Ancient Egypt*, vol. 1, pp. 450–4. New York: Oxford University Press, 2001

Lehner, Mark and Zahi Hawass, *Giza and the Pyramids*. London: Thames and Hudson, 2017

Leprohon, Ronald J., *The Great Name: Ancient Egyptian Royal Titulary*. Atlanta: Society of Biblical Literature, 2013

Lesko, Leonard H., 'Ancient Egyptian cosmogonies and cosmology', in Byron E. Shafer (ed.), *Religion in Ancient Egypt: Gods, Myths, and Personal Practice*, pp. 88–122. London: Routledge, 1991

Lesko, Leonard H., 'Book of Going Forth by Day', in Donald B. Redford (ed.), *The Oxford Encyclopedia of Ancient Egypt*, vol. 1, pp. 193–5. New York: Oxford University Press, 2001

Lesko, Leonard L., *King Tut's Wine Cellar*. Berkeley: BC Scribe, 1977

Lichtheim, Miriam, *Ancient Egyptian Literature, Volume II: The New*

Kingdom. Berkeley, Los Angeles and London: University of California Press, 1976

Lilyquist, Christine, 'Egypt and the Near East: Evidence of Contact in the Material Record', in Catharine H. Roehrig (ed.), *Hatshepsut: From Queen to Pharaoh*, pp. 60–7. New York/New Haven and London: The Metropolitan Museum of Art/Yale University Press, 2005

Littauer, M. A. and J. H. Crouwel, *Chariots and Related Equipment from the Tomb of Tut'ankhamun*. Oxford: Griffith Institute, 1985

Lurker, Manfred, *The Gods and Symbols of Ancient Egypt*. London: Thames and Hudson, 1980

Manley, Deborah and Sahar Abdel-Hakim (eds), *Traveling Through Egypt from 450 BC to the Twentieth Century*. Cairo and New York: The American University in Cairo Press, 2004

Manniche, Lise, *Musical Instruments from the Tomb of Tutankhamun*. Oxford: Griffith Institute, 1976

Manniche, Lise, *Sexual Life in Ancient Egypt*. London: Kegan Paul International, 1987

Manniche, Lise, *An Ancient Egyptian Herbal*. London: British Museum Press, 1989

Manniche, Lise, *Music and Musicians in Ancient Egypt*. London: British Museum Press, 1991

Mariette, Auguste, *Notice des principaux monuments exposés dans les galeries provisoires du Musée d'Antiquités Égyptiennes de S.A. le Vice-Roi à Boulaq*. Alexandria: Mourès, Rey & Cie, third edition. Paris: A. Franck, 1868

Martin, Geoffrey T., *The Hidden Tombs of Memphis*. London: Thames and Hudson, 1991

McDowell, A. G., *Village Life in Ancient Egypt: Laundry Lists and Love Songs*. Oxford: Oxford University Press, 1999

McGovern, Patrick E., Ulrich Hartung, Virginia R. Badler, Donald L. Glusker and Lawrence J. Exner, 'The beginnings of winemaking and viniculture in the ancient Near East and Egypt', *Expedition* 39/1 (1997), pp. 3–21

McGreal, Chris, 'Tutankhamun statues among priceless items stolen from Cairo museum', *Guardian*, 13 February 2011. http://www.theguardian.com/culture/2011/feb/13/tutankhamun-statues-cairo-museum-looted, accessed 15 July 2020

McLeod, W., *Composite Bows from the Tomb of Tut'ankhamun*. Oxford: Griffith Institute, 1970

McLeod, W., *Self Bows and Other Archery Tackle from the Tomb of Tut'ankhamun*. Oxford: Griffith Institute, 1982

Meskell, Lynn, *Private Life in New Kingdom Egypt*. Princeton and Oxford: Princeton University Press, 2002

Metropolitan Museum of Art, *Egyptian Art in the Age of the Pyramids*. New York: Metropolitan Museum of Art, 1999

Midant-Reynes, Béatrix, tr. I. Shaw, *The Prehistory of Egypt: From the First Egyptians to the First Pharaohs*. Oxford: Blackwell, 2000

Montagu, Jeremy, 'One of Tutankhamun's Trumpets', *Journal of Egyptian Archaeology* 64 (1978), pp. 133–4

Montserrat, Dominic, *Akhenaten: History, Fantasy and Ancient Egypt*. London and New York: Routledge, 2000

Moran, William L., *The Amarna Letters*. Baltimore and London: The Johns Hopkins University Press, 1992

Morrison, Richard, 'How *The Times* caused the curse of King Tut', *The Times*, 22 July 2014, pp. 8–9

Murnane, William J., 'The Return to Orthodoxy', in Rita E. Freed, Yvonne J. Markovitz and Sue D'Auria (eds), *Pharaohs of the Sun: Akhenaten, Nefertiti, Tutankhamen*, pp. 177–85. London: Thames and Hudson, 1999

Murray, Mary Anne, 'Cereal production and processing', in Paul T. Nicholson and Ian Shaw (eds), *Ancient Egyptian Materials and Technology*, pp. 505–36. Cambridge: Cambridge University Press, 2000a

Murray, Mary Anne, 'Fruits, vegetables, pulses and condiments', in Paul T. Nicholson and Ian Shaw (eds), *Ancient Egyptian Materials and Technology*, pp. 609–55. Cambridge: Cambridge University Press, 2000b

Murray, Mary Anne, Neil Bolton and Carl Heron, 'Viticulture and wine production', in Paul T. Nicholson and Ian Shaw (eds), *Ancient Egyptian Materials and Technology*, pp. 577–608. Cambridge: Cambridge University Press, 2000

Nicholson, Paul T. and Julian Henderson, 'Glass', in Paul T. Nicholson and Ian Shaw (eds), *Ancient Egyptian Materials and Technology*, pp. 195–224. Cambridge: Cambridge University Press, 2000

Nicholson, Paul T., Caroline M. Jackson and Katharine M. Trott, 'The Ulu Burun Glass Ingots, Cylindrical Vessels and Egyptian Glass', *Journal of Egyptian Archaeology* 83 (1997), pp. 143–53

Norrie, Philip, *An Account of Diseases in the Near East During the Bronze Age – An Historical View*, Doctor of Medicine thesis, University of New South Wales, 2014

Nunn, John F., *Ancient Egyptian Medicine*. London: British Museum Press, 1996

Nunn, John F., 'Disease', in Donald B. Redford (ed.), *The Oxford Encyclopedia of Ancient Egypt*, vol. 1, pp. 396–401. New York: Oxford University Press, 2001

O'Connor, David, 'New Kingdom and Third Intermediate Period, 1552–664 BC', in B. G. Trigger, B. J. Kemp, D. O'Connor and A. B. Lloyd,

Ancient Egypt: A Social History, pp. 183–278. Cambridge: Cambridge University Press, 1983

O'Connor, David and D. Silverman (eds), *Ancient Egyptian Kingship*. Leiden: Brill, 1995

Ockinga, Boyo, 'Piety', in Donald B. Redford (ed.), *The Oxford Encyclopedia of Ancient Egypt*, vol. 3, pp. 44–7. New York: Oxford University Press, 2000

Ockinga, Boyo G., 'Morality and ethics', in Toby Wilkinson (ed.), *The Egyptian World*, pp. 252–62. Abingdon: Routledge, 2007

Ogden, Jack, 'Metals', in Paul T. Nicholson and Ian Shaw (eds), *Ancient Egyptian Materials and Technology*, pp. 148–76. Cambridge: Cambridge University Press, 2000

Osman, Ahmed, *Moses Pharaoh of Egypt: The Mystery of Akhenaten Resolved*. London: Grafton Books, 1990

Otto, Eberhard, 'Der Gebrauch des Königstitels *bjtj*', *Zeitschrift für Ägyptische Sprache und Altertumskunde* 85 (1960), pp. 143–52

Parkinson, Richard, *Voices from Ancient Egypt: An Anthology of Middle Kingdom Writings*. Norman, OK: University of Oklahoma Press, 1991

Parkinson, Richard, '"Homosexual" desire and Middle Kingdom literature', *Journal of Egyptian Archaeology* 81 (1995), pp. 57–76

Parkinson, Richard and Louise Schofield, 'Akhenaten's Army?', *Egyptian Archaeology* 3 (1993), pp. 34–5

Peden, A. J., *The Reign of Ramesses IV*. Warminster: Aris & Phillips, 1994

Petrie, W. M. F., *Koptos*. London: Quaritch, 1896

Pinch, Geraldine, *Egyptian Myth: A Very Short Introduction*. Oxford: Oxford University Press, 2004

Poo, Mu-Chou, *Wine and Wine Offering in the Religion of Ancient Egypt*. London and New York: Kegan Paul International, 1995

Postgate, Nicholas, Tao Wang and Toby Wilkinson, 'The evidence for early writing: utilitarian or ceremonial?', *Antiquity* 69 (1995), pp. 459–80

Quirke, Stephen, *Who Were the Pharaohs?* London: British Museum Press, 1990

Quirke, Stephen, *Ancient Egyptian Religion*. London: British Museum Press, 1992

Redford, Donald B., 'The Beginning of the Heresy', in Rita E. Freed, Yvonne J. Markovitz and Sue D'Auria (eds), *Pharaohs of the Sun: Akhenaten, Nefertiti, Tutankhamen*, pp. 50–9. London: Thames and Hudson, 1999

Reeves, Carole, *Egyptian Medicine*. Princes Risborough: Shire Publications, 1992

Reeves, Nicholas, *The Complete Tutankhamun*. London: Thames and Hudson, 1990

Reeves, Nicholas and Richard H. Wilkinson, *The Complete Valley of the Kings*. London: Thames and Hudson, 1996

Reid, Donald M., *Whose Pharaohs? Archaeology, Museums, and Egyptian National Identity from Napoleon to World War I*. Berkeley, Los Angeles and London: University of California Press, 2002

Reid, Donald M., 'Remembering and Forgetting Tutankhamun. Imperial and National Rhythms of Archaeology, 1922–1972', in William Carruthers (ed.), *Histories of Egyptology. Interdisciplinary Measures*, pp. 157–73. New York and London: Routledge, 2015

Ritner, Robert K., 'Medicine', in Donald B. Redford (ed.), *The Oxford Encyclopedia of Ancient Egypt*, vol. 2, pp. 353–6. New York: Oxford University Press, 2001

Roaf, Michael, *Cultural Atlas of Mesopotamia and the Ancient Near East*. Oxford: Andromeda, 1990

Robins, Gay, 'Gender Roles', in Donald B. Redford (ed.), *The Oxford Encyclopedia of Ancient Egypt*, vol. 2, pp. 12–16. New York: Oxford University Press, 2000

Roehrig, Catharine H., 'Glass', in Catharine H. Roehrig (ed.), *Hatshepsut: From Queen to Pharaoh*, p. 67. New York/New Haven and London: The Metropolitan Museum of Art/Yale University Press, 2005

Roehrig, Catharine H. (ed.), *Hatshepsut: From Queen to Pharaoh*. New York/New Haven and London: The Metropolitan Museum of Art/Yale University Press, 2005

Roth, Ann Macy, 'The *pss-kf* and the "opening of the mouth" ceremony: a ritual of birth and rebirth', *Journal of Egyptian Archaeology* 78 (1992), pp. 113–47

Roth, Ann Macy, 'Fingers, stars, and the "opening of the mouth": the nature and function of the *ntrwj*-blades', *Journal of Egyptian Archaeology* 79 (1993), pp. 57–79

Roth, Ann Macy, 'Funerary ritual', in Donald B. Redford (ed.), *The Oxford Encyclopedia of Ancient Egypt*, vol. 1, pp. 575–80. New York: Oxford University Press, 2001a

Roth, Ann Macy, 'Opening of the Mouth', in Donald B. Redford (ed.), *The Oxford Encyclopedia of Ancient Egypt*, vol. 2, pp. 605–9. New York: Oxford University Press, 2001b

Sagrillo, Troy Leiland, 'Bees and honey', in Donald B. Redford (ed.), *The Oxford Encyclopedia of Ancient Egypt*, vol. 1, pp. 172–4. New York: Oxford University Press, 2001

Samuel, Delwen, 'Brewing and baking', in Paul T. Nicholson and Ian Shaw (eds), *Ancient Egyptian Materials and Technology*, pp. 537–76. Cambridge: Cambridge University Press, 2000

Samuel, Delwen, 'Beer', in Donald B. Redford (ed.), *The Oxford Encyclopedia of Ancient Egypt*, vol. 1, pp. 171–2. New York: Oxford University Press, 2001a

Samuel, Delwen, 'Bread', in Donald B. Redford (ed.), *The Oxford Encyclopedia of Ancient Egypt*, vol. 1, pp. 196–8. New York: Oxford University Press, 2001b

Sattin, Anthony, *Lifting the Veil: British Society in Egypt 1768–1956*. London: J. M. Dent & Sons, 1988

Satzinger, Helmut, 'Zwei Wiener Objekte mit bemerkenswerten Inschriften', in *Melanges Gamal Eddin Mokhtar*, vol. 2, pp. 249–59. Cairo: Institut Français d'Archéologie Orientale, 1985

Saulnier, M., fils, *A Journey in Egypt, by M. Lelorrain; And Observations on the Circular Zodiac of Denderah*, in *New Voyages and Travels: Consisting of Originals and Translations*, vol. 3, pp. 75–96. London: Sir Richard Phillips & Co. (English translation of *Notice sur le voyage de M. Lelorrain en Egypte; et observations sur le zodiaque circulaire de Denderah*. Paris: Chez l'Auteur), 1822

Serpico, Margaret and Raymond White, 'Oil, fat and wax', in Paul T. Nicholson and Ian Shaw (eds), *Ancient Egyptian Materials and Technology*, pp. 390–429. Cambridge: Cambridge University Press, 2000

Shafer, Byron E., 'Introduction', in Byron E. Shafer (ed.), *Religion in Ancient Egypt: Gods, Myths, and Personal Practice*, pp. 1–6. London: Routledge, 1991

Silverman, David P., 'Divinity and deities in ancient Egypt', in Byron E. Shafer (ed.), *Religion in Ancient Egypt: Gods, Myths, and Personal Practice*, pp. 7–87. London: Routledge, 1991

Sleigh, Sophia, 'Rosetta Stone will never return to Egypt, says expert at £1bn museum in Cairo', *Evening Standard*, 25 February 2020. http://www.standard.co.uk/london/arts/rosetta-stone-return-egypt-museum-a4370731.html, accessed 15 July 2020

Smith, H. S., *The Fortress of Buhen: The Inscriptions*. London: Egypt Exploration Society, 1976

Smith, Stuart Tyson, 'Ethnicity and culture', in Toby Wilkinson (ed.), *The Egyptian World*, pp. 218–41. Abingdon: Routledge, 2007

Smythe, Jane, 'Moments in Mud', *Nekhen News* 17 (2005), pp. 21–3

Stevens, Anna and Mark Eccleston, 'Craft production and technology', in Toby Wilkinson (ed.), *The Egyptian World*, pp. 146–59. Abingdon: Routledge, 2007

Strabo, tr. Horace Leonard Jones, *Geography*, Book 17. Cambridge, MA and London: Harvard University Press, 1949

Strouhal, Eugen, 'Deformity', in Donald B. Redford (ed.), *The Oxford Encyclopedia of Ancient Egypt*, vol. 1, pp. 364–6. New York: Oxford University Press, 2001

Tait, W. John, *Game Boxes and Accessories from the Tomb of Tutankhamun*. Oxford: Griffith Institute, 1982

Tallet, Pierre, 'Les étiquettes de jarres à vin de Nouvel Empire', in C. J. Eyre (ed.), *Proceedings of the Seventh International Congress of Egyptologists*. Leuven: Peeters, 1998

Tallet, Pierre, *Les Papyrus de la Mer Rouge I: 'Le Journal de Merer' (Papyrus Jarf A et B)*, MIFAO 136. Cairo: Institut Français d'Archéologie Orientale, 2017

Taylor, John H., *Egyptian Coffins*. Princes Risborough: Shire Publications, 1989

Taylor, John H., *Sir John Soane's Greatest Treasure: The Sarcophagus of Seti I*. London: Pimpernel Press, 2017

Taylor, John H. and Daniel Antoine, *Ancient Lives, New Discoveries: Eight Mummies, Eight Stories*. London: The British Museum Press, 2014

Tyldesley, Joyce, *Tutankhamen's Curse: The Developing History of an Egyptian King*. London: Profile Books, 2012

Vivian, Cassandra, *The Western Desert of Egypt*. Cairo: The American University in Cairo Press, 2000

Vogelsang-Eastwood, Gillian, 'Textiles', in Paul T. Nicholson and Ian Shaw (eds), *Ancient Egyptian Materials and Technology*, pp. 268–98. Cambridge: Cambridge University Press, 2000

Wegner, Josef, 'A decorated birth-brick from South Abydos', *Egyptian Archaeology* 21 (2002), pp. 3–4

Weigall, Arthur, *The Glory of the Pharaohs*. London: Thornton Butterworth, 1923

Wells, Ronald A., 'Horoscopes', in Donald B. Redford (ed.), *The Oxford Encyclopedia of Ancient Egypt*, vol. 2, pp. 117–19. New York: Oxford University Press, 2000

Wendrich, Willeke and René Cappers, 'Egypt's earliest granaries: evidence from the Fayum', *Egyptian Archaeology* 27 (2005), pp. 12–15

Wendrich, Willemina Z., 'Basketry', in Paul T. Nicholson and Ian Shaw (eds), *Ancient Egyptian Materials and Technology*, pp. 254–67. Cambridge: Cambridge University Press, 2000

Wengrow, David, 'Rethinking "cattle cults" in early Egypt: towards a prehistoric perspective on the Narmer Palette', *Cambridge Archaeological Journal* 11 (2001), pp. 91–104

Wente, E., *Letters from Ancient Egypt*. Atlanta: Scholars Press, 1990

Wilfong, Terry G., 'Gender and sexuality', in Toby Wilkinson (ed.), *The Egyptian World*, pp. 205–17. Abingdon: Routledge, 2007

Wilkinson, John Gardner, *Modern Egypt and Thebes. Being a Description of Egypt, Including the Information Required for Travellers in That Country*. 2 vols. London: John Murray, 1843

Wilkinson, Richard H., *The Complete Temples of Ancient Egypt*. London: Thames and Hudson, 2000

Wilkinson, Richard H., *The Complete Gods and Goddesses of Ancient Egypt*. London: Thames and Hudson, 2003

Wilkinson, Toby, *Early Dynastic Egypt*. London: Routledge, 1999a

Wilkinson, Toby, 'Ostriches, elephants and aardvarks', *Shemu*, 3.3 (July 1999b), pp. 3–5

Wilkinson, Toby, 'What a king is this: Narmer and the concept of the ruler', *Journal of Egyptian Archaeology* 86 (2000), pp. 23–32

Wilkinson, Toby, 'Reality versus ideology: the evidence for "Asiatics" in Predynastic and Early Dynastic Egypt', in Edwin C. M. van den Brink and Thomas E. Levy (eds), *Egypt and the Levant: Interrelations from the 4th Through the Early 3rd Millennium BCE*, pp. 514–20. London and New York: Leicester University Press, 2002

Wilkinson, Toby, *Genesis of the Pharaohs: Dramatic New Discoveries That Rewrite the Origins of Ancient Egypt*. London: Thames and Hudson, 2003a

Wilkinson, Toby, 'Did the Egyptians invent writing?', in Bill Manley (ed.), *The Seventy Great Mysteries of Ancient Egypt*, pp. 24–7. London: Thames and Hudson, 2003b

Wilkinson, Toby, *Lives of the Ancient Egyptians*. London and New York: Thames and Hudson, 2007

Wilkinson, Toby, *The Rise and Fall of Ancient Egypt*. London: Bloomsbury, 2010

Wilkinson, Toby, *The Nile: Downriver through Egypt's Past and Present*. London: Bloomsbury, 2014

Wilkinson, Toby, *Writings from Ancient Egypt*. Harmondsworth: Penguin, 2016

Wilkinson, Toby, *A World Beneath the Sands: Adventurers and Archaeologists in the Golden Age of Egyptology*. London: Picador, 2020

Yoyotte, Jean, 'Les pelerinages dans l'Egypte ancienne', in Jean Yoyotte *et al.*, *Les pelerinages*, pp. 17–74. Paris: Seuil, 1960

Zeuner, F. E., *A History of Domesticated Animals*. London: Hutchinson & Co., 1963

Zivie, Alain, 'The tomb of the lady Maïa, wet-nurse of Tutankhamun', *Egyptian Archaeology* 13 (1998), pp. 7–8

Index

Numbers in **bold** refer to pages with illustrations